MERRILL Science

AUTHORS

Dr. Jay K. Hackett
University of Northern Colorado

Dr. Richard H. Moyer
University of Michigan-Dearborn

Dr. Donald K. Adams
University of Northern Colorado

Reading Consultant
Barbara S. Pettegrew, Ph.D.
Director of the Reading/Study Center
Assistant Professor of Education
Otterbein College
Westerville, Ohio

Safety Consultant
Gary E. Downs, Ed.D.
Professor
Iowa State University
Ames, Iowa

Gifted and Mainstreaming Consultants
George Fichter
Educational Consultant
Programs for Gifted
Ohio Department of Education
Worthington, Ohio

Timothy E. Heron, Ph.D.
Professor
Department of Human Services, Education
The Ohio State University
Columbus, Ohio

Content Consultants
Robert T. Brown, M.D.
Associate Professor of Clinical Pediatrics
Director, Section for Adolescent Health
The Ohio State University/Children's Hospital
Columbus, Ohio

Henry D. Drew, Ph.D.
Chemist
U.S. FDA, Division of Drug Analysis
St. Louis, Missouri

Judith L. Doyle, Ph.D.
Physics Teacher
Newark High School
Newark, Ohio

Todd F. Holzman, M.D.
Child Psychiatrist
Harvard Community Health Plan
Wellesley, Massachusetts

Knut J. Norstog, Ph.D.
Research Associate
Fairchild Tropical Garden
Miami, Florida

James B. Phipps, Ph.D.
Professor, Geology/Oceanography
Grays Harbor College
Aberdeen, Washington

R. Robert Robbins, Ph.D.
Associate Professor of Astronomy
Astronomy Department, University of Texas
Austin, Texas

Sidney E. White, Ph.D.
Professor
Department of Geology & Mineralogy
The Ohio State University
Columbus, Ohio

ACKNOWLEDGEMENT

The authors are deeply indebted to the late Robert B. Sund for his inspiration and guidance in the early development of this series.

MERRILL
PUBLISHING COMPANY

Merrill Science Program Components

Student Editions, K-6
Teacher Editions, K-6
Teacher Resource Books, K-6
  (Reproducible Masters)
Big Books, K-2
SkillBuilders: A Process & Problem Solving
  Skillbook, Student Editions, K-6
SkillBuilders: A Process & Problem Solving
  Skillbook, Teacher Editions, K-6

Poster Packets: Science in Your World, K-6
Color Transparencies, K-6
Activity Materials Kits, K-6
Activity Materials Management System
Awards Stickers
Science Words Software, 1-6
In-service Videotapes
Mr. Wizard Videos, 3-7
Science Fair Package

Dr. Jay K. Hackett is Professor of Earth Science Education at the University of Northern Colorado. He holds a B.S. in General Science, an M.N.S. in Physical Science, and an Ed.D. in Science Education with support in Earth Science. A resource teacher for elementary schools, he conducts numerous workshops and professional seminars. With over 20 years of teaching experience, he has taught and consulted on science programs across all levels and remains active in local, state, and national science professional organizations.

Dr. Richard H. Moyer is Professor of Science Education at the University of Michigan, Dearborn. He holds a B.S. in Chemistry and Physics Education, an M.S. in Curriculum and Instruction, and an Ed.D. in Science Education. With more than 19 years of teaching experience at all levels, he is currently involved in teacher training. He was the recipient of two Distinguished Faculty Awards. He conducts numerous workshops and in-service training programs for science teachers. Dr. Moyer is also the author of Merrill's *General Science* textbook.

Dr. Donald K. Adams is Professor of Education and Director, Education Field Experiences at the University of Northern Colorado. He holds a B.S. in Liberal Arts Social Science, an M.S. in Biological Science, and an Ed.D. in Science Education with support in Earth Science. In over 20 years of teaching, he has been instrumental in implementing personalized science and outdoor education programs and has served as a consultant to teacher preparation and science programs throughout the United States, Australia, and New Zealand.

Reviewers: Teachers and Administrators   **Annette Barzal,** Walter Kidder Elementary School, Brunswick, OH; **Jack Finger,** Waukesha Public Schools, Waukesha, WI; **Shirley Gomez,** Luling Elementary School, Luling, LA; **Dr. Madelyn Jarvis,** West Carrollton School District, Dayton, OH; **Eddie Jordan,** Miami Edison Middle School, Miami, FL; **Shirley Larges,** Azalea Middle School, St. Petersburg, FL; **David Larwa,** Michigan Department of Education, Lansing, MI; **Janet McDonald,** Pine Middle School, Los Alamitos, CA; **Marsha McKinney,** Pope Elementary School, Arlington, TX; **Corinne Measelle,** Palm Beach County School Board, West Palm Beach, FL; **Sister Pauline Elizabeth Neelon,** St. Teresa Elementary School, Providence, RI; **Barbara Panzer,** P.S. 279, Brooklyn, NY; **Donald Paul,** Vineland Board of Education, Vineland, NJ; **Dr. Rosa White,** Cutler Ridge Elementary School, Miami, FL; **Jay Woodard,** Waukesha Public Schools, Waukesha, WI

Cover Photo: Rainbow/VLA radio telescope, copyright © 1981 by Douglas W. Johnson, Battelle Observatory
Series Editors: Karen S. Allen, Janet L. Helenthal; **Project Editor:** Teresa Anne McCowen; **Editor:** Angela E. Priestley, Ph.D.; **Project Designer:** Joan Shaull; **Series Artist:** Dennis L. Smith; **Project Artist:** David L. Gossell; **Illustrators:** Nancy Heim, Intergraphics, Kirchoff/Wohlberg, Inc., Jeanine S. Means, Jim Shough; **Photo Editor:** Ruth E. Bogart; **Series Production Editor:** Joy E. Dickerson

ISBN 0-675-03516-3

Published by
Merrill Publishing Co.
Columbus, Ohio

Table of Contents

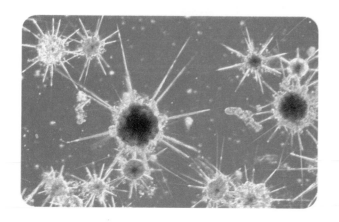

UNIT 3

UNIT 4

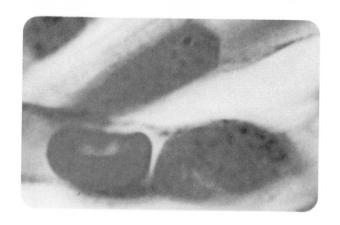

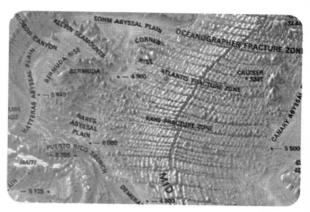

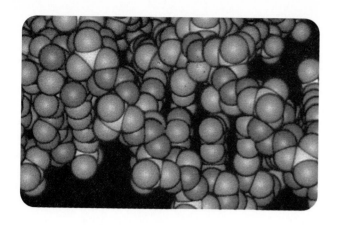

UNIT 9

UNIT 10

Science in Your World

What is science? Is it a class? Is it the activities of scientists in laboratories? Science is much more. Science is a way of learning. It is a way of thinking. It is also a process of organizing our knowledge of the world.

Science provides us with skills that we can use throughout our lives. We learn how to be good observers and how to ask good questions. The processes we use in science lead us to a better understanding of our world. We learn about matter and energy all around us. From science we can learn how to use matter and energy in new ways to produce new products and new processes.

Science begins with information that we obtain from our senses. The boy in the picture is observing red peonies. He is photographing the flowers. The image of these flowers will appear on the film in his camera. Careful study of the film in the camera before and after the photograph is taken reveals that physical and chemical changes produce the image of the flowers on the film. Knowing what happens during this process has led to the design of better film and better cameras. Photography has improved the observations we can make of the world around us.

A study of science can introduce you to many of the scientific discoveries of the past. It can also lead you to the possibilities of future discovery. Perhaps you will be the person who designs the rocket engine and fuel that will allow us to travel to Mars or other planets. You may help solve our air and water pollution problems. You may be the scientist who develops a cure for cancer. Perhaps you will make new plastics, build safer automobiles, or develop crops that resist insects and grow in dry regions. Whatever you decide to do in your life, knowledge and your ability to use that knowledge will always be important resources. The study of science can provide both.

UNIT 1
The Variety of Life

Carolus Linnaeus brought order to the confusion in classification of plants and animals. The naming system he proposed is still in use today. It is called the *binomial system*. In this system, each organism is given two special names. Radiolarians are one kind of one-celled organism. There are thousands of radiolarians. Using the system of Linnaeus, one kind of radiolarian can be distinguished from all others. How are organisms named using the binomial system?

Carolus Linnaeus—1754

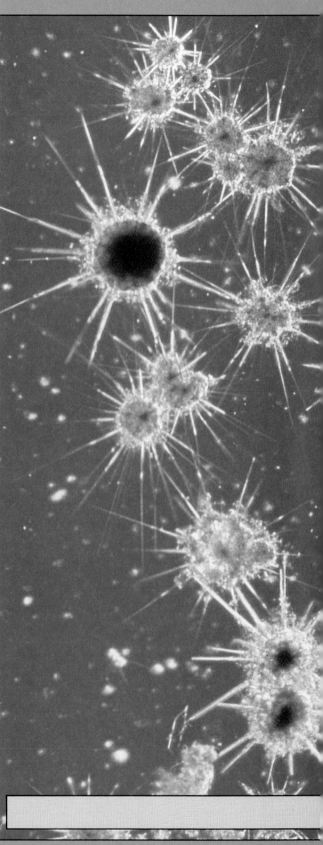

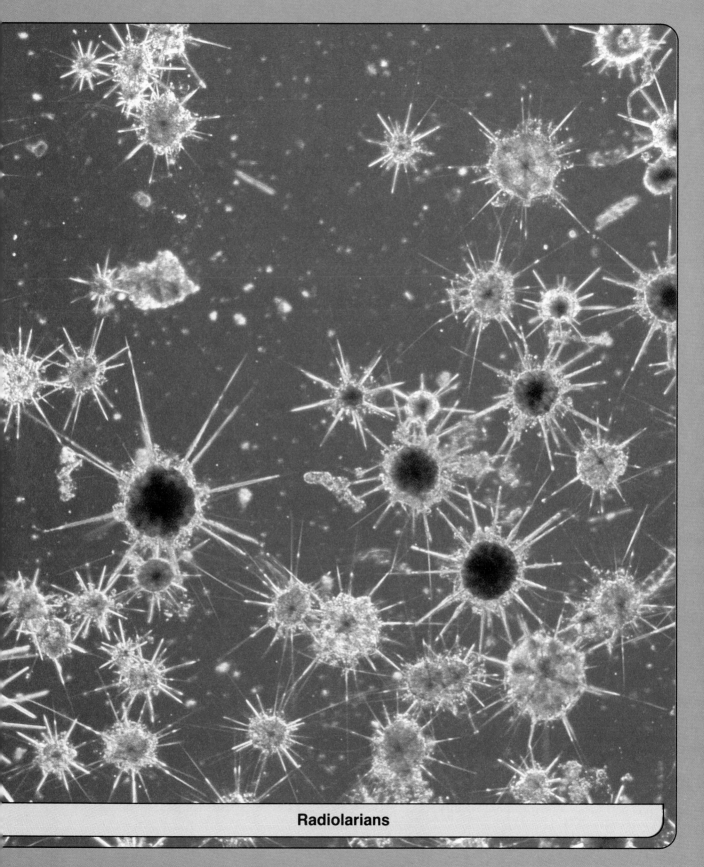

Radiolarians

Chapter 1
Classification

Life exists in many thousands of different forms. To study all these organisms, scientists group those with like characteristics together. Two of these groups are plants and animals. In which group would you place this sea anemone? What characteristics helped you make your choice?

Sea anemone

Features of Life

LESSON GOALS

In this lesson you will learn
- living things have six features in common.
- cells have specific structures.
- the nucleus, cell membrane, and cell wall have certain functions.

What living things do you see near you? There are many kinds of life. All living things have certain characteristics in common. These characteristics may be called features of life. Anything that has all the features of life is an **organism** (OR guh nihz um). Dogs, trees, worms, and frogs are organisms. The features of life shared by all living things are listed as follows.

What is an organism?

Feature 1. *Organisms reproduce.* They produce more of their own kind. Reproduction allows traits to be passed from parent to offspring.

Feature 2. *Organisms grow.* Growth adds mass. Over the life span of a living thing, growth may be great, such as in a redwood tree. The growth of an organism such as grass may be small.

Feature 3. *Organisms develop.* They change in shape or form as they grow. As you grow, your brain and muscles develop. At first you could not walk. Then, you learned to crawl. Your muscles and nerves developed further. They worked together allowing you to learn to walk.

Feature 4. *Organisms use energy.* All life processes use energy. Any action of a living thing uses energy. Even sleeping requires energy!

Feature 5. *Organisms need food.* Food contains energy. Most of the energy for life comes from the sun. Some organisms make food using the sun's energy. Energy is used in photosynthesis. In photosynthesis, carbon dioxide and water combine to produce food and oxygen. Energy is released from food in a process called respiration. In respiration, food and oxygen combine to produce carbon dioxide and water.

Figure 1-1. Evidence of the features of life is easy to observe in elephant seals.

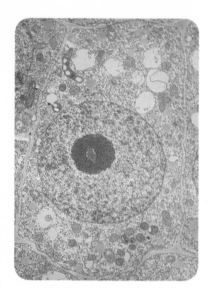

Figure 1-2. A plant cell has a nucleus, cell membrane, and cell wall.

What are some of the basic parts of a cell?

Feature 6. *Organisms are made of cells.* The **cell** is the basic unit of life. An organism may be made of only one cell. If so, all life processes are carried out in that one cell. Many-celled organisms have groups of cells that carry out certain functions.

Cell Structure

Each cell has structures for certain life processes such as respiration and waste removal. These functions are controlled by the nucleus (NEW klee us). The **nucleus** is the control center of a cell. The nucleus controls reproduction, growth, development, and energy use. The material of the nucleus is usually enclosed by a membrane. Look at Figure 1-2. Describe the nucleus of this cell.

A cell is enclosed by a cell membrane. The **cell membrane** is a flexible structure that holds the contents of the cell together. The cell membrane regulates the materials entering and leaving the cell. All cells have cell membranes.

Some types of cells have a wall-like structure around the cell membrane. The **cell wall** is a stiff structure that provides protection and support for the cell. Plant cells are one type of cell that have cell walls. Animal cells do not have cell walls. How do you think plants might be aided by cell walls?

Lesson Summary

- All organisms reproduce, grow, develop, use energy, need food, and are made of cells.
- Cells have structures for specific functions.
- A nucleus controls cell activities, while a cell membrane and cell wall provide protection.

Lesson Review

Review the lesson to answer these questions.

1. What is an organism?
2. Name the six features of life.
3. Describe one difference between a plant cell and an animal cell.

Activity 1-1 Graphing Magnification

What does a microscope do?

Materials
graph paper
pencil and paper

What to do
1. Draw a one-celled organism that fills one square on the graph paper. Assume this is the real size of the organism.
2. Pretend you are looking at the organism through a microscope. The microscope magnifies the size of an object, making it *look* much larger. To draw your organism so it is magnified five times, outline an area that is five squares on each side. Draw the organism so it fills the outlined area.
3. Pretend you are looking through a microscope that makes objects look ten times larger than they really are. Draw the organism as it would appear through the microscope. (Hint: Outline an area that is ten squares on each side.)
4. Pretend you are looking through a microscope that makes objects look 40 times larger than they really are. Draw the organism as it would appear through the microscope.

What did you learn?
1. How many times larger does the organism appear in step 2? Step 3? Step 4?
2. How many squares does an organism cover that has been magnified five times? 10 times? 40 times?

Using what you learned
1. How do your drawings show what a microscope does?
2. Why is a microscope useful to scientists?

LESSON GOALS

In this lesson you will learn
- organisms can be grouped according to their characteristics.
- all organisms can be grouped into five kingdoms.

Figure 1-3. Accurate observations aid the classification of organisms.

What is the largest grouping of organisms?

Figure 1-4. Monerans (a), protists (b), fungi (c), plants (d), and animals (e) are classified by their characteristics.

Organisms can be grouped or classified by their characteristics. **Classification** is the process of grouping organisms by their characteristics. There are many ways organisms can be grouped. Scientists classify organisms by grouping those that have similar characteristics in either body structure or cell structure. Classification shows how closely two organisms may be related, because grouping is based on similar structures.

The organisms in each group are similar in their cell structures and in the way they get food. A **producer** is a living thing that makes its own food. Producers contain chlorophyll that captures the sun's energy. A **consumer** is a living thing that eats other organisms. Consumers do not contain chlorophyll.

Each organism can be classified into one of five groups. Each of the five kinds of organisms is placed into a group called a kingdom. A **kingdom** is the largest grouping of living things used in classification. There are five kingdoms.

a

b
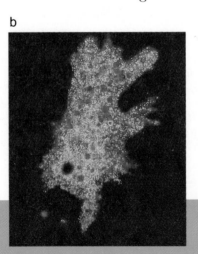

c

SIMPLE

Moneran Kingdom. The smallest living things are monerans. A **moneran** (muh NIHR un) is a one-celled organism that has no nucleus. Material found in the nucleus of other cells is present in monerans however. Monerans do not have cell organelles as do other living things. Organelles are cell structures bounded by membranes. Life processes in monerans are carried out by different structures. Monerans may be producers or consumers. They are the simplest organisms.

What is an organelle?

Protist Kingdom. A **protist** (PROH tihst) is a one-celled organism with a nucleus. Some protists are plantlike. They are producers and have cell walls. Other protists are animallike. They are consumers, show movement, and do not have cell walls. Protists have cell organelles for carrying out life processes.

Fungus Kingdom. A **fungus** is a consumer with cell walls. Fungi may be one-celled or many-celled. Each cell in a fungus has a nucleus and organelles for carrying out life processes.

Plant Kingdom. Recall that most plants are producers. They are many-celled. Each cell has a nucleus, a cell membrane, and a cell wall. Organelles for carrying out life processes are present in each cell.

Animal Kingdom. Recall that animals are consumers. They are many-celled. Each cell has a nucleus and a cell membrane, but no cell wall. Organelles for carrying out life processes are present in each cell.

d

e

COMPLEX

9

Monerans, protists, and fungi are often referred
to as simple organisms. This is because of their cell
structure and the way their life processes are carried
out. Plants and animals are said to be complex
organisms. Life processes in complex organisms are
carried out by groups of cells. Complex organisms
may be made of tissues, organs, or organ systems.
Review the characteristics of simple and complex
organisms in Table 1–1.

Table 1–1 Five-Kingdom Classification					
	Simple Organisms			Complex Organisms	
	Monerans	Protists	Fungi	Plants	Animals
producers	some	some	no	most	no
consumers	some	some	yes	some	yes
one-celled	yes	yes	some	no	no
many-celled	no	no	most	yes	yes
nucleus	no	yes	yes	yes	yes
cell membrane	yes	yes	yes	yes	yes
cell wall present	most	some	yes	yes	no
cell organelles	no	yes	yes	yes	yes

Lesson Summary

● Classification is the process of grouping organisms
by their characteristics.
● A kingdom is the largest group of living things.
● Monerans, protists, fungi, plants, and animals are
the five kingdoms of organisms.

Lesson Review

Review the lesson to answer these questions.
1. How do scientists classify organisms?
2. Describe the differences in cell structure and ways
of getting food among the organisms of the five
kingdoms.
3. What organisms are said to be simple in structure?
Complex in structure?

Activity 1-2 Classifying Cells

QUESTION How do you use the structure of cells to classify organsims?

Materials
microscope   prepared slides A, B, C, D, E
pencil and paper

What to do
1. Focus the microscope on a cell on slide A. Compare the structures you see on the slide with the structures you see in picture A.
2. Draw one cell from slide A. Label the structures. Use reference books if needed.
3. Repeat steps 1 and 2 using each pair of slides and pictures.
4. Make a chart like the one shown. Compare your drawings. Record which structures are present in each cell.

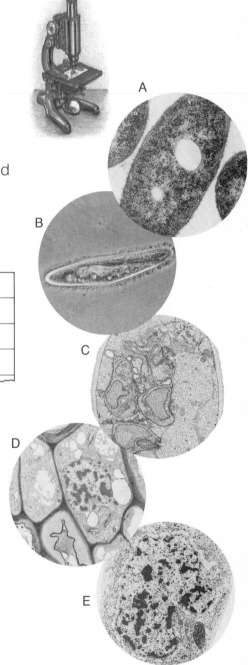

A

B

C

D

E

Observations of Cell Structures					
	A	B	C	D	E
nucleus					
cell membrane					

5. Identify the kingdom to which each cell belongs.

What did you learn?
1. Which cell did not have a nucleus?
2. Which cells had cell membranes only?
3. Which cells had cell walls?

Using what you learned
1. Which cell was the simplest in structure? Why?
2. Look at the drawing and picture of the protist cell. Is it animallike or plantlike? Why?
3. a. How might you know if a cell is a producer?
   b. Which pictures showed cells that can make food?

LESSON GOALS

In this lesson you will learn
- a naming system is used in classification.
- each type of organism has a scientific name.

How is classification aided by a naming system?

A naming system or scheme is used to identify organisms in a classification. Scientists classify similar organisms together by giving them a common name. Each name refers to a certain set of characteristics that are shared by all members of a group. All living things can be grouped into five kingdoms. What are the general characteristics used to place an organism in a kingdom? Think of a white oak tree. To what kingdom does it belong?

Each kingdom is made up of many smaller groups. A phylum (FI lum) is a group within a kingdom. Certain characteristics are used to place living things into kingdoms. Other characteristics are used to place living things in a phylum within a kingdom. Again, think of the white oak. Plants are either vascular (VAS kyuh lur) or nonvascular. A vascular plant has tubes or vessels that carry food, water, and minerals to all parts of the plant. A tree is a vascular plant. Therefore it is grouped in phylum Tracheophyta. What other plants have vascular tissue?

Figure 1–5. There are many kinds of vascular plants.

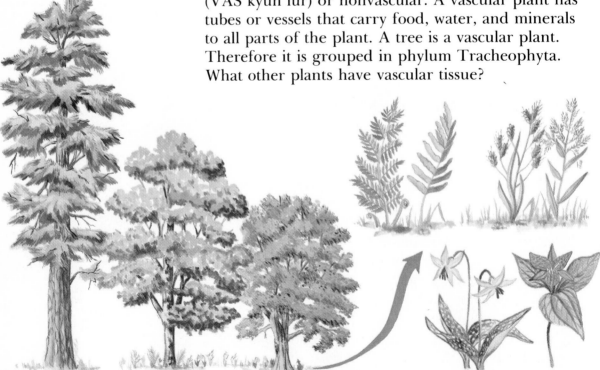

Each phylum is made up of many smaller groups. A class is a group within a phylum. More specific characteristics are used to place an organism in a class than in a phylum. A white oak tree is a vascular plant that produces seeds in flowers. Therefore, it is placed in class Angiospermae. What other plants do you know that produce seeds in flowers?

Within a class are smaller groups. An order is a group within a class. A family is a group within an order. More specific characteristics are used to place organisms in these groups. Look at Table 1-2 for the names of the order and family of the white oak.

Figure 1-6. Ferns and conifers do not produce seeds in flowers.

Table 1-2 Classification of White Oak Tree		
Group	Group Name	Common Name
Kingdom	Plantae	Plant
Phylum	Tracheophyta	Vascular
Class	Angiospermae	Flowering
Order	Fagales	Beeches, Birches, Alders, Oaks
Family	Fagaceae	Beeches, Oaks
Genus	*Quercus*	Oaks
Species	*alba*	White

A family also contains smaller groups. A genus is a group within a family. Characteristics that distinguish oaks from other kinds of trees are used to place the white oak in the genus *Quercus*. One of these characteristics is flower structure.

A genus is made up of smaller groups. A species is a group within a genus. The species name of the white oak is *alba*. One characteristic used to place white oaks in this species is leaf structure.

Figure 1-7. Compare the shape of a white oak leaf (a) with a red oak leaf (b).

a

b

13

Figure 1-8. A birdfoot violet has some characteristics that are slightly different from other violets.

How are scientific names written?

A scientific name is given to every kind of organism. The scientific name of the white oak tree is *Quercus alba*. Notice that this name is the genus and species names written together. The characteristics used to place an organism in these groups are very specific. They can be used to describe it. No other species has exactly the same traits as *Quercus alba*.

When an organism is classified in a group, many of its characteristics can be predicted. All species of violet will have a set of characteristics in common. The scientific name of the birdfoot violet is *Viola pedata*. What characteristics might be used to distinguish the birdfoot violet from other violets?

There are rules for writing scientific names. The genus and species names are always written together. The genus name always begins with a capital letter. The species name begins with a small letter. People all over the world use the same naming system. How is this helpful?

Most names of the groups in the classification scheme come from another language, such as Latin. We translate many of these names into English. The English names are referred to as common names. Look at Table 1-2 for the group and common names of the classification of the white oak tree.

Lesson Summary
- A classification scheme, based on structure, is used by people all over the world.
- The classification scheme, beginning with the largest group, is kingdom, phylum, class, order, family, genus, and species.
- All living things with the same scientific name, genus and species, are the same type of organism.

Lesson Review
Review the lesson to answer these questions.
1. To what kingdom, phylum, and class does a dandelion belong? Use both group and common names.
2. What is the group name of the genus to which a red oak tree belongs?

Activity 1-3 Classifying Objects

QUESTION How are characteristics used in classification?

Materials
box of items
pencil and paper

What to do

1. Place the contents of the box on your desk. List each item on a piece of paper.
2. Closely observe each object. List characteristics of each object beside the object's name.
3. Make a chart like the one shown. Consider that all the objects in the box belong to the same kingdom. Give the kingdom a name. Place this name at the top of the chart.
4. Look at the characteristics of each object. Divide the kingdom into phylum A and phylum B. Name each phylum. List the objects you classified in each phylum.
5. Look at the objects placed in phylum A. Divide these objects into two classes. Name each class. List the objects classified in each class.
6. Repeat step 5 with the objects in phylum B.

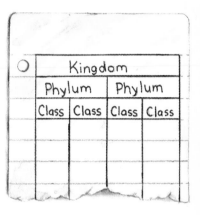

What did you learn?

1. What characteristics did you use to classify the objects into each phylum?
2. What characteristics did you use to classify the objects of phylum A into two classes? Phylum B into two classes?

Using what you learned

1. At what level of classification did the objects included have the most characteristics in common?
2. At what level of classification did the objects included have the fewest characteristics in common?
3. Make up a scientific name for each object.

1:4

Viruses

LESSON GOALS

In this lesson you will learn
- characteristics of viruses are different from those of living things.
- humans produce antibodies that fight diseases caused by viruses.

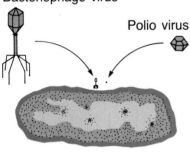

Bacteriophage virus

Polio virus

E. coli bacterium

Figure 1–9. Viruses are much smaller than monerans.

How may a virus affect a cell?

Viruses are special types of matter. A **virus** is a particle that has characteristics of both living things and nonliving matter. Scientists do not classify viruses as organisms. Therefore they are not grouped with any type of life.

Viruses are made of some of the same substances found in living things. However, viruses are not made of cells. A virus can reproduce, but only if it is inside a living cell. A virus needs energy, which must be obtained from a cell. When a virus is not inside a living cell, it cannot carry on any life processes.

Viruses are extremely small. Compare the size of the virus and the moneran in Figure 1–9. Viruses have very odd shapes when compared with shapes of cells. They may be rod-shaped, round, or have many sides. Some viruses also have spikes or tails. Viruses can be identified by their shapes and sizes.

Viruses cause many diseases. After a virus enters a cell, changes occur. The virus may take control of the cell's activities. The virus reproduces many times. The number of viruses in a cell becomes so great that the cell bursts. The viruses are then free to enter other cells. Each cell entered by a virus no longer carries out its job. The cells may finally be destroyed. Look at Table 1–3. How many diseases caused by viruses have you had? Which diseases affect both humans and other animals?

When a virus enters the body of a bird or mammal, antibodies are produced. An **antibody** is a chemical produced in the blood when foreign matter is present. In the case of virus-caused diseases, the foreign matter in the blood is a virus. The body makes a different kind of antibody for each kind of virus.

Table 1–3 Some Virus-Caused Diseases	
In Humans	In Other Animals
hepatitis, polio, encephalitis, flu, measles, shingles, colds, chicken pox, rabies, smallpox, mumps, warts	foot-and-mouth disease (cows) flu (pigs, cows, birds) Newcastle disease (chickens) distemper (dogs, cats) rabies (bats, dogs, other mammals) leukemia (cats, mice, cows)

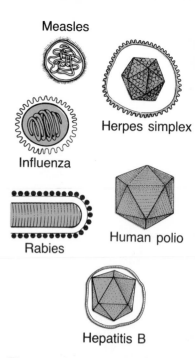

Figure 1–10. Viruses have many different shapes.

Perhaps you have been sick with chicken pox. Chicken pox is caused by a virus. When you got chicken pox, your body began making antibodies to destroy the viruses. As the viruses were destroyed by the antibodies, you began to get well.

Cells that produce antibodies stay in your blood even after you no longer have a disease. They keep you from getting that disease again. Most people have a disease like chicken pox only once. However, people who have had chicken pox may get shingles as adults.

Vaccines are used to help your body make certain antibodies. A **vaccine** (vak SEEN) is a dead or weak virus used to help the body fight a certain disease. When a vaccine is put into your body, you do not get the disease. Your body makes antibodies that destroy the viruses quickly. The antibodies stay in your blood and keep you from getting the disease later. Vaccines can be given to prevent some diseases caused by viruses. What vaccines have you received to protect you from diseases caused by viruses?

From what is a vaccine made?

Lesson Summary

- Viruses cannot carry on life processes unless they are inside living cells.
- Viruses cause many diseases in animals.
- Birds and mammals produce antibodies that destroy viruses.

Lesson Review

Review the lesson to answer these questions.
1. Why are viruses not classified as organisms?
2. How do viruses compare in size to monerans?
3. How does a vaccine aid in keeping you healthy?

People and Science

Viruses Against Hungry Insects

Professor Maria Martino is a scientist doing research on ways to use viruses to help control crop pests. Insects cause millions of dollars of damage to farm crops each year.

For many years, insect pests were controlled by using chemicals such as DDT. Scientists now know that some of these chemicals are dangerous and can harm people, livestock, and wild animals. It is important to find new ways to protect crops from harmful insects.

In the laboratory, Maria studies the ways that viruses affect the growth of insects. One of the instruments she uses is an electron microscope. This powerful microscope can magnify the image of a virus thousands of times.

The electron microscope has shown that viruses are surrounded by a tough coating of protein. When the virus enters the cells of an insect, this coating is broken down and the virus reproduces. As the virus takes over, the insect dies.

Maria and her co-workers have tested the virus in careful experiments. A special mixture of the virus and a liquid was sprayed on several test fields. Healthy plants grew in the test fields because there were very few insects eating the plants. The insects had been killed by the virus. Maria's results show that the virus can be used to rid crops of harmful insect pests.

"We already know that the virus is not dangerous to any organism except the insect host," she says. "We are working closely with the government to make the virus available to farmers for a low cost. Their crops will be healthier and we won't have to worry about the pollution caused by chemical insect-killers."

Chapter 1 Review

Summary

1. All organisms reproduce, grow, develop, use energy, need food, and are made of cells. 1:1
2. The cell is the basic unit of life. 1:1
3. Cell activities are controlled by the nucleus. 1:1
4. The cell membrane and cell wall provide support for the cell. 1:1
5. Organisms can be grouped, or classified, by their characteristics. 1:2
6. A kingdom is the largest grouping of organisms. 1:2
7. The five kingdoms of organisms are monerans, protists, fungi, plants, and animals. 1:2
8. The classification scheme is kingdom, phylum, class, order, family, genus, and species. 1:3
9. Living things with the same genus and species name are the same type of organism. 1:3
10. Viruses must be inside living cells in order to carry on life processes. 1:4
11. Many diseases in animals are caused by viruses. 1:4
12. Antibodies that destroy viruses are produced by birds and mámmals. 1:4

Science Words

antibody	consumer	organism
cell	fungus	producer
cell membrane	kingdom	protist
cell wall	moneran	vaccine
classification	nucleus	virus

Understanding Science Words

Complete each of the following sentences with a word or words from the Science Words that will make the sentence correct.

1. A one-celled organism with a nucleus is a _moneran_ .
2. Anything that shows all the features of life is an _cell_ .
3. The basic unit of life is the _nucleous_ .

4. The system of grouping organisms by their characteristics is
   classification .

5. Dead or weak viruses that cause a certain disease are made into a
   vaccine .

6. A particle that has characteristics of both living things and
   nonliving matter is a _antibody_ .

7. A living thing that makes its own food is a _producer_ .

8. A stiff structure that provides protection and support for the cell is
   a _cell wall_ .

9. A consumer with cell walls and a nucleus is a _virus_ .

10. The flexible structure that holds the contents of the cell together is
    the _protist_ .

11. A one-celled organism that has no nucleus is a _fungus_ .

12. The largest grouping of living things is a _kingdom_ .

13. A chemical produced in the blood when foreign matter is present
    is an _organism_ .

14. The control center of a cell is the _cell membrain_ .

15. A living thing that eats other living things is a _consumer_ .

========================= Questions =========================

A. Checking Facts

*Determine whether each of the following is true or false. Rewrite the false
statements to make them correct.*

1. The energy needed for life comes from the sun. *nutrients* f

2. One-celled organisms have nothing in common with many-celled f
   organisms.

3. All living things can be grouped into five families. +

4. Reproduction, growth, development, and energy use are controlled
   by each cell's nucleus. f

5. A structure that provides protection and support for a plant cell is
   a cell membrane. *wall* f

6. Scientists classify organisms by grouping those that share places to
   live. *characteristics* f

7. Monerans, protists, and fungi are made up of tissues, organs, and
   organ systems. +

8. Vaccines cause the body to make antibodies that destroy viruses. f

20

B. Recalling Facts

Choose the word or phrase that correctly completes each of the following sentences.

1. All living things reproduce, grow, develop, use energy, are made of cells, and
   (a) make noise.　　(c) have lungs.
   (b) need food.　　(d) make food.

2. *Quercus alba* is the scientific name for
   (a) mule deer.　　(c) white oak.
   (b) birdfoot violet.　　(d) white birch.

3. The human body fights viral diseases by producing
   (a) monerans.　　(c) vaccines.
   (b) antiseptics.　　(d) antibodies.

4. Anything that shows all the features of life is an
   (a) organism.　　(b) antibody.　　(c) virus.　　(d) *alba.*

5. A virus has characteristics of
   (a) living matter.　　(c) both living and nonliving matter.
   (b) nonliving matter.　　(d) an organism.

6. In respiration, food and oxygen are combined, releasing energy and producing
   (a) carbon dioxide.　　(c) water.
   (b) carbon dioxide and water.　　(d) alcohol.

C. Understanding Concepts　− Do NOT Do

Answer each of the following questions using complete sentences.

1. Compare the organisms in the five kingdoms on the basis of cell structure and properties of the organisms.
2. List the groupings of the classification scheme on the basis of size from largest to smallest.
3. Compare the characteristics of viruses with those of living things.
4. Why is a naming system used in classification?

D. Applying Concepts　− Do NOT Do

Think about what you have learned in this chapter. Answer each of the following questions using complete sentences.

1. Plants and animals are said to be the most complex organisms. Tell why you agree or disagree. Discuss cell structures and the six features of life in your statement.
2. You have just gotten the measles. Explain how your body is fighting this disease. How could this disease have been prevented?

21

Chapter 2
Simple Organisms

One-celled organisms exist in more environments than any other type of organism. They are found in soil, in air, in water, and in other living things. Cyanobacteria can exist at widely different temperatures. They are important producers in water environments. What is a producer? What compound do all producers contain?

Cyanobacteria around hot spring

Monerans

LESSON GOALS

In this lesson you will learn

- cyanobacteria are important in water environments.
- bacteria are consumers found in many places.
- some communicable diseases are caused by bacteria.
- different methods can be used to control growth of bacteria.

There are many kinds of organisms in our environment. Each organism meets a need or plays a role in the environment. Complex organisms—plants and animals—are very important. You know that plants make food from sunlight, water, and carbon dioxide. This process, called photosynthesis, releases oxygen. Animals and plants produce carbon dioxide through respiration. Both plants and animals play important roles as food sources. It is easy to understand how plants and animals affect the environment.

Simple organisms, the monerans, protists, and fungi, are also very important in our environment. Plants and animals are affected by simple organisms each day. Simple organisms serve as food sources, make food, and recycle matter. They may also cause disease.

Monerans are the simplest organisms. Recall the characteristics of the living things in the moneran kingdom learned in Lesson 1:2. Cyanobacteria are monerans that contain the green pigment, chlorophyll. Therefore, they can carry on photosynthesis. Other pigments, such as blue, red, or yellow, may be present along with chlorophyll. Cyanobacteria are important producers in many water environments. Other organisms depend on them for food.

Cyanobacteria live in water or other places where moisture is present. Most live in fresh water, though some are found in oceans. Others live on dead logs and the bark of trees. They are very hardy organisms. Some cyanobacteria live in hot springs where the temperature may reach 74°C. Other kinds live in cold Antarctic pools. Still other species are common in soil, where they use nitrogen from the air.

Figure 2–1. The red bracket fungi on this rotting log are simple organisms.

What are cyanobacteria?

Where can cyanobacteria be found?

23

Figure 2-2. A colony of cyanobacteria forms when many cells stick together.

Perhaps you have seen a slimy green mass on the surface of a lake, pond, or swimming pool. This green mass may be a colony of cyanobacteria. A **colony** is several cells stuck to each other in a group or chain. Each cell in a cyanobacteria colony could live by itself. The colony forms because of a jellylike layer around the cell wall of each cell. These colonies may be a sign of a polluted body of water. If growth has occurred very quickly, it may be because of excess nutrients in the water. Cyanobacteria grow very well in many polluted lakes and ponds.

Bacteria

Bacteria are monerans that are mostly consumers. They are found everywhere! Bacteria can live in many places. Some species are adapted to withstand drought. Other species can withstand lack of oxygen, while still others withstand extremes of temperature and air pressure.

Bacteria are very important in our environment. Much matter could not be recycled without bacteria. Some bacteria change the nitrogen in the air into a form that plants can use. Other bacteria break down dead organisms. Breaking down dead organisms is very important in recycling matter for other living things to use. Many types of food are produced using bacteria. Cheese, yogurt, vinegar, and sauerkraut are examples. Bacteria are also used to make linen, rope, and leather.

What foods are produced using bacteria?

Figure 2-3. Bacteria are important in producing insulin, detergents, fabrics, rope, and foods.

Bacteria live inside the bodies of some organisms. They can be found in the digestive systems of some animals that are plant eaters. Plant cell walls are hard to break down. Bacteria in the stomachs of cows and goats, for example, aid in the breakdown of cell walls. The nutrients in the cell walls can then be used by the animal.

Escherichia coli is a species of bacteria that lives in the intestines of humans. In humans, this species makes vitamins and produces materials that may kill other bacteria. Materials that aid the movement of nutrients into tissues are also released.

Many species of bacteria are harmful. One species, *salmonella*, is a cause of food poisoning. Harmful bacteria are often referred to as "germs." Harmful bacteria may spread among groups of people, causing diseases. A **communicable** (kuh MYEW nih kuh bul) **disease** is one that can be passed from one person to another. Many diseases caused by bacteria are communicable. Look at Table 2–1. How many of these communicable diseases have you or someone in your family had?

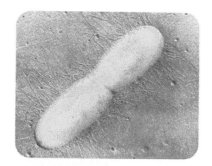

Figure 2–4. *Escherichia coli* are shown in the intestine, where they aid digestion.

How are bacteria harmful?

Table 2–1 Some Communicable Diseases Caused by Bacteria	
Disease	How disease affects the body
meningitis	infection of lining around brain and spinal cord; possible death
scarlet fever	sore throat; rash of tiny red spots; can lead to kidney and other infections
strep throat	sore throat; can lead to scarlet fever
whooping cough	violent cough; can lead to ear and lung infections

Figure 2–5. Much food spoilage is due to the growth of bacteria.

Besides causing diseases, bacteria may cause food to spoil. Bacteria use many of the same food sources that people do. Appearance and smell of food may show that bacteria are using it as an energy source. Look at Figure 2–5. Which sample of hamburger would you rather prepare to eat?

Figure 2-6. Food canners use high temperatures to kill bacteria.

Controlling Growth of Bacteria

Although bacteria can grow in many places, they have certain needs. Each species has certain temperature and moisture ranges and food sources in which it grows best. When any of these needs are not met, most bacteria cannot survive.

Very high temperatures kill most bacteria. Perhaps you have seen someone prepare food using a food canner. Canners are used to sterilize food that has been placed in jars with special lids. The jars are placed in boiling water for several minutes to kill the bacteria. As the jars cool, the lids seal tightly. Because the jars are airtight, no more bacteria can enter and the food does not spoil. A similar process is used to preserve food in cans you see at the grocery store.

Milk is processed at high temperatures. **Pasteurization** (pas chuh ruh ZAY shun) is the process of heating and then quickly cooling milk to kill disease-causing bacteria. Other bacteria do survive though, because the milk is not boiled. Milk will spoil eventually, even if it is sealed in a carton or jug.

How can low temperatures be used to control the growth of bacteria?

Lowering the temperature of food to 5°C or below is another method of controlling growth of bacteria. At low temperatures, growth and reproduction of bacteria are slowed. Freezing will kill any species not adapted to this extreme temperature. Bacteria adapted to low temperatures will survive and begin to reproduce once the food is thawed. How do you think bacteria are affected by refrigeration?

Figure 2-7. Cooling slows the growth of most bacteria.

Changing the amount of moisture present in food may keep bacteria from using it as a food source. **Dehydration** is the removal of water from a material. Bacteria will not use dried fruit or beans as a food source even if the container lid is left open.

Sometimes disease-causing bacteria enter your body. When this occurs, your body makes antibodies. Your body makes different kinds of antibodies for different kinds of disease-causing bacteria. Vaccines, which cause antibodies to form, may be used to prevent these diseases. What vaccines have you had for diseases caused by bacteria?

Figure 2–8. Disinfectants kill simple organisms on many surfaces.

Describe dehydration.

For what are disinfectants used?

Scientists have learned other ways to prevent the growth of bacteria. One way to control growth is to use disinfectants. A **disinfectant** is a chemical that kills many simple organisms. Rubbing alcohol, hydrogen peroxide, and chlorine bleach are used as disinfectants. Disinfectants are used to control growth of bacteria in hospitals and homes. Where might disinfectants be used in your school?

Perhaps you can recall getting a cut on your knee. Someone may have disinfected the cut with an antiseptic. An **antiseptic** is a disinfectant used on living things. An antiseptic kills any simple organisms that might have entered the cut. Your cut also may have been bandaged. This not only slows bleeding, but also keeps out harmful bacteria.

Lesson Summary

- Cyanobacteria are producers in water environments.
- Bacteria are important consumers that cause recycling of matter and are used in some industrial processes.
- Many diseases are caused by bacteria.
- The growth of bacteria can be controlled in many ways.

Lesson Review

Review the lesson to answer these questions.
1. Why do cyanobacteria form colonies?
2. How do bacteria aid digestion in some animals?
3. How is the growth of bacteria controlled in food?

27

Activity 2-1 Growing Bacteria

QUESTION **Where are bacteria found and how can their growth be controlled?**

Materials

2 agar dishes, with lids
tape
glass-marking pencil
2 cotton swabs
forceps
2 paper circles
antiseptic
pencil and paper

What to do

1. Choose one dish to use as your control. Label the lid A. Tape the dish closed.

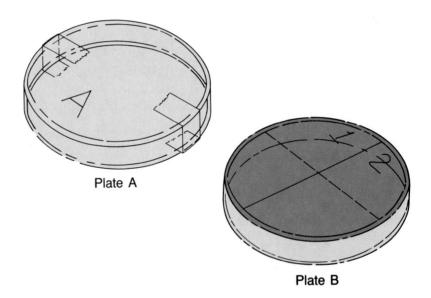

Plate A

Plate B

2. Label a second dish B. Carefully turn the dish over, making sure it stays closed. Use the marking pencil to divide the bottom of the dish into four parts. Use solid and dashed lines as shown. Label one side of the solid line 1 and the other side 2.

3. Carefully turn the dish back over. Do not allow it to come open.

4. Choose a bacteria source. Rub a swab across it several times. Lift the lid of dish B slightly. Rub the swab lightly over side 1 in a zigzag pattern. Replace the lid.

5. Soak one of the paper circles in the antiseptic. Using the forceps, place the circle in one half of side 1. Lightly press it to the agar.

6. Choose a different source of bacteria. Repeat step 4 using a clean swab. Place the bacteria on side 2.

7. Soak one of the paper circles in the antiseptic. Using the forceps, place the circle in one-half of side 2. Lightly press it to the agar.

8. Tape dish B shut. Place your name on top of both dishes.

9. Carefully turn over each dish. Place the dishes in a warm, dark place for five days.

10. After five days, observe the growth. Do **not** open the dishes. Bacteria colonies usually appear as shiny dots. Colonies of other simple organisms may be present. Do not count these in your results.

What did you learn?

1. a. Describe the growth in control dish A.
   b. What was the purpose of this dish?

2. Look only at the sections without the antiseptic circles.
   a. Which source supplied the most bacteria?
   b. How do your results compare with the rest of the class?

3. Compare the sections that contained antiseptic circles. Which of the sources of bacteria was affected most by the antiseptic?

Using what you learned

1. Using class results, determine the most likely place in your classroom that you would find bacteria.

2. Based on class results, where is the most likely place on the body that you would find bacteria?

3. How can the growth of bacteria be controlled?

LESSON GOALS

In this lesson you will learn

• protists are important in our environment.

• algal protists and protozoans have some different characteristics.

• protozoans use certain structures for movement.

An algal protist is a one-celled plantlike protist. It has a nucleus, cell wall, and chlorophyll. Algal protists are producers in many water environments. They are also important animal food sources. Different species are adapted to live in fresh water or ocean water. Algal protists are classified according to color, type of cell wall, and method of movement.

Diatoms are algal protists found in fresh water and in the ocean. Diatoms are called "golden algae" because of a yellow pigment in the cells. The yellow color appears along with the green color of chlorophyll. Each diatom cell has two parts, giving it a boxlike shape. The cell wall is made of a glasslike material. When the cells die, they settle on the bottom of the ocean. Huge deposits of diatom "shells" have formed in some areas. These deposits can be mined. The material is used to make products such as swimming pool filters and scouring powder.

Dinoflagellates are a type of algal protist found mostly in the ocean. The name *dinoflagellate* suggests how the cells move. A **flagellum** (fluh JEL um) is a long whiplike structure used for movement.

What is an algal protist?

Figure 2–9. The boxlike structure is common to all diatoms (a), some of which are shown (b).

a

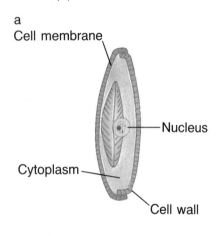

Cell membrane

Nucleus

Cytoplasm

Cell wall

b

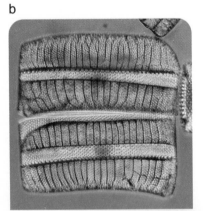

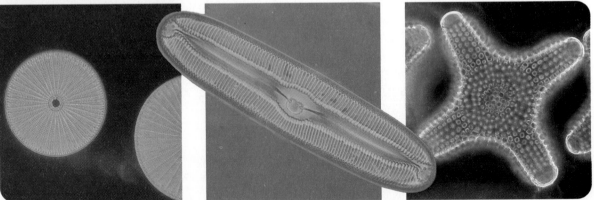

Dinoflagellates have two flagella. Look at the flagella shown in Figure 2-11a. Many dinoflagellates have pigments other than chlorophyll. Some appear red because the red pigment hides the green pigment of chlorophyll. The cell wall is made of a substance like that of plant cell walls.

Dinoflagellates can be harmful. A "red tide" is a rapid growth of dinoflagellates in the ocean. Look at Figure 2-10. Why do you think this rapid growth is called a red tide? Poisons produced by the algae that make up a red tide cause the death of fish and other ocean animals.

Figure 2-10. A red tide can be poisonous to fish and other ocean animals.

Protozoans

A protozoan is a one-celled animallike protist. It has a nucleus but no cell wall or chlorophyll. Protozoans are consumers found in fresh water and ocean water. Why are protozoans not producers? Many larger organisms use protozoans as food sources. Protozoans are classified according to how they move.

What is a protozoan?

One group of protozoans moves by means of pseudopodia (sewd uh POHD ee uh). An *amoeba* belongs to this group. A **pseudopodium** is a fingerlike extension of a cell that enables movement and feeding. Look at the pseudopodia in Figure 2-11b.

How does an amoeba move?

A *paramecium* is one of a group of protozoans that move with cilia (SIHL ee uh). A **cilium** is a tiny hairlike structure. Cilia on a paramecium enable it to move. Cilia also direct food into the paramecium's "mouth." Look at the cilia in Figure 2-11c. Other types of protozoans move by flagella while still others do not move at all.

How does a paramecium move?

Figure 2-11. Movement in protists is aided by flagella (a), pseudopodia (b), and cilia (c).

a

b

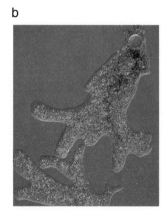

c

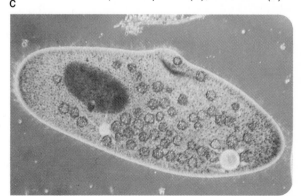

Protozoans are helpful to the environment as a food source. Some form limestone deposits and can be used as scouring agents. One type of protozoan lives inside the digestive system of termites. By itself, a termite cannot digest the food it eats. The protozoan produces a chemical to break down the wood eaten by the termite.

The protozoan that causes malaria lives inside mosquitoes. Malaria is spread from person to person through the bite of a female mosquito. The disease can be controlled by draining swampy areas where the mosquitoes breed. Many diseases caused by protozoans can be controlled by using disinfectants. Some of the protozoan-caused diseases are listed in Table 2–2.

Table 2–2 Some Protozoan-Caused Diseases		
Human Disease	Body Part in Which Protozoan Lives	How the Disease Affects the Body
Sleeping sickness	Blood	loss of body tissues; coma, death
Malaria	Blood	chills, nausea, vomiting, headache, fever
Dysentery	Large intestine	diarrhea, fever, chills
Amoebic keratitis	Eye	pain, clouding of cornea

Lesson Summary

- Algal protists are important producers in water environments.
- Algal protists are plantlike while protozoans are animallike.
- Pseudopodia, flagella, and cilia are used for movement by protozoans.

Lesson Review

Review the lesson to answer these questions.
1. Why are algal protists considered to be plantlike?
2. Why are protozoans considered to be animallike?
3. What human diseases are caused by protists?

Science and Technology

Undersea Bacteria— Food and Flashlights

Scientists have discovered bacteria living deep beneath the ocean, providing food and light for some of nature's most unusual creatures. Not long ago, a team of scientists explored an area of the Pacific Ocean floor several kilometers below the surface. The scientists observed huge tubeworms up to 3.5 meters long living near volcanic vents in the ocean floor.

Unlike other tubeworms, these huge worms have no way to catch, eat, or digest food. Instead, they have a special relationship with bacteria. The bacteria live within the cells of the tubeworms. The bacteria obtain nutrients from the chemicals produced during volcanic eruptions. As the bacteria digest these chemicals, other chemicals are released into the cells of the tubeworms. These chemicals are the "food" that the tubeworms need to grow.

Colonies of bacteria are also found in patches on the bodies of some fish. The bacteria obtain food from the water. They digest the food in complex chemical reactions. As the bacteria digest their food, they begin to glow. The glowing patches on the skin of the fish act like flashlights, lighting the area around the fish. The fish can locate food and attract others of their kind, thanks to their bacterial guests.

Predators may be attracted to a brightly lighted fish. To escape predators, some fish cut off the flow of blood to the colony of bacteria. Without blood, it is impossible for the chemical reactions that produce the glow to occur. Other fish cover the colonies of bacteria with a flap of skin until the danger has passed.

As deep sea exploration continues, scientists hope to find more animals that have developed ways of using bacteria for food or light. The discoveries of giant tubeworms and "flashlight" fish are probably just the first of many exciting discoveries.

LESSON GOALS

In this lesson you will learn
- fungi are important in our environment.
- there are many kinds of fungi.
- fungi may cause disease.

What are some different types of fungi?

Figure 2-12. Examples of fungi include white (a), winter (b), turkey tail (c), and morel (d) mushrooms as well as yellow fungus (e).

Fungi are plantlike consumers. Each fungus cell has a nucleus and a cell wall. Some fungi are one-celled, although most are many-celled. You may be familiar with many kinds of fungi. Molds, mildew, yeast, and mushrooms are kinds of fungi.

Fungi are helpful organisms. They break down dead organisms, using this matter for food. Fungi are also very important in the food industry. Mushrooms of various types are used as food by people. Another type of fungi, yeast, produces carbon dioxide that causes bread to rise. The flavor of some cheeses, such as Roquefort, is due to the action of fungi during aging.

People may be kept healthy by fungi. Some medicines are made from a fungus called *Penicillium*. What common medicine do you think is made from this fungus? Some vitamins are made by yeasts and are used by people to supplement their diets. Molds are used to make citric acid for use in medicines, flavorings, and ink.

a

b

e

c

d

34

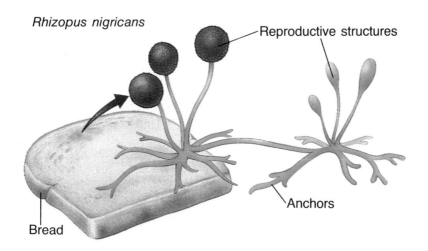

Rhizopus nigricans

Reproductive structures

Anchors

Bread

Figure 2-13. *Rhizopus nigricans* is a fungus that attacks bread.

Fungi can also be harmful. They break down cotton cloth, leather, and other products made from organisms. Some plastics may be destroyed by fungi. Many foods may also be affected by fungi. Fruit stored in humid places is often spoiled by fungi. The fungi changes the taste and appearance of the fruit. Bread is another food often attacked by fungi.

How are fungi harmful?

Many fungi cause diseases in animals and plants. You may have had a fungus-caused disease such as athlete's foot or ringworm. Animals may be poisoned by eating food that has molded. Plants are also affected by fungus-caused diseases. Rusts, smuts, and Dutch elm disease are examples of plant diseases caused by fungi.

Figure 2-14. Corn smut is one disease caused by a fungus.

Lesson Summary

- Fungi are important in recycling matter and producing foods and medicines.
- Molds, mildew, yeast, and mushrooms are kinds of fungi.
- Diseases caused by fungi affect many kinds of plants and animals.

Lesson Review

Review the lesson to answer these questions.

1. What kind of fungi are often used as food by people?
2. Why should bread be stored in a dry, cool place?

Activity 2-2 Growing Fungi

QUESTION What are the growth needs of fungi?

Materials

4 plastic cups
glass-marking pencil
1 slice fresh bread
moldy bread
4 swabs
4 plastic wrap squares

4 rubber bands
dropper
distilled water
hand lens
pencil and paper

What to do

1. Label each cup with your names. Label the cups A, B, C, and D.

2. Divide the fresh bread into four parts. Place one piece in cup A. Lightly brush a swab over the surface of the molded bread. Lightly rub the mold swab across the bread in cup A. Cover the cup with plastic wrap, and secure with a rubber band.

3. Place one piece of bread in cup B. Lightly brush a different swab over the surface of the molded bread. Lightly rub the surface of the bread in cup B with the mold swab. Using the dropper, moisten the bread with distilled water. Cover the cup with plastic wrap and secure it with a rubber band.

36

4. Repeat step 2, placing the bread in cup C.
5. Repeat step 3, placing the bread in cup D.
6. Place cups A and B in a lighted area such as on the windowsill.
7. Place cups C and D in a dark closet.
8. Make a table like the one shown in which to record your observations.

Observing Mold Growth				
Day	Variables			
	Cup A	Cup B	Cup C	Cup D
1				
2				
3				
4				
5				

9. Observe the bread each day for five days without removing the plastic wrap. Estimate the amount of the piece of bread covered by mold each day. Record your observations. Moisten the bread in cups B and D if needed.

What did you learn?

1. On what day did you first observe mold growth? In which cup?
2. In which cup was there the greatest amount of mold growth after 3 days? After 5 days?
3. In which cup was there the least amount of mold growth after 3 days? After 5 days?

Using what you learned

1. What are the best growing conditions for mold?
2. How should bread be stored so there is as little mold growth as possible?
3. Predict what would happen if you used bread that contained preservatives. Test your prediction.

Language Arts Skills

Reading a Table

Information presented in the form of a table provides a comparison of two or more items for a reader. Tables can help readers understand what they read. The information is brief and is arranged so that it is easy to read.

Look at the table below. This table compares cyanobacteria and bacteria. The information about these organisms is presented in two kinds of columns. The headings *cyanobacteria* and *bacteria* identify which kind of organism the information concerns. The headings down the side of the table, *environment, function in environment,* and *appearance,* identify the kinds of information that is presented about each organism.

When reading the table, remember both headings. This will help you find information about a particular organism. The arrangement of the material in a table allows you to see quickly some of the similarities and differences between the two types of organisms.

Use the table to answer the following questions.
1. What three characteristics of these organisms are compared?
2. Why are the terms *cyanobacteria* and *bacteria* over the rows of boxes?
3. Which organism is the consumer and which is the producer?
4. Which organism is found in the digestive systems of animals?
5. Was the information in questions 3 and 4 easy to find? Why?
6. Why might information presented in a table help readers to understand it?

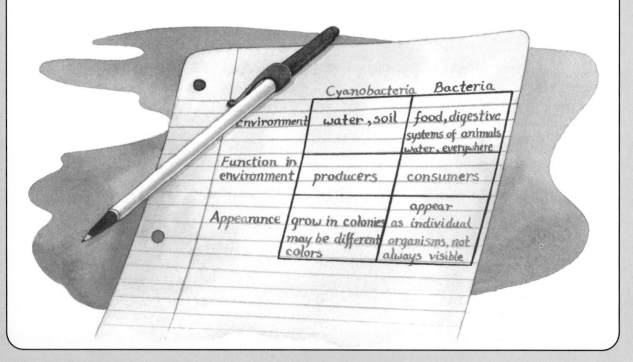

	Cyanobacteria	Bacteria
Environment	water, soil	food, digestive systems of animals, water, everywhere
Function in environment	producers	consumers
Appearance	grow in colonies may be different colors	appear as individual organisms, not always visible

Chapter 2 Review

1. Cyanobacteria are monerans that contain chlorophyll. 2:1
2. Cyanobacteria live in water or other moist places. 2:1
3. Bacteria are important in recycling matter for other organisms to use. 2:1
4. Many species of bacteria are harmful and can cause diseases. 2:1
5. Scientists have learned ways to prevent growth of bacteria. 2:1
6. Algal protists are producers in many water environments. 2:2
7. Algal protists are one-celled plantlike protists, while protozoans are one-celled animallike protists. 2:2
8. Flagella, pseudopodia, and cilia are used by one-celled organisms for movement. 2:2
9. Fungi are important in the recycling of dead organisms. 2:3
10. Fungi are important in the production of certain foods and medicines. 2:3
11. Fungi may cause certain foods to spoil and may cause diseases in plants and animals. 2:3

Science Words

antiseptic	communicable disease	flagellum
cilium	dehydration	pasteurization
colony	disinfectant	pseudopodium

Understanding Science Words

Complete each of the following sentences with a word or words from the Science Words that will make the sentence correct.

1. A chemical that kills many simple organisms is a _____.
2. A long whiplike structure used by protozoans for movement is a _____.
3. The process of heating and quickly cooling milk to kill disease-causing bacteria is _____.
4. The removal of water from a material is _____.
5. A fingerlike extension of a cell that enables movement and feeding is a _____.
6. A disinfectant used on living things is an _____.

7. Several cells stuck to each other in a group or chain are a
_____ .

8. A disease that can be passed from one person to another is a
_____ .

9. A tiny hairlike structure used by a paramecium for movement is a
_____ .

Questions

A. Checking Facts

Determine whether each of the following is true or false. Rewrite the false statements to make them correct.

1. Cyanobacteria are important producers in water environments.
2. One-celled animallike protists are dinoflagellates.
3. Animals produce oxygen through respiration.
4. Bacteria can live only where there are mild temperatures and plenty of water.
5. Scarlet fever is caused by a fungus.
6. A red tide made up of dinoflagellates can be harmful.
7. Colonies of cyanobacteria in a pond may indicate pollution.
8. Dutch elm disease, athlete's foot, and ringworm are caused by fungi.
9. Bacteria are involved only in spoilage of food products.
10. Protozoans are producers.
11. Bacteria in the digestive system of an animal will cause it to be ill.
12. Fungi are important producers in land environments.

B. Recalling Facts

Choose the word or phrase that correctly completes each of the following sentences.

1. Simple organisms provide food sources, make food, recycle matter, and
   (a) have special organs.   (c) do not reproduce.
   (b) can cause disease.   (d) all live in water.
2. Cyanobacteria are monerans that contain
   (a) a nucleus.   (c) chlorophyll.
   (b) a flagellum.   (d) pseudopodia.
3. Bacteria are mostly
   (a) producers.   (c) algal protists.
   (b) protozoans.   (d) consumers.

4. Two methods used to control the growth of bacteria are dehydration and
   (a) reproduction.   (c) fertilization.
   (b) pasteurization.   (d) respiration.
5. Two types of algal protists are diatoms and
   (a) dinoflagellates.   (c) fungi.
   (b) amoebas.   (d) bacteria.
6. There are many kinds of fungi, such as mushrooms, mildew, mold, and
   (a) cyanobacteria.   (c) protozoans.
   (b) amoebas.   (d) yeast.
7. Some medicines are made from a genus of fungi called
   (a) *Escherichia.*   (b) *Quercus.*   (c) *Penicillium.*   (d) *Viola.*
8. When food is canned, growth of bacteria is controlled by
   (a) heat.   (c) freezing.
   (b) pressure.   (d) antiseptics.

C. Understanding Concepts

Answer each of the following questions using complete sentences.

1. Identify two different kinds of monerans and tell why each is important in the environment.
2. How do cyanobacteria form colonies?
3. Identify one important use of algal protists.
4. Compare and contrast algal protists and protozoans.
5. Describe the structures used for movement in algal protists and protozoans.
6. Explain several ways in which fungi can be helpful and harmful to humans.
7. Distinguish between a disinfectant and an antiseptic.

D. Applying Concepts

Think about what you have learned in this chapter. Answer each of the following questions using complete sentences.

1. Why should foods made with meat, mayonnaise, eggs, or milk be kept in a cooler at a picnic?
2. Suppose a scientist has developed a product that will kill all fungi. The scientist is excited because food will be prevented from spoiling and certain diseases will be eliminated. Do you share this scientist's excitement? Explain why or why not.

UNIT 1 REVIEW

CHECKING YOURSELF

Answer these questions on a sheet of paper.
1. Classify each of the following organisms into the proper kingdom: spider, diatom, bacteria, mold, evergreen.
2. What is an antibody?
3. What is the purpose of a vaccine?
4. How is an algal protist different from a protozoan?
5. What is a colony?
6. How are fungi helpful?
7. What characteristics do all living things have in common?
8. Why are viruses not classified as organisms?
9. Give several examples of communicable diseases.
10. How do scientists classify organisms?
11. Under what circumstance can a virus reproduce?
12. When are bacteria harmful?
13. Describe the major cell structures.
14. Explain the classification scheme.
15. What are some ways to control bacteria?
16. Name the five kingdoms and give one characteristic of each.
17. What organisms are referred to as simple organisms?
18. What is the difference between a producer and a consumer?

RECALLING ACTIVITIES

Think about the activities you did in this unit. Answer the questions about these activities.
1. What does a microscope do? 1–1
2. How do you use the structure of cells to classify organisms? 1–2
3. How are characteristics used in classification? 1–3
4. Where are bacteria found and how can their growth be controlled? 2–1
5. What are the growth needs of fungi? 2–2

IDEAS TO EXPLORE

1. What are warts? What are some of the causes and remedies for warts that have been suggested by folklore? What is known today about warts, and how are they treated?

2. How do the cell walls of plants, bacteria, fungi, and diatoms differ? Use books to find the major cell wall component of each of these four groups of organisms.

3. How can bacteria be helpful? Read books to make a report about how bacteria are used in the food industry, how they keep soil fertile, and how they aid in digestion.

PROBLEM SOLVING

What observations can you make that could be used to prove that yeast cells are living things? One of the features of life is that all organisms use energy. Most organisms obtain their energy from food by respiration. Some organisms, such as species of yeasts and bacteria, can obtain their energy without oxygen. Using dry yeast from a grocery store, mix yeast, corn syrup, and warm water in a narrow-necked bottle. Obtain a balloon. Stretch it several times. Then attach it to the neck of the bottle. Observe changes at the surface of the yeast mixture. Observe the effect on the balloon. Remove a small sample of the yeast cells and observe them under a microscope. Use books to answer the question, what is fermentation?

BOOKS TO READ

Hidden Worlds: Pictures of the Invisible by Seymour Simon, Morrow, William, & Co., Inc.: New York, © 1983.
   See photographs of microscopic objects.

Milk: The Fight for Purity by James Cross Giblin, Crowell Junior Books: New York, © 1986.
   Read about efforts to make milk a safe product.

Viruses by Alan E. Nourse, Franklin Watts, Inc.: Danbury, CT, © 1983.
   Read about the mysterious virus.

UNIT 2
Interactions of Matter

As early as the ninth century, the Chinese observed that reactions between certain materials would produce beautiful displays of colored light that today we call fireworks. People can now make light displays using lasers. Different colors of laser light are produced by atoms of different substances. What happens during a chemical reaction? What is an atom?

Chinese fireworks

Laser light

Chapter 3
Matter and Its Changes

Wood burns. Acorns become oak trees. Cows produce milk. Animals convert food into bone and muscle. Oil is used to make plastics, run cars, and heat homes. A glowworm lights up. What kind of change is common to all these processes? What other kinds of change are there?

Glowworm

LESSON GOALS

In this lesson you will learn

- the composition of substances varies from one substance to another.
- substances have chemical properties that affect the way they interact with other substances.
- matter cannot be created or destroyed in chemical reactions.
- substances have physical properties that can be observed without changing their identities.

Think about all of the different kinds of matter you see and use every day. Each object you use is matter. You are matter. The food you eat and the air you breathe are also matter.

A list of all the different kinds of matter you use or see in one day would be very long. There are millions of different kinds of matter. Recall that matter is anything that has mass and takes up space. You may not be able to see some kinds of matter. Air cannot be seen, but it is matter because it has mass and takes up space. Not everything you can see is matter. You can see light, but it is not matter. Light does not have mass or take up space.

A way is needed to classify matter, because there are so many different kinds. There are several ways scientists classify matter. One way to classify matter is by its state. Matter can be solid, liquid, or gaseous. Water is matter. It can exist as ice, liquid water, or water vapor. Another way to classify matter is whether or not it is pure. Pure matter is always the same in composition and is known as a **substance.** The composition of something is what is in it. A baseball team is composed of nine players. A story is composed of words, and music is composed of notes.

Water is a substance. All pure water has the same composition. It is made of two parts hydrogen and one part oxygen. All pure water contains only these two kinds of matter in these amounts. Water is a substance needed by all living things.

What is matter?

Figure 3-1. Written themes and music are compositions.

Figure 3-2. Water is involved in many changes that occur in organisms.

You may think glass is a substance. Glass is matter, but it is not a substance. The composition of glass varies. Two pieces of glass may contain different *kinds* of matter. The pieces may contain the same kinds of matter, but in different *amounts*.

Iron and sugar are also substances. Each substance has the same composition throughout. Table 3-1 shows some substances. How are they used?

Table 3-1 Substances and Their Uses	
Substance	Uses
Aluminum	building material, aircraft and ships
Copper	electrical wire, plumbing
Gold	jewelry, coins, dentistry
Table Salt	flavoring food, making other chemicals
Baking Soda	cooking/baking, industry
Iodine	medicines, dyes
Propane	fuel

Chemical Properties

Objects are different because they are made of different substances. Substances have properties. Properties are characteristics such as color, hardness, and ability to combine with other substances. We use properties to tell one substance from another.

A **chemical property** is one that relates to how a substance changes to a new substance. Most often, chemical properties are observed when substances react with one another. That one substance may break apart when heated is also a chemical property.

Oxygen in air can cause a new substance called rust to form on objects that contain iron. The ability to rust is a chemical property of iron. The ability to burn is a chemical property of substances such as wood and cotton. When some substances burn, smoke, ash, and gases are formed. The burning of substances forms different kinds of matter.

When are chemical properties observed?

Chemical Reactions

A **chemical change** is the formation of a new substance with different chemical properties. Suppose wood is burned in a fireplace. What new substances would form? Think of the properties of a wooden log. How are the properties of ash different from the properties of the log?

A **chemical reaction** is the process of chemical change. Two or more substances may combine to form a new substance that has different properties. Each of the original substances will be chemically changed. Hydrogen and oxygen are both clear, colorless gases. A chemical reaction between hydrogen and oxygen can form water. The properties of water are very different from the properties of either hydrogen or oxygen. Some chemical reactions may also cause a substance to be broken down into simpler substances. Water can be broken down into hydrogen and oxygen. Chemical reactions can build up or break down substances.

What is formed in a chemical reaction?

a

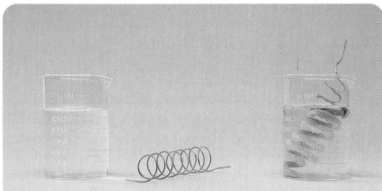

b

Figure 3-3. When silver nitrate reacts with copper (a), silver and copper(II) nitrate form. When silver nitrate reacts with sodium chloride (b), white silver chloride results.

49

Figure 3–4. The law of conservation of mass is demonstrated by making an apple pie.

What is the law of conservation of mass?

Chemically combining substances is a little like making a pie. You combine flour, apples, sugar, and butter and bake them to make an apple pie. What happens to the flour and the apples? What happens to the sugar and the butter? They are not destroyed. They are changed into an apple pie. There is the same total amount of substances you started with.

The **law of conservation of mass** states that mass is neither created nor destroyed in a chemical reaction. All the mass present in substances before a chemical reaction is present in the new substances after the chemical reaction. Conservation of mass applies to all chemical reactions. For this reason, scientists say that conservation of mass is a law.

Energy is involved in all chemical changes. Energy is either released or absorbed during a chemical reaction. The energy may be in the form of heat, light, or electricity. Burning is an example of a chemical reaction that releases energy. In what forms is energy released when a substance burns? A chemical reaction inside a flashlight battery also releases energy. What kinds of energy are produced by this reaction?

50

Physical Properties

A **physical property** is one that can be observed without referring to another substance. The volume, mass, and boiling point of a substance are examples of physical properties. How are physical and chemical properties different?

Color is a physical property. What color is the park bench in Figure 3–5? The color of the park bench is a physical property. The park bench may be hard. Hardness is a physical property of the park bench, too. What are some other physical properties of the park bench?

The state of a substance is another physical property. Rain is liquid water. It is not a solid or a gas. Look at Figure 3–6. Which picture shows water as a solid? Which picture shows where water as a gas is present? When a substance changes state, its physical properties change.

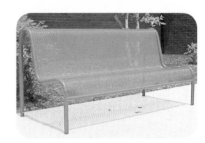

Figure 3-5. This park bench has physical properties of color and hardness.

Figure 3-6. The three states of water—gas (a), liquid (b), and solid (c)—are shown.

a

b

c

A **physical change** is a process that does not change the chemical composition of a substance. A physical change does not cause a new substance to be formed. Look at Figure 3–7. The boy has changed the size and shape of the wood. A physical change has taken place. The substance has not changed. It is still wood. What kind of change takes place if the wood is painted?

Figure 3–7. This boy has physically changed the wood.

Lesson Summary

- A substance is composed of the same matter throughout.
- Chemical properties of substances depend on the behavior of those substances in a chemical reaction.
- The law of conservation of mass states that matter is neither created nor destroyed in a chemical reaction.
- Physical properties of substances can be observed without referring to another substance.

Lesson Review

Review the lesson to answer these questions.
1. What is a substance? Give an example.
2. What is a chemical reaction?
3. How are chemical and physical properties different?

Activity 3-1   Observing Properties

QUESTION   How are properties useful?

Materials
apple
pencil and paper

What to do

1. Observe and record as many properties of your apple as you can.
2. Your teacher will collect your apple and place it in a pile with other apples.
3. Locate your apple in the pile.
4. Replace your apple in the pile.
5. Trade your record of observations for another student's record of observations.
6. Locate the other student's apple using only the record of observations you have been given. Check with the student to be sure you have found the correct apple.
7. Trade the record of observations with a different student and repeat step 6.

What did you learn?

1. How were you able to locate your apple and the apples of other students?
2. How were your observations different from other students' observations?
3. What are some physical properties of apples?
4. What are some chemical properties of apples?

Using what you learned

1. What kinds of observations are most useful for finding objects?
2. What kinds of observations are not useful for finding objects?
3. What are some chemical and physical properties of other foods? Of clothing?

LESSON GOALS

In this lesson you will learn

● all matter is composed of atoms.

● different elements have different properties.

● atoms are composed of small particles.

Figure 3–8. Atoms, like bricks, can be arranged in different ways to form different structures.

What is an element?

All matter is made of tiny particles called **atoms.** Atoms are like the bricks of a house. There are many kinds of bricks. The bricks can be arranged in many ways to make different kinds of houses.

There are many kinds of atoms, too. Scientists have found 109 kinds of atoms. Atoms combine in different ways to make many kinds of substances.

A substance made of just one kind of atom is an **element.** Iron is an element. Iron is made of only iron atoms. Each atom in iron is the same. Iron is the only element made of iron atoms. Gold is an element made of gold atoms. Gold is a costly element because of its special properties and because there is not much gold on Earth. Oxygen is an element needed for life. You use oxygen from the air you breathe. What kind of atoms make up oxygen?

People have found 90 elements in Earth's crust and atmosphere. Scientists have made 19 elements in laboratories. Scientists may find or make more elements. What are some elements you have seen? How are they used? What kinds of atoms are in them?

Table 3-2 Some Common Natural Elements

Element	Symbol	State of Matter*	Some Properties and Uses	
Aluminum	Al	Solid	Lightweight metal	
Carbon	C	Solid	Found as coal, graphite, diamonds	
Chlorine	Cl	Gas	Greenish, poisonous gas	
Hydrogen	H	Gas	Lightest element, colorless, odorless	
Nitrogen	N	Gas	Colorless, odorless gas	
Oxygen	O	Gas	Colorless, odorless gas needed for life	

*at room temperature, 25°C

The Structure of Atoms

All atoms are alike in some ways. All atoms have a core called the **nucleus,** which contains protons and neutrons. A **proton** is a particle in an atom that has a positive electric charge. A **neutron** is a particle in an atom with no electric charge. Protons and neutrons have similar masses. Together they make up most of the mass of an atom.

The number of protons in an atom is called the atomic number. Each kind of atom has a certain number of protons. This is why the atomic number of an atom can be used to identify it. Hydrogen has just one proton in its nucleus. Its atomic number is 1. All atoms of hydrogen have one proton. Helium atoms have two protons and an atomic number of 2. An atom with atomic number 47 is a silver atom. How many protons are in a silver atom?

A particle with a negative electric charge called an **electron** moves around the nucleus. Electrons have a very small mass. It would take almost 2,000 electrons to equal the mass of one proton or one neutron.

What is the charge of an electron?

Figure 3-9. Protons and neutrons compose the nucleus of an atom, which is circled by electrons.

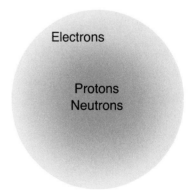

Electrons

Protons
Neutrons

The electrons are always moving around the nucleus of the atom. Scientists say the electrons form a "cloud" around the nucleus. We cannot be sure just where the electrons are found in the cloud. The electron cloud model is what scientists think atoms look like. Atoms are very small and cannot be seen. The model may change as we learn more about atoms.

How does the number of protons compare to the number of electrons in an atom?

Although the mass of a proton is much greater than that of an electron, the amount of charge each has is the same. In an atom, the number of positively charged protons equals the number of negatively charged electrons. Therefore, the charge of the atom for each element is zero. Hydrogen has one proton and one electron. Helium has two protons and two electrons. A silver atom has 47 protons. How many electrons would you find in a silver atom?

Electron Cloud Model

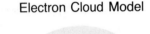

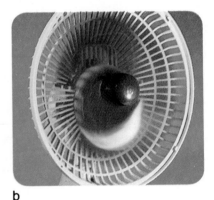

Nucleus

Electron cloud

a

b

Figure 3-10. The electron cloud model (a) is similar to the cloudlike appearance created by the moving blades of a fan (b)

Lesson Summary

- All matter is composed of atoms.
- Different elements are composed of different atoms.
- Protons are particles with a positive charge. Neutrons are particles with no charge. Electrons are particles with a negative charge.

Lesson Review

Review the lesson to answer these questions.

1. What is an element?
2. Carbon has 6 protons. How many electrons does it have?
3. Why do atoms not have an electric charge?

Activity 3-2 Electron Cloud Model

QUESTION Where are electrons found in an atom?

Materials
large sheet of paper
metric ruler
10 paper dots
pencil and paper

What to do

1. Place the sheet of colored paper on your desk. Mark an X in the center of the paper.
2. Hold the paper dots in your hand about 30 cm above the X. Drop the dots on the paper.
3. Make a mark on the paper where each dot falls.
4. Rotate the paper one-fourth turn.
5. Repeat steps 2 through 4 until you have 100 marks on the paper.
6. Draw a circle that encloses all of the marks and the X.

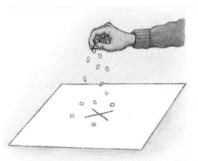

What did you learn?

1. If the circled area on the colored paper stands for an atom, what does the X stand for?
2. What particles would be found in that part of the atom represented by the X?
3. What do the marks on the paper surrounding the X stand for?
4. Where did most of the dots fall?

Using what you learned

1. How are the marks on the paper like a cloud of electrons in an atom?
2. How is your electron cloud model different from a real atom?

LESSON GOALS

In this lesson you will learn

● elements can be grouped into a special table.

● each element can be represented by a symbol.

● there are different methods of grouping elements.

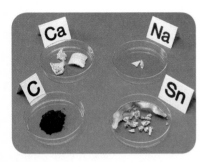

Figure 3-11. Each element is represented by a symbol.

Scientists classify elements into a table called the **periodic** (pihr ee AHD ihk) **table.** All elements that have been found or made are listed in order of atomic number. The table is shown on pages 60 and 61. Each element has a symbol. The symbol is usually made of one or two letters. If you were an element, what might your symbol be? How could you be sure your symbol is different from that of other students in your class?

A symbol may be the first letter in the name of an element. Look at the periodic table. What is the symbol for carbon? Sometimes the first two letters in a name are the symbol. The symbol for helium is He. What is the symbol for neon? When a symbol is two or three letters, the first letter is written as a capital letter. The remaining letters are written as small letters.

What is the symbol for iron? Some symbols come from the name of an element in another language. *Ferrum* is the Latin word for iron. What is the symbol for gold? The symbol comes from the Latin word *aurum*.

The elements in the periodic table can be classified in many ways. One way to classify elements is by their atomic structure. Elements with similar arrangements of electrons in their atoms are grouped together. These groups are called families. The elements in a chemical family have similar properties.

How are elements in chemical families alike?

Families of elements are like families of people. You may have brothers or sisters who look a little like you. Maybe they do some things the same way you do. The people in a family have similar properties. As a result, they are alike in some ways. However, they are different in some ways, too. How do the people in your family differ, or vary, from you?

The elements in chemical families are alike in some ways. They also vary in some ways. The elements in a chemical family are listed in columns in the periodic table. All of the elements in a column have similar properties, but the elements are not exactly the same. The elements with the least amount of mass are at the top of each column. The more massive elements are at the bottom.

Another way to classify elements is to group them into metals and nonmetals. Metals are usually shiny. They are good conductors of heat and electricity. They can be bent or hammered into many shapes. Metals are found on the left side of the periodic table. All metals are solids at room temperature (25°C) except mercury, Hg, which is a liquid. The symbol for mercury comes from the Latin name for quicksilver. About 75 percent of the elements are metals.

Except for hydrogen, nonmetals are found on the right side of the periodic table. Nonmetal solids usually have dull surfaces and are brittle. Brittle substances cannot easily be hammered or bent into another shape. Nonmetals are poor conductors of heat and electricity. At room temperature, 10 nonmetals are solids, 11 are gases, and 1 is a liquid.

a

b

Figure 3–12. Metals (a) and nonmetals (b) have different properties.

Lesson Summary

- The periodic table is a table that shows how scientists classify elements.
- Symbols for elements may be one, two, or three letters, with the first letter always capitalized.
- Elements may be classified as metals or nonmetals or according to the electron structure of their atoms.

Lesson Review

Review the lesson to answer these questions.

1. From where do you think the symbol for mercury comes? Why is the symbol for mercury not M?
2. How might scientists use the symbols that stand for the elements?
3. What are some elements that have properties like those of calcium?
4. What is the lightest element that has properties like those of iodine?

Which are better conductors, metals or nonmetals?

Table 3–3
The Periodic Table
(Based on Carbon 12 = 12.0000)

Metals

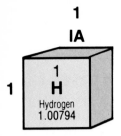

1 IA

| 1 H Hydrogen 1.00794 |

Transition Elements

	1 IA	2 IIA	3 IIIB	4 IVB	5 VB	6 VIB	7 VIIB	8	9 VIIIB
1	1 H Hydrogen 1.00794								
2	3 Li Lithium 6.941	4 Be Beryllium 9.01218							
3	11 Na Sodium 22.98977	12 Mg Magnesium 24.305							
4	19 K Potassium 39.0983	20 Ca Calcium 40.078	21 Sc Scandium 44.95591	22 Ti Titanium 47.88	23 V Vanadium 50.9415	24 Cr Chromium 51.9961	25 Mn Manganese 54.9380	26 Fe Iron 55.847	27 Co Cobalt 58.9332
5	37 Rb Rubidium 85.4678	38 Sr Strontium 87.62	39 Y Yttrium 88.9059	40 Zr Zirconium 91.224	41 Nb Niobium 92.9064	42 Mo Molybdenum 95.94	43 Tc Technetium 97.9072*	44 Ru Ruthenium 101.07	45 Rh Rhodium 102.9055
6	55 Cs Cesium 132.9054	56 Ba Barium 137.33	71 Lu Lutetium 174.967	72 Hf Hafnium 178.49	73 Ta Tantalum 180.9479	74 W Tungsten 183.85	75 Re Rhenium 186.207	76 Os Osmium 190.2	77 Ir Iridium 192.22
7	87 Fr Francium 223.0197*	88 Ra Radium 226.0254	103 Lr Lawrencium 260.1054*	104 Unq Unnilquadium 261*	105 Unp Unnilpentium 262*	106 Unh Unnilhexium 263*	107 Uns Unnilseptium 262*	108 Uno Unniloctium 265*	109 Une Unnilennium 266*

Lanthanide Series

57 La Lanthanum 138.9055	58 Ce Cerium 140.12	59 Pr Praseodymium 140.9077	60 Nd Neodymium 144.24	61 Pm Promethium 144.9128*	62 Sm Samarium 150.36

Actinide Series

89 Ac Actinium 227.0278*	90 Th Thorium 232.0381	91 Pa Protactinium 231.0359*	92 U Uranium 238.0289	93 Np Neptunium 237.0482	94 Pu Plutonium 244.0642*

Nonmetals

10	11 IB	12 IIB	13 IIIA	14 IVA	15 VA	16 VIA	17 VIIA	18 VIIIA
								2 He Helium 4.002602
			5 B Boron 10.811	6 C Carbon 12.011	7 N Nitrogen 14.0067	8 O Oxygen 15.9994	9 F Fluorine 18.998403	10 Ne Neon 20.179
			13 Al Aluminum 26.98154	14 Si Silicon 28.0855	15 P Phosphorus 30.97376	16 S Sulfur 32.06	17 Cl Chlorine 35.453	18 Ar Argon 39.948
28 Ni Nickel 58.69	29 Cu Copper 63.546	30 Zn Zinc 65.39	31 Ga Gallium 69.723	32 Ge Germanium 72.59	33 As Arsenic 74.9216	34 Se Selenium 78.96	35 Br Bromine 79.904	36 Kr Krypton 83.80
46 Pd Palladium 106.42	47 Ag Silver 107.8682	48 Cd Cadmium 112.41	49 In Indium 114.82	50 Sn Tin 118.710	51 Sb Antimony 121.75	52 Te Tellurium 127.60	53 I Iodine 126.9045	54 Xe Xenon 131.29
78 Pt Platinum 195.08	79 Au Gold 196.9665	80 Hg Mercury 200.59	81 Tl Thallium 204.383	82 Pb Lead 207.2	83 Bi Bismuth 208.9804	84 Po Polonium 208.9824*	85 At Astatine 209.98712*	86 Rn Radon 222.017*

63 Eu Europium 151.96	64 Gd Gadolinium 157.25	65 Tb Terbium 158.9254	66 Dy Dysprosium 162.50	67 Ho Holmium 164.9304	68 Er Erbium 167.26	69 Tm Thulium 168.9342	70 Yb Ytterbium 173.04
95 Am Americium 243.0614*	96 Cm Curium 247.0703*	97 Bk Berkelium 247.0703*	98 Cf Californium 251.0796*	99 Es Einsteinium 252.0828*	100 Fm Fermium 257.0951*	101 Md Mendelevium 258.986*	102 No Nobelium 259.1009*

Language Arts Skills

Using Context Clues

Predicting the meaning of unfamiliar words can be done by using the meaning of the surrounding words. When doing this, you are using context clues. For example, determine the meaning of *periodic table* from its use in the following sentence.

> Ellen looked at the **periodic table** to find the symbol and mass of silver.

From the rest of the sentence, you know that the periodic table is a table that gives you the symbol and mass of an element.

Read the following sentences. Then, use the clues in each sentence to define the word or words in boldfaced type.

> **Atoms,** the tiny particles that make up matter, are composed of even smaller particles.

What part of the sentence helped you define the word *atoms?* In this case, the unfamiliar word is defined for you in the sentence.

> Iron, copper, and aluminum are all classified as **metals.**

How did you define *metals?* What elements of the sentence helped you to determine the meaning? In what way did you need to apply your knowledge from previous experience to help you determine the meaning?

When you encounter unfamiliar words while reading or listening, you can often determine the meaning by finding clues in the sentence or paragraph in which the words are used. Sometimes the words are defined. Sometimes you must combine other clues with knowledge you already have.

Chapter 3 Review

Summary

1. Substances have the same composition throughout. 3:1
2. The chemical properties of a substance affect the way the substance reacts to form new substances. 3:1
3. Chemical reactions produce new substances. 3:1
4. Mass is neither created nor destroyed in a chemical reaction. 3:1
5. The physical properties of a substance can be observed without referring to another substance. 3:1
6. In a physical change, the same substance is present before and after the change. 3:1
7. All matter is made of atoms. 3:2
8. An element is made of only one kind of atom. 3:2
9. Atoms have a nucleus that contains protons and neutrons. 3:2
10. The number of protons in an atom is its atomic number. 3:2
11. Negatively charged particles called electrons move around the nucleus of an atom. 3:2
12. Scientists use the electron cloud model to help explain atoms. 3:2
13. Each element has a symbol, and scientists classify these elements into a table called the periodic table. 3:3
14. Scientists group elements with similar arrangements of electrons into families. 3:3
15. The elements in a chemical family have similar properties and are listed in a column on the periodic table. 3:3

Science Words

atoms	element	periodic table
chemical change	law of conservation	physical change
chemical property	of mass	physical property
chemical reaction	neutron	proton
electron	nucleus	substance

Understanding Science Words

Complete each of the following sentences with a word or words from the Science Words that will make the sentence correct.

1. Matter is made of very tiny units called _____.

2. A characteristic that can be observed only when a substance changes to another substance is called a _____.
3. A negatively charged particle moving around the nucleus of an atom is called an _____.
4. Matter that has the same composition throughout is a _____.
5. The central core of an atom is the _____.
6. The particle in the nucleus with a positive charge is the

_____.

7. A characteristic that can be observed without a substance being changed to a different substance is a _____.
8. Matter that is made of only one type of atom is an _____.
9. When a substance is changed into a different substance, a

_____ has occurred.
10. A particle in the nucleus with no electrical charge is the

_____.

11. A change in the size, shape, or state of matter is a _____.
12. The statement that says mass is neither created nor destroyed in a chemical reaction is the _____.
13. The process of chemical change is a _____.
14. Elements are classified in the _____.

Questions

A. Checking Facts
Determine whether each of the following statements is true or false. Rewrite the false statements to make them correct.
1. When water freezes, a physical change takes place.
2. Air is matter, because it has mass and takes up space.
3. Light can be solid, liquid, or gaseous.
4. Elements are substances.
5. Physical properties depend on the way substances affect each other.
6. A new substance forms in a physical change.
7. Energy is involved in all chemical changes.
8. Elements are made of atoms.
9. The nucleus of an atom contains protons and electrons.
10. Elements with similar properties are placed in the same column on the periodic table.

B. Recalling Facts

Choose the word or phrase that correctly completes each of the following sentences.

1. All atoms of an element have the same number of
   (a) protons.   (c) neutrons and electrons.
   (b) neutrons.   (d) neutrons and protons.
2. Pure matter is always the same and is known as
   (a) an element.   (b) a compound.   (c) a substance.   (d) a solid.
3. Which of the following is a correct match of the element name and symbol?
   (a) I—iron   (c) Hg—mercury
   (b) H—helium   (d) Ne—nitrogen
4. What part of the atom has a negative electrical charge?
   (a) electron   (b) proton   (c) neutron   (d) the nucleus
5. Rusting is an example of a
   (a) physical property.   (c) physical change.
   (b) chemical property.   (d) chemical change.
6. Elements that are usually shiny and good conductors of heat and electricity are known as
   (a) gases.   (b) metals.   (c) solids.   (d) nonmetals.
7. The ability of a substance, such as wood, to burn is a
   (a) physical property.   (c) physical change.
   (b) chemical property.   (d) chemical change.

C. Understanding Concepts

Answer each of the following questions using complete sentences.

1. What kind of property is the state of a substance?
2. How are all atoms alike?
3. How are the elements in a chemical family different?
4. An atom of platinum, Pt, has 78 protons. How many electrons does it contain?
5. What is the law of conservation of mass?
6. How is a physical property different from a chemical property?

D. Applying Concepts

Think about what you have learned in this chapter. Answer each of the following questions using complete sentences.

1. Explain the electron cloud model of atoms.
2. What are some elements that have properties similar to helium? Explain how you know.

Chapter 4
Combinations of Matter

The chairs on a Ferris wheel move as the hub of the wheel turns. Ribs or spokes connect the rim and hub so that the Ferris wheel moves as a unit. Atoms of different elements may attach to each other by bonds to form new substances. What are these substances called? What forms when atoms of the same element bond?

Ferris wheel

Compounds

LESSON GOALS

In this lesson you will learn

- elements combine to form compounds.

- there are different kinds of compounds.

- symbols may be grouped in a formula to show the elements in a compound.

How many words do you know? Language experts think that most sixth-graders know about 50,000 words. It would be hard to make a list of all the words you understand when you hear or read them. To list this many words, one on each line, would take more than 1,750 sheets of paper. The number of words in the English language has been estimated at one million. If one million words were listed on lined paper, more than 35,000 sheets would be needed. All of these words are made by using one or more of the 26 letters of the alphabet.

Figure 4–1. Elements, like letters of the alphabet, can be combined.

Just as the letters of the alphabet can be combined to form words, elements can be combined to form compounds. A **compound** is a substance formed when atoms of different elements combine chemically. Scientists have discovered about four million compounds formed from two or more of the 109 elements. Many new compounds are made each year.

What is a compound?

Atoms combine in chemical reactions because of the activity of their electrons. Some atoms share electrons with other atoms, forming a particle called a **molecule** (MAHL ih kyewl). A water molecule is made of the atoms of two elements. These elements are hydrogen and oxygen. The atoms join in a chemical reaction to form a molecule of water. Trillions of water molecules are found in a single drop of water. Compounds made of molecules, such as water, are called molecular compounds. In molecular compounds, the atoms share electrons.

Sugars are a group of molecular compounds. All sugars are made of the atoms of three kinds of elements. These elements are carbon, hydrogen, and oxygen. Each compound of sugar forms when a certain number of carbon, hydrogen, and oxygen atoms join in a certain way. The properties of a compound are different from the properties of the elements that make up the compound.

Figure 4–2. Sugar granules can be divided into very small pieces, and still have the properties of sugar.

Suppose you cut a cube of table sugar into smaller and smaller pieces. There is a limit to how many times a sugar cube can be divided and still be sugar. A sugar molecule is the smallest amount of a compound of sugar that still has all the properties of sugar. What is the smallest amount of water that still has all the properties of water?

Chemical reactions can separate a sugar molecule into hydrogen, oxygen, and carbon atoms. The atoms will not have the same properties as the sugar molecule. Hydrogen and oxygen are odorless, colorless gases. Charcoal and soot are carbon. How are the properties of the compound sugar different from the properties of the elements that form it?

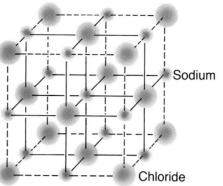

Sodium

Chloride

Figure 4-3. Salt is a compound formed of ions of sodium and chlorine.

Why does an ion have an electric charge?

What is an ionic compound?

Some compounds are formed when an electron is transferred from one atom to another. An atom that has gained or lost an electron is an **ion** (I ahn). An ion has an electric charge. The numbers of protons and electrons in an ion are not the same. When an atom gains an electron, an ion with a negative charge is formed. Nonmetals often gain electrons when they form compounds. An atom that loses an electron forms an ion with a positive charge. In general, metals lose electrons when they form compounds. Ions with opposite charges attract each other to form compounds. Ionic compounds are those compounds formed of ions. Ionic compounds do not contain molecules.

Table salt is an ionic compound. An atom of sodium gives an electron to an atom of chlorine in a chemical reaction. The sodium atom becomes a sodium ion when it loses the electron. The chlorine atom gains one electron, forming a chloride ion. Sodium ions and chloride ions join to make sodium chloride. This compound is called table salt. The properties of salt are not the same as those of chlorine and sodium. Chlorine is a green gas and sodium is a shiny metal. What are some properties of salt?

Atoms of the same element can combine to form a molecule. The molecules of oxygen in the air you breathe are made of oxygen atoms. Two oxygen atoms join to form one molecule of oxygen. An oxygen molecule is not a compound. Oxygen molecules are made of only oxygen atoms. To be a compound, a molecule must have atoms of at least two different elements. Why is carbon dioxide a compound?

Figure 4-4. Each oxygen molecule is composed of two oxygen atoms.

Oxygen Molecule

Oxygen   Oxygen

Activity 4-1 Forming Compounds

How is a compound formed?

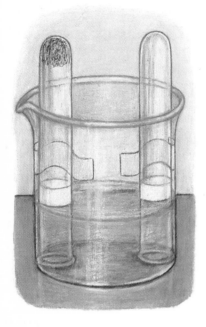

Materials

steel wool
2 test tubes
beaker
water

masking tape
metric ruler
pencil and paper

What to do

1. Place a small, wet ball of steel wool in one test tube. Use the eraser end of a pencil to gently push the steel wool to the bottom of the test tube. Do not put anything in the other test tube.
2. Record the properties of the steel wool.
3. Place both test tubes upside down in a beaker that is half full of water. Tape the test tubes so they will remain standing upside down in the beaker.
4. Measure and record the height of the water level in each tube.
5. Observe the test tubes once a day for five days. Measure any change in the water levels. Make a table for each test tube in which to record your observations and measurements.

What did you learn?

1. Describe the changes in the steel wool.
2. What compound was formed?
3. Explain any changes in the water level of the tubes.

Using what you learned

1. Where else have you seen this compound formed?
2. What combined to make the compound?
3. From where did the atoms of the compound come? What is your evidence?
4. How might the compound be prevented from forming?

Formulas

A symbol is used to stand for an atom of an element. Symbols put together a certain way to show the elements in a compound make a **formula.** Look at Table 4–1. What elements make each compound?

There are rules for writing chemical formulas. The formula for a water molecule is H_2O. H is the symbol for a hydrogen atom and O is the symbol for an oxygen atom. The small number 2 after the H means two hydrogen atoms. The O has no number after it. No number means only one atom of oxygen. The number 1 is not written in a formula. H_2O shows that a water molecule contains two atoms of hydrogen combined with one atom of oxygen. A different combination of hydrogen and oxygen atoms is a different compound. The formula for the compound hydrogen peroxide is H_2O_2. This compound is used as a bleach and a disinfectant. How is the formula of hydrogen peroxide different from that of water?

The formula for carbon dioxide is CO_2. How many atoms of each element are in the compound carbon dioxide? CO is the formula for carbon monoxide. Carbon monoxide is made of the same elements as carbon dioxide. Compare the formulas for both compounds. How are they different?

Table 4–1 Some Compounds and Their Formulas	
Compound	Formula
Water	H_2O
Carbon dioxide	CO_2
Table salt	NaCl
Table sugar	$C_{12}H_{22}O_{11}$
Vitamin A	$C_{20}H_{30}O$

Carbon Dioxide

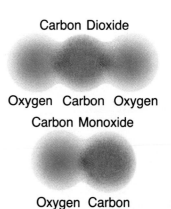

Oxygen Carbon Oxygen

Carbon Monoxide

Oxygen Carbon

Figure 4–5. Carbon dioxide and carbon monoxide are composed of the same elements.

Lesson Summary

- A compound is formed when the atoms of different elements combine in a chemical reaction.
- In molecular compounds, atoms share electrons. Ionic compounds contain ions, formed when electrons are transferred from one atom to another.
- A formula shows the kind of atoms and number of atoms in a compound.

Lesson Review

Review the lesson to answer these questions.
1. What is an ion?
2. How are elements different from compounds?
3. Vitamin C has the formula $C_6H_8O_6$. How many atoms of each of its elements does it have?

Mixtures

LESSON GOALS

In this lesson you will learn

- mixtures are formed without chemical reactions.
- there are different kinds of mixtures.
- how mixtures can be separated.

Scott is helping his parents with lunch by making fruit salad. Scott has sliced apples, grapes, and oranges for the salad. Fruit salad is a combination of different substances, but it is not a compound. There is no chemical reaction. Fruit salad is a mixture. A **mixture** is a combination of substances that forms without a chemical reaction.

Mixtures can be combinations of solid, liquid, and gaseous substances. Fruit punch is a mixture of liquids. The air you breathe is a mixture of gases. Soil is mostly a mixture of solids. Ocean water is an example of solids and gases mixed with a liquid. What are some substances in ocean water? A carbonated beverage is an example of gas mixed with a liquid. What other mixtures can you name?

What is a mixture?

Figure 4-6. Most of the matter around you is in the form of mixtures.

a

b

c

Solutions

A **solution** is a special kind of mixture in which a substance is spread evenly throughout another substance. A solution is exactly the same all the way through. Why is fruit salad not a solution?

Watch someone put a lump of sugar into a glass of tea. The lump of sugar sinks to the bottom of the glass and begins to dissolve. The sugar and tea in the glass are a mixture, but are not yet a solution. At first, the tea is sweeter at the bottom of the glass than at the top. The tea may be stirred. What happens to the lump of sugar? When the dissolved sugar is present evenly throughout the tea, the entire mixture is a solution. All parts of the tea will taste sweet.

Some people put two lumps of sugar in tea. Two lumps of sugar can easily dissolve in a glass of tea. It is not possible, however, to keep on dissolving sugar into the tea. After a few lumps, no more sugar will dissolve. The tea-sugar solution is said to be saturated. A **saturated solution** is a solution in which no more of a substance can be dissolved at that temperature. Temperature is important in forming a saturated solution. More of a substance can usually be dissolved in a warmer liquid than in a cooler one. It is easier to dissolve sugar in hot tea than in iced tea. The dissolving liquid, the tea, is called the solvent.

Figure 4-7. Sugar in tea forms a mixture (a), then a solution (b) when completely dissolved. Adding more sugar may form a saturated solution (c).

How is a solution different from other mixtures?

What is a saturated solution?

73

Activity 4-2 Making Solutions

Which solvent dissolves the most materials?

Materials
20 labels
20 small jars
safety goggles
4 solvents (water, rubbing alcohol, vegetable oil, vinegar)
5 spoons
5 materials (sugar, cocoa, petroleum jelly, flour, baking soda)
pencil and paper

What to do

1. Label five jars *Water*. Label five more jars *Alcohol*. Label five jars *Oil*. Label five jars *Vinegar*.
2. Make a table like the one shown. Predict which solvents will dissolve each material. Record your predictions in the table by using a check mark.
3. Put on your safety goggles. Fill each jar half full of the solvent named on its label.
4. Put a spoonful of sugar in one of the jars labeled *Water*. Stir carefully. Record your observations.

Solvent	Prediction/Result	Dissolving Materials				
		Sugar	Cocoa	Petroleum Jelly	Flour	Baking Soda
Water	Prediction					
	Result					
Alcohol	Prediction					
	Result					
Oil	Prediction					
	Result					
Vinegar	Prediction					
	Result					

5. Put a spoonful of sugar in a jar of another solvent. Record your observations in the table. Repeat this step with each solvent.

6. Repeat steps 4 and 5 with the remaining materials. Use a new spoon for each material.

What did you learn?

1. In which solvent did the most materials dissolve?
2. In which solvent did the fewest materials dissolve?
3. How did your predictions compare with your results?

Using what you learned

1. Which solvent would be most useful for cleaning food stains from clothing?
2. Which material would be the most difficult stain to remove from clothing?
3. Which solvent might be called the universal solvent? Explain.

Suspensions

A **suspension** (suh SPEN chun) is another kind of mixture in which the substances that make it up are not dissolved. When a suspension is left undisturbed, the materials in it separate. The force of gravity causes the heavier materials to slowly settle to the bottom of the container.

What happens to a suspension that is left undisturbed?

Salad dressing that contains only oil and vinegar is a suspension. Why do you shake a bottle of vinegar and oil salad dressing before you use it? What happens when you stop shaking it? Many medicines are also suspensions. For this reason, they must be shaken before they are used.

Figure 4-8. Dust particles in air are a commonly-seen suspension.

Dust particles in air also form a suspension. You may see the dust when a ray of sunlight shines through a window. Dust particles are much larger than atoms. Therefore, light is scattered as it strikes the dust. A beam of light passing through clean air cannot be seen because the light is not scattered. For a length of time, dust will be suspended in the air. Eventually, the force of gravity will cause dust to settle onto the furniture and floor.

Separating Mixtures

Substances in a mixture are not chemically combined. Each substance still has its own properties. The physical properties of substances can be used to separate mixtures. What properties could you use to separate a mixture of buttons?

Some mixtures can be separated by a filter. A strainer is a kind of filter. What have you seen filtered with a strainer? Some solids that are mixed with liquids can be separated with a filter. The liquids pass through holes in the filter. The solids do not go through. They are trapped in the filter.

Some mixtures of solids can be separated by dissolving one of the substances. A mixture of salt and sand can be separated by adding water to the mixture. The salt will dissolve in the water; the sand will not. Then the mixture of sand, salt, and water can be poured through a filter. The sand will be trapped in the filter. The salt and water solution will go through the filter. The salt may then be separated from the water by evaporation. Evaporating the water from the solution leaves only the salt. Many solutions can be separated by evaporation.

A different method may be used with suspensions. Many suspensions can be separated by allowing them to remain undisturbed. The heavier materials will settle to the bottom of the liquid.

Figure 4–9. Some mixtures can be separated by filtering.

How can a mixture of salt and sand be separated?

Lesson Summary

- Mixtures form without chemical reactions.
- Solutions and suspensions are special types of mixtures.
- Mixtures may be separated by filtering, evaporaton, or settling.

Lesson Review

Review the lesson to answer these questions.
1. What is a mixture?
2. How is a mixture different from a compound?
3. How could you use a filter to separate a mixture of raisins and flour?
4. How is a solution different from a suspension?

Activity 4-3 Separating Mixtures

QUESTION   How can you separate and compare mixtures?

Materials

paper towel	water
metric ruler	beaker
scissors	tape
black felt-tip pens	pencil and paper

What to do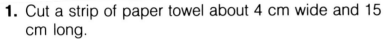

1. Cut a strip of paper towel about 4 cm wide and 15 cm long.
2. Make a large ink dot with a felt-tip pen about 5 cm from the bottom of the strip.
3. Put about 3 cm of water in your glass or beaker.
4. Dip the bottom of the strip into the water. The ink dot must be above the water. Bend the top of the strip over the edge of the glass or beaker. Secure the end with tape.
5. Wait for the water to soak up to the top of the strip.
6. Observe the ink dot. Record your observations.
7. Repeat steps 1 through 6 using different pens. Record your observations.

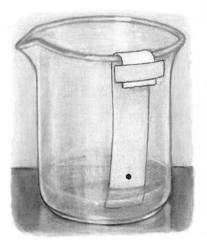

What did you learn?

1. What color ink was in each pen you used?
2. What did you observe when you placed the paper towel strip in the water?
3. What colors were found in the different inks?

Using what you learned

1. What evidence do you have that the ink in the pens is a mixture instead of a compound?
2. How do you know the black inks in the different pens are not the same?
3. Why did the ink move up the paper towel?
4. Suppose you stain your clothing. You try to clean the stain with water and a ring forms around the stained area. Explain why this happened.

Science and Technology

How is a Tire Like a Record and Gum?

Do you know what tires, phonograph records, and chewing gum have in common? Each object is made from organic compounds called polymers. A polymer is a compound made up of simpler chemicals called monomers. Each monomer unit in the materials above contains carbon, hydrogen, and oxygen atoms arranged in a chainlike sequence. When several different monomers are combined and heated under pressure, a polymer forms.

A car's tires are made up of the polymer we know as rubber. One type of rubber is made by combining monomers of a substance called isoprene with sulfur. This mixture is heated in a process called vulcanization. Rubber, the product of vulcanization, is easily molded into durable automobile tires.

Orlon® is another type of polymer. The polymer molecules are very long chains that form fibers. Orlon® fibers can be woven into a number of fabrics, including the fabric used to produce some types of carpeting. Perhaps you have a sweater or blanket made of Orlon®.

Your favorite musical group has made recordings of its music using a polymer. Phonograph records are made of a polymer that is nicknamed PVC. This compound is excellent for recording music.

Chewing gum gets its "chewiness" from a polymer. The monomers from which the polymer is formed are found in chicle, the sap collected from certain tropical trees. The polymer in chewing gum is soft and stretchy and does not break apart easily. These characteristics make the polymer ideal for blowing bubbles with bubble gum.

From tires to chewing gum, carbon, hydrogen, and oxygen atoms are the building blocks for millions of polymer compounds.

Chapter 4 Review

Summary

1. A compound is formed when the atoms of different elements combine in a chemical reaction.   4:1
2. All compounds are formed by combining two or more of the 109 elements.   4:1
3. Atoms that share electrons form molecules.   4:1
4. A compound has properties different from the elements that form it.   4:1
5. Atoms that lose or gain electrons become ions.   4:1
6. Electrons are transferred from one atom to another to form the ions in ionic compounds.   4:1
7. Compounds have formulas that show what elements are in them.   4:1
8. Mixtures contain two or more substances and are formed without chemical reactions.   4:2
9. A solution is a mixture in which a substance is dissolved in, evenly spread throughout, another substance.   4:2
10. A suspension is also a mixture, but the substances do not dissolve in one another.   4:2
11. The substances in many mixtures can be separated by filtering, evaporation, or settling.   4:2

Science Words

compound	**ion**	**molecule**	**solution**
formula	**mixture**	**saturated solution**	**suspension**

Understanding Science Words

Complete each of the following sentences with a word or words from the Science Words that will make the sentence correct.

1. A special mixture in which the substances are evenly mixed throughout is a _____.
2. When two or more atoms combine by sharing electrons, they form a _____.
3. Symbols combined to represent the elements in a compound make a _____.
4. The atoms of different elements may combine chemically to form a _____.

5. Any combination of substances that are not chemically combined is a _____.

6. An atom that has lost or gained an electron is called an _____.

7. A mixture in which heavier materials may settle to the bottom is a _____.

8. When no more of one substance can be dissolved in another substance, a _____ has formed.

Questions

A. Checking Facts

Determine whether each of the following sentences is true or false. Rewrite the false statements to make them correct.

1. Atoms of different elements may combine physically to form a compound.
2. Atoms that share electrons with other atoms form ionic compounds.
3. If an atom loses an electron, it becomes a molecule.
4. Symbols put together in a certain way to show the elements in a compound make a formula.
5. A solution is a special kind of mixture in which a substance is spread evenly throughout another substance.
6. Salt can be separated from a salt water solution by settling.
7. A mixture is a combination of substances that forms during a chemical reaction.
8. More sugar can be dissolved in cold water than in hot water.

B. Recalling Facts

Choose the word or phrase that correctly completes each of the following sentences.

1. A copper atom that has lost two electrons is
   (a) a molecule.   (c) an alloy.
   (b) a compound.   (d) an ion.
2. Compounds are made of at least two
   (a) mixtures.   (b) ions.   (c) suspensions.   (d) elements.
3. What is the formula for a compound that has one sodium atom, one oxygen atom, and one hydrogen atom?
   (a) SH_2O (b) $NaOH$ (c) SOH (d) HO_2Na

4. Electrons are shared in
   (a) an element.   (c) a molecule.
   (b) an ion.   (d) an ionic compound.
5. A solution in which no more substances can be dissolved is
   (a) saturated.   (b) filtered.   (c) ionic.   (d) separated.
6. Which one of the following is a compound?
   (a) Co   (b) N_2 (c) NO   (d) Fe

C. Understanding Concepts

Answer each of the following questions using complete sentences. Use the table to answer the questions.

Some Compounds and Formulas	
Compound	Formula
Ammonia	NH_3
Baking soda	$NaHCO_3$
Copper(II) sulfate	$CuSO_4$
Hydrogen peroxide	H_2O_2
Rust	Fe_2O_3

1. What elements combine to form rust?
2. How many elements are in baking soda?
3. How many hydrogen atoms are there for every nitrogen atom in ammonia?
4. What makes hydrogen peroxide different from water?
5. What kinds of atoms make copper sulfate?

D. Applying Concepts

Think about what you have learned in this chapter. Answer each of the following questions using complete sentences.

1. How can you separate each of the following mixtures?
   (a) sand and water   (d) salt and water
   (b) oil and vinegar   (e) salt and sand
   (c) pennies and nickels
2. The formula for one kind of soap, sodium stearate, is $C_{17}H_{35}COONa$. How many atoms of each element are present in two of these formula units?

Chapter 5
Investigating Compounds

Over six million chemical compounds are known. Without classification, study and use of these compounds would be almost impossible. Scientists use both the structure and properties of compounds to classify them. How are the items in a grocery store classified? What problem might Jake have if the items in the grocery store were not organized?

Jake in a grocery store

LESSON GOALS

In this lesson you will learn
- properties and composition of compounds are important in their classification.
- all organic compounds contain carbon.

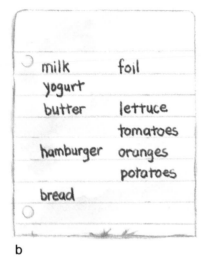

a   b

Figure 5-1. Items in a grocery store (a) may be grouped (b) to aid shopping.

Jake's mother asked him to go to the grocery store. She gave him a list of ten items to buy. Jake was worried that he would not be able to find everything. He knew, though, that items in the grocery store are grouped, or classified, to make shopping easier.

Jake thought about the characteristics of each item on his list. He put all items with similar properties together. Jake knew he could find milk in the dairy case. What other items on his list have properties similar to milk? What properties did Jake use to classify the rest of the items on his list?

The periodic table shows how scientists group elements. Recall that some mixtures may be grouped with solutions. Scientists also group compounds. All compounds are formed by chemical reactions, but no two compounds are the same. Atoms of different elements react with each other in many ways to form the millions of compounds on Earth.

How are compounds formed?

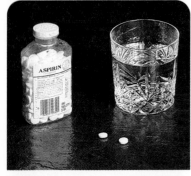

Each compound has a set of properties that scientists use to classify it. Physical and chemical properties of a compound affect how it can be used. A compound may also be classified by its composition. You can tell the composition of a compound by looking at its formula. The formula for limestone is $CaCO_3$. Of what elements is limestone composed?

Figure 5-2. Each compound contains at least two different elements. Carbon, hydrogen, and oxygen make up aspirin and sugar. Rust contains oxygen and iron. The compound P_2S_3 is in the tips of strike-anywhere matches.

What element besides carbon do most organic compounds contain?

Organic Compounds

Scientists have a special name for compounds that are made with carbon. An **organic compound** is one that contains carbon. The word *organic* suggests life. At one time scientists thought that carbon compounds could be found only in organisms or in matter that was once alive. This is why carbon compounds are known as organic compounds.

Carbon is combined with other elements in organic compounds. Most organic compounds also contain hydrogen. Others may contain oxygen, nitrogen, phosphorus, sulfur, or a few other elements. Many organic compounds are made in nature. About 150 years ago, scientists discovered they could make organic compounds in laboratories. Since that time, several million organic compounds have been made in laboratories. Many compounds in everyday use are organic compounds. All of the materials shown in Figure 5-3 contain organic compounds. Vitamins and plastics are organic compounds.

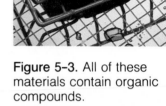

Figure 5-3. All of these materials contain organic compounds.

An organic compound that contains only carbon and hydrogen is called a **hydrocarbon.** Hydrocarbons are often used for fuels. One common hydrocarbon is methane. Methane is common in marshes. When organisms in the marsh die and decay, methane is produced. Methane is sometimes called "marsh gas." Its formula is CH_4. How many atoms of hydrogen are there for each atom of carbon in methane?

Natural gas is a mixture of gases that contains methane. People use natural gas as a fuel for heating and cooking in their homes. Campers often use another hydrocarbon called propane for heating and cooking. The formula for propane is C_3H_8.

Petroleum is a mixture of hydrocarbons. Many useful products are made from petroleum. Gasoline and other fuels are petroleum products. Many medicines, cosmetics, dyes, paints, plastics, clothes, and camera films are also made from petroleum.

What are compounds that contain only hydrogen and carbon called?

Lesson Summary

- Scientists classify compounds by their physical and chemical properties and by their composition.
- Organic compounds contain carbon.

Lesson Review

Review the lesson to answer these questions.
1. What do scientists need to know about a compound in order to classify it?
2. Why are there so many more compounds than there are elements?

Inorganic Compounds

LESSON GOALS

In this lesson you will learn

- most inorganic compounds are compounds of any elements except carbon.
- inorganic compounds may be classified into four groups: oxides and inorganic acids, bases, and salts.
- indicators are compounds that may be used to determine if a solution is an acid or a base.

Inorganic compounds are all compounds made from any elements except those carbon compounds classified as organic. Examples of inorganic compounds that contain carbon are carbon dioxide (CO_2) and carbonic acid (H_2CO_3). Inorganic compounds are sometimes classified into four groups because of their composition and properties: oxides, acids, bases, and salts.

Oxides

Oxygen combined with one other element is an **oxide** (AHK side). One oxide is aluminum oxide. Aluminum oxide forms when oxygen combines with the element aluminum. This oxide, Al_2O_3, forms a protective coating on aluminum. Silicon can combine with oxygen to form silicon dioxide, SiO_2. Perhaps you have built a castle out of silicon dioxide at a beach. What is another name for silicon dioxide?

Most elements can combine with oxygen to form oxides. What is the composition of each oxide listed in Table 5-1? How are the oxides used?

Figure 5-4. This sculpture is made of silicon dioxide (SiO_2).

How are inorganic compounds classified?

Table 5-1 Some Oxides and Their Uses		
Oxide	Formula	Some Uses
Zinc oxide	ZnO	skin cream, cosmetics, ceramics
Lead(IV) oxide	PbO_2	batteries
Tin(IV) oxide	SnO_2	putty, perfumes, cosmetics
Copper(I) oxide	Cu_2O	colored glass (red), ceramics

Some oxides are harmful. Oxides of nitrogen are produced when some fuels are burned. Two common ones are nitrogen oxide (NO) and nitrogen dioxide (NO_2). They are produced in high temperature engines. They can kill plants and may be harmful to animals, including people. High amounts of nitrogen oxides in the air can lead to lung diseases. These pollutants in the air also aid in forming smog. Oxides of sulfur are also pollutants from burning fuels. These oxides are the main cause of acid rain.

Figure 5-5. Many foods contain weak acids.

Acids

An **acid** is a substance that forms hydrogen ions (H^+) as it dissolves in water. Because of these ions, all acids have many of the same properties. Acids cause some foods to taste sour. Vinegar, for example, owes its sour taste to acetic acid, an organic compound. When dissolved in water, acids conduct electricity. A chemical property of some acids is that they react with many metals.

What causes all acids to have many of the same properties?

Some acids are poisonous. Some cause burns on skin and destroy other materials. **CAUTION:** *NEVER taste or touch a substance to find out if it is an acid. Also, you should always wear safety goggles when working with strong acids.* Acids are useful in many ways. Table 5-2 shows some inorganic acids and their uses.

Table 5-2 Some Inorganic Acids and Their Uses		
Acid	Formula	Some Uses
Sulfuric acid	H_2SO_4	fertilizers, pigments, explosives, car batteries
Hydrochloric acid	HCl	stomach acid, cleaning metals and bricks
Hydrofluoric acid	HF	polishing, etching, and shining glass
Nitric acid	HNO_3	refining ores, making drugs
Phosphoric acid	H_3PO_4	soft drinks, needed for plant and animal cell growth

Red ants contain the substance formic acid. This acid is injected when the insect stings an animal. Many animal body fluids contain acids. Stomach acid aids food digestion. Conifers and cranberries are examples of plants that grow best in acid soils.

Figure 5-6. Bases have many uses. Some, however, must be used with caution.

What are some properties of bases?

Soft drinks often contain carbonic acid. Soft drinks, however, taste sweet because they contain sugar or other sweeteners. Carbonic acid is also present in blood and ocean water. Some acids may be used to clean metals. Paints and fertilizers are made from acids and other substances. Sulfuric acid is often present in acid precipitation. It is an acid widely used in industry. The United States produces more sulfuric acid than it does any other chemical.

Bases

A **base** is a substance that dissolves in water to form hydroxide ions. A hydroxide ion is a unit of hydrogen and oxygen. Its formula is OH^-. An example of a base is sodium hydroxide, NaOH. When dissolved in water, bases conduct electricity. Bases taste bitter and feel slippery. **CAUTION:** *NEVER taste or touch a substance to find out if it is a base. You should always wear safety goggles when working with strong bases.* Bases are especially harmful if splashed into the eyes. Like acids, bases are important compounds, but some can be dangerous.

Many household chemicals are bases. Bases can dissolve fats and oils. What use does this suggest for bases? Baking soda dissolved in water is a base. Antacids such as milk of magnesia are bases. Ammonia is a base used for cleaning floors and windows. Lye, sodium hydroxide, is a strong base. Lye is used to make some soaps and drain cleaners. There are strong warnings on drain cleaner containers. Why do you think these warnings are there? Look at Table 5-3 for some inorganic bases and their uses.

Table 5-3 Some Inorganic Bases and Their Uses		
Base	Formula	Some Uses
Sodium hydroxide	NaOH	making soap and detergents, drain and oven cleaners
Magnesium hydroxide	$Mg(OH)_2$	stomach antacid, sugar refining
Ammonia	NH_3	cleaning agent, textiles
Potassium hydroxide	KOH	making soap, matches, medicine
Calcium hydroxide	$Ca(OH)_2$	plasters, mortars, cements

Acid and Base Indicators

Scientists never taste or touch a substance to find out if it is an acid or a base. There is a safe way to find out if a substance is an acid or a base. An **indicator** (IHN duh kayt ur) is a compound that changes color when added to acids and bases. Often indicators are organic compounds. The color change indicates whether a substance is an acid or a base.

Litmus is an indicator made from lichens. People use paper treated with litmus to find out if substances are acids or bases. Litmus paper can be red or blue. Blue litmus paper turns red when dipped in an acid. Red litmus paper turns blue when dipped in a base. Another common indicator is a compound called phenolphthalein (feen ul THAYL een). Phenolphthalein is clear in an acid and pink in a base.

Name two indicators.

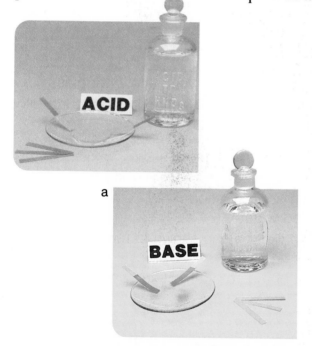

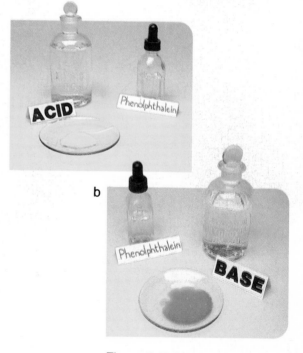

a

b

Figure 5-7. Litmus paper (a) or phenolphthalein (b) can be used to indicate acids and bases.

A special scale called the **pH scale** can be used to indicate the strength of acids and bases. The pH scale ranges between 0 and 14. A pH between 0 and 7 indicates an acid. A pH between 7 and 14 indicates a base. A substance that is neither an acid nor a base has a pH of 7. A substance with a pH of 7 is called **neutral.** Water is a neutral substance. Pure water has a pH of 7.

For what is the pH scale used?

Activity 5-1 Identifying Acids and Bases

How does litmus paper indicate acids and bases?

Materials

5 small jars
labels
safety goggles
vinegar
lemon juice
liquid detergent
baking soda solution
distilled water
litmus paper, red and blue
pencil and paper

What to do

1. Label the jars 1–5. Put on your safety goggles.
2. Do not touch the liquids. Fill each jar one-fourth full of the following liquids.
   Jar 1: vinegar
   Jar 2: lemon juice
   Jar 3: detergent
   Jar 4: baking soda solution
   Jar 5: distilled water
3. Make a table like the one shown to record your observations.
4. Dip one end of a strip of red litmus paper into the liquid in jar 1.

Jar Number	Contents	Litmus Paper	
		Red	Blue
1	vinegar		
2	lemon juice		
3	detergent		
4	baking soda solution		
5	distilled water		

5. Dip one end of a strip of blue litmus paper into the liquid in jar 1.
6. Using new strips of red and blue litmus paper for each test, repeat steps 4 and 5 with each liquid.

What did you learn?

1. What happened to the red litmus paper in each liquid?
2. What happened to the blue litmus paper in each liquid?
3. Which solutions are neutral? Acids? Bases?

Using what you learned

1. How can you use litmus paper to find out if a substance is an acid or a base?
2. What does the litmus paper test tell you about distilled water?
3. Some of the liquids used in this experiment may be combined to form a neutral solution. Predict a combination of two liquids that will form a neutral solution. Combine these liquids. Use litmus paper to test your prediction.

Salts

An acid and a base can be combined in a chemical reaction. The chemical changes that occur produce water and a salt. Water is neutral. It has a pH of 7. The salt produced may also be neutral.

What is produced when an acid and a base react?

The water and salt have properties different from those of the acid and the base from which they were formed. You know many properties of water. There are many kinds of salts. Most salts are composed of a metal and a nonmetal. Each salt can be made by combining a certain acid and base.

Some salts are common in your home. The most common salt is sodium chloride. Sodium chloride is a salt often used to flavor food. Some "salt substitutes" used to flavor food are made of potassium chloride. You may use baking soda when you cook. Baking soda is a salt called sodium hydrogen carbonate.

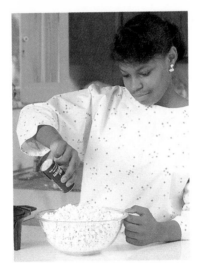

Figure 5-8. Salts have many practical uses.

How do some salts affect ice?

The toothpaste you use may contain a salt called tin(II) fluoride. Tin(II) fluoride is also called stannous fluoride. Why is this salt important?

Another salt you may have seen is calcium chloride. It, along with sodium chloride, can be used to melt snow and ice on streets and sidewalks. When either of these salts mixes with ice, the freezing point of water is lowered. Thus, the ice becomes liquid water. Salts can only be used to lower the freezing point of water so far. At temperatures below $-10°C$, salts no longer cause ice to melt.

Lesson Summary

- Most inorganic compounds do not contain carbon atoms.
- Oxides, acids, bases, and salts are four kinds of inorganic compounds.
- Indicators are compounds that change color to indicate whether a solution is an acid or a base.

Lesson Review

Review the lesson to answer these questions.
1. How are inorganic compounds often classified?
2. What are some properties of acids? Of bases?
3. Why are some solutions called neutral?
4. If a solution has a pH of 8, is the solution acidic, basic, or neutral?

Activity 5-2   Acid/Base Indicators

How can you make an indicator?

Materials

safety goggles
red cabbage (shredded)
2 beakers
hot water
spoon
strainer

3 jars
labels
3 mystery
  liquids
dropper
pencil and paper

What to do

1. Put on your safety goggles. Place some shredded red cabbage into a beaker.
2. Pour enough hot water into the container to cover the cabbage. Carefully stir the mixture until the water is bright red.
3. Use a strainer to separate the cabbage from the juice mixture. Collect the juice in the other beaker.
4. Label the jars 1, 2, and 3. Fill each jar one-half full of the following liquids.
   Jar 1: mystery liquid 1
   Jar 2: mystery liquid 2
   Jar 3: mystery liquid 3
5. Make a chart to record your observations.
6. Add five drops of red cabbage juice to each jar. Observe.

What did you learn?

1. What does the red cabbage juice act as? How do you know?
2. What changes did you observe in each liquid?
3. Which liquid is neither an acid nor a base? Explain.

Using what you learned

1. How do indicators help scientists learn about compounds?
2. Predict which mystery liquid is an acid and which is a base. Use litmus paper to test your prediction.

Soil Scientist

Every morning Donald R. Ballinger laces his sturdy hiking boots and packs a knapsack with an assortment of bottles and small tools. His daily work assignments take him to many of the farms and fields in the county in which he works. Don is a soil scientist. He studies the chemical properties of soil.

When he arrives at a work site, Don assembles the equipment he will need. He tests the soil at several sampling locations. At each location, Don collects a small jar of soil and prepares the soil for chemical analysis.

One of the chemical properties Don studies is soil pH. Acidic soil contains compounds that produce hydrogen ions in water. Basic soils contain compounds that produce hydroxide ions in water.

To determine the pH of a soil sample, Don uses an indicator solution. Don places a few drops of the solution in a vial containing a small amount of soil. If the soil is acidic, the colorless indicator solution will turn dark green. If the soil is basic, the solution will turn bright red.

Don then takes another small soil sample and compares its natural color to special color charts. These charts are used to determine the exact soil pH.

It is important to know the pH of soil. Farmers who rely on the soil for raising crops need to know what types of plants will grow best on their land. For example, tomatoes and asparagus require slightly acidic soil with pH between 5.5 and 6.0. Cranberries also need an acidic soil. Certain types of wheat, on the other hand, require slightly basic soil with a pH between 7.5 and 8.0. Soil scientists, like Don, can help farmers make decisions about which crops to grow.

Chapter 5 Review

Summary

1. The properties and composition of compounds are used for classification. 5:1
2. Organic compounds are made of carbon combined with other elements. 5:1
3. Some organic compounds are formed in nature; some are made in laboratories. 5:1
4. Hydrocarbons, compounds of carbon and hydrogen, are often used for fuels. 5:1
5. Compounds that do not contain carbon are called inorganic. 5:2
6. Inorganic compounds may be classified as oxides, acids, bases, and salts. 5:2
7. A compound of oxygen and another element is an oxide. 5:2
8. Acids and bases are chemical opposites. 5:2
9. Scientists use indicators that change color to find out safely if a substance is an acid or a base. 5:2
10. The pH scale from 0–14 is used to indicate the strength of acids and bases. 5:2
11. Neutral substances are neither acids nor bases; they have a pH of 7. 5:2
12. Water and a salt form when an acid and a base react. 5:2

Science Words

acid	indicator	pH scale
base	inorganic compound	organic compound
hydrocarbon	neutral	oxide

Understanding Science Words

Complete each of the following sentences with a word or words from the Science Words that will make the sentence correct.

1. A compound that contains carbon is called an _____.
2. A compound that contains only carbon and hydrogen is known as a _____.
3. A compound containing oxygen and one other element is an _____.

95

4. A substance that produces hydrogen ions as it dissolves in water is an _____.
5. A substance that dissolves in water to form hydroxide ions is a _____.
6. A compound that changes color when added to acids or bases is an _____.
7. A range of numbers used to measure the strength of acids and bases is the _____.
8. A compound that is neither an acid nor a base is said to be _____.
9. A compound that does not contain carbon is classified as an _____.

Questions

A. Checking Facts
Determine whether each of the following sentences is true or false. Rewrite the false statements to make them correct.
1. A chemical compound may be classified by its physical and chemical properties.
2. Most organic compounds do not contain carbon.
3. Salts can be made by combining water and acids.
4. A pH value of 4 indicates that a solution is neutral.
5. Blue litmus paper turns red when dipped into acid.
6. Bases taste sour and feel slippery.
7. A hydrocarbon is a compound of carbon and water.
8. Scientists may use indicators to find out if a solution is an acid or a base.

B. Recalling Facts
Choose the word or phrase that correctly completes each of the following sentences.
1. A substance with a pH of 7 is
   (a) neutral.   (b) an acid.   (c) a base.   (d) saturated.
2. Litmus turns red in
   (a) a salt.   (b) a base.   (c) an acid.   (d) an element.

3. Sand is an example of
   (a) an oxide.   (b) an acid.   (c) a base.   (d) a salt.
4. Which is the chemical opposite of a base?
   (a) water   (b) a salt   (c) an oxide   (d) an acid
5. What two compounds are formed when an acid reacts with a base?
   (a) water and oxide   (c) salt and oxide
   (b) water and salt   (d) organic and inorganic
6. All of the following are hydrocarbons **EXCEPT**
   (a) CH_3COOH.   (b) CH_3CH_3.   (c) C_8H_{18}.   (d) CH_4.

C. Understanding Concepts

Answer each of the following questions using complete sentences.

1. How is the composition of every oxide alike?
2. How are the properties of acids and bases different?
3. Which of the following household items contain acids? Which contain bases?
   (a) orange juice   (d) tea
   (b) ammonia   (e) soap
   (c) tomato sauce
4. Why does litmus paper not change color in distilled water?
5. Which of the following are NOT organic compounds?
   (a) alcohol (C_2H_6O)
   (b) water (H_2O)
   (c) antifreeze ($C_2H_6O_2$)
   (d) table sugar ($C_{12}H_{22}O_{11}$)
   (e) zinc oxide (ZnO)
   (f) methane (CH_4)
   (g) octane (C_8H_{18})

D. Applying Concepts

Think about what you have learned in this chapter. Answer each of the following questions using complete sentences.

1. How are all compounds alike?
2. How do scientists classify compounds?
3. What are two ways that organic compounds are made?
4. Explain why sodium bicarbonate (baking soda) is often sprinkled over acids that have been spilled.

UNIT 2 REVIEW

Answer these questions on a sheet of paper.
1. How are all atoms alike?
2. State the law of conservation of mass.
3. How is a solution different from a suspension?
4. Air cannot be seen. How do we know it is matter?
5. How does an ion form?
6. Choose an object and list its physical properties.
7. Describe the four groups of inorganic compounds.
8. The atomic number of calcium is 20. How many protons and electrons are in an atom of calcium?
9. Define organic compound and hydrocarbon.
10. Name the kind of change that occurs in each of the following: (a) wood burning, (b) paper tearing, (c) ice melting, (d) glass breaking.
11. How are elements classified in the periodic table?
12. Distinguish elements, compounds, and mixtures.
13. What is the pH scale?
14. The formula for vitamin B_{12} is $C_{63}H_{84}N_{14}O_{14}PCo$. List the kind and number of each element in the compound.

RECALLING ACTIVITIES

Think about the activities you did in this unit. Answer the questions about these activities.
1. How are properties useful?   3–1
2. Where are electrons found in an atom?   3–2
3. How is a compound formed?   4–1
4. Which solvent dissolves the most materials?   4–2
5. How can you separate and compare mixtures?   4–3
6. How does litmus paper indicate acids and bases?   5–1
7. How can you make an indicator?   5–2

IDEAS TO EXPLORE

1. Collect pictures from old magazines that show changes in matter. Label each picture as a physical change or a chemical change.
2. Prepare a list of common household materials. Separate the list into substances and mixtures. Find the formulas of the substances. Print the names and formulas on pieces of colored poster board. Make a mobile to hang in your classroom.
3. Do some library research to find out more about organic compounds. How are they used as fuels? Medicines? Other products? Prepare a written or oral report for your class.

PROBLEM SOLVING

What test could you use to tell the difference between a solution and a colloid? Solutions and suspensions are two kinds of mixtures. The particles in a suspension are much larger than those in solutions. For this reason, a suspension can be separated by filtering. There is a third type of mixture called a *colloid*. Its particles are larger than those in a solution, but smaller than the particles in a suspension. A colloid cannot be separated by filtering. Homogenized milk is an example of a colloid. Use some high school chemistry books to find a simple means of determining if a certain mixture is a colloid. Perform the test on several liquids found in your home.

BOOKS TO READ

Fireworks! Pyrotechnics on Display by Norman D. Anderson and Walter R. Brown, Dodd, Mead & Co.: New York, © 1983.
  This is an explosively entertaining book!

Gobs of Goo by Vicki Cobb, Lippincott Junior Books: New York, © 1983.
  Try some "gooey" experiments and learn about chemical reactions at the same time.

Marie Curie: Brave Scientist by Keith Brandt, Troll Associates: Mahwah, NJ, © 1983.
  This biography may inspire you to become a scientist.

UNIT 3
Exploring the Universe

On November 21, 1873, the first free flight took place in a hot air balloon. Joseph and Jacques Montgolfier, French paper manufacturers, built the balloon out of linen pasted with paper. By the 1990s, scientists plan to have a space station ready to be occupied. In 125 years we will have advanced from the first free flight, in which two men traveled 8 km in 25 minutes, to living in space. What are some problems that had to be solved to reach this point?

Montgolfier balloon flight—1873

Space station—future

Chapter 6
Space Frontiers

The study of space is often exciting. There is always the possibility of some new discovery, of going where no one has gone before. What we call space contains millions of stars, planets, and other structures, such as this nebula. What is a nebula? How is our sun related to a nebula?

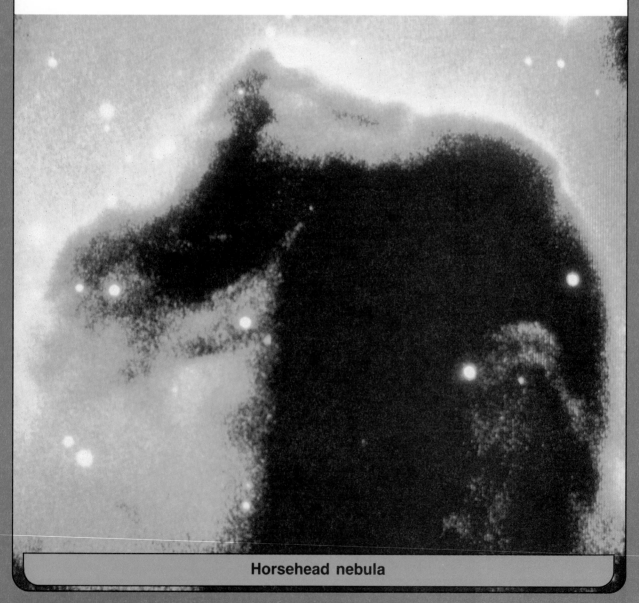

Horsehead nebula

LESSON GOALS

In this lesson you will learn
- space is all the area beyond Earth's atmosphere.
- the universe is composed of planets, stars, galaxies, and space.

People use the word *space* in many different ways. Drivers spend time trying to find a parking space. People talk about conserving open space in our environment. Objects take up space. Each of these spaces can be measured and compared. What is the largest "space" you have ever seen?

Figure 6-1. A parking space is just one kind of space.

To astronomers, the word *space* has a special meaning. **Space** is all the area beyond Earth's atmosphere. Space is so large it is hard to imagine. Space is much larger than our solar system. It is even larger than the Milky Way and its neighboring galaxies. Astronomers are not sure just how large space is.

How large is space?

It is fun to imagine traveling in space. You can compare it to traveling on Earth. The speed limit of cars on many highways is 88 kilometers per hour. If you could drive at 88 kilometers per hour, 24 hours per day, on a highway to the sun, it would take almost 200 years to get there. You could not get very far in space traveling that slowly. Suppose you could travel at 40,200 kilometers per hour. This is the speed at which spacecraft must travel to escape Earth's gravity. Traveling at 40,200 kilometers per hour, it would still take over five months to get to the sun. It would take nearly 17 years to get out of our solar system. At this speed the nearest star, Proxima Centauri, would be nearly 11,700 years away. Even then you would not have traveled very far into space.

At what speed must a spacecraft travel to escape Earth's gravity?

Activity 6-1 Identifying a Location

Materials
globe or world map
pencil and paper

What to do

1. Write your name and school address by listing the following information in order:
   - (a) name
   - (b) desk position
   - (c) room number
   - (d) school name
   - (e) school address
   - (f) city
   - (g) county
   - (h) state or province
   - (i) nation
   - (j) continent
   - (k) hemisphere
   - (l) longitude
   - (m) latitude
   - (n) planet
   - (o) solar system
   - (p) galaxy
2. Compare your address in space to the addresses of other students in your class.
3. Compare your address to the addresses of other students in the school.

What did you learn?

1. How did you find the information for each part of your address?
2. How is your address like the addresses of other students in your class?
3. How is your address different from the addresses of other students in the school?

Using what you learned

1. Why might you need to know your address in the universe?
2. How might you address a letter to a friend living on the moon?
3. Design a universal zip code for your address.

Figure 6–2. Our solar system is a small part of the Milky Way galaxy, which is just one of many galaxies in the universe.

The Universe

Space and all matter and energy in space are called the **universe.** Earth and other planets in the solar system are part of the universe. Our sun and other stars in the Milky Way are part of the universe. The countless number of other galaxies are scattered throughout the universe. Earth is just a tiny speck in the universe. How does this make you feel?

What is the universe?

Lesson Summary

- Space is all the area beyond Earth's atmosphere.
- The universe contains all space, matter, and energy.

Lesson Review

Review the lesson to answer these questions.

1. Arrange these distances in order of smallest to largest: Earth to Proxima Centauri, sun to Earth, width of the Milky Way, sun to Pluto.
2. What is the universe?
3. Why is it so hard for people to imagine the size of the universe?

The Life Cycle of Stars

LESSON GOALS
In this lesson you will learn
* stars go through a series of stages.
* there are different kinds of stars.

Figure 6–3. People show various features related to age.

On what is the star life cycle based?

What occurs during fusion?

Look at the people in Figure 6–3. Who is the oldest? Who is the youngest? How do you know? People go through stages as they grow older. You can tell by observing whether a person is very young, a teenager, middle aged, or elderly. People in each stage have certain features. Height, weight, and general appearance are features related to age.

Stars also go through a series of stages. Different features of stars are related to different stages. Stars vary in size, brightness, and color. They also vary in composition. Some stars contain mostly hydrogen. Others contain mostly helium. Astronomers have observed that, like people, younger stars have features different from older stars.

Astronomers have used the features of stars to build a star life cycle. The life cycle of stars is a model used to explain how stars form and change. Large clouds of hydrogen gas and dust have been seen in space. A large cloud of dust and gas in space is called a **nebula**. Astronomers believe stars like our sun begin in nebulas rich in hydrogen. Figure 6–4 shows the five stages in the star life cycle.

Stage 1. The force of gravity causes the gas and dust in a nebula to come closer and closer together. This contraction of the nebula causes the gases to become very hot. The gravitational attraction causes the gases to become more densely packed to form a core.

Stage 2. When the contracted gases reach a certain temperature, some nuclei join, or fuse, together. In **fusion,** the nuclei of two atoms are combined to form a different nucleus. As the core of a star forms, hydrogen nuclei fuse into helium nuclei. Fusion produces huge amounts of energy. Most astronomers believe stars are "born" during this stage. After a star

is born, fusion continues in the core. Young stars have lots of hydrogen in the core, while older stars have more helium than hydrogen. For a star like our sun, this stage may last for ten billion years. Our sun is a middle-aged star. It is about halfway through this stage.

Stage 3. When most of the hydrogen in the core of the star has changed to helium, the core contracts further and the outer layer of gases begins to expand. The star grows very large. The outer layer cools and glows red as it grows larger. Such a very large red star is called a **red giant.** Helium in the core fuses into some of the other elements during the red giant stage. Red giants are hundreds of times larger than our sun.

Stage 4. As the fuel of many red giants is used up, the force of gravity causes the star to shrink. This shrinking causes the star to become hotter. As the star becomes hotter, it glows white. The very hot, white star is about the size of Earth and is called a **white dwarf.** White dwarfs are very old stars.

Stage 5. White dwarfs slowly lose energy until they give off no heat or light. This cooling state may last trillions of years. The small, dense, cold star is called a **black dwarf.** The black dwarf stage is the last stage in the life cycle of stars similar to our sun.

Figure 6–4. Astronomers believe that stars like our sun have five stages in their life cycle. Our sun, now in the second stage, began as a nebula. In time it will become a red giant, then shrink to a white dwarf and, finally, a black dwarf.

What is the last stage in most star life cycles?

Black hole

Neutron star

Other Kinds of Stars

What is a nova?

One very special type of star suddenly becomes much brighter than it normally is. Then it slowly fades. A star that bursts into brightness and then fades is called a **nova.** Some astronomers suggest that a nova may be a pair of stars. For example, if white dwarfs and expanding red giants are found close together, the force of the white dwarf's gravity pulls hydrogen and other matter from the red giant. Hydrogen is fused into helium, which causes the white dwarf to flare up explosively. The star may be up to 1,000,000 times brighter than normal. Soon this extra bright star fades to its normal brightness. The star may flare up and fade many times. Novas are observed about once every ten years.

Some stars are born many times larger than our sun. These very massive stars do not form white dwarfs at the end of their life cycles. They explode. A very large exploding star is called a **supernova.** A supernova may be up to 1,000 times brighter than a nova.

Supernovas are not seen very often. A supernova was seen by Chinese astronomers in 1054. The exploding star could even be seen during the day. A nebula formed where the supernova occurred. It is called the Crab Nebula because some people thought it looked like a crab.

Astronomers have built a model of the events after a supernova occurs. First, the force of gravity causes the core to collapse. The outer layer of gases also collapses and explodes. The very small and dense star formed by a supernova is called a **neutron star.** The force of gravity is so strong that matter in a neutron star is forced into a very small space. A neutron star is very small compared to a white dwarf. How big is a white dwarf? The diameter of a neutron star is about 20 kilometers.

Figure 6–6. The Crab Nebula was formed by a supernova in 1054.

108

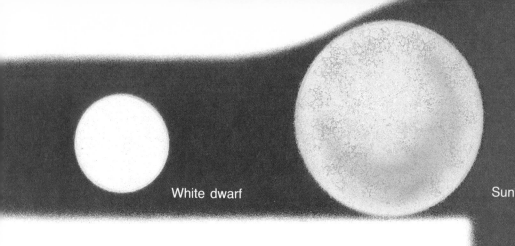

White dwarf   Sun

Red giant

A **pulsar** is a neutron star that spins quickly and gives off radio waves. The radio waves seem to blink off and on many times a second. The "blinks" form a pattern much like the beacon of a lighthouse. The pattern is used by astronomers to find out how fast the pulsar is spinning. A pulsar has been observed in the Crab Nebula by astronomers using a special telescope. This pulsar is rotating about 30 times per second.

Not all supernovas produce neutron stars. Sometimes the matter in the core has a great mass. As the force of gravity of this large mass becomes very strong, the core collapses on itself. Nothing can escape the star's gravity field. A **black hole** is a star with a gravity field so strong that light cannot escape.

No matter or energy can escape a black hole. Therefore, astronomers cannot observe it. However, astronomers believe they have seen the effects of black holes on other stars. Studying black holes may help us find out how the universe began.

Why are black holes invisible?

Lesson Summary

- There are five stages in the life cycle of most stars.
- Novas, supernovas, neutron stars, pulsars, and black holes are special kinds of stars.

Lesson Review

Review the lesson to answer these questions.

1. At what stage in its life cycle is the sun?
2. Which is observed more often, a nova or a supernova?
3. Why can astronomers not see black holes with large telescopes?

An Expanding Universe

LESSON GOALS

In this lesson you will learn

- star spectra can be used to identify which elements make up a star.
- star spectra can be used to determine how stars move in relation to each other.
- a theory that astronomers use to explain how the universe began.

a

b

Figure 6-7. A spectrum can be produced from white light (a) or gases when they are passed through special instruments (b).

What causes dark lines in a star's spectrum?

What does a "red shift" of spectral lines indicate?

White light can be separated into colors. This band of colors is called a spectrum. Light from the sun forms a spectrum when the light is passed through a prism. You see the spectrum colors in sunlight when you see a rainbow. Where else have you seen the sun's spectrum?

A tool that works like a prism can be put on a telescope. It splits light from stars into spectra. These spectra look like rainbows with dark lines in certain places. The dark lines are caused by elements in the star. The lines are in definite patterns for each element. Real spectra have many dark lines. The spectrum in Figure 6-7b has only two lines to make it easier to understand. Scientists use star spectra to find out which elements are in stars. The spectra can also be used to show the direction in which a star is moving.

Look at spectrum **a** in Figure 6-8. Notice where the dark lines are placed. The spectrum represented is that of a star like the sun. The sun stays at a certain distance from Earth. It does not move closer or farther away.

Now look at spectrum **b** in Figure 6-8. Spectrum **b** represents the spectrum of a star that scientists think is moving away from Earth. Look closely at spectra **a** and **b.** Compare the dark lines. They have moved or shifted toward the red part of the spectrum. Scientists have observed that the "red shift" of dark lines shows a star is moving away from Earth. The faster it moves away, the greater the red shift, or movement of dark lines.

a

b

c

Figure 6–8. A shift in the dark lines of a star spectrum shows the direction of movement of that star with respect to Earth.

Look closely at spectrum **c** in Figure 6–8. It represents the spectrum of a star that is moving closer to Earth. Compare the dark lines in **c** with those in spectrum **a.** Why do you think astronomers call this a "blue shift"?

Some galaxies can be seen through large telescopes. The light needed to see the galaxies comes from the billions of stars in each galaxy. The mixture of light from these stars can be split into a spectrum. Scientists have studied the spectra of many galaxies. Each spectrum shows a red shift of dark lines. This evidence supports the idea that galaxies are moving away from each other. Galaxies farthest from Earth are moving away faster than those nearby. This indicates that the universe is expanding.

What evidence supports the idea that the universe is expanding?

Figure 6–9. Spiral Galaxy NGC6946 is moving away from all other galaxies in the universe.

111

Activity 6-2 Model Universe

QUESTION   How do galaxies move in the universe?

Materials

round balloon
clothespin
felt-tip marker
metric ruler
string
pencil and paper

What to do

1. Make a chart like the one shown to record your data.

Model of the Universe Data			
Distance between dots (in mm)	Size of balloon		
	small	medium	large
A to B			
A to C			
A to D			
A to E			
A to F			

2. Inflate a balloon to a small, rounded shape. Fold the neck and clip it shut with the clothespin so the air does not escape.
3. Draw six dots on the balloon. The dots should be about evenly spaced apart. Label the dots A through F.
4. Use the string and ruler to measure the distance in mm from A to each of the other dots. Record the distances in the chart.

5. Remove the clothespin from the balloon neck. Inflate the balloon to a medium size. Clip the neck shut. Repeat step 4.

6. Remove the clothespin from the balloon neck. Inflate the balloon to a larger size. Clip the neck shut. Repeat step 4.

What did you learn?

1. What happens to the distance between the dots as the balloon expands?
2. Which distances increased the most?
3. Which distances increased the least?

Using what you learned

1. Let dot A be our Milky Way and the other dots be other galaxies in the universe. How would you describe the motion of the galaxies?
2. How is the model like the universe?
3. How would the spectra from each of these galaxies appear?
4. Suppose you lived in a galaxy at spot C. What would you observe about the spectra of the other galaxies?

People and Science

Messages From Space

Where Phillip A. Mines works, the desert is dry and hot during the day and cool during the night. Twenty-seven dish-shaped antennas rise above the landscape and face a clear, cloudless sky. Phillip is a computer technician. He works at a laboratory where scientists study space using radio astronomy.

The large antennas receive radio signals from space. Television monitors linked to computers "translate" the radio signals into pictures. The pictures, or color images, are used to interpret data about stars and galaxies far away. Phillip makes sure the computers and monitors are working correctly and repairs any problems he finds. The antennas can receive signals whether it is dark or light outside. Phillip's schedule changes, so that sometimes he works at night and sometimes during the day.

Scientists use other computers at the laboratory to decide where to place the antennas. When the antennas are placed close together, they can record large-scale images such as whole galaxies. When they are spaced farther apart, they can record details from a single star's radio signals. Scientists would like to launch an orbiting radio telescope. It would be free from interference in the atmosphere. Phillip knows the project will require complex computer technology. He hopes his experience will be needed on the project.

Phillip already knows a great deal about computers. Through his work at the radio astronomy laboratory, he is learning about space also. For example, one galaxy whose radio signals were displayed on a monitor was computed to be 350 million light-years away. Often, during a break from work, Phillip steps outside at night and looks up at the sky. He feels very small when he thinks about how far the light from the stars travels before it reaches his eyes.

Origin of the Universe

For centuries, people have wondered how the universe began. One answer that scientists propose is the big bang theory. The **big bang theory** is a model that states that the universe began with an explosion. Scientists suggest that all energy and matter were together in one place at one time. They were packed in an extremely small volume. The universe began to expand. As it expanded, it cooled. Energy began to form more matter. Then, more than ten billion years ago, the matter exploded. Pieces of matter were thrown in all directions. As the matter cooled, hydrogen formed. The hydrogen collected and formed stars. These stars formed other matter. The galaxies that formed are still moving away from each other today. Some astronomers believe that the universe will continue to expand forever.

Other astronomers suggest that the universe will stop expanding and begin to shrink some day. This idea is called the pulsating theory. The **pulsating theory** model states that the universe will expand and shrink, over and over. In time, all the galaxies would start moving toward each other. When all the matter in the universe is in one place, an explosion might occur. Then the universe would start expanding again. Compare the pulsating theory with the big bang theory.[1] How are they different?

What is the big bang theory?

What is the pulsating theory?

Lesson Summary

- Star spectra can be used to determine star composition.
- The red shifts shown by star spectra indicate that all stars are moving away from each other.
- The big bang theory is one explanation of the way in which the universe could have begun.

Lesson Review

Review the lesson to answer these questions.

1. How can astronomers tell if a star is moving away from us?
2. Why do astronomers believe the universe is expanding?
3. What is the big bang theory?

Language Arts Skills

Reading a Diagram

Sometimes a picture can aid a reader in better understanding certain facts or ideas. One kind of picture is called a diagram. A diagram is a drawing rather than a photograph. It has labels for the various parts of the item in the picture. The diagram aids understanding of how a machine works, how two ideas are alike, or what makes up the skeleton of a cow.

Look at the diagram at the bottom of this page. It is a drawing that shows how a solar eclipse occurs. The moon orbits, or circles, Earth in the same way that Earth orbits the sun. Sometimes the moon passes between Earth and the sun. When this occurs, our view of the sun is blotted out. The side of Earth that is experiencing daytime falls in the moon's shadow. One part of the moon's shadow is called the umbra. People in the area of the umbra see a total eclipse. No part of the sun can be seen. The other part of the moon's shadow is the penumbra. People in the penumbra see only a part of the sun. The sun may seem to have a splotch on its surface.

Use the diagram to answer the following questions.

1. What part of this diagram tells readers that the drawing shows a solar eclipse?
2. Would more people see a total eclipse of the sun or a partial eclipse? Why?
3. Where would people not be able to see anything of the eclipse?
4. Why is the right side of Earth shaded in this picture?
5. What did the artist draw to show what the labels name?
6. Why is the umbra shaded a darker color than the penumbra?
7. Why might eclipses not happen very often?

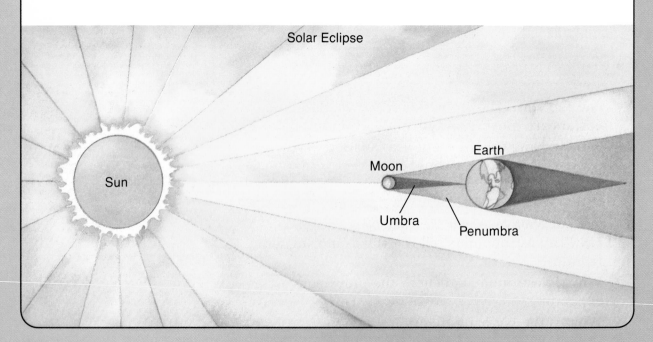

Solar Eclipse

Sun

Moon

Earth

Umbra

Penumbra

Chapter 6 Review

Summary

1. Scientists consider space as all the area beyond Earth's atmosphere. 6:1
2. The universe contains planets, stars, galaxies, and space. 6:1
3. Earth is a very small part of the universe. 6:1
4. Most of the universe is empty space because there are large distances between stars and between galaxies. 6:1
5. Most stars go through five stages in a life cycle. 6:2
6. Stars are born in nebulas. 6:2
7. Most stars end life as black dwarfs. 6:2
8. Novas, supernovas, neutron stars, pulsars, and black holes are special stages in the life cycles of some stars. 6:2
9. Scientists find out what elements make up stars by studying star spectra. 6:3
10. The "red shift" in spectra indicate that stars are moving away from Earth. 6:3
11. The universe is expanding. 6:3
12. The big bang theory is a possible explanation of the origin of the universe. 6:3

Science Words

big bang theory	neutron star	space
black dwarf	nova	supernova
black hole	pulsar	universe
fusion	pulsating theory	white dwarf
nebula	red giant	

Understanding Science Words

Complete each of the following sentences with a word or words from the Science Words that will make the sentence correct.

1. Our sun may someday expand to a _____.
2. A large cloud of gas and dust in space is called a _____.
3. Space and everything in it is called the _____.
4. A theory that states the universe will expand and shrink over and over is the _____.
5. A very hot star the size of Earth is called a _____.

6. The combination of the nuclei of two atoms to form a different nucleus is called _____.

7. Nothing, not even light, can escape from a _____.

8. A star that bursts into brightness and then fades is called a _____.

9. All of the area beyond the atmosphere of Earth is called _____.

10. A neutron star that spins quickly and gives off radio waves is called a _____.

11. A scientific model that states all matter in the universe was together in one place more than 10 billion years ago and then exploded is the _____.

12. A very large exploding star is called a _____.

13. The remaining core of an exploded supernova is called a _____.

14. When a white dwarf no longer gives off heat or light, it becomes a _____.

Questions

A. Checking Facts

Determine whether each of the following is true or false. Rewrite the false statements to make them correct.

1. As a red giant star shrinks, it becomes cooler.
2. The core of a star forms when hydrogen atoms fuse into helium atoms.
3. A black hole is a star with a strong gravity field from which light cannot escape.
4. According to the big bang theory, the universe is contracting.
5. Space is larger than our solar system.
6. It would be possible to visit Proxima Centauri in a modern spacecraft in your lifetime.
7. A star's composition can be determined by its spectrum.
8. A pulsar is a neutron star that rotates and gives off radio waves.
9. The last stage in the life cycles of most stars is a black hole.
10. A supernova may be one thousand times brighter than a nova.

B. Recalling Facts

Choose the word or phrase that correctly completes each of the following sentences.

1. Stars are thought to form from
   (a) empty space.   (c) white dwarfs.
   (b) nebulas.   (d) black holes.
2. Our sun is thought to be
   (a) very old.   (c) very young.
   (b) middle aged.   (d) almost dead.
3. Young stars are mostly
   (a) hydrogen.   (b) helium.   (c) carbon.   (d) oxygen.
4. Rainbows show the colors of the sun's
   (a) core.   (b) surface.   (c) spectrum.   (d) tail.
5. The spectra from galaxies give evidence the universe is
   (a) shrinking.   (c) expanding.
   (b) very small.   (d) coming together.
6. Compared to the size of the universe, Earth is the size of a
   (a) tennis ball.   (b) moon.   (c) speck.   (d) marble.
7. When the nucleus of one atom is joined with the nucleus of a different atom, the process is called
   (a) fission.   (b) gravitation.   (c) formation.   (d) fusion.
8. A large exploding star is a
   (a) supernova.   (c) neutron star.
   (b) white drawf.   (d) red giant.

C. Understanding Concepts

Answer each of the following questions using complete sentences.

1. Why is it so hard to imagine the size of the universe?
2. How do astronomers tell younger stars from older ones?
3. Where in its life cycle is our sun?
4. What can scientists learn from studying the spectrum of a star?
5. How is a pulsar different from other neutron stars?

D. Applying Concepts

Think about what you have learned in this chapter. Answer each of the following questions using complete sentences.

1. What kind of evidence would indicate the universe was contracting or shrinking?
2. Why is the big bang idea considered to be a theory instead of a law?

Chapter 7
Studying Space

These four images of Venus were made by the *Pioneer* spacecraft in August, 1984. Light reflected from the planet was split into its spectrum. Thus, the colors in these images give information about what the atmosphere of Venus contains. Why do you think the images are different? What advantages do spacecraft have over Earth telescopes for studying space objects?

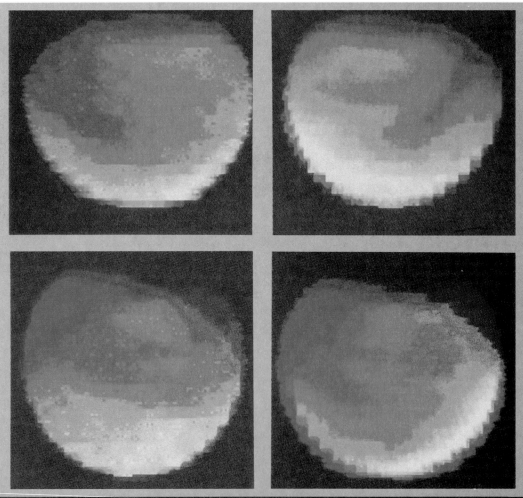

Spectral images of Venus

Tools for Space Study

LESSON GOALS

In this lesson you will learn
- telescopes of different types aid in the observation of space objects.
- rockets are used to carry spacecraft into space.
- satellites have many uses.
- space probes aid in the study of the planets.

Much of what we know is learned by observing. Observing requires the use of our senses. Sight, hearing, and touch are the senses we use most to learn new information. We also learn from our sense of smell and our sense of taste.

Astronomers learn about space by observing objects in space. The more astronomers observe, the more they can learn. Astronomers use telescopes to observe space objects. How might astronomers observe more about space objects?

People have always wondered about the stars, the planets, and the moon. The more they observed the night sky, the more questions they had. Ancient people could observe stars only with their eyes. They had no tools like binoculars or telescopes.

One of the first people to use a telescope was Galileo Galilei, who lived in Italy about 400 years ago. He was able to see objects in space that no one had ever seen before. Galileo was the first person to see moons around Jupiter. The telescope Galileo used was an optical telescope. An **optical telescope** is a tube with glass lenses or mirrors that collect, focus, and transmit light. You may have looked through binoculars. Binoculars are small optical telescopes.

Telescopes aid people in overcoming two problems of observing space objects. First, the eye is too small to collect much light. Second, the lens in the eye cannot magnify what is seen. Telescopes use large lenses and mirrors that gather much light. More light makes it easier to study dim objects. They appear brighter. Telescopes also magnify objects.

Why was Galileo's telescope important?

Figure 7-1. Galileo used this optical telescope to observe stars.

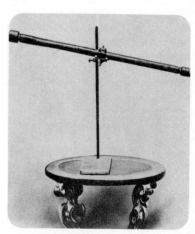

121

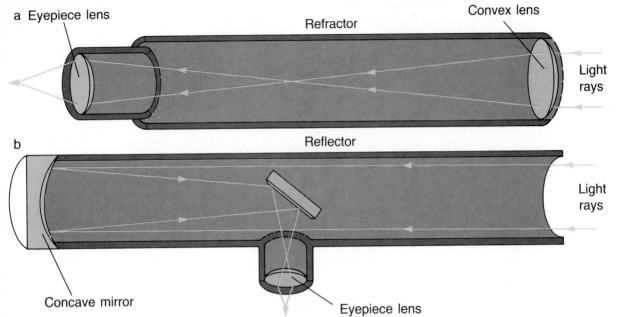

a Eyepiece lens

Refractor

Convex lens

Light rays

b

Reflector

Light rays

Concave mirror

Eyepiece lens

Figure 7-2. Refracting telescopes (a) use lenses and reflecting telescopes (b) use mirrors to magnify objects.

Optical telescopes today are much better than the ones used by Galileo. Some people have optical telescopes at home for studying space objects. The telescopes used by astronomers for research are very large. Most are too large to fit inside a house. They are mounted in special buildings called observatories. The Hale Telescope at Mount Palomar Observatory in California has a mirror 508 centimeters across. This telescope is so large that astronomers can walk *inside* the telescope to look into the eyepiece. However, many large telescopes are not made to look through with your eye. Instead, cameras, televisions or computers act as the astronomer's eyes.

How are observations made through many large telescopes?

Figure 7-3. The Hale Telescope is located at Mt. Palomar Observatory in California.

Satellites

Any space object that moves in an orbit around a more massive object is called a satellite. The moon is a natural satellite. Artificial satellites are objects placed in Earth orbit by people. Artificial satellites vary greatly in size. Some are round and range from 15 centimeters to more than 30 meters in diameter. Not all satellites are round, however. Many are oddly shaped, with antennas and panels of light collectors attached to them that serve as power sources.

Once a satellite enters space, it tends to travel in a straight line at a certain speed. The force of Earth's gravity causes the satellite to fall toward Earth. The result of these two actions is that the satellite travels, or freely falls, in a curved orbit around Earth. If the satellite slowed down, the force of gravity would cause the satellite to fall back toward Earth. Thrust produced by small rockets on the satellite is used to guide the direction and size of its orbit.

Satellites have many uses. The first satellite used for communication was *Echo 1*. The satellite was a large, round, silver-colored balloon. It worked like a mirror for radio and television signals. Signals were beamed at *Echo 1* from a sending station on Earth. *Echo 1* reflected the signals back to a different place on Earth.

Compare artificial and natural satellites.

How did *Echo 1* send signals to Earth?

Figure 7-8. A satellite is held in orbit by the interaction of its speed and the force of Earth's gravity.

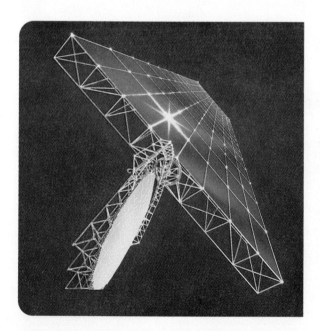

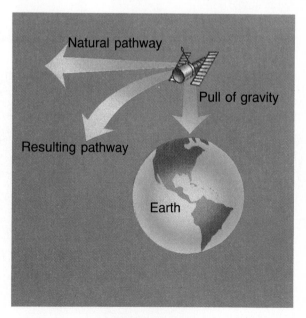

Natural pathway

Pull of gravity

Resulting pathway

Earth

How do satellites aid
communications?

How do scientists use weather
satellites?

Modern communications satellites do more than reflect signals. They may also receive and store signals. *INTELSAT* and *Comstar D* are two satellites that aid communications by receiving and storing signals. These satellites relay messages, such as telephone calls and television programs, between the United States and other countries.

Weather satellites provide scientists with pictures of clouds and Earth's surface. The pictures provide data about temperature, humidity, and the speed and direction of winds. Scientists use the information from pictures produced by weather satellites to understand and forecast weather on Earth. You can see pictures from weather satellites in newspapers or on television each day.

Figure 7-9. *Comstar D* (a) is one satellite that aids telephone communication (b). Other satellites provide details of weather such as this picture of the eye of a hurricane (c).

a

b

c

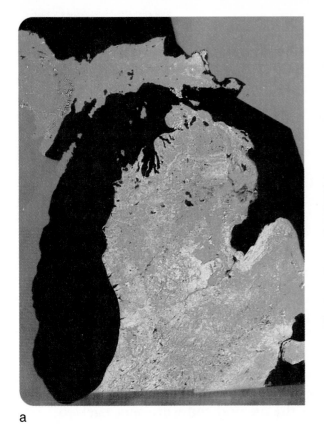

a

b

Figure 7-10. *Landsat* photos provide information on vegetation in Michigan (a) and the Mississippi River delta at the Gulf of Mexico (b).

Why are false colors used in many *Landsat* pictures?

Landsat satellites are also used for studying Earth's surface. They send radio signals back to computers on Earth. The computers change the signals into pictures. Many of these pictures are made with "false colors." Using false colors, healthy plants may appear red while unhealthy plants are gray. Other objects appear in unusual colors. False colors make it easier for people to interpret the pictures.

Landsat 5 is orbiting Earth at an altitude of 710 kilometers. The satellite can clearly pick out objects that are larger than 80 meters across. Many facts can be learned from *Landsat* pictures. The types of crops in an area can be surveyed. Crops that are diseased or affected by insects can be identified. *Landsat* pictures can be used to estimate the amount of water that will run off when winter snows melt. Why do you think this is an important fact? *Landsat* pictures also show fractures beneath the surface of Earth. Earthquakes may occur along fractures. *Landsat* pictures show where ores can be found. Mining companies use the data to plan where to dig.

Figure 7-11. Information about Mars was obtained from this *Viking* space probe shown on the Martian surface.

Space Probes

Not all spacecraft become Earth satellites. A **space probe** is a spacecraft sent beyond Earth to gather data about space objects. The United States launched spacecraft *Viking 1* and *Viking 2*, which landed on Mars in 1976. These space probes tested samples of Martian air and soil. Data about the composition and temperature of the air and soil were sent back to Earth.

Voyager 1 and *Voyager 2* have been very important space probes. Both probes were launched in 1977. Their flights took them past Jupiter in 1978 and Saturn in 1980 and 1981. The probes sent back data to computers that produced spectacular television pictures. Scientists learned much about the composition of the rings around Jupiter and Saturn. Some of the pictures showed eight volcanoes erupting on one of Jupiter's moons. These were the first volcanic eruptions seen anywhere except on Earth.

What data from Mars were sent to Earth by the *Viking* space probes?

On what space object have volcanoes been observed?

Figure 7-12. *Voyager 1* photographed the volcanic eruption on Io, one of Jupiter's moons.

Voyager 1 will not fly past any more planets. It is headed toward space outside the solar system. In 1986 *Voyager 2* flew past Uranus. For the first time people were able to see Uranus. Pictures sent to Earth showed surface features on five of Uranus's largest moons. *Voyager 2* is scheduled to fly past Neptune in 1989. From Neptune, *Voyager 2* will move out of the solar system into deep space.

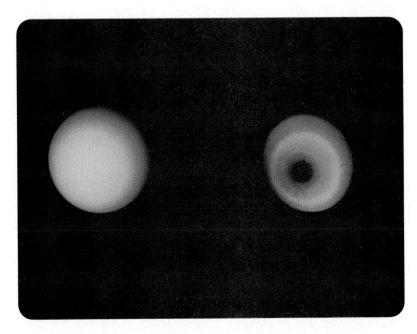

Figure 7–13. These pictures of Uranus were made by *Voyager 2* in January 1986. On the left is the way Uranus would look to a person on board *Voyager 2*. The right picture shows what could be a polar haze.

Lesson Summary

- Two types of telescopes are optical and radio.
- Thrust is the force that pushes a rocket forward.
- Satellites orbit Earth and aid people in many ways.
- Space probes have been used to study most of the other planets.

Lesson Review

Review the lesson to answer these questions.

1. Why are observatories usually found on high mountaintops?
2. What produces thrust in a rocket?
3. What keeps a satellite in orbit?
4. How are satellites useful?
5. How are space probes different from satellites?

Activity 7-2 Directing Space Probes

QUESTION **How does distance affect accuracy?**

Materials

wastebasket
small rubber ball
meter stick

masking tape
pencil and paper

What to do

1. Mark a tape line on the floor. Place the wastebasket 1 meter from the line. Stand at the line.

2. Toss the ball underhanded into the wastebasket 10 times. Record the number of times the ball landed in the wastebasket.

3. Move the wastebasket 2 meters from the line. Repeat Step 2.

4. Predict the number of times you can toss the ball in the wastebasket from 4 meters. Move the wastebasket to 4 meters from the line. Repeat Step 2.

5. Predict the number of times you can toss the ball in the wastebasket from 6 meters. Move the wastebasket to 6 meters from the line. Repeat Step 2.

6. Predict the number of times you can toss the ball in the wastebasket from 37 meters. Move the wastebasket to 37 meters from the line. Repeat Step 2.

7. Make a bar graph from your data that shows the number of times the ball landed in the wastebasket from each distance.

What did you learn?

1. How close were your predictions to the actual number of times you tossed the ball into the wastebasket at each distance?

2. At which distance was the wastebasket easiest to hit?

Using what you learned

1. Why is the target harder to hit as the distance increases?

2. Suppose the target were moving. How would this affect your ability to hit the target?

3. The apparent size of the wastebasket at 37 meters is about the same as the apparent size of the full moon from Earth. What problems do scientists have when they try to land a spacecraft on the moon?

4. Mars is 2,000 times farther from Earth than the moon is. In 1976, *Viking 1* and *Viking 2* landed on Mars. How did the problems involved in landing these space probes compare with those involved in landing a spacecraft on the moon?

LESSON GOALS

In this lesson you will learn

- exploring space requires special preparation.
- there are special spacecraft for living in space.
- many products have resulted from knowledge gained from the space program.

Figure 7–14. Early spacecraft were not very roomy. Here, Alan Shepard fits snugly inside.

Who was the first U.S. astronaut to orbit Earth?

How many lunar landings were completed?

An exciting chapter of space exploration began for the United States in 1961. In that year, Alan Shepard became the first astronaut from the United States to ride into space. His flight into space and back to Earth took 15 minutes. In early 1962, John Glenn became the first astronaut to orbit Earth. Glenn's flight was followed by a series of more complex missions in space. The early missions were called Mercury, Gemini, and Apollo. These were used to prepare for landing people on the moon.

On July 20, 1969, astronauts Neil Armstrong and Edwin Aldrin, Jr., landed on the moon's surface. They were the first people to walk on the moon. Between 1969 and 1972, six lunar landings were completed. Astronauts did experiments and gathered rock and soil samples for testing on Earth. We have been able to learn much about the solar system by traveling in space.

Figure 7–15. American astronauts were the first humans to walk on the moon.

Exploring space requires special preparation. On Earth, people have air to breathe, food to eat, and water to drink. Space does not provide the air, food, or water that people need. The environment in space is very different from that on Earth. An earthlike environment must be made in a spacecraft so astronauts can live in space.

Astronauts often need to wear spacesuits. The atmosphere inside a spacesuit is like Earth's atmosphere. A spacesuit has an oxygen supply. It even has an air conditioner! Why do you think an air conditioner is needed?

a

b

c

Figure 7-16. Weightlessness can be imitated by working underwater (a) and jumping on a trampoline (b). Objects float freely under weightless conditions (c).

Astronauts have a special problem when their spacecraft is falling freely, or is in orbit, in space. This problem is weightlessness. **Weightlessness** is a condition of objects that are falling freely. For example, if you jump on a trampoline, your body is falling freely while it is going both up and down. You are weightless because you do not feel the pull of gravity. Look at Figure 7-16. What problems do you think weightlessness causes for astronauts?

Why must astronauts exercise while they are in space?

Astronauts in a spacecraft may be weightless for long periods of time. Long periods of weightlessness can cause people's muscles to become weak, and their bones can become soft from loss of minerals. Astronauts must exercise in space to keep their bones and muscles healthy. Proper diet and sleep are also necessary for good health in space.

Why do astronauts go through much training?

Astronauts go through much training before they travel in space. Weightlessness can be imitated by working underwater. Other conditions of space travel can be imitated so astronauts learn how to work in space. Each step of a space mission is rehearsed so the astronauts can react calmly and correctly in a crisis.

Living in Space

Figure 7–17. The *Skylab* project showed that humans could live and work well in space.

A **space station** is a spacecraft used for living and working in space. Rockets have launched space stations into orbit around Earth. A space station called *Skylab* was launched in 1973. Three crews of astronauts lived in *Skylab* at different times while it orbited Earth. Each crew traveled in an Apollo spacecraft to *Skylab*. They lived in the space station for several weeks, one crew for 84 days.

Skylab had several small rooms on different levels. The astronauts had a room for sleeping and a kitchen for fixing and eating meals. *Skylab* had a laboratory, too, where the astronauts did experiments. The astronauts observed the growth of plants and animals in space. Why might growth in space be different from growth on Earth? *Skylab* had a telescope that the astronauts used to observe the sun and other stars. Views of objects in space were very good from *Skylab*. Why do you think the views were better from *Skylab* than from Earth?

One of the most useful spacecraft is a space shuttle. A **space shuttle** is a system composed of a giant fuel tank, two large rockets, and an orbiter. The orbiter is a reusable spacecraft with its own rockets. It can orbit Earth. The orbiter can also glide and land like an airplane when in Earth's atmosphere. The two large rockets launch the orbiter into space. These rockets soon separate and drop into the ocean. The rockets can be recovered and used in future launches. About

nine minutes after launch, the fuel tank separates from the orbiter. The fuel tank burns up as it falls through Earth's atmosphere. The orbiter goes into orbit, completes its mission, and returns to Earth. Look at the events of a space shuttle mission shown in Figure 7–18.

Space shuttle orbiters can be launched into space and returned to Earth many times. They can carry satellites, space laboratories, and supplies. Space shuttle crews record much data during experiments conducted while in space.

The United States has plans to build a large space station in the near future. This space station will be in an orbit about 300 miles above Earth. People and equipment will be brought from Earth to the space station by a space shuttle. Scientists will conduct experiments that cannot be done on Earth. One type of experiment involves preparing certain medicines. These medicines must be prepared in a weightless environment. The space station will also serve as a base to launch and repair satellites.

Figure 7–18. The stages of a space shuttle mission include: liftoff (a), separation of rocket boosters (b), separation of fuel tanks (c), completion of daily activities while orbiting Earth (d), and landing (e).

What is the main advantage of the space shuttle?

Space Technology and You

Scientists have learned a lot as a result of building spacecraft and sending people into space. What scientists have learned has changed life on Earth. New products have been made using the knowledge scientists have learned. Using scientific knowledge to develop new products is called **technology** (tek NAHL uh jee).

Many products that people use daily were developed with space technology. One of the first uses of space technology was in building tiny electronic circuits. Spacecraft of all kinds use much electronic equipment. Because the equipment must be lifted into space, it must be small. Electronic circuits, whose parts are so small they can be seen only with a microscope, were developed for spacecraft. This technology made the microcomputer and the hand-held calculator possible. You may have used a tiny portable radio or tape player. You may have a digital watch with an alarm. These are all products of space technology.

Making the *Echo 1* satellite led to the development of a lightweight material that reflects light and heat. The material has been used to make special blankets and food packages. Technology from developing spacesuits has been used to make warm clothing. Why are these products important?

What application of space technology is used in digital watches and calculators?

Figure 7-19. A heart pacemaker (a), edible toothpaste (b), and a spacesuit used to maintain a germ-free atmosphere (c) are products of space technology.

b
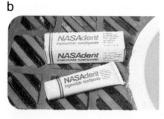

c

a
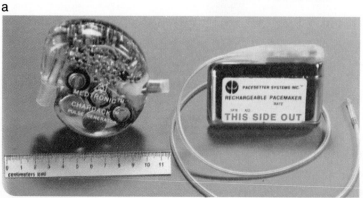

Space technology has also been useful in developing devices that aid health and the handicapped. Heart pacemakers, which have saved many lives, were the result of space technology. Pacemakers are used to keep a person's heart beating with a steady rhythm. A device that converts ink to a vibrating form allows a person who is blind to read any printed material. The person can feel the vibrating letters to determine what they are. Another device that aids persons who are blind is one that scans paper money and "announces" what the amount is. Switches have been developed that can be worked by eye movements. The switches allow a person who is paralyzed to control objects such as a television, a light, or a book page turner.

Space technology has produced many new products. Freeze-dried foods and vacuum-sealed foods that were prepared for use in space have led to packaged foods that need not be refrigerated. Better batteries, paints, and plastics have been made. Stereo speakers, cameras, and communications systems have been improved. Solar cells, smoke detectors, and metal alloys have also been developed with space technology. How many products developed with space technology can you find at school? At home?

Figure 7-20. Space technology provided the knowledge to develop the Optacon, which converts the image of print into a form that a blind person can read by touch.

What applications of space technology are used in health care of people who are disabled?

Lesson Summary

- An earthlike environment must be made in a spacecraft so astronauts can survive in space.
- *Skylab* and the space shuttle have served as space stations.
- Technology from the space program has produced many products that improve people's lives.

Lesson Review

Review the lesson to answer these questions.
1. What is an earthlike environment? How is it important in space travel?
2. What was *Skylab?*
3. What is technology?
4. Why are microscopic electronic circuits so important to people?

Science and Technology

Lightsailing Through Space

People have been dreaming of space travel for centuries. In the 1950s, the dream became a reality when the first satellite orbited Earth. In 1969, astronauts walked on the surface of the moon. Scientists are constantly studying ways to improve space travel.

The vehicle for propelling things into space has been the rocket. Rockets must travel at great speeds to escape Earth's gravitational force. Large amounts of fuel are needed to accelerate ships to those speeds. Once in space, ships are often drained of fuel and can only coast. Because distances in space are so vast, travel is very time-consuming. Scientists are developing the technology that will enable vehicles to travel in space without bringing large quantities of fuel from Earth.

One promising method for space travel resembles the type used by early explorers like Columbus and Magellan. Scientists would like to hoist sails to power space vehicles. Instead of using wind, however, spaceships would use light energy.

The pressure of the sun's energy would exert force against a "lightsail." Although the force of sunlight is weak, a ship in space would have a constant supply of it. The quantity of sunlight would make up for its weakness. Eventually, the ship would pick up speed. The ship would not have to work against friction. A lightsail could accelerate a vehicle steadily. Conventional rockets, on the other hand, must coast at a set rate of speed after using up their fuel supply. Lightsails could reduce the time needed to travel to other planets.

Chapter 7 Review

Summary

1. Scientists learn about the universe by observing.   7:1
2. Optical telescopes collect light from space objects.   7:1
3. Radio telescopes collect radio waves from space objects.   7:1
4. The development of rockets has made it possible to explore space.   7:1
5. Rockets that produce enough thrust to overcome gravity are used to launch spacecraft.   7:1
6. Artificial satellites are placed in Earth orbit by people.   7:1
7. Satellites are used to improve communications and weather forecasting and for studying Earth's surface.   7:1
8. Space probes help scientists learn about the universe beyond Earth.   7:1
9. Astronauts live in an earthlike environment in spacecraft.   7:2
10. *Skylab* and the space shuttle have served as space stations.   7:2
11. Space technology has many uses in everyday life on Earth.   7:2

Science Words

optical telescope
radio telescope
rocket
space probe

space shuttle
space station
spacecraft

technology
thrust
weightlessness

Understanding Science Words

Complete each of the following sentences with a word or words from the Science Words that will make the sentence correct.

1. The application of science knowledge to improve products is called _____.

2. A spacecraft sent into orbit to gather information about other planets is called a _____.

3. The force that pushes rockets into space is called _____.

4. An orbiting base for people working in space is a _____.

5. Objects that fall freely in space are said to be in a condition of _____.

6. A device used to launch objects into space is a _____.
7. Radio waves from space are collected by a _____.
8. Any vehicle made by people to travel in space is called a

   _____.

9. A tube with lenses or mirrors to collect light is an _____.
10. The spacecraft that can be launched like a rocket and land back on Earth like an airplane is the _____.

Questions

A. Checking Facts

Determine whether each of the following is true or false. Rewrite the false statements to make them correct.

1. One advantage of a space shuttle is that the orbiter and rockets can be launched, returned to Earth, and reused.
2. Optical telescopes gather radio waves.
3. Modern communications satellites only reflect signals from Earth.
4. Long periods of weightlessness do not cause any health problems.
5. A rocket's thrust must be equal to its weight for it to leave the ground.
6. Mars has been explored by *Viking 1* and *Viking 2*.
7. A space station is a spacecraft sent beyond Earth to gather data about space objects.
8. Radio waves from space can be collected and focused in the dishes of radio telescopes.
9. Astronauts and many other people benefit from space technology.
10. *Landsat* satellites show fractures where earthquakes may occur.

B. Recalling Facts

Choose the word or phrase that correctly completes each of the following sentences.

1. Galileo was able to see new objects in space by using
   (a) a radio telescope.
   (b) an optical telescope.
   (c) a satellite.
   (d) binoculars.
2. America's first orbiting space station was called
   (a) the space shuttle.
   (b) the orbiter.
   (c) *Landsat.*
   (d) *Skylab.*

3. Pictures of Jupiter, Saturn, and Uranus were sent to Earth by
   (a) *Voyager 2*.
   (b) *Viking*.
   (c) *Mariner*.
   (d) the space shuttle.
4. *Echo 1, Comstar D,* and *INTELSAT* are examples of
   (a) telescopes.
   (b) space probes.
   (c) rockets.
   (d) communications satellites.
5. Astronauts can suffer from weak muscles and bones because of
   (a) their diet in space.
   (b) the difficult launch.
   (c) weightlessness.
   (d) high temperatures.
6. All of these are products of space technology EXCEPT
   (a) lightweight insulating material.
   (b) electronic circuits.
   (c) heart pacemakers.
   (d) aluminum.
7. A device used to launch objects into space is
   (a) a radio telescope.
   (b) a satellite.
   (c) a rocket.
   (d) an orbiter.
8. A device used with a radio telescope to obtain useful information is
   (a) a computer.
   (b) an optical telescope.
   (c) binoculars.
   (d) a satellite.
9. A rocket can move faster by increasing its
   (a) weightlessness.
   (b) thrust.
   (c) mass.
   (d) volume.
10. Facts about Earth's surface are learned from a satellite called
    (a) *Voyager 1*.   (b) *Viking 2*.   (c) *Landsat*.   (d) *Echo 1*.

C. Understanding Concepts

Answer each of the following questions using complete sentences.
1. Why is Earth's gravity a problem in exploring space?
2. Why do satellites stay in orbit?
3. List special preparations astronauts make for space.
4. In what ways is the space shuttle different from other spacecraft?
5. What is the advantage of putting a telescope in space?

D. Applying Concepts

Think about what you have learned in this chapter. Answer each of the following questions using complete sentences.
1. Why are weather satellites important to people?
2. How has space technology aided in improving the lives of people?

UNIT 3 REVIEW

Answer these questions on a sheet of paper.
1. What is collected with radio telescopes?
2. Compare the sizes of our sun, red giants, white dwarfs, and neutron stars.
3. Why can astronomers not see black holes?
4. How does Newton's third law of motion explain how rockets work?
5. How are stars different from each other?
6. How has space technology been useful to people other than astronauts?
7. What evidence leads to the idea of an expanding universe?
8. Compare the size of Earth with the size of the universe.
9. How are star spectra useful?
10. Compare the big bang theory to the pulsating theory.
11. How are rockets used?
12. What are the stages in the life of a star?
13. Why are weather satellites valuable?
14. Why must astronauts exercise in space?
15. Describe a nova and a supernova.
16. Why are space probes such as *Voyager* and *Viking* important?
17. What is the purpose of an optical telescope?
18. How are *Landsat* pictures used?
19. What are the parts of the space shuttle system?
20. What is a pulsar?

RECALLING ACTIVITIES

Think about the activities you did in this unit. Answer the questions about these activities.
1. How can you describe your location in space? 6–1
2. How do galaxies move in the universe? 6–2
3. How does a rocket work? 7–1
4. How does distance affect accuracy? 7–2

IDEAS TO EXPLORE

1. How did the big bang theory of the universe come into being? There were, of course, no Earth scientists present when the universe began. What data have scientists used to construct the theory that the universe began with a "big bang?" Research this theory and write a report on it.

2. Consider everything that is required for an astronaut to exist in outer space. Design a spacesuit that would allow an astronaut to function freely on the moon. Draw a picture of your suit.

3. A large number of satellites are presently in orbit around Earth. Try to find out how many satellites there are and their purposes. Also try to find out how many satellites fall into Earth's atmosphere and burn up each year.

CHALLENGING PROJECT

The ratios of the diameters of stars are estimated as follows: 1 = black hole; 3 = neutron star; 2,100 = white dwarf; 210,000 = sun; 52,500,000 = red giant. Thus, the diameter of a neutron star is 3 times that of a black hole. The sun's diameter is 100 times that of a typical white dwarf. Where do Jupiter, Earth, and Earth's moon fit in this scale? You will need the diameters of each of these three bodies. The diameter of the sun is about 1,380,000 kilometers.

BOOKS TO READ

From Sputnik to Space Shuttles: Into the New Space Age by Franklyn M. Branley, Crowell Junior Books: New York, © 1986.
  Discover the past, present, and future of space technology.

The Macmillan Book of Astronomy by Roy A. Gallant, Macmillan Publishing Co.: New York, © 1986.
  See our solar system from the cameras of *Voyager 2*.

To Space and Back by Sally Ride, with Susan Okie, Lothrop, Lee & Shepard Books: New York, © 1986.
  Learn about the daily activities of astronauts on a space shuttle flight, from lift-off to landing.

UNIT 4
Energy Resources

Windmills have used wind energy to do work for centuries. Some early windmills were used to pump water from the land in Holland. Many others were used to turn grinding stones that ground wheat and corn. The energy of the wind is a valuable resource. This windmill farm provides energy for part of central California. What are the advantages and disadvantages of using windmill farms to supply energy?

Windmills in Holland

Windmills in California

Chapter 8

Fossil Fuels

Coal, oil, and natural gas supply about 90 percent of all the energy used in the United States. Scientists and others are working to solve the problems related to the burning, mining, and transportation of fossil fuels. For what is coal used in the United States? How is coal obtained?

Coal barges on the Mississippi River

LESSON GOALS

In this lesson you will learn
- fossil fuels are important energy resources.
- there are three kinds of fossil fuels.

Energy is needed for many chemical reactions to occur. Many compounds could not be formed or broken down without an input of energy. Energy is needed to carry on the life processes of organisms. Energy for all organisms is stored in food. Energy from the sun is stored in food made by plants and certain monerans and protists. When these organisms are eaten, a chemical reaction takes place that releases the energy. The stored energy in food supplies energy to do work.

There are many forms of energy. Two types are light energy and chemical energy. People use energy to do work. This work may be carrying books to class, solving a jigsaw puzzle, or cleaning out the garage. Work is also done when machines use energy. This work may be making a vacuum clean the floor or turning wheels so you can bike to the park.

An energy resource is a supply of energy that can be used to do work. Before 1900, plants and animals were the main energy resources. There were few machines. Horses were used for transportation. Axes and handsaws were used to cut trees. Wood was burned to cook food and provide warmth. What other types of energy resources did people use?

What energy resources were used before 1900?

Figure 8-1. Many machines that require fuel have replaced machines drawn or powered by animals.

149

More energy is used today than ever before for doing work. Machines now do most of the work that was once done by animals. These machines require a different kind of energy resource than animals do. Energy resources used for machines are usually called fuels.

A **fossil fuel** is an energy resource formed from the remains of plants and animals that lived millions of years ago. Why do you think it is called a fossil fuel? As the organisms died and began to decay, they became buried in Earth. Heat and pressure caused the decaying organisms to change into coal, oil, or natural gas. When fossil fuels are burned, the energy in them is released.

What is a fossil fuel?

Figure 8-2. Millions of years are required for the formation of coal.

Plants die and are buried with new plants on top.

Pressure and heat result in chemical changes.

Coal is formed in layers.

Coal

Coal is a brown or black rock that contains stored energy. Coal was formed from plants that once grew in swamps and bogs. The plants were preserved because they were buried under thick layers of mud and sediment. Millions of years of heat and pressure slowly changed the plant material into coal. Figure 8-2 shows the chemical changes that produced coal. Coal is found in layers called seams. Seams range in thickness from about two centimeters to more than 30 meters. Coal seams may be deep underground or near the surface of Earth.

People have burned coal as an energy resource since at least the 1200s. In the early 1900s, coal supplied most of the energy in the United States. In 1985 coal supplied only 24 percent of all the energy consumed in the United States.

150

Coal is not only used for heating. Compounds from coal are used in plastics, medicines, dyes, and many other products. Today most coal is used in power plants to produce electricity. Heat from burning coal boils water that turns to steam. The steam turns the blades of turbines. A **turbine** is a machine with blades like a fan that turns generators to produce electricity.

For what is most coal used today?

Crude Oil

Crude oil is a liquid fossil fuel formed from microscopic ocean organisms. These organisms lived in seas millions of years ago. When the organisms died, they settled to the bottom and were preserved in the mud. Thick layers of dead organisms were covered by sediments. As time passed, new layers of dead organisms and mud formed on top of older layers. Millions of years of heat and pressure caused the dead organisms to change into oil. The heat and pressure caused the sediment to harden into rock.

From what was crude oil formed?

The newly formed oil squeezed out of the mud and into nearby sandstone rocks. The oil moves through the sandstone. Often, the movement is stopped by a bend or blockage in the sandstone. The oil is trapped at that spot. An area where oil is trapped is an **oil reservoir** (REZ urv wor). An oil reservoir is like a giant sandstone "sponge" full of oil. Crude oil is often called petroleum. The word *petroleum* comes from the Latin word that means "rock oil."

People drill deep below Earth's surface to find oil reservoirs. The reservoirs may be several thousand meters down. Pipes are placed in the drill holes and oil is forced up through them. These holes through which oil is pumped are called oil wells.

Crude oil is a mixture of hydrocarbons. In Lesson 5:1 you learned that hydrocarbons contain only carbon and hydrogen. The hydrocarbons in oil are made of long chains of carbon and hydrogen atoms. When oil is found, it is pumped out of the ground and taken to a refinery. A **refinery** is a place where the oil mixture is separated into different products. Figure 8-3 shows some of the products that can be made from a barrel of oil. Other products made from crude oil include plastics, rubber, and organic chemicals.

Figure 8-3. One barrel of petroleum (152.5 liters) yields many products.

Gasoline

Fuel for heating/industry

Jet fuel

Diesel fuel

Lubricants

Other

151

Natural Gas

Natural gas is formed in the same way oil is formed. It is also a mixture of hydrocarbons. The hydrocarbons in natural gas, however, are made of short carbon and hydrogen chains. The shortest chain contains one carbon atom and is called methane. Methane (CH_4) makes up the greatest part of natural gas. Also present are the hydrocarbons, propane (C_3H_8) and butane (C_4H_{10}). Often natural gas and oil form at the same time. The natural gas will be trapped at the top of the oil reservoirs. Why do you think the natural gas rises above the oil?

After natural gas is brought to the surface, the propane and butane are made liquid. The methane is then pumped into pipelines for distribution. Natural gas is the easiest of the fossil fuels to process. It is also the easiest to transport in pipelines.

Using natural gas as a fuel has advantages over oil and coal in other ways. Coal and oil smoke when burned, while natural gas does not. Natural gas does not take up much storage space. Also, natural gas does not have to be refined. Most importantly, natural gas has a higher heat value than other fossil fuels. **Heat value** is a measure of the heat released when a certain amount of fuel is burned. More heat is released from a given mass of natural gas than is released from the same mass of coal or oil. How do you think the heat value of natural gas relates to the amount of energy stored in it?

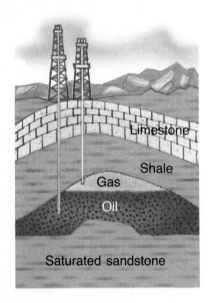

Figure 8-4. Natural gas often exists over oil reservoirs.

What is heat value of a fuel?

Lesson Summary

- Fossil fuels are fuels formed from the remains of plants and animals that lived long ago. Fossil fuels release energy when burned.
- Coal, oil, and natural gas are fossil fuels.

Lesson Review

Review the lesson to answer these questions.
1. What is an energy resource?
2. Why are coal, oil, and natural gas called fossil fuels?
3. Which fossil fuel has the greatest heat value?

Activity 8-1   Locating Resources

QUESTION   How easy are energy resources to locate?

Materials
200 pennies   clock with second hand
pencil and paper

What to do
1. Make a table like the one shown in which to record your data.

Number of Pennies Found in 30-Second Periods		
Time Period		Number of Pennies Found
Start	Finish	
A B C D		

2. Pennies have been hidden around the room. Record your start time for period A. Look for pennies for 30 seconds. Record the number of pennies you found during time period A.
3. Repeat step 2 for periods B, C, and D. Record the number of pennies you found during each period.
4. Make a graph of your results. Graph the number of pennies found against the time period.

What did you learn?
1. In which 30-second period were the most pennies found?
2. What is the shape of your graph?

Using what you learned
1. Why were fewer pennies found in each 30-second period as time passed?
2. What would happen if more people were looking for the pennies at the same time?
3. How is this activity like looking for supplies of fossil fuels or other resources?

Fossil Fuel Supplies

LESSON GOALS

In this lesson you will learn
- some energy resources can be replaced after they are used while others cannot.
- there are many ways that people are trying to make fossil fuel supplies last longer.

What is the difference between a renewable resource and a nonrenewable resource?

Some energy resources can be replaced after they are used. When trees are cut down and used for firewood, new trees can be planted. The new trees can produce more wood in about 25 years. Trees are a renewable energy resource. A **renewable resource** is one that can be replaced within the foreseeable future.

An energy resource that cannot be replaced within the foreseeable future is called a **nonrenewable resource.** Because fossil fuels take millions of years to form, they are nonrenewable. Earth's supply of fossil fuels is limited.

There is more coal than oil or natural gas. However, as the supplies of oil and natural gas are used up, more coal will be used. The supply of coal can also be used up. Many power plants burn natural gas or fuel made from oil to produce electricity. Some of these power plants have been changed so they burn coal instead.

Scientists predict that if oil continues to be used at the present rate, 80 percent may be used up in 30 years. Some scientists think that oil is too scarce to be used for fuel. They think it should be used to make other important products. Paints, plastics, and some medicines are made from oil. Think about how many substances you use that are made from oil.

What is coal gasification?

Supplies of natural gas are also limited. A substitute for natural gas can be made from coal. The process of making natural gas from coal is called coal gasification. In this process, coal is crushed into a powder. A gas is formed when the coal powder is heated under high pressure. Another type of coal gasification converts coal to gasoline. Both of these processes are complex and, at this time, expensive. They are not commonly used.

Even though coal is the most plentiful fossil fuel, the supply is not renewable. What problems might be solved by using coal as a substitute for oil or natural gas? What new problems might result?

Conserving Fossil Fuels

One way to make our fossil fuel supplies last longer is to conserve. To conserve resources means to use them wisely. Using cars less often conserves gasoline. We can walk, ride a bike or bus, or form a carpool to conserve gasoline. Lowering the temperature in our homes in winter conserves fossil fuels used for heating. Fuel is also conserved by insulating homes and buildings. Less energy is needed to heat or cool a building that has been insulated. We can turn off lights, televisions, radios, and other electric devices when we are not using them. How does using electric devices wisely conserve fossil fuels? What are some other ways you can conserve fossil fuels?

Figure 8–5. There are many ways you can conserve in your use of fossil fuels.

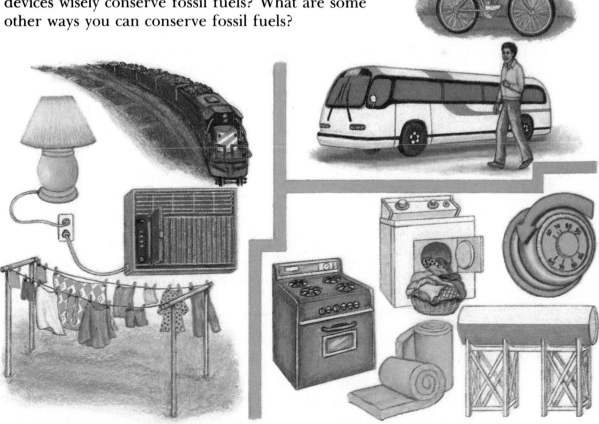

a

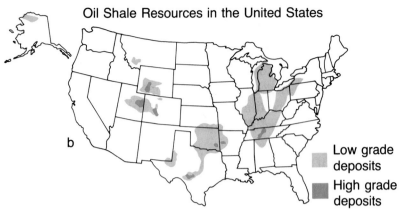

b

Oil Shale Resources in the United States

Low grade deposits

High grade deposits

Figure 8-6. Most oil shale (a) is found in three general areas of the United States (b).

What is oil shale?

How is kerogen removed from oil shale?

Scientists are trying to develop new energy resources. One possible resource is called oil shale. Oil shale is a sedimentary rock made from microscopic organisms that lived in ancient lakes. Oil shale formed millions of years ago from the organisms and mud. Thick layers of this mud-organism mixture came to rest on lake bottoms. In time, these layers were buried by other sediments. The pressure of the overlying sediments caused the mud to change into oil shale. The organic matter changed to **kerogen,** a rubbery hydrocarbon mixture that releases oil when heated.

When oil shale is heated to very high temperatures, kerogen forms a liquid mixture. The mixture can be refined to produce gasoline and other products. Figure 8-6 shows the location of oil shale supplies in the United States. As crude oil supplies decrease, the supplies of oil shale may be developed as an energy resource.

Lesson Summary

- Resources are classified as renewable or nonrenewable.
- Conserving and developing new resources are two ways to make fossil fuel supplies last longer.

Lesson Review

Review the lesson to answer these questions.
1. Why is wood called a renewable resource?
2. Why do some people think we should not use oil for fuel?
3. How can people conserve energy resources?

Science and Technology

Fuel-Producing Plants

All forms of fossil fuels were once living organisms. People have been extracting and burning fossil fuels at an increasing rate, and known resources are shrinking. Scientists have been working to discover and improve ways to use renewable, or replaceable forms of energy. Fossil fuels took millions of years to form, but some scientists are working to speed the process of obtaining fuels from plants.

Brazil obtained nearly half its fuel needs for the 1980s from sugarcane. The juice from the plants is fermented, a process that produces alcohol. Then the alcohol is burned, producing energy. Many plants, including grain crops like corn, can be fermented to produce alcohol.

Recent discoveries have brought other plant species into the role of fuel producers without the costly, time-consuming step of fermentation. The *Copaifera* tree from the Amazon region can be tapped, or drilled into, to produce a fluid. This fluid can be used as diesel fuel without any processing.

These tropical trees are maturing on experimental plantations in Brazil. It will soon be known if fuel can be produced at a reasonable cost to replace some petroleum diesel fuel. If so, scientists will begin to "improve" the species by growing only the best fuel-producing varieties. Scientists will try to grow the tree in other locations.

Other plants are being tested along the western coast of the United States and in the Philippines. However, many problems will have to be overcome if these plants are found to be productive fuel producers. One question to be answered is how much land can be reserved to grow plants for fuel without seriously reducing food-crop harvests. Some of the fuel-producing plants are expensive to grow because they require a lot of care and fertilization. Some have an annual cycle and must be replaced each year. Because fossil fuels are not renewable resources, the importance of these experimental fuel plants increases each year.

LESSON GOALS

In this lesson you will learn

- use and mining of fossil fuels cause problems in our environment.
- scientists are working to solve some problems of using fossil fuels.

Fossil fuels provide energy to do work. They also provide needed products such as medicines. Some of this work makes our lives more comfortable. For example, if you have air conditioning run by fossil fuel in your school, it is easier to study in warm weather. We would have many changes in our lives if there were no more fossil fuels. Yet, the use of fossil fuels can cause problems in our environment.

Burning coal and oil produces smoke and gases that form smog and pollute the air. Coal and oil contain compounds of sulfur and nitrogen. When these fossil fuels are burned, oxides of sulfur and nitrogen are formed. Nitrogen oxides are also produced as cars burn gasoline. Sulfur and nitrogen oxides are two compounds in smog. Smog is harmful to plants and animals and is very harmful to people with breathing problems.

How does the burning of fossil fuels form smog?

Figure 8-7. Smog in the atmosphere can be harmful to plants, humans, and other animals.

Figure 8–8. Acid precipitation affects both organisms and nonliving things.

Acid Precipitation

Sulfur and nitrogen oxides cause another major problem in our environment. **Acid precipitation** consists of sulfur and nitrogen oxides combined with water in the air. Recall that pure water has a pH of 7, which is neutral. Rainwater normally has a pH of 5.6 because it combines with CO_2 in the air to form carbonic acid. Acid rain has an average pH of 4 to 4.5. Acid snow may be formed when the temperature is below freezing.

Acid rain or snow dissolves substances needed for plant life. This can cause the death of large areas of plants such as forests. Animals that depend on these plants for food may also die. Much of the acid rain that falls to Earth collects in lakes. As acid rain continues to fall, the lake water becomes more acidic. This high acidic content is harmful to most organisms that live in water, so they die. Only some algae, fungi, and insects may survive.

How does acid precipitation affect plant life?

The problem of acid rain is very serious in some parts of the world. Serious effects of acid rain have been observed in the eastern United States, eastern Canada, and northern Europe. Oxides produced in industrialized areas may be carried hundreds of kilometers due to wind patterns. Therefore, acid rain can fall to Earth far from where the fossil fuels are being burned.

Where are serious effects of acid rain being observed?

Activity 8-2   The Effects of Acid Precipitation

QUESTION   How does acid rain affect plants?

Materials

2 small watering cans
2 young potted plants
distilled water

vinegar
pencil and paper
red and blue litmus paper

What to do

1. Label the watering cans 1 and 2. Label the plants 1 and 2.
2. Add distilled water to watering can 1 until it is full. Add distilled water to watering can 2 until it is three-fourths full. Add vinegar until can 2 is full.
3. Test the liquid in each watering can with red and blue litmus paper. Record your results.
4. Place the plants in a sunny location. Water each plant two times a week for one month. Use each watering can to water only the plant with the same number. Repeat steps 2 and 3 whenever you need more liquid to water the plants.
5. Observe the growth and appearance of each plant. Record your observations.

What did you learn?

1. Compare the liquids in each watering can. How is vinegar different from distilled water?
2. Compare the growth of the plants.

Using what you learned

1. How do you think acid rain affects the growth of plants?
2. What might happen if you watered a plant with only acid rainwater? Explain.
3. Predict how the acid rainwater could be neutralized. Test your prediction.
4. Predict what you could add to the soil that would neutralize the effects of the acid rain. Test your prediction.

Mining

Coal seams deep under Earth's surface must be removed by people and machines. Underground mines are called shaft mines. Working in a shaft mine can be dangerous. Breathing coal dust can cause a disease called black lung. Sometimes a pocket of natural gas may explode when miners try to remove the coal. Explosions may also be caused by coal dust catching on fire.

What is a shaft mine?

Many coal seams are located at or near Earth's surface. Removal of the soil and rock above such a coal seam is called **strip mining.** What do you think the landscape looks like after the coal has been mined? If the soil and rock are not replaced in layers similar to the way they were before mining, it will be hard for plants to grow. There are few nutrients in the rocky soil that remains after the coal is removed. If there are few plants to hold this rocky soil in place, erosion occurs easily.

Figure 8-9. Much coal is removed from Earth through strip mining.

Oil shale can be mined much like coal. After the oil shale is mined, it is taken to a processing plant where it is crushed and treated to remove the kerogen. Large amounts of water are needed to remove the kerogen. In the areas of oil shale deposits, water is usually scarce. Also a large amount of waste rock is produced. If we begin using oil shale as an energy resource, how might these problems be solved?

161

Figure 8-10. The transportation of oil may cause problems in the environment.

Transportation

Much of the oil used in the United States must be moved great distances. The largest oil deposits in the world are in the Middle East. Another large oil reservoir is located under the North Sea, which borders Norway and Germany.

Much oil is transported in large ships called tankers. Sometimes tankers accidentally spill oil into the ocean. The oil floats on top of the water. The floating oil harms those organisms that live on or near the surface. When the oil is washed on shore, birds may become trapped in it.

Large amounts of oil were discovered under Prudhoe Bay in northern Alaska. The problem was how to move the oil to where many people could use it. A decision was reached to build a pipeline across the state of Alaska to carry the oil. What problems could there be with a pipeline in a cold climate?

Solving Fossil Fuel Problems

What are gas scrubbers?

Scientists are finding ways to solve some of the problems of burning, mining, and transporting fossil fuels. Special equipment has been designed to clean the smoke and remove some of the pollutants produced from burning fossil fuels. Devices called gas scrubbers are being used on smokestacks to remove harmful gases. Most cars built after 1976 have a device in the exhaust system called a catalytic converter. Catalytic converters reduce the amount of carbon monoxide, nitrogen oxides, and hydrocarbons released into the air.

a

b

Coal companies must now replace the rock and soil removed during strip mining. This is called reclamation. **Reclamation** is the reconstruction of strip-mined land. The layers of soil and rock are replaced in the opposite order in which they were removed. The soil layers that contain nutrients are placed on top. Then trees and other plants are replanted. Why is reclamation important?

Scientists are also searching for new energy resources. Other types of energy resources can be used instead of fossil fuels. What energy resources may be used most in the future?

Figure 8–11. After coal has been stripped from Earth (a), coal companies are required to reclaim the land (b).

How do coal companies reclaim land after stripping the coal?

Lesson Summary

- Acid precipitation, which results when fossil fuels are burned, can harm many kinds of organisms. Strip mining and transportation of oil can also cause problems in the environment.
- Scientists are working to solve some problems caused by the mining and use of fossil fuels.

Lesson Review

Review the lesson to answer these questions.
1. What causes acid rain?
2. How can strip mine sites be reclaimed?
3. What is the purpose of a catalytic converter on an automobile?

Language Arts Skills

Distinguishing Fact and Opinion

When you hear or read information, it is important to be able to decide if the information is fact or opinion. A fact is real. A factual statement is one that is true and can be proved. A statement of opinion reflects what the speaker or the writer thinks is true. An opinion may or may not be true.

Read the following sentences about fossil fuels. Decide which is a fact and which is an opinion.

- Fossil fuels are burned to produce energy.
- More oil is used in the United States each year than either coal or natural gas.
- Burning coal is the best way to make electricity.

The first two sentences are factual statements. Oil, coal, and natural gas are all used as energy sources. Likewise, records of the United States Department of Energy show that coal is the most used fossil fuel in the United States. The third sentence, however, is an opinion. It is a fact that coal is used to produce electricity, but someone else may think that hydroelectricity is better. The statement that coal is best cannot be proved.

Read the following paragraph and determine which statements are fact and which are opinion.

Drilling an oil well is hard and dangerous work. The men and women who do the hard, physical work are called *roughnecks*. They must work with pieces of drill pipe that weigh hundreds of pounds. They operate the machinery that turns the drill bit. Most people would not want to do the work of a roughneck.

Chapter 8 Review

Summary

1. Energy is needed for some chemical reactions and is released in others.   8:1
2. An energy resource is a supply of energy that can be used to do work.   8:1
3. Fossil fuels are energy resources formed from the remains of plants and animals that lived millions of years ago.   8:1
4. Coal, petroleum, and natural gas are fossil fuels.   8:1
5. Resources are classified as renewable or nonrenewable.   8:2
6. Fossil fuel supplies are limited.   8:2
7. Conserving and developing new resources are two ways to make fossil fuel supplies last longer.   8:2
8. Acid precipitation, which results from burning fossil fuels, can harm many kinds of organisms.   8:3
9. Strip mining and the transportation of oil can cause problems in the environment.   8:3
10. Scientists are working to solve some of the problems caused by the mining and use of fossil fuels.   8:3

Science Words

acid precipitation	nonrenewable resource	renewable resource
fossil fuel	oil reservoir	strip mining
heat value	reclamation	turbine
kerogen	refinery	

Understanding Science Words

Complete each of the following sentences with a word or words from the Science Words that will make the sentence correct.

1. Restoring strip-mined land is called _____.
2. The removal of soil and rock above a coal seam is _____.
3. A measure of the heat released when a certain amount of fuel is burned is _____.
4. When sulfur and nitrogen oxides mix with water in the air, _____ results.

5. A rubbery hydrocarbon material in oil shale is _____.
6. Petroleum mixtures are separated at a _____.
7. A machine with blades like a fan that turns generators to produce electricity is a _____.
8. A resource that can be replaced in the foreseeable future is called a _____.
9. An energy resource that was formed from living organisms over millions of years is a _____.
10. The area where oil is trapped in sandstone is an _____.
11. A resource that cannot be replaced in the foreseeable future is called a _____.

Questions

A. Checking Facts

Determine whether each of the following is true or false. Rewrite the false statements to make them correct.

1. An energy resource is a supply of energy that can be used to do work.
2. Today most coal is used to heat homes.
3. The mixture of hydrocarbons in crude oil is separated in a turbine.
4. Coal, oil, and natural gas were formed from the remains of plants and animals by heat and pressure over millions of years.
5. Coal has a higher heat value than natural gas.
6. Coal gasification is an inexpensive way to convert coal to gasoline or natural gas.
7. Sulfur and nitrogen oxides produced from burning fossil fuels cause acid precipitation.
8. The hydrocarbons in crude oil are made of short chains of carbon and hydrogen atoms.
9. Petroleum is the fossil fuel that is easiest to transport in pipelines.
10. Smog is produced by the burning of fossil fuels.
11. Rainwater is naturally slightly acidic.
12. Coal is the easiest of the fossil fuels to process.
13. Heat value is a measure of the heat released when a certain amount of fuel is burned.

B. Recalling Facts

Choose the word or phrase that correctly completes each of the following sentences.

1. Another name for petroleum is
   (a) natural gas. (b) gasoline. (c) crude oil. (d) oil shale.
2. Which has the greatest heat value?
   (a) petroleum (b) natural gas (c) coal (d) crude oil
3. Which fossil fuel is most plentiful?
   (a) crude oil (b) natural gas (c) petroleum (d) coal
4. All of the following are used to solve problems caused by fossil fuel use EXCEPT
   (a) reclamation. (c) conservation.
   (b) catalytic converter. (d) strip mining.
5. Which of the following is a renewable resource?
   (a) natural gas (b) oil (c) coal (d) wood
6. In using coal to generate electricity, what other resource is also needed?
   (a) oil (b) water (c) trees (d) natural gas
7. Crude oil reservoirs are found in rock layers of
   (a) limestone. (b) shale. (c) granite. (d) sandstone.

C. Understanding Concepts

Answer each of the following questions using complete sentences.

1. How are fossil fuels alike?
2. Why do some scientists think that petroleum should not be used as a fuel?
3. How can oil shale be used to produce fuel?
4. Why is conserving energy important?
5. How does acid rain affect lakes?

D. Applying Concepts

Think about what you learned in this chapter. Answer each of the following questions using complete sentences.

1. Explain five ways in which people use energy today that is different from the ways people in the early 1900s used energy.
2. Explain the importance of reclamation.
3. What are some problems that result from using fossil fuels?

Chapter 9
Energy Alternatives

Fossil fuel supplies are gradually being used up. Some other sources of energy are solar, wind, hydroelectric, geothermal, tidal, and nuclear fission energy. Nuclear fusion may provide energy in the future. Scientists are now working to control the energy of fusion. What is fusion? Why is it better than nuclear fission?

Tokamak—core of a fusion reactor

Wind, Water, and Geothermal Energy 9:1

LESSON GOALS

In this lesson you will learn

- alternative energy resources are those other than fossil fuels.
- wind and water, as well as heat in Earth's crust, can be energy resources.

There is a continuing demand for energy. Yet, fossil fuel reserves are not increasing. In fact, they are decreasing. Conserving fossil fuels will make the reserves last longer, but will not make them last forever. Alternate energy resources are needed. An **energy alternative** is an energy resource that is *not* a fossil fuel. Energy alternatives can help meet the constant demand for energy.

Most energy alternatives are not "new" resources. People have been using resources such as wind for centuries. Scientists have found ways to make these resources produce more energy. Other energy alternatives, such as energy in the nucleus of an atom, have gained widespread use only recently. Not until the 1950s did scientists learn how to use and control energy in the nuclei of atoms.

What is an energy alternative?

Wind Energy

Wind energy was first used to power sailing ships. Since that time, we have learned to control wind energy for other kinds of work. Wind energy has been used to grind grain and pump water. Some people use wind energy to supply their homes with electricity. Wind turns the turbines of a windmill to produce electricity. This method can be used to produce electricity in areas where winds are strong and frequent. The Great Plains, mountainous areas, and some coastal areas are places where wind can be used to supply energy.

The use of wind energy has advantages. Wind energy produces little pollution. It does not have to be mined or pumped from Earth. What are some other advantages of wind energy?

Figure 9-1. Wind energy has been used for centuries.

169

What wind speed is needed to produce electricity?

Wind energy may sound like the perfect energy resource but there are some disadvantages. Wind speed must be greater than 12 kilometers per hour to produce useful amounts of electricity. In many places, winds are too weak or not frequent enough.

There are places where the wind speed would produce electricity. Many places where the wind speed is strong enough are far from cities where people need the electricity. The electricity must be transported great distances. In the proper area, one large windmill may supply electricity to about 1,000 homes. However, many windmills are needed to supply a large community. Many people think that a large number of windmills in one place would spoil the beauty of natural areas. People who live nearby may be bothered by noise. What do you think? Electricity produced when the wind is blowing must be stored for later use. Storing electricity is costly and requires special equipment.

Figure 9-2. This field of wind turbines in California supplies a nearby community with electricity.

170

Activity 9-1　Using Wind Energy

QUESTION　How may wind energy be used?

Materials

empty milk carton　　　construction paper
scissors　　　　　　　　masking tape
3 straws　　　　　　　　stapler
2 large thread spools　　pencil and paper

What to do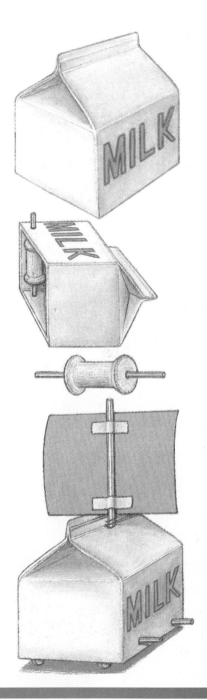

1. Cut off the bottom of the milk carton. Punch four holes in the carton as shown in the diagram.
2. Insert a straw through each pair of holes and a spool as shown in the diagram. Flatten the ends of the straws.
3. Cut a large square of construction paper and attach the paper to a straw with masking tape. Leave part of the straw sticking out to form a mast.
4. Staple the mast to the top of the milk carton.
5. Test your car by blowing into the paper sail.
6. Experiment with your car to see if you can make it travel faster, slower, or farther. You may change the structure of the car or sail if needed.

What did you learn?

1. List the variables that affect how fast and how far the car moves.
2. Which of these variables are easiest to control?

Using what you learned

1. Design and carry out an experiment to test the effect of one variable. Record your results.
2. List two reasons why people might want to use wind-powered cars and two reasons why they may not.
3. What other wind-powered vehicles do people use?

Water Energy

The energy of moving water can also be used as an energy resource. Water energy has been used to power machines such as mills for grinding grain. Most water energy is now used for generating electricity. Electricity produced when water falls from a high place to a low place is called **hydroelectric energy.** *Hydro* means water.

Hydroelectric power plants may be large or small. Electricity may be supplied to millions of people, or only hundreds. Most hydroelectric power plants require the building of a dam across a river. The water held behind the dam contains potential energy. The potential energy changes to kinetic energy as the water flows through the dam. The kinetic energy

How is most water energy now used?

Figure 9-3. An area (a) undergoes many changes after the building of a dam (b). In some rivers, dams prevent salmon from going upstream to spawn. Salmon ladders (c) have been built to overcome this problem.

a

b

c

causes the paddles of the turbines to turn. Electricity is generated. The farther the water falls, the more electricity can be produced. Also, the more water that falls, the more electricity can be produced.

The use of water energy has advantages. It causes little pollution. Water energy does not have to be mined or pumped from Earth. After the electricity is produced, the water can be used for other needs. Also, electricity produced with falling water does not cost any more than that produced with fossil fuels.

The use of hydroelectric power plants is limited, however. There are some disadvantages to using water energy to produce electricity. Few rivers have good locations for building power plants or dams. Some locations are far from cities. It is costly to build power lines to transport the electricity. Other possible locations for hydroelectric power plants are wilderness areas. Damming the rivers or building power plants would change these natural areas forever.

Why is hydroelectric power limited?

Tidal Energy

Another form of energy is present in the rise and fall of ocean water along a coast. You may have seen the changes in water level at a beach. These changes are called tides. **Tidal energy** is energy of moving water caused by the tides. Tides are caused by the gravitational attraction of the sun and moon on Earth.

Low tide is the lowest level of ocean water along a coast. Why do you think people say the tide is "out" at low tide? From low tide, the level of the ocean water rises for about six hours until it reaches its highest level along the coast. The highest level of ocean water is called high tide. People often say the tide is "in" at high tide. From high tide, the level of ocean water falls for about six hours until it reaches low tide again. Ocean tides usually rise and fall twice in about 24 hours.

Along some seacoasts, the tidal waters flow through narrow inlets. The difference between high tide and low tide may be more than eight meters at these places. Tidal power plants have been built in some of these places. The moving water of the tides is used to turn turbines and produce electricity.

Figure 9-4. In the Bay of Fundy, Nova Scotia, the difference between high (a) and low (b) tides is very large.

a

b

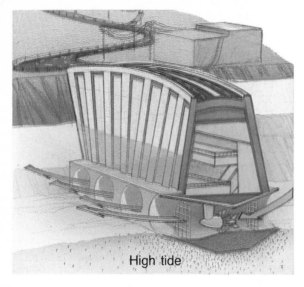
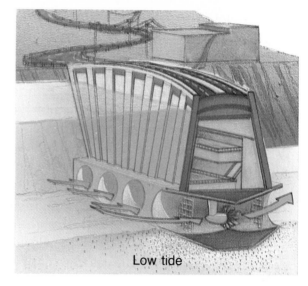

High tide

Low tide

Figure 9-5. In a tidal power plant, water moves through a turbine as the tide rises and falls.

In how many areas could tidal power plants be built?

The use of energy from tides is limited. There are few places in the world that are suited for tidal power plants. Some scientists think there are as few as 25 suitable places. Also, the cost of building tidal power plants is very high. For this reason, the electricity produced is more costly than that produced by other power plants.

Geothermal Energy

Perhaps you have seen or heard of Old Faithful in Wyoming. Old Faithful is a geyser. Geysers and hot springs are places where underground steam and hot water come to Earth's surface naturally. A huge burst of steam erupts from Old Faithful about every hour.

Geothermal (jee oh THUR mul) **energy** is heat from rocks and water deep inside the Earth. *Geo* means Earth and *thermal* means heat. Rocks in some areas below Earth's surface are very hot. The rocks heat underground water to high temperatures. Sometimes the water boils and produces steam. Geothermal water and steam can be brought to the surface to heat buildings.

In some places, steam and hot water are trapped in the rocks below Earth's surface. Holes can be drilled into the rocks to release the geothermal energy. Geothermal power plants have been built in some places where geothermal energy is present. The steam released by drilling into rocks is used to turn turbines.

Figure 9-6. Water is forced upward by steam pressure to produce the Beehive Geyser in the upper basin of Yellowstone National Park.

174

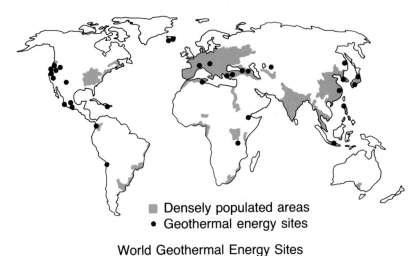

Figure 9–7. Most geothermal energy is not located near heavily populated areas.

■ Densely populated areas
• Geothermal energy sites

World Geothermal Energy Sites

Geothermal energy has advantages. Electricity produced with geothermal energy often costs less than electricity made with fossil fuels. Also, it causes little pollution. Like tidal energy, geothermal energy is limited. Only a small part of the energy demand can be satisfied with geothermal energy. Also, geothermal energy must be used near the source, or the electricity must be stored and transported great distances. Unfortunately, little geothermal energy has been found near large population centers.

Why is geothermal energy limited?

Lesson Summary

- Alternative energy resources are needed to replace the decreasing supplies of fossil fuels.
- Wind, water, and geothermal energy are energy alternatives that can be used to produce electricity. Geothermal energy can also be used directly to heat buildings.

Lesson Review

Review the lesson to answer these questions.
1. What does *energy alternative* mean?
2. Why are energy alternatives important to people?
3. Why is it a disadvantage that some energy alternatives are located far from cities?
4. List some disadvantages of using wind, tidal, hydroelectric, and geothermal energy sources.

LESSON GOALS

In this lesson you will learn
- atoms can be split or fused to release energy.
- energy from the sun may be used by people.
- wise choices concerning energy use must be made.

Atoms are an energy resource. The nucleus of every atom has stored energy. The nuclei of some kinds of atoms change naturally. A new nucleus with a different number of protons may form. When the number of protons changes, a new element is formed. A **radioactive element** is one whose atoms change naturally to different atoms. This change gives off energy in the form of radiation.

Figure 9-8. Atoms undergoing fission (a) produce large amounts of heat in a nuclear reactor (b).

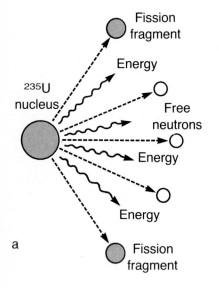

For what are nuclear reactors used?

Scientists have found ways to release large amounts of energy from the nuclei of some atoms. An atom's nucleus can be split in a process called **fission.** In fission, large amounts of energy are released in the form of heat. This heat can be used to make steam. The steam can turn turbines to produce electricity.

Fission can be controlled in a nuclear reactor. The nuclei of atoms are split in the core of the reactor. Fission in nuclear reactors supplies energy to produce electricity in many parts of the world. Small nuclear reactors are used to power some submarines, ships, and spacecraft.

Uranium is a radioactive element. It is used as fuel in nuclear reactors. Uranium is strip-mined from Earth. After it is mined, the uranium must be refined. It is then made into fuel. One kilogram of uranium has as much stored energy as 3,000,000,000 kilograms of coal.

How much energy is stored in one kilogram of uranium?

Splitting uranium atoms produces wastes that are radioactive. Because radiation is harmful to living things, the waste products are kept inside thick walls at the nuclear reactor site. In time, though, the wastes must be removed. To protect the environment, the radioactive wastes are sealed in airtight drums, then transported and stored. Great care must be taken during storage so that the containers do not break open and leak wastes into the environment. What might happen if the wastes got into the environment? The problem of how to store these wastes is a major disadvantage of using nuclear fission energy.

Another way to release the energy in the nuclei of atoms is to join atoms together. In fusion, the nuclei of atoms are combined to form the nucleus of a different atom. Recall from Lesson 6:2 that this reaction occurs in the sun. Nuclei of hydrogen atoms fuse into helium nuclei, producing huge amounts of energy.

What occurs in fusion?

Fusion produces much more energy than fission, and it does not produce as much of the harmful wastes. At this time, though, scientists are not able to control this great amount of energy. A temperature of several million degrees is needed for fusion to take place. When these problems are solved, fusion may become an important energy alternative.

Figure 9–9. Fusion of atoms releases much energy that, at this time, is not easily controlled.

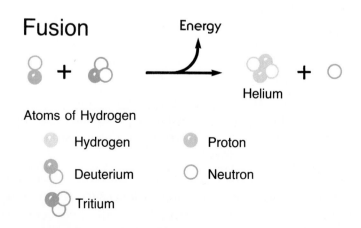

Fusion

Energy

Helium

Atoms of Hydrogen

Hydrogen

Deuterium

Tritium

Proton

Neutron

177

Solar Energy

Large amounts of energy from the sun strike Earth each day. The energy is produced by fusion of hydrogen nuclei in the sun. Energy from the sun is called **solar energy.** Each day, the amount of solar energy that strikes the United States is more than the energy in 22 million barrels of oil. Solar energy, however, is scattered over a wide area. It is often not available when it is needed. Solar energy must be collected, concentrated, and stored.

Special equipment is not always needed to concentrate solar energy. Think of a home built in the Northern Hemisphere with the longest sides facing north and south. Few windows are placed on the north side. Large windows are placed on the south side. In winter, the solar energy can pass through the large windows, warming the inside of the house. Shades that cover the windows in summer reduce the amount of solar energy entering the house. This aids in keeping the inside of the house cool. Why are few windows placed on the north side? If you lived in the Southern Hemisphere, on which side of the house would you place large windows if you wanted to collect solar energy?

Special equipment may be used to control solar energy. A **solar reflector** is a curved shiny surface that reflects and focuses sunlight on one spot. Solar reflectors can be used to start fires or to heat water. They can also be used to cook food.

A **solar collector** is a device that gathers the sun's energy. It is a dark-colored material covered by glass or plastic. Sunlight passes through the glass or plastic covering. The material underneath absorbs the solar energy. The solar energy is changed to heat. The heat is trapped by the glass. Air or a liquid is heated as it moves through the collector. The hot air or liquid can be circulated to heat a building. Solar collectors can also provide hot water for washing and bathing. Many modern buildings are being designed with solar collectors on their roofs.

One device used to concentrate solar energy is a solar cell. A **solar cell** produces electricity from solar energy. It is made from a thin layer of silicon coated on one side with aluminum. The other side is coated

How can solar energy be made more useful?

How is heat from a solar collector circulated?

a

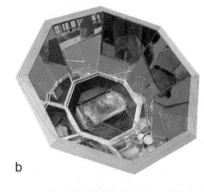
b

c

with a film often made from a metal such as silver. When light strikes a solar cell, electrons flow between the film and the aluminum, producing electricity. Solar cells are used to power calculators and watches. Many solar cells are needed to produce enough electricity to light a lamp or run a motor. Solar cells have been used on space satellites. Electricity made by the solar cells is used to send and receive radio signals between the satellite and Earth.

Solar energy has advantages and disadvantages. Use of solar energy reduces the need for fossil fuels. In many locations, sunlight is plentiful. It causes no pollution. All parts of Earth, though, do not receive the same amounts of sunlight. Solar energy must be collected and stored for use on cloudy days or at night. How useful do you think solar energy is for heating homes or water where you live?

Figure 9-10. South-facing windows and roof collectors provide some homes with solar energy (a). Energy from the sun is also used in solar cookers (b) and to produce electricity in solar cells (c).

Our Energy Future

No energy resource is perfect for every need. The advantages and disadvantages of each must be judged before a choice can be made. The choices that are made are often called *trade-offs.* Why do you think people use this term? Energy alternatives may be combined with fossil fuels to meet energy demands in many areas. No single energy resource can meet all demands for energy. Wise use of all energy resources is the best solution to the problem of increasing energy needs. What energy resources can be used to best supply the energy needs of your community?

179

Activity 9-2   Making Solar Collectors

QUESTION   Which color material absorbs the most solar energy?

Materials

cardboard
4 widemouthed jars
scissors
aluminum foil
black paper
white paper
4 thermometers
masking tape
clock or watch
pencil and paper

What to do

1. Mark and cut out four cardboard lids for the jars.
2. Cut a piece of aluminum foil to line three-fourths of one jar. Cut a piece of black paper to line three-fourths of another jar. Cut a piece of white paper to line three-fourths of a third jar. Do not line the fourth jar with anything.
3. Use a pencil to poke a hole in the center of each cardboard lid. Tape a lid on each jar.
4. Carefully insert a thermometer into each jar through the hole in the cardboard lid. Tape the thermometers in place. Do not let the thermometers touch the bottoms or sides of the jars.
5. Make a table to record the starting temperature and ten more temperatures for each jar.

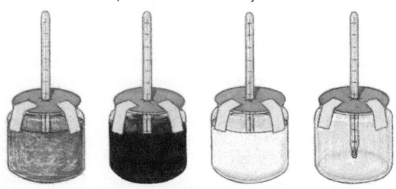

6. Set the jars together in a sunny place. The jars should not touch.

7. Record the starting temperature in each jar. Continue to record the temperature in each jar every minute for ten minutes.

What did you learn?

1. Compare the starting temperatures in each jar.
2. What temperature changes did you observe?
3. In which jar did the temperature change the most in ten minutes?

Using what you learned

1. How can you explain the temperature changes you observed?
2. What color is best for the lining of the solar collector?
3. What is the purpose of the jar that was not lined?
4. What might happen if you left the cardboard lids off each jar? How could you find out?
5. How might you use the solar energy you collected in the jars?

Lesson Summary

- Fission and fusion are two processes in which energy can be released from atoms. In fission, the nucleus of an atom is split. In fusion, the nuclei of atoms combine to form a new nucleus.
- Solar energy can be used directly, or it can be used to produce electricity.
- No one energy resource can meet every need.

Lesson Review

Review the lesson to answer these questions.
1. What is fission?
2. What is fusion?
3. Explain the major advantages and disadvantages of nuclear energy.
4. What special equipment might be used to make solar energy more useful?

People and Science

Getting Rid of a Hazard

How is your home or school kept warm during the winter and cool in the summer? Most buildings have some insulation in the walls and ceilings. Good insulation lowers energy loss from a building.

Asbestos is a fibrous mineral that was used in the past for insulation, fireproofing, and absorbing sound. In many cases, it was mixed in a form that could be sprayed on a surface. Small fibers of asbestos floated free in the air. It has been found that these fibers are the source of some forms of lung cancer. Now asbestos has to be removed from all public buildings.

Thomas R. Byington works for an asbestos removal company. Before Tom was hired, he had to have a physical examination. Tom was in good health, had not worked with asbestos before, and had never smoked. He attended a training program and had to pass a written exam before being considered for the job. Part of Tom's training involved learning how to protect himself from the asbestos dust. He had to learn how to seal off a room to cut down on airborne fibers. He was taught how to wet down the asbestos and dispose of it safely.

Tom has to follow strict procedures for what he wears. He has to wear either a mask or respirator, along with special clothing that protects his entire body. He may be fined if he does not follow these guidelines. People like Tom, who work with hazardous materials, have to follow safety regulations to protect themselves and others.

Chapter 9 Review

Summary

1. The world supply of fossil fuels is decreasing.   9:1
2. Conserving fuel and finding energy alternatives can help meet the constant demand for energy.   9:1
3. An energy alternative is an energy resource that is not a fossil fuel.   9:1
4. Wind energy is used to produce electricity in some places where strong winds blow regularly.   9:1
5. Water flowing over dams or waterfalls can be used to produce electricity in hydroelectric power plants.   9:1
6. Tidal energy is an important energy alternative in places where the difference between high tide and low tide is large.   9:1
7. Geothermal energy is heat from rocks and water deep inside Earth that can be used to produce electricity or heat buildings.   9:1
8. Nuclear energy is released by fission and fusion of the nuclei of certain kinds of atoms.   9:2
9. Nuclear fission is controlled in nuclear reactors to produce electricity.   9:2
10. Solar energy can be used to produce electricity, cook food, heat water, and heat buildings.   9:2

Science Words

energy alternative
fission
geothermal energy
hydroelectric energy

radioactive element
solar cell
solar collector

solar energy
solar reflector
tidal energy

Understanding Science Words

Complete each of the following sentences with a word or words from the Science Words that will make the sentence correct.

1. An element whose atoms change naturally to different atoms, giving off energy in the form of radiation, is a _____.
2. An energy resource that is not a fossil fuel is an _____.
3. Energy present in the regular rise and fall of ocean water is called _____.
4. A device that produces electricity from solar energy is a _____.

5. Heat from rocks and water in Earth is _____.
6. A curved shiny surface that reflects and focuses sunlight on one spot is called a _____.
7. Energy from the sun is called _____.
8. Electricity produced when water falls from a high place to a low place is _____.
9. Atoms can be split to release energy in a process called _____.
10. A dark-colored material that gathers the sun's energy is a _____.

Questions

A. Checking Facts

Determine whether each of the following is true or false. Rewrite the false statements to make them correct.

1. In nuclear fission, the nuclei of atoms are combined to form the nucleus of a different atom.
2. Wind energy and solar energy are alternative energy sources.
3. Wind energy can be used to produce electricity in any location.
4. Solar energy must be collected and concentrated to be useful.
5. The cost of building tidal power plants is very high.
6. A major disadvantage of fusion energy is the production of large amounts of radioactive wastes.
7. A fossil fuel is an alternative energy source.
8. Electricity produced with geothermal energy is usually more expensive than that made with fossil fuels.
9. Nuclear fusion is not yet an important energy alternative.
10. Most hydroelectric power plants require the building of a dam across a river.

B. Recalling Facts

Choose the word or phrase that correctly completes each of the following sentences.

1. Electricity can be produced from the sun's energy in
   (a) solar flares.
   (c) solar collectors.
   (b) solar reflectors.
   (d) solar cells.

2. Which type of energy produces the most pollution?
   (a) wind   (b) oil   (c) hydroelectric   (d) solar
3. Solar collectors are usually made of
   (a) light-colored materials.   (c) dark-colored materials.
   (b) mirrors.   (d) silicon.
4. The type of energy that produces radioactive wastes that are difficult to store is
   (a) oil.   (b) solar.   (c) wind.   (d) nuclear.
5. Which releases the most energy?
   (a) fission   (c) burning coal
   (b) fusion   (d) geothermal water
6. Which type of energy has the fewest practical locations available?
   (a) tidal   (b) solar   (c) nuclear   (d) hydroelectric
7. A hydroelectric plant produces electricity from
   (a) hot water.   (c) solar energy.
   (b) moving water.   (d) nuclear energy.
8. Which of the following is an alternative energy source?
   (a) natural gas   (b) wind   (c) coal   (d) oil
9. Energy produced by the fusion of hydrogen nuclei is
   (a) solar.   (b) fission.   (c) wind.   (d) geothermal.

C. Understanding Concepts

Answer each of the following questions using complete sentences.
1. What is meant by saying that uranium is a radioactive element?
2. Compare the use of wind energy today with the ways people used it in the past.
3. How is falling water an energy resource?
4. Describe the tides in places where tidal energy is an important energy alternative.
5. Describe the differences between nuclear fission and nuclear fusion.

D. Applying Concepts

Think about what you learned in this chapter. Answer each of the following questions using complete sentences.
1. Why is there no perfect energy resource?
2. What is the best solution to meet the constant demands for energy on Earth?

UNIT 4 REVIEW

Answer these questions on a sheet of paper.

1. Match each energy resource with the most appropriate description.

   coal   petroleum
   fission   solar energy
   fusion   tidal energy
   geothermal energy   water energy
   natural gas   wind energy
   oil shale

   (a) our main source of energy on Earth
   (b) found in underground seams
   (c) uranium nuclei split to produce energy
   (d) a source of hydroelectric power
   (e) burns cleaner than other fossil fuels
   (f) can be refined into gasoline
   (g) formed from hot water and steam
   (h) contains kerogen
   (i) nuclei join together and produce energy
   (j) has been used to sail boats and produce electricity
   (k) only possible along a few seacoast areas

2. How can the use of fossil fuels cause problems in our environment?

3. Why is energy conservation important?

4. Discuss some possible advantages of energy alternatives over fossil fuels.

5. What is a nonrenewable resource?

RECALLING ACTIVITIES

Think about the activities you did in this unit. Answer the questions about these activities.

1. How easy are energy resources to locate?   8–1
2. How does acid rain affect plants?   8–2
3. How may wind energy be used?   9–1
4. Which color material absorbs the most solar energy?   9–2

IDEAS TO EXPLORE

1. Use solar energy to dry fruits or vegetables or to cook food. A simple solar cooker is not difficult to construct. Consult a natural food or camping cookbook for instructions.

2. Research tidal energy. Discover how tidal energy is produced and why this energy resource is available only in very few regions of the world. Obtain a world map and indicate on the map the areas where tidal energy is, or might be, a good energy alternative.

3. There are a variety of other energy alternatives not discussed in this unit. Among them are biomass conversion, ocean thermal conversion, and solar satellites. Do some research to find out what these alternatives are, how they can be used, and whether or not they are in use at present. Choose one on which to write a report.

CHALLENGING PROJECT

Contact the air quality control office in your area. Find out which air pollutants are measured and what the major pollutants in your area are. What is the pollutant standard index? Find out if automobiles in your area must have regular inspections to see if the vehicles are producing too much of some pollutants. If a vehicle does not pass inspection, what happens? Prepare a report on your findings for the class.

BOOKS TO READ

Coal by Wilbur Cross, Childrens Press: Chicago, © 1983.
   Read about this important energy resource.

Oil by Nigel Hawkes, Franklin Watts, Inc.: Danbury, CT, © 1985.
   Learn more about an essential energy source.

Petroleum: How It Is Found and Used by William R. Pampe, Enslow Publishers, Inc.: Hillside, NJ, © 1984.
   Learn about petroleum from its discovery to its present uses.

UNIT 5
Inside the Body

William Harvey conducted many systematic tests in animals to find out how blood flows. In 1628, he published his findings on circulation. This paper stated that the heart acts as a pump to keep blood flowing in the body. Today, scientists can see and photograph individual blood cells using tools that Harvey never imagined. How has the microscope been used to increase our understanding of circulation?

William Harvey—1628

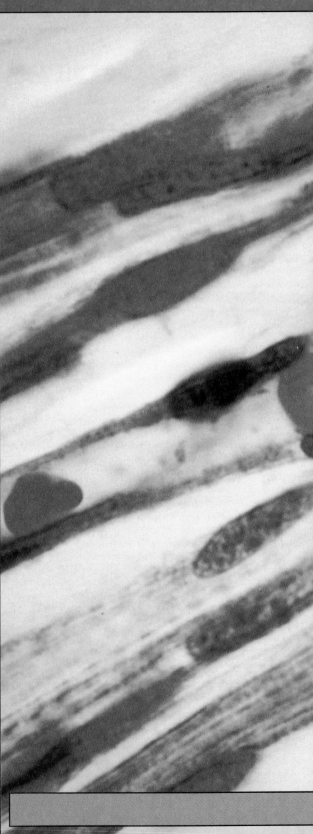

188

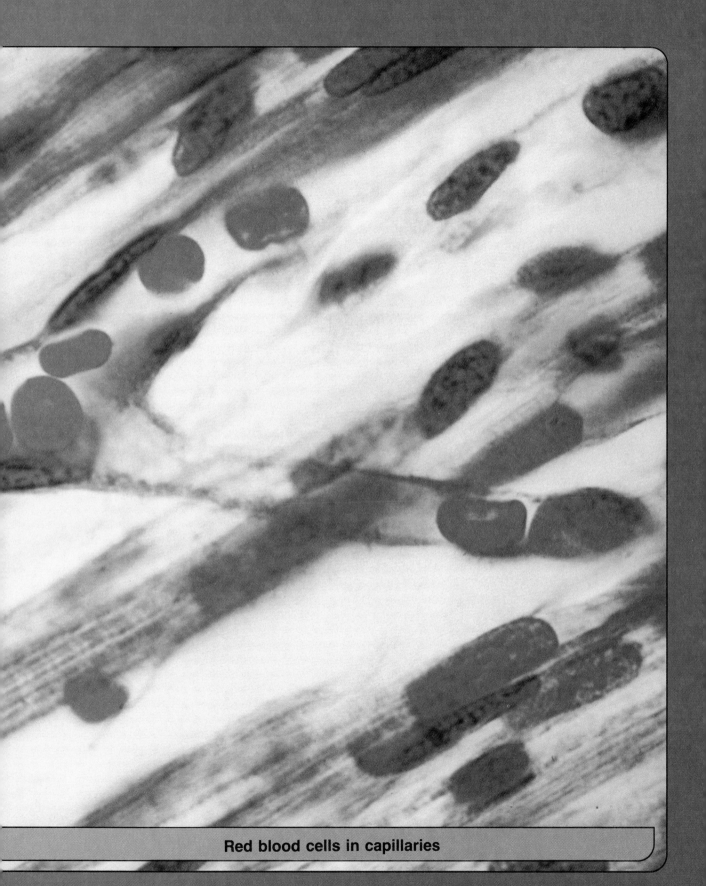

Red blood cells in capillaries

Chapter 10
Circulation and Digestion

Blood transports digested food to body cells and removes wastes. Blood contains red and white blood cells, plasma, and platelets, along with a variety of other materials. Each person's blood is different. An automatic analyzer can identify blood types. Why is blood typing needed? How many main blood types are there?

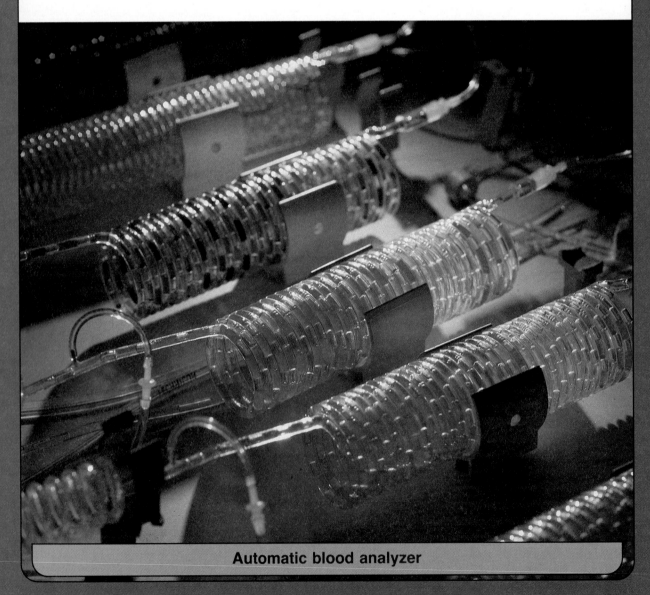

Automatic blood analyzer

Circulation

LESSON GOALS
In this lesson you will learn
- the parts and purpose of the circulatory system.
- the parts of blood and how it circulates in the body.
- the four main blood types.

Of what kingdom are you a member? Are you a simple or complex organism? Recall from Lesson 1:2 that complex organisms are made of cells that are organized into tissues, organs, and organ systems.

The basic building blocks of living things are cells. Your body is made up of over 70 trillion cells. Groups of cells called tissues work together to do certain jobs. Bones, muscles, and blood are examples of tissues. Tissues form organs that work together to perform certain jobs. The brain, stomach, and heart are examples of organs. Organs that work together to do certain jobs form systems. What are some of your organ systems?

Humans show all the features of life. They are made of cells. They grow, develop, use energy, need food, and reproduce. Organ systems are used in each of these features of life. Look at Figure 10–1. This picture shows the organization of one of your organ systems. How is the circulatory system important?

Figure 10-1. Muscle cells form heart tissue. Heart tissue forms the heart. The heart and blood vessels form the circulatory system.

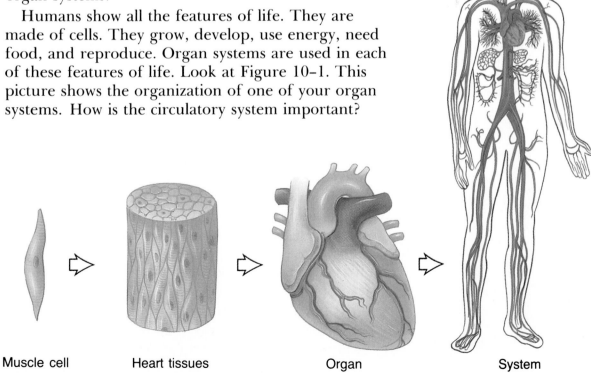

Muscle cell   Heart tissues   Organ   System

The **circulatory system** is a system that transports materials in the blood to and from the cells of the body. Your circulatory system transports food, water, and oxygen to each cell in your body. These materials are used in cells for growth and repair. While growth and repair take place, wastes are produced. The wastes must be removed. Your circulatory system removes the wastes from your cells. The wastes are transported to organs that release the wastes from your body.

The circulatory system has three parts: the blood, the heart, and the blood vessels. The heart pumps blood through blood vessels to the cells. The blood then flows back to the heart. Why is *circulatory* a good name for this body system?

What are the parts of the circulatory system?

Parts of the Circulatory System

The heart is the organ that pumps blood around the body. Your heart is about the size of your fist. The heart is located near the center of your chest. It is behind the breastbone and between the lungs. The bottom tip of the heart points toward the left side of your body.

How many chambers make up your heart?

Your heart has four chambers, two upper and two lower. Each upper chamber is called an atrium (AY tree um). There is a right and a left atrium. Lower chambers are called ventricles (VEN trih kulz). There is a right and a left ventricle. A thick wall, the septum, separates the right and left sides of the heart. The left atrium and left ventricle are separated by a valve. A valve also separates the right atrium and right ventricle. Find each atrium, the ventricles, and the valves in the drawing of the heart.

Your heart is made of muscle and other tissues. When the muscles of an atrium contract, blood is forced into a ventricle. When a ventricle contracts, blood is forced into the blood vessels. Your heart pumps constantly and normally beats 60 to 80 times each minute.

Blood flows through a network of tubes called blood vessels. There are three kinds of blood vessels. They are arteries, veins, and capillaries. An **artery** is a blood vessel that carries blood away from the heart. A

Figure 10–2. The heart has four chambers. Valves separate the upper chambers from the lower chambers. A thick wall divides the left and right sides.

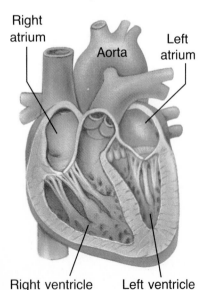

Right atrium

Aorta

Left atrium

Right ventricle   Left ventricle

192

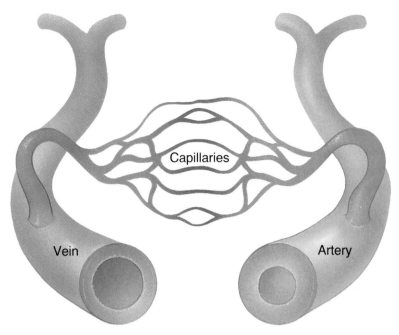

Figure 10–3. Arteries and veins connect in the tiny capillaries.

Capillaries

Vein

Artery

vein is a blood vessel that carries blood to the heart. A **capillary** is a small blood vessel that connects arteries and veins.

Arteries transport blood from your heart to your lungs and all other parts of your body. Each ventricle of your heart is connected to a large, thick-walled artery. The largest artery in your body is the aorta (ay ORT uh). The aorta leads out of the left ventricle. When the left ventricle contracts, blood is pumped through the aorta into many smaller arteries. The regular flow of blood from the heart makes a rhythmic pressure on the walls of the arteries called a pulse. Where on your body can you feel a pulse?

As blood moves farther away from the heart, the arteries become smaller. They branch into microscopic blood vessels called capillaries. Capillaries are in every tissue of your body. Capillary walls are only one cell thick. Materials pass between your body cells and your blood through the capillary walls.

Capillaries connect arteries to veins. Veins carry blood back to the heart. There are many valves on the walls of the veins. Valves stop blood from flowing back and keep blood flowing toward the heart. See Figure 10–4. Look at the inside of your wrist or the back of your hand. The blue lines under your skin are veins.

What is the largest artery in your body?

Figure 10–4. The opening (a) and closing of valves (b) in veins control the flow of blood.

a   b

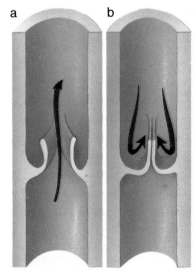

Activity 10-1 Pulse Rate

QUESTION How does exercise affect your pulse rate?

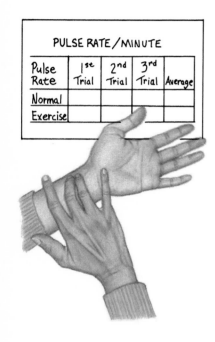

PULSE RATE / MINUTE

Pulse Rate	1st Trial	2nd Trial	3rd Trial	Average
Normal				
Exercise				

Materials

watch or clock with second hand
aerobic music
pencil and paper

What to do

1. Place the tips of your two middle fingers on the inside of your wrist. Feel for your pulse.
2. Count the number of pulse beats you feel in your wrist for 10 seconds. Multiply this number of beats by 6 and record this number as your pulse rate.
3. Repeat step 2 two more times. Find the average of the three counts. Record the average as your normal pulse rate.
4. Exercise in place to music for two minutes. Immediately repeat step 2 and record your pulse rate.
5. Repeat step 4 two more times. Find the average of the three counts. Record the average as your exercise pulse rate.

What did you learn?

1. What is your normal average pulse rate? Your exercise average pulse rate?
2. What effect did exercise have on your pulse rate?

Using what you learned

1. Find your pulse rate immediately after outdoor recess or physical education class. How does it compare to the exercise pulse rate of this activity?
2. Find your pulse rate when you wake up in the morning. How does it compare to your normal and exercise pulse rates?
3. About how many times does your heart beat in one day?

Blood is a mixture of four main parts. They are plasma, red blood cells, white blood cells, and platelets. **Plasma** is the liquid part of the blood. It is mostly water and contains many other substances. Plasma transports food and other materials to your cells. It also takes wastes such as carbon dioxide away from your cells.

There are many microscopic cells in plasma. A **red blood cell** is a cell in the plasma that transports oxygen to your body cells. It also takes carbon dioxide away from your cells. Red blood cells contain a chemical called hemoglobin (HEE muh gloh bun). Hemoglobin turns bright red when combined with oxygen. The blood in the vessels from the lungs contains much oxygen. This blood is bright red. When the oxygen is used up by the cells, the hemoglobin turns a dark purplish red.

Of what is blood a mixture?

When is hemoglobin bright red?

a
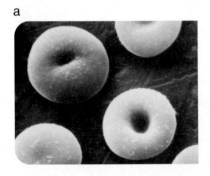
b
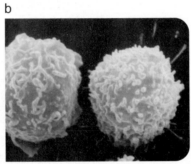

Figure 10-5. Red blood cells (a) and white blood cells (b) are two parts of whole blood.

A **white blood cell** is a cell in the plasma that destroys foreign matter in the blood. This cell also produces antibodies. White blood cells fight infections and diseases of the body. White blood cells usually remain in the bloodstream. Sometimes they squeeze between the cells of blood vessel walls and enter the tissues of the body. This occurs when a splinter or other object enters the tissue. White blood cells surround the splinter and sometimes form pus.

When a blood vessel is cut, the blood that flows out soon forms clots. A **platelet** is a small cell in the plasma that causes blood clots to form. In the clotting process, platelets collect around injured tissue and produce chemicals that form a protein. **Fibrin** is a threadlike protein that forms a blood clot. You have seen blood clots and scabs form on the surface of skin. Why is a scab important?

Figure 10-6. Platelets play an important part in blood clotting.

195

Blood Circulation

Look at Figure 10–7. Notice that the blood vessels have two main paths. Trace the blood through the shorter path. Start at the right ventricle. The right ventricle contracts and pumps blood into a large artery. This artery branches into smaller arteries that lead to the even smaller capillaries in the lungs. Here carbon dioxide is released and oxygen is picked up.

Blood flows from the lung capillaries into many small veins. Trace these veins to the left atrium of the heart. The left atrium contracts and pumps oxygen-rich blood into the left ventricle. The left ventricle contracts and pumps this blood into the aorta.

From the aorta, blood flows into small arteries to the rest of the body. Trace the blood through the arteries to the capillaries. In the capillaries food and oxygen are exchanged for wastes between the blood and body cells. Red blood cells give up oxygen to the cells. Carbon dioxide is picked up by the red blood cells and plasma.

The blood flows from the capillaries into many small veins and then into two large veins. Trace the blood from these two large veins to the right atrium of the heart. Where does blood go from the right atrium? A complete circulation of blood through the body takes about one minute.

What chamber of the heart pumps blood into the aorta?

What processes take place in the capillaries?

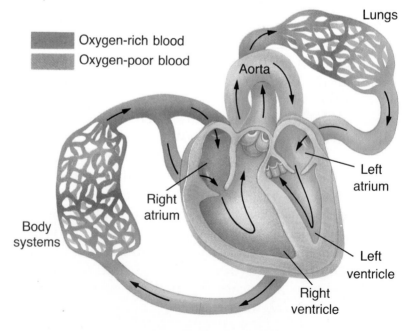

Figure 10–7. The right side of the heart pumps blood to the lungs. The left side then pumps this oxygen-rich blood to the rest of the body.

Blood Types

Every person has blood with the same four basic parts. All human blood has red cells, white cells, plasma, and platelets. There are, however, differences in the blood of different people. Two substances, known as A and B, are used to classify human blood into four main types. People with only substance A in their red blood cells have type A blood. People with only substance B in their red blood cells have type B blood. People with both substances A and B have type AB blood. People with neither substance A nor B have type O blood. What is your blood type? If you do not know, how can you find out?

When people are injured or have surgery, they may need a transfusion. A **blood transfusion** is the process of receiving blood from a donor. If certain blood types are mixed, the red blood cells will clump together. Clumped red blood cells can block blood vessels. People may die if given a blood type that does not mix safely with their own. See Table 10-1.

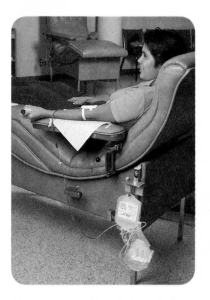

Figure 10-8. Blood donations provide blood to be used in transfusions.

What may happen if certain blood types are mixed?

Table 10-1 Blood Transfusions	
A person with blood type	Can receive blood types
AB	AB, A, B, O
A	A, O
B	B, O
O	O

Lesson Summary

- The circulatory system is made up of the heart, the blood, and blood vessels. It transports food, water, and oxygen to, and removes wastes from, each cell of the body.
- Blood is a mixture of red blood cells, white blood cells, platelets, and plasma. Blood is pumped by the heart into arteries that carry blood to all body cells, and is returned to the heart through veins.
- A, B, AB, and O are the four main blood types.

Lesson Review

Review the lesson to answer these questions.

1. Name the structures that make up the circulatory system in your body.
2. What are the two important purposes of the circulatory system?
3. Trace the flow of blood from the right ventricle to the left atrium of the heart.
4. What types of blood could a person with type A blood safely receive in a transfusion?

LESSON GOALS

In this lesson you will learn

- the parts of the digestive system.
- how food is digested and passed into the blood.
- what enzymes are and how they work.

Every cell in your body uses energy. The energy comes from the food you eat. The **digestive system** is the system that changes food to forms that cells can use for all life activities. How do you think energy is obtained from food?

Your digestive system includes all the parts of your body that break down food. Some of the organs of the digestive system form a continuous tube. Other organs make enzymes (EN zimez) that help break down food as it passes through the tube. An **enzyme** is a molecule that speeds up a chemical reaction in an organism. With enzymes your body can digest most food in a few hours.

Food is changed as soon as it is placed in the mouth. Chewing causes a physical change. As you chew, your teeth break food into smaller pieces. Food is also changed chemically by an enzyme in saliva (suh LI vuh). Saliva is the liquid in your mouth. It is made in glands that have ducts leading to the mouth. A duct is a tube made of cells. The tongue and teeth mix the food with saliva. Moist food is easier to swallow. The enzyme in saliva aids in breaking starch molecules into smaller molecules of sugar. If you chew a cracker for thirty seconds, what happens to its taste?

When you swallow food, it moves from your mouth into your esophagus (ih SAHF uh gus). The **esophagus** is a tube that connects the mouth with the stomach. Look at Figure 10–9. Notice how the esophagus and the windpipe are close together. When you swallow, a flap of tissue called the epiglottis covers the windpipe and food passes down the esophagus. Muscles on the inside of the esophagus move the food toward the stomach.

Figure 10–9. Food, moistened with saliva, moves into the esophagus as you swallow. Notice the flap of tissue that covers the windpipe.

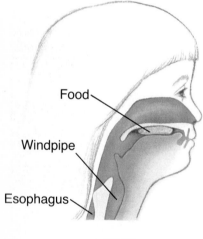

Food
Windpipe
Esophagus

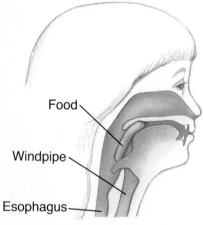

Food
Windpipe
Esophagus

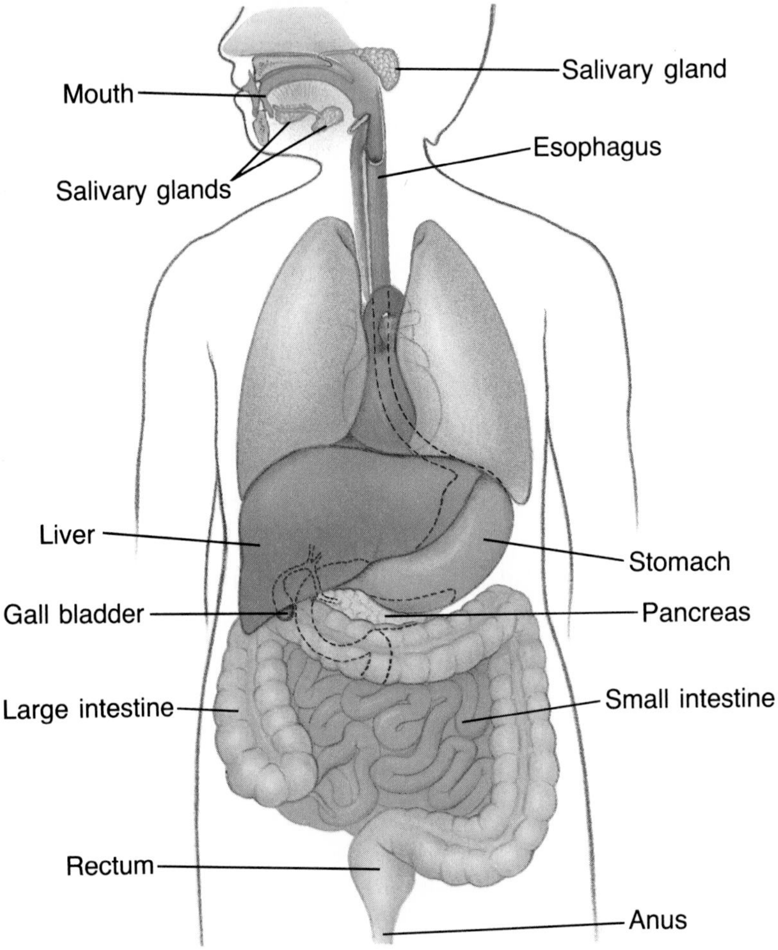

Figure 10–10. Organs of the digestive system

Mouth

Salivary glands

Salivary gland

Esophagus

Liver

Gall bladder

Large intestine

Rectum

Stomach

Pancreas

Small intestine

Anus

The **stomach** is a small, saclike organ that holds and digests food. The muscles of the stomach contract and relax when food is present. This muscle action causes churning that breaks food into smaller pieces. The food is mixed with hydrochloric acid and enzymes that are made in the stomach walls. The acid and enzymes break down large molecules of protein into smaller molecules. Food stays in the stomach for about four hours. The muscles of the stomach then move the food along into the small intestine. The food is now a soupy mixture called chyme.

The small intestine is a long, narrow, tubelike organ. It is about seven meters long and has many folds. Notice how it fits into a very small body space. Most of the chemical processes of digestion take place in the first part of the small intestine.

What is mixed with food in the stomach?

What is the small intestine?

Where does most of the chemical process of digestion occur?

199

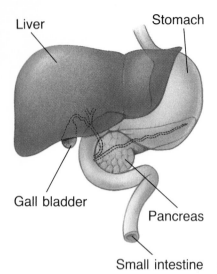

Figure 10-11. Ducts lead from the gall bladder and pancreas into the small intestine.

The food we eat consists of many large molecules. Most are molecules of fats, proteins, and carbohydrates. Enzymes in the small intestine break these molecules apart. Some of these enzymes are made in the walls of the small intestine. Others come from the pancreas (PAN kree us). This is an organ that lies close to the stomach. A duct leads from the pancreas to the small intestine. The enzymes from the pancreas pass through this duct.

Bile also aids digestion. Bile is made in the liver and stored in the gall bladder. It travels through ducts to the small intestine. Bile is a yellow to greenish fluid that separates fatty food into small droplets. These droplets are easier for enzymes to digest.

Digestion is completed in the small intestine. Digested food is then ready to be used by the body. Inside the walls of the stomach and small intestine are many capillaries. Food molecules pass from the digestive system into the blood by diffusion (dihf YEW zhun). **Diffusion** is the movement of molecules from where they are present in large amounts to where they are present in small amounts.

Most food molecules enter the blood from the small intestine. The inner lining of the small intestine is not smooth. Instead, it has millions of tiny folds called villi. These villi stick out like tiny fingers into the interior of the intestine. Inside the villi are capillaries. Food molecules pass through the villi walls into the capillaries. The blood carries the food molecules to all body cells.

How do food molecules move from the digestive system to the cells where they are used?

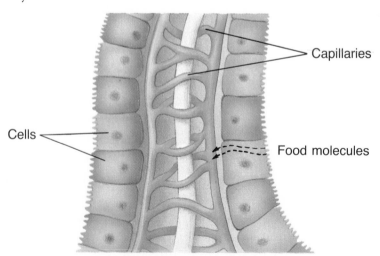

Figure 10-12. Food molecules pass through the walls of the small intestine into the bloodstream.

200

Movement of Food Through the Digestive System

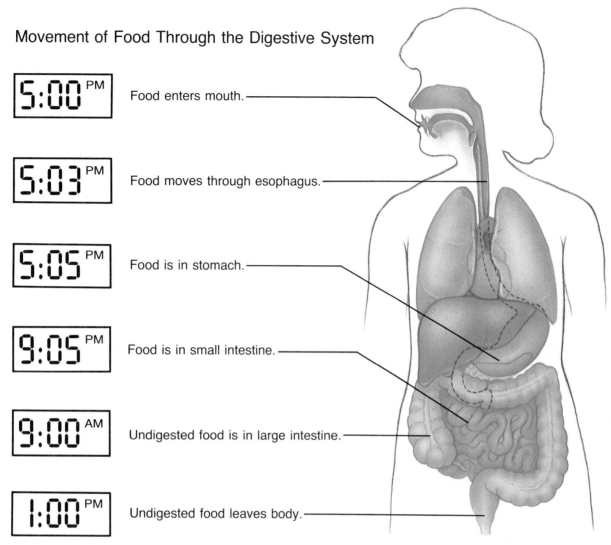

5:00 PM — Food enters mouth.

5:03 PM — Food moves through esophagus.

5:05 PM — Food is in stomach.

9:05 PM — Food is in small intestine.

9:00 AM — Undigested food is in large intestine.

1:00 PM — Undigested food leaves body.

Figure 10-13. Food moves through the digestive system in about 20 hours. This time varies for different people.

Some food is not digested and passes into the large intestine. The large intestine is about two meters long. It is shorter and wider than the small intestine. How is the large intestine arranged in your body?

Food wastes that enter the large intestine contain much water. Most of the water passes through the walls of the large intestine into the blood. Bacteria in the intestine decompose the food wastes. They also make vitamin K and some B vitamins that your body needs. The solid wastes are stored in the enlarged end of the large intestine called the rectum. The wastes pass out of the body through the anus (AY nus) about 20 hours after food first enters the body. This time varies from person to person.

What substances pass from the large intestine into the blood?

201

Activity 10-2 Diffusion

How does diffusion take place?

Materials

3 paper cups
starch solution
water
safety goggles
iodine solution in dropper bottle
2 small cellophane bags
2 marbles
string
twist ties
2 small widemouthed jars
pencils
masking tape
paper towels
pencil and paper

What to do

Part A

1. Label one cup *Starch* and another cup *Water*. Fill the starch cup with starch solution. Fill the water cup with water.

2. Put safety goggles on. Add three drops of iodine solution to each cup. **CAUTION:** *Do not touch the iodine solution.* Record your observations. Then empty the cups in a sink and throw them away.

Part B

1. Put a marble in each bag. Fill the bags half full of water. Tie the bags tightly shut with a twist tie. Then use string to tie the bags to the pencils so the bags hang down freely.

2. Put the pencils across the mouths of the jars. The bags should hang down inside the jars. Tape the pencils in place.

3. Fill one jar almost to the top with starch solution. Fill the second jar with water. This will be your control. Let the jars stand overnight.

4. The next day observe both bags. Remove the bag from the starch solution. Dry off the outside of the bag. Pour some of the water from the bag into a cup.

5. Add three drops of iodine solution to the cup. Record your observations.

What did you learn?

1. In Part A, what happened to the starch solution when iodine solution was added?
2. In Part A, what happened to the water when iodine solution was added?
3. In Part B, what happened when you added iodine solution to the water that was in the bag?
4. Does the amount of water in the bags change?

Using what you learned

1. How do your results show the importance of digestion for getting food into cells?
2. How do food molecules move from your small intestine into your blood?
3. How do you think food molecules move from your blood into your cells?

Lesson Summary

- The mouth, esophagus, stomach, small intestine, and large intestine, along with the liver and pancreas, form the digestive system of your body.
- Food goes through physical and chemical changes so that it can be used by body cells.
- Enzymes are substances that speed up chemical reactions and allow your body to digest food faster.

Lesson Review

Review the lesson to answer these questions.

1. In what parts of the digestive system are enzymes made?
2. What happens to food in the small intestine?
3. Explain what happens to digested and undigested food.

People and Science

Saving Hearts

The steady beep of the heart rate monitor above the patient's bed assured Dr. Seymour Bardo that the patient was doing well. Hours before, Dr. Bardo led a team of doctors in performing open heart surgery on this patient.

Dr. Bardo's goal in performing the delicate surgery was to repair a small hole between the left and right ventricles of the patient's heart. In most humans, this hole closes permanently within hours after birth. But in this patient, the hole did not close. Without surgery, the patient's blood would not have circulated properly. Oxygen-rich blood from the lungs would have mixed with oxygen-poor blood from the body. Without efficient blood circulation, the patient, a 2-day-old baby boy, would not have survived.

Dr. Bardo and a skilled team of doctors and nurses worked for many hours during the operation. Special surgical tools were used because the baby was so small. Dr. Bardo even used a magnifying lens to make it easier to see tiny arteries and veins.

As the team worked, a special machine pumped oxygen-rich blood through the boy's circulatory system. Another machine helped him breathe. Through a small incision in the heart muscle, Dr. Bardo found the hole in the ventricle wall. Using very thin, strong thread, Dr. Bardo closed the hole. He then repaired the incision in the heart muscle.

Later that day, Dr. Bardo paused at the door to the baby's hospital room. The sleeping baby sighed gently. Dr. Bardo could see the rosy color in his cheeks, a sure sign that the baby's heart was, at last, healthy and strong.

Chapter 10 Review

Summary

1. The circulatory system transports food, water, and oxygen to body cells and removes wastes from the cells. 10:1
2. The circulatory system has three parts: the blood, the heart, and the blood vessels. 10:1
3. The heart has four chambers, two upper chambers called atria and two lower chambers called ventricles. 10:1
4. There are three kinds of blood vessels: arteries, veins, and capillaries. 10:1
5. Blood is a mixture having four main parts: plasma, red and white blood cells, and platelets. 10:1
6. There are four main human blood types: A, B, AB, and O. 10:1
7. The digestive system changes food to forms that cells can use for all life activities. 10:2
8. The mouth, esophagus, stomach, small and large intestines, along with the liver and pancreas, form the digestive system of the body. 10:2
9. Food goes through physical and chemical changes so that it can be used by the cells of the body. 10:2
10. Enzymes are substances that speed up chemical reactions and allow the body to digest food faster. 10:2
11. Some parts of food cannot be digested and leave the body as wastes. 10:2

Science Words

artery	digestive system	platelet
blood transfusion	enzyme	red blood cell
capillary	esophagus	stomach
circulatory system	fibrin	vein
diffusion	plasma	white blood cell

Understanding Science Words

Complete each of the following sentences with a word or words from the Science Words that will make the sentence correct.

1. The system that transports materials in the blood to and from the cells of the body is the _____.

2. A small blood vessel that connects arteries and veins is a

   _____.

3. A cell in the plasma that transports oxygen to body cells is a

   _____.

4. A threadlike protein that forms a blood clot is _____.
5. The movement of molecules from where they are present in large
   amounts to where they are present in small amounts is

   _____.

6. The tube that connects the mouth with the stomach is the

   _____.

7. A blood vessel that carries blood to the heart is a _____.
8. A molecule in an organism that speeds up a chemical reaction is
   known as an _____.
9. A small saclike organ that holds and digests food is the

   _____.

10. A blood vessel that carries blood away from the heart is an

    _____.

11. The system that changes food to forms the cells can use is called
    the _____.
12. The liquid part of the blood is the _____.
13. The process of receiving blood from a donor is a _____.
14. A cell in the plasma that causes blood clots to form is a _____.
15. A cell that destroys foreign matter in the blood is a _____.

Questions

A. Checking Facts

Determine whether each of the following is true or false. Rewrite the false
statements to make them correct.

1. Your circulatory system transports food, water, and carbon dioxide
   to each cell of your body.
2. Valves separate the upper and lower chambers of the heart.
3. The large intestine is a narrow, tubelike organ about 7 meters long.
4. The process of digestion is completed in the large intestine.
5. Veins transport blood from the heart to the lungs and all other
   parts of the body.
6. The largest artery in your body is the aorta.

7. Materials pass between your body cells and your blood mainly through the walls of arteries.
8. Hemoglobin in red blood cells is bright red when combined with oxygen.
9. A person with type O blood can safely receive O and AB blood.
10. Saliva is an enzyme in the mouth.

B. Recalling Facts

Choose the word or phrase that correctly completes each of the following sentences.

1. Food is changed to forms your cells can use by the
   (a) circulatory system.
   (b) digestive system.
   (c) large intestine.
   (d) capillaries.
2. The tube that connects your mouth with your stomach is the
   (a) epiglottis.   (b) aorta.   (c) esophagus.   (d) atrium.
3. Oxygen is added to the blood and carbon dioxide released in the
   (a) lungs.   (b) heart.   (c) liver.   (d) small intestine.
4. Which of the following is NOT a human blood type?
   (a) AB   (b) B   (c) AO   (d) O
5. Each upper chamber of your heart is called
   (a) an aorta.   (b) a valve.   (c) a ventricle.   (d) an atrium.
6. The movement of molecules from where they are present in large amounts to where they are in smaller amounts is called
   (a) circulation.   (b) transfusion.   (c) diffusion.   (d) digestion.

C. Understanding Concepts

Answer each of the following questions using complete sentences.

1. What is the order in which blood flows through the heart when it returns to the heart from the body?
2. What happens to the water in "food" while the "food" is in the large intestine?
3. What are the functions of the stomach?

D. Applying Concepts

Think about what you learned in this chapter. Answer each of the following questions using complete sentences.

1. Explain how the food digested in the small intestine gets to the cells of the body.
2. How is the circulatory system like a transportation system of a large city?

Chapter 11

Respiration and Excretion

When humans breathe, air moves into and out of their lungs. The incoming air provides cells with oxygen. The outgoing air removes waste carbon dioxide. When whales surface to breathe, they first clear water from their air passages, and then inhale. How does oxygen move from the lungs to body cells? Where is carbon dioxide produced?

Humpback whale "breathing"

LESSON GOALS

In this lesson you will learn
- how respiration is a process that releases energy.
- how you breathe.
- the parts of the respiratory system.
- how gases are exchanged in the body.

Everything you do uses energy. Recall from Lesson 10:2 that your body uses food to obtain the energy it needs. In the digestive system, food is broken into smaller molecules. The cells use some of these molecules for energy. These molecules are glucose, a kind of sugar. When glucose and oxygen molecules combine in the cells, energy is released. At the same time, wastes such as carbon dioxide are produced.

What molecules do cells use for energy?

$$\text{ENERGY}$$
$$C_6H_{12}O_6 \quad + \quad 6O_2 \quad \xrightarrow{\quad\quad} \quad 6CO_2 \quad + \quad 6H_2O$$
$$\text{Glucose} \qquad\qquad \text{Oxygen} \qquad \text{Carbon dioxide} \qquad \text{Water}$$

Figure 11–1. This equation is the sum of all the chemical reactions by which the body uses glucose to produce energy.

What body systems remove wastes? What body systems supply oxygen to your cells? The respiratory system passes oxygen from the air to the cells. It also rids the body of waste gases. Other body wastes are removed mainly through the digestive and urinary (YOOR uh ner ee) systems. Food, gases, and wastes move through the body in the circulatory system.

What system removes waste gases from the body?

Breathing

Place your hands on your rib cage. Take a deep breath, then exhale. What do you observe? As you inhale, your chest expands. When you exhale, your chest contracts.

A muscle called the diaphragm (DI uh fram) aids in breathing. The **diaphragm** is a sheet of muscle that separates the chest from the lower part of the body. If you put your hand on your ribs when you have hiccups, you may feel this muscle jerk up and down. Normally your diaphragm moves up and down smoothly. When it relaxes, it moves up. When it contracts, it moves down.

What muscle aids in breathing?

209

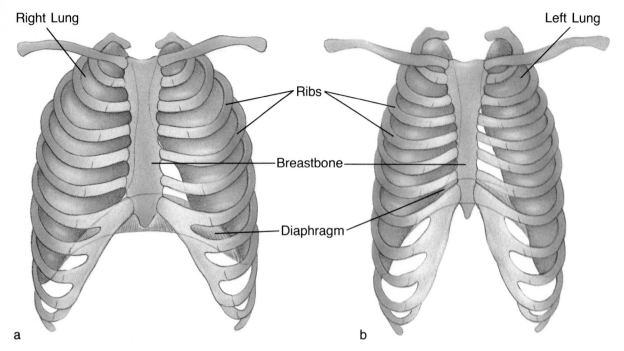

Right Lung

Left Lung

Ribs

Breastbone

Diaphragm

a   b

Figure 11-2. As you inhale (a), the lungs and rib cage expand. When you exhale (b), the diaphragm relaxes and your chest moves in.

When you breathe in, your diaphragm contracts and muscles pull your ribs apart. Air moves into your lungs. When you exhale, your diaphragm relaxes. Your ribs move together and air is pushed out of your lungs.

Breathing results in an exchange of gases. The air you inhale has more oxygen than the air you breathe out. The air you exhale has more carbon dioxide than the air you breathe in.

Parts of the Respiratory System

Air enters your body through your nose or mouth. The nasal cavity is lined with mucus and hairlike structures called cilia. **Mucus** is a moist, sticky fluid. The mucus and cilia trap dust and other objects as air passes through. The nasal passages also warm and moisten the air.

From the nasal cavity air passes into the pharynx (FER ingks). The **pharynx** is a passage that connects the nasal cavity with the trachea (TRAY kee uh). The **trachea,** or windpipe, is a stiff tube that leads to the lungs. The pharynx and trachea are also lined with mucus and cilia. These trap and move small particles away from the lungs.

What are cilia?

Figure 11-3. Cilia aid mucus in trapping particles and moving them out of air passages.

210

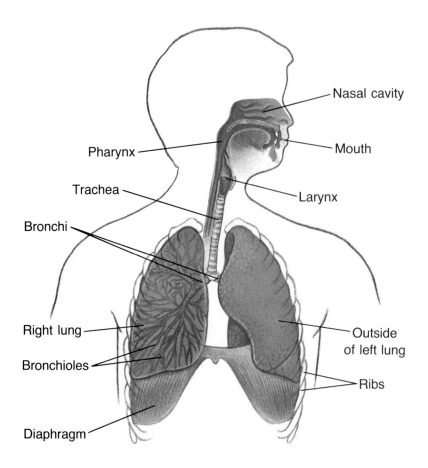

Figure 11-4. Air passes into the respiratory system through these structures.

Nasal cavity

Pharynx

Mouth

Trachea

Larynx

Bronchi

Right lung

Outside of left lung

Bronchioles

Ribs

Diaphragm

At the top of the trachea is the larynx (LER ingks). The **larynx** is a structure in your throat that contains the vocal cords. Air passing over the vocal chords may cause them to vibrate, making sounds. The greater the force of air, the louder the sounds. Movements of the mouth and pharynx control the patterns of the sounds. Why does singing sound different from talking?

In the chest the trachea branches into two tubes called bronchi (BRAHN ki). **Bronchi** are short tubes that direct air into the right and left lungs. Inside the lungs the bronchi branch many times into bronchioles (BRAHN kee ohlz). The bronchioles lead into tiny air sacs. An **alveolus** (al VEE uh lus) is an air sac in the lungs where gases are exchanged. Each alveolus is surrounded by blood capillaries. See Figure 11–5. There are about 300 million alveoli in the lungs. If these air sacs were opened up and spread out, they would cover an area about the size of an average classroom floor.

Figure 11-5. Gases are exchanged between the air and blood in the alveoli.

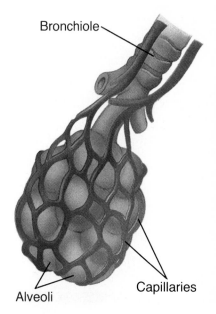

Bronchiole

Capillaries

Alveoli

211

Activity 11-1 The Products of Respiration

QUESTION **What do we exhale?**

Materials

safety goggles
graduated cylinder
limewater
2 test tubes
test tube rack
drinking straw
mirror
pencil and paper

What to do

1. Put on safety goggles. Pour 6 mL of limewater into each of two test tubes in the test tube rack. Label one test tube *C* for control.
2. Place a drinking straw in the other test tube. Blow your breath out *gently* through the straw several times. A steady stream of air should bubble through the limewater. Continue this process for 5 minutes.
3. Observe any change in the limewater.
4. Take a deep breath through your nose. Blow your breath onto a mirror held close to your mouth.
5. Observe what happens to the mirror. Rub your finger across the spot that has formed.

What did you learn?

1. What happened to the limewater through which you exhaled?
2. Why did you need a control test tube?
3. Describe what you saw on the mirror.

Using what you learned

1. What do you exhale that could have caused the change in the limewater?
2. What evidence shows that we exhale water vapor?

Respiration

When wood or any other fuel burns, it reacts with oxygen. The burning process releases energy. What happens in respiration is similar. **Respiration** is the process of using oxygen to combine with food and release energy. There are five main steps in the respiration process.

Step 1. As we breathe, oxygen from air enters the lungs. Oxygen diffuses through capillary walls into the blood.

Step 2. The blood transports oxygen through the blood vessels to body cells. Red blood cells carry the oxygen. Oxygen diffuses into body cells.

Step 3. In the cells, oxygen and glucose combine. Energy is released. Water and carbon dioxide form.

Step 4. Body cells get rid of carbon dioxide. Carbon dioxide diffuses into the blood.

Step 5. Blood transports carbon dioxide to the lungs. Carbon dioxide diffuses into the lungs and is exhaled.

Figure 11–6. Oxygen and carbon dioxide move between an alveolus and surrounding capillaries.

How does oxygen from the air get into the blood?

Gas Exchange and Transport

The air you inhale is a mixture of gases. Most of it is nitrogen. Only about 20 percent is oxygen. There is less oxygen in the blood of the lungs than in the air. So oxygen diffuses from the alveoli into the capillaries around them. Particles from cigarette smoking or air pollution may decrease the amount of oxygen that can enter the bloodstream. Some of these particles break down the walls of air sacs.

What percent of inhaled air is oxygen?

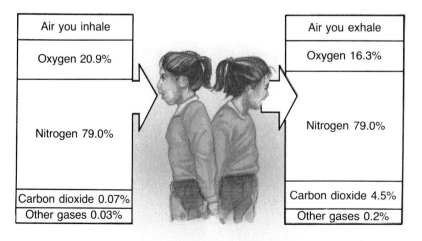

Air you inhale	Air you exhale
Oxygen 20.9%	Oxygen 16.3%
Nitrogen 79.0%	Nitrogen 79.0%
Carbon dioxide 0.07%	Carbon dioxide 4.5%
Other gases 0.03%	Other gases 0.2%

Figure 11–7. The content of inhaled air is different from that of exhaled air.

Why does oxygen diffuse from the blood into body cells?

Oxygen is carried by red blood cells from capillaries around each alveolus to the body cells. Because the oxygen content of the blood is higher, oxygen diffuses into body cells. Here oxygen and food go through chemical changes. Water, carbon dioxide, and energy are produced. Look again at the equation on page 209. The amount of carbon dioxide is higher in body cells than in the blood. This gas diffuses out of the cells into the blood. What happens to carbon dioxide in the blood when it reaches the alveoli? The air you exhale contains more carbon dioxide than the air you inhale. It also contains water vapor.

When you exercise, what triggers the nervous system to speed up the breathing rate?

The body controls the amounts of oxygen and carbon dioxide in the blood. When you start to run or do other exercise, you need more oxygen. The carbon dioxide level increases. This increase triggers the nervous system to cause an increase in fast, deep breathing. You inhale and exhale more often. Deep breathing lowers the amount of carbon dioxide in the blood. It also keeps your cells supplied with oxygen.

Lesson Summary

- Respiration is the process of combining oxygen with glucose and releasing carbon dioxide, water, and energy.
- When you breathe, the diaphragm contracts and relaxes, and air is drawn into and pushed out of the lungs.
- The respiratory system includes the nose, pharynx, larynx, trachea, bronchi, bronchioles, and alveoli in the lungs.
- Oxygen in the lungs diffuses into the blood and is carried to body cells where waste carbon dioxide diffuses into the blood and then out of the blood in the lungs.

Lesson Review

Review the lesson to answer these questions.

1. Explain why the air you exhale contains more carbon dioxide than the air you inhale.
2. In what part of the lung does oxygen diffusion take place?

Language Arts Skills

Understanding Sequence

To understand how a scientific process happens, a reader or an observer must understand its sequence. **Sequence** means the order of the steps in which a process or an event happens. One step occurs. The first step causes something else to happen. Then, one after another, other steps happen. The order in which these steps occur is the sequence of the process.

Sequence can also mean the order of importance. In the United States Army, the rank of sergeant is considered more important than that of private. A lieutenant is considered more important than a sergeant, and so on.

Order of degree is also a kind of sequence. Imagine that you start with navy blue paint. You add some white paint to it. You now have royal blue paint. You add more white paint. You now have sky blue paint. The order of blues, from very dark to light, is a sequence.

On page 213 of this chapter, you will find the sequence of respiration described. The following paragraph describes a sequence involving the respiratory tract.

The respiratory tract is made up of several parts. Air comes into the body through the nasal cavities. These cavities warm and filter the inhaled air. The air then travels into the pharynx. From the pharynx, air flows into the larynx. The larynx is the structure that produces the voice. Air then moves into the trachea, or windpipe. This is a tube that connects the larynx with the bronchi. Bronchi are the branches of tubes that carry air into the lungs. When the air flows through the bronchi, it is inside the lungs themselves.

- List the parts of the respiratory tract in their correct sequence.

First Aid for Choking

1 Object lodges in person's airway.

2 Hold person in standing position from behind with thumb side of fist against victim's abdomen just below breastbone. Place other hand over fist and quickly push hard and up. Repeat as needed.

LESSON GOALS
In this lesson you will learn
• what excretion is.
• the organs involved in excretion.
• the structures of the urinary system.
• how wastes are removed from the body.

As your body uses food, wastes build up in and around body cells. If these wastes are not removed, cells may be poisoned and die. Wastes are removed from the body in a process called **excretion** (ihk SKREE shun).

In Lesson 10:2 you learned that solid wastes from digestion leave the body through the anus. In Lesson 11:1 you learned that cells produce carbon dioxide. Where does this waste gas leave the body? Extra water and salts such as sodium chloride are also waste materials. The body must get rid of these wastes. It must also get rid of urea (yoo REE uh). **Urea** is a cell waste that contains nitrogen. Part of the urea comes from the breakdown of proteins. Excess water, salts, and urea are removed mainly by the urinary system.

Solid, liquid, and gaseous wastes are excreted from the body in four steps.

Step 1. The wastes are removed from the cells.

Step 2. The blood transports the wastes to the organs of excretion.

What system removes excess water from the body?

Figure 11–8. A system of wastewater treatment is necessary to maintain the health of the people who live in a city. Likewise, the health of the human body requires the removal of wastes.

Step 3. Wastes move from the blood into organs for removal from the body.

Step 4. Wastes leave the body.

The Urinary System

The **urinary system** is the group of organs that remove liquid wastes from the body. The urinary system consists of the kidneys, the bladder, and connecting tubes. A **kidney** is a bean-shaped organ that filters wastes from the blood. You normally have two kidneys. They are located on each side of your spine just above the waist. Each kidney is about ten centimeters long and five centimeters wide.

The kidneys produce urine. **Urine** is a liquid that is made up mainly of water, with urea, some salts, and other wastes. Urine leaves each kidney through a tube called a **ureter** (YOOR ut ur). The ureters lead into the bladder. The **bladder** is a sac that stores urine for a few hours. The bladder expands as it fills with urine. When the bladder contracts, urine is pushed into the urethra. The **urethra** (yoo REE thruh) is a duct through which urine leaves the body.

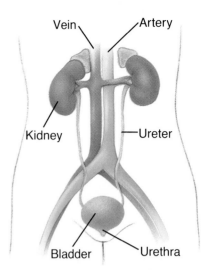

Figure 11-9. Ureters lead from the kidneys to the bladder. The urethra leads from the bladder to the outside of the body.

What forms the urinary system?

Figure 11-10. Each kidney contains over a million filtering units called nephrons.

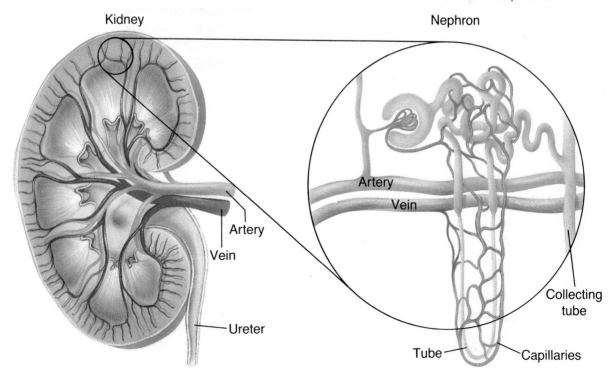

217

How many nephrons does a kidney contain?

Urine is produced as the kidneys clean the blood. Blood enters each kidney through an artery. The blood flows into a network of capillaries in the nephrons. A **nephron** (NEF rahn) is the filtering unit of the kidneys. Each kidney has over a million of these nephrons. See Figure 11–10 on page 217. A nephron has a bundle of capillaries inside a cup-shaped capsule. The capsule leads into a U-shaped tube. The U-shaped tube is surrounded by capillaries. Food molecules, water, urea, and salts are forced out of the blood into the cup-shaped tubes. As these substances move through the U-shaped tubes, the food molecules pass back into the capillaries. Some of the salts and most of the water also return to the blood. The cleansed blood leaves the kidney through a vein. The wastes left behind in the kidney form urine. The kidneys filter all the blood in the body more than 50 times each day, but only about 1 to 1.5 liters of urine are produced in 24 hours.

How can urine be used to learn about one's health?

Even though urine is a waste product, it can be used to learn about your health. Chemical tests on urine can be used to find out if certain body processes are working correctly. For example, if sugar is present in urine, it may mean that a person has diabetes. If parts of bile are in the urine, a person may have a liver problem.

Your kidneys play a major role in keeping you healthy. Sometimes one kidney may no longer function. This may happen as the result of accident or illness. The other kidney may enlarge and do the work of both. If both kidneys fail to work properly, a person may be placed on a dialysis machine. This machine takes over the function of the kidneys. A tube connects this machine to one of the person's arteries. The person's blood flows into the machine. Wastes are removed. Another tube carries the blood back into one of the person's veins. Dialysis is usually done two or three times a week.

Figure 11–11. Some dialysis machines are portable and can be used while on vacation.

Instead of dialysis, a person may have a kidney transplant. During a kidney transplant operation a person is given a healthy kidney. The kidney often comes from a relative. This makes it more likely that the person's body will accept the new kidney.

Activity 11-2 Filtration

Materials

filter paper	sandy soil
funnel	spoon
2 jars	pencil and paper
water	

What to do

1. Fold the filter paper in half. Then fold it again, almost in half.
2. Open the folded filter paper to form a cone. Place the cone in the funnel. Moisten the top of the filter paper so it will stick to the inside of the funnel.
3. Place the funnel in one of the jars.
4. Put a spoonful of sandy soil in the other jar. Fill this jar halfway with water. Stir the water until it becomes muddy.
5. Slowly pour half of the muddy water into the funnel lined with filter paper. Be careful not to let the water go over the top of the filter paper. Observe the water that comes through the filter paper. Record your observations.

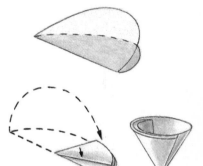

What did you learn?

1. What changes did you observe in the water when it passed through the filter paper?
2. What was filtered out of the water?

Using what you learned

1. Why does water pass through the filter, but soil does not?
2. How is this activity like the action of kidneys?
3. Why is filtering an important process in the urinary system?

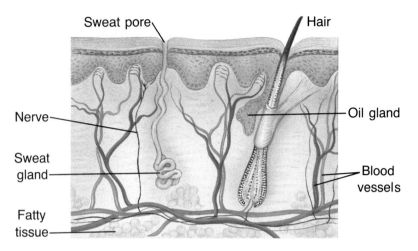

Figure 11-12. Sweat glands in the skin act as organs of excretion.

Sweat pore

Hair

Nerve

Oil gland

Sweat gland

Blood vessels

Fatty tissue

The Skin

Your skin covers and protects your body systems. It is also an organ of excretion. Sweat glands are located in the fatty tissue of the skin. Some urea, salts, and water are taken from the blood by the sweat glands. These wastes move through ducts to pores in the skin and form perspiration, or sweat. Sweat is mostly water. As the water evaporates, it uses energy. This process cools the body. The salts and urea stay on the skin until they are washed away. How are sweat glands similar to your kidneys? Why do you sweat more when you exercise?

Lesson Summary

- Excretion is the process in which wastes are removed from the body.
- The organs of excretion include the kidneys, the large intestine, the lungs, and the skin.
- The structures of the urinary system are the kidneys, the ureters, the bladder, and the urethra.
- Wastes are carried by the blood to excretory organs where the wastes are removed.

Lesson Review

Review the lesson to answer these questions.

1. List the excretory organs that remove each of these wastes from the blood: carbon dioxide, water, salts, urea.
2. What is the filtering unit of the kidneys called?

220

Chapter **11** Review

Summary

1. Respiration is the process of combining oxygen with glucose and releasing carbon dioxide, water, and energy.   11:1

2. When you breathe, the diaphragm contracts and relaxes, and air is drawn into and pushed out of the lungs.   11:1

3. Breathing results in an exchange of oxygen and carbon dioxide.   11:1

4. The respiratory system includes the nose, pharynx, larynx, trachea, bronchi, bronchioles, and the alveoli in the lungs.   11:1

5. In respiration, oxygen diffuses into the blood in the alveoli of the lungs and is carried to body cells where waste carbon dioxide diffuses into the blood.   11:1

6. The waste carbon dioxide from body cells is carried by the blood to the lungs where it is released.   11:1

7. Excretion is the process of removing wastes from the body.   11:2

8. The organs of excretion include the kidneys, the large intestine, the lungs, and the skin.   11:2

9. The urinary system is the group of organs that remove liquid wastes from the body.   11:2

10. The structures of the urinary system are the kidneys, the ureters, the bladder, and the urethra.   11:2

11. Wastes are carried by the blood to excretory organs where the wastes are removed from the body.   11:2

Science Words

alveolus	kidney	pharynx	ureter
bladder	larynx	respiration	urethra
bronchi	mucus	trachea	urinary system
diaphragm	nephron	urea	urine
excretion			

Understanding Science Words

Complete each of the following sentences with a word or words from the Science Words that will make the sentence correct.

1. A moist, sticky substance that lines the nose and trachea is

   _____.

2. A liquid made up mostly of water containing urea, some salts, and other wastes is _____.
3. The process by which food and oxygen are combined and energy is released is _____.
4. One of the pair of bean-shaped organs in your back that filter wastes from your blood is a _____.
5. The process of removing wastes from the body is _____.
6. An air sac in the lungs where gases are exchanged is an _____.
7. The sheet of muscle that separates the chest from the lower part of the body is the _____.
8. The passage that connects the nasal cavity with the trachea is the _____.
9. The structure in your throat that contains your vocal chords is the _____.
10. A tube that carries urine from a kidney to the bladder is a _____.
11. A sac that stores urine for a few hours is the _____.
12. A stiff tube that leads from the throat to the lungs is the _____.
13. The filtering unit of the kidneys is a _____.
14. A cell waste containing nitrogen is _____.
15. The duct through which urine leaves the body is the _____.
16. Short tubes that direct air into the right and left lungs are the _____.
17. The group of organs that remove liquid wastes from the body make up the _____.

Questions

A. Checking Facts
Determine whether each of the following is true or false. Rewrite the false statements to make them correct.
1. Your diaphragm relaxes as you inhale and contracts as you exhale.
2. Mucus and cilia lining the trachea trap and move small particles away from the lungs.

3. The air we inhale is mostly nitrogen.
4. Solid wastes from digestion leave the body through the ureters.
5. Urine is produced in the bladder.
6. Each kidney contains ten small filtering units called nephrons.
7. The skin is an organ of excretion.
8. Oxygen and carbon dioxide are exchanged between blood capillaries and the alveoli of the lungs.

B. Recalling Facts

Choose the word or phrase that correctly completes each of the following sentences.

1. Which of these is NOT involved in the excretion of body wastes?
   (a) kidneys   (b) stomach   (c) lungs   (d) skin
2. A muscle that helps control breathing is the
   (a) alveolus.   (b) trachea.   (c) diaphragm.   (d) pharynx.
3. Which of the following is NOT part of the urinary system?
   (a) bladder   (b) ureter   (c) kidney   (d) larynx
4. The structures for air exchange in the lungs are
   (a) alveoli.   (b) nephrons.   (c) veins.   (d) cilia.
5. Which of the following structures are NOT part of the respiratory system?
   (a) lungs   (b) bronchi   (c) ventricles   (d) alveoli
6. Which of the following is NOT a body waste product?
   (a) enzyme   (b) carbon dioxide   (c) urea   (d) water
7. The process of combining oxygen with glucose to release energy is known as
   (a) digestion.   (b) excretion.   (c) respiration.   (d) breathing.

C. Understanding Concepts

Answer each of the following questions using complete sentences.

1. How do the circulatory and respiratory systems work together?
2. How does your skin excrete body wastes?
3. What happens to inhaled air before it gets into the lungs?

D. Applying Concepts

Think about what you learned in this chapter. Answer each of the following questions using complete sentences.

1. How are the systems of respiration and excretion related?
2. How are the systems of digestion and excretion related?

Chapter 12
Control of Body Systems

Each human body system carries out certain functions. All of these systems work together in harmony in a body that is healthy. In a rowing shell, each crew member must work in harmony with the other crew members to be successful. The steersman is responsible for control of the rowing system. What two body systems control the other body systems? How is their control different?

Racing shell and crew

LESSON GOALS

In this lesson you will learn

- how the endocrine system controls many body processes.
- how hormones move throughout the body.
- the names and functions of some endocrine glands.
- about problems caused by too much or too little of certain hormones.

Two systems help control the other body systems. They are the nervous system and the endocrine (EN duh krun) system. The nervous system controls other systems by relaying impulses along nerves. The endocrine system releases chemicals into the bloodstream. These chemicals travel through the bloodstream to their targets. The endocrine system works more slowly than the nervous system. Its effects, however, usually last longer than those of the nervous system. In general, the nervous system is involved in quick reactions. The endocrine system produces effects that may last for hours, days, or even years.

What two systems help control other body systems?

Figure 12–1. An athlete feels a burst of energy as a hormone from the adrenal glands enters the bloodstream.

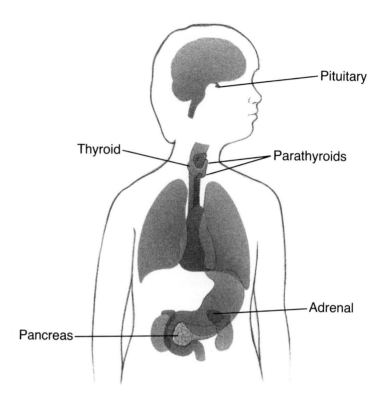

Figure 12–2. The glands of the endocrine system are not connected with one another.

Pituitary

Thyroid

Parathyroids

Adrenal

Pancreas

The Endocrine System

The **endocrine system** is a system of glands in the body that release hormones (HOR mohnz) into the bloodstream. A **hormone** is a chemical produced by the endocrine glands. In Lesson 11:2 you learned that glands in the skin produce sweat. This sweat passes through tubes called ducts to the surface of the skin. Endocrine glands are ductless. The hormones they produce do not travel through tubes. They pass directly from gland cells into blood capillaries.

Hormones pass into the blood from a gland in one part of the body, but have an effect somewhere else in the body. They are sometimes called "chemical messengers." There are many different kinds of hormones present in the blood at one time. Each one is recognized by special molecules in the tissue that the hormone controls. This tissue is called *target tissue*. A hormone may increase the activity of a target tissue. At another time, it may decrease or stop the activity of a target tissue. Hormones regulate the way the body grows and reproduces. They control the rate at

Why are endocrine glands called ductless glands?

What is the name of the tissue controlled by a hormone?

226

which the body uses food. Hormones also control the amounts of water and salts in the body. Hormones aid the body in dealing with stress.

Endocrine glands produce hormones when they are needed. How does the body know when to produce a certain hormone? The system works something like the thermostat that controls the heating of your house. When the temperature gets too low, the thermostat turns the furnace on. When would the thermostat shut off the furnace? Body signals cause endocrine glands to release hormones. If the level of water in the body becomes too high, a certain gland will release a hormone. This hormone will cause the body to rid itself of extra water.

The endocrine system is different from most other organ systems in the body in that its glands are not connected with one another. The glands form a system because they act in a similar way. The glands in your endocrine system control many different types of activities. If the body fails to produce a certain hormone, disease may result. Likewise, disease may occur if too much or too little of a certain hormone is released into the bloodstream.

Figure 12–3. Hormones control the way the body grows.

The Thyroid Gland

The **thyroid gland** is a butterfly-shaped endocrine gland in the throat. It lies just below the voice box in front of the trachea. It is a dark red structure, richly supplied with blood vessels.

The thyroid gland produces several hormones. These hormones are needed for normal growth and development. The main function of the thyroid is to control cell metabolism (muh TAB uh lihz um). **Metabolism** is the total of all the chemical reactions that take place in the body. The thyroid hormones control the rate at which cells use food. If a person's thyroid makes too much of these hormones, a person's metabolism may increase. The cells use food too fast. The person may eat well and yet lose weight. How might a person's metabolism change if the thyroid made too little of these hormones?

Figure 12–4. The thyroid gland produces hormones that regulate metabolism.

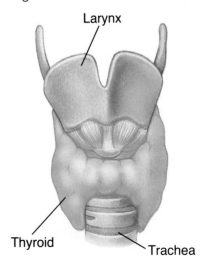

Larynx

Thyroid

Trachea

227

Iodine is important for keeping your thyroid gland healthy. The thyroid gland cannot make thyroid hormones without iodine. Iodine has to be supplied by a person's diet. People who do not have enough iodine in their diets may develop goiters. A goiter is an enlarged thyroid gland. The most common way to prevent goiters is to use iodized salt. Iodized salt is table salt to which a small amount of potassium iodide has been added. Fish is also a good source of iodine.

What is iodized salt?

Figure 12-5. Fish is a good source of iodine in the diet.

The Parathyroid Glands

What do the parathyroid glands control?

Figure 12-6. The four small parathyroid glands lie in the back of the thyroid gland. They control calcium and phosphate ion levels in the body.

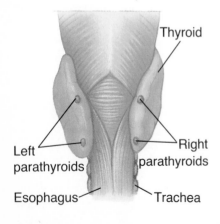

Thyroid

Left parathyroids

Right parathyroids

Esophagus

Trachea

Located on the back of the thyroid are four tiny endocrine glands called the **parathyroid glands.** These glands are each about the size of a pea. The parathyroids make a hormone that controls the amounts of calcium and phosphate ions in the blood. Both of these ions are needed for proper growth and general health.

Calcium is needed for teeth and bones. It is also involved in blood clotting. It is used by nerves and muscles. Too much of the parathyroid hormone may cause bones to lose too much calcium and become brittle. Phosphate is needed to make several important compounds. It aids in maintaining the pH of the blood. The parathyroid hormone raises or lowers the levels of calcium and phosphate as needed.

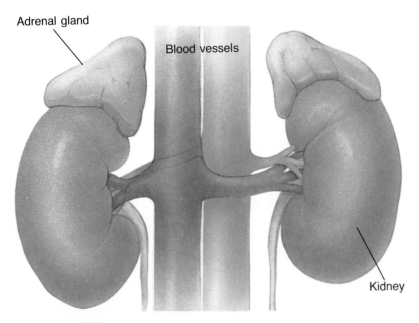

Adrenal gland

Blood vessels

Kidney

Figure 12-7. The adrenal glands are located on top of the kidneys.

The Adrenal Glands

The **adrenal** (uh DREE nul) **glands** are two endocrine glands on the top of the kidneys. Each gland has inner and outer layers. A hormone made in the inner layer is adrenaline (uh DREN ul un). **Adrenaline** is a hormone that helps the body react to emergencies. Adrenaline is released in times of sudden fear, anger, or pain. Adrenaline causes metabolism to speed up. It makes the heart beat faster. It increases the release of stored food by the liver. There is an increase in sweating and rate of breathing. Why is adrenaline sometimes called the "fight or flight" hormone?

The outer layer of each adrenal gland makes over thirty different hormones. Separate hormones control the amounts of salt and sugar in the blood. Other hormones provide relief for swollen joints. Some of the hormones aid in keeping water balance.

Figure 12-8. Adrenaline flows into the bloodstream when a person experiences sudden fear.

What effects does adrenaline produce in the body?

The Pancreas

The pancreas, located behind the stomach, is an organ of digestion. It is also an endocrine gland. Recall from Lesson 10:2 that the pancreas makes enzymes to digest food. These enzymes travel through ducts into the small intestine. Other cells in the pancreas release hormones into the blood.

What is the location of the pancreas?

229

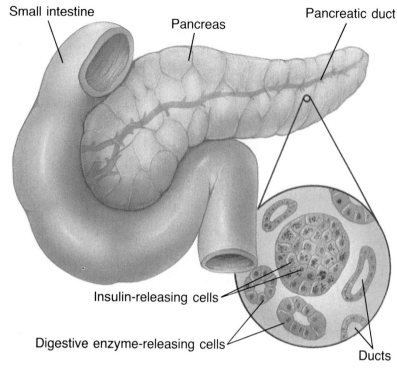

Figure 12-9. The pancreas is both a duct and a ductless gland. Cells release insulin directly into the bloodstream.

Small intestine

Pancreas

Pancreatic duct

Insulin-releasing cells

Digestive enzyme-releasing cells

Ducts

What do the hormones of the pancreas control?

Two hormones produced by the pancreas control the amount of glucose in the blood. Recall that glucose is a sugar that your cells use for energy. After you have exercised or if you have not eaten for a few hours, the amount of glucose in your blood may be low. When this happens, the pancreas releases a hormone that causes the glucose level to increase. What else might increase the amount of glucose in the blood?

What hormone aids the movement of glucose into cells?

The pancreas makes another hormone called insulin. **Insulin** is a hormone that allows glucose to move from the bloodstream into body cells. When the amount of glucose in the blood increases, the pancreas releases insulin. This allows a certain amount of glucose to move into the cells. This happens after you eat a meal. More insulin is produced after a big meal than after a snack. Extra glucose may be stored in the liver.

Without insulin, glucose cannot move into body cells. **Diabetes** (di uh BEET us) is an illness that occurs when the pancreas does not produce enough insulin. In diabetes, the level of glucose in the blood rises. Some glucose leaves the body in the urine. Body cells do not get enough glucose and cannot produce energy for the body's activities. Most people with diabetes can be helped by taking insulin. They must eat special diets to match the amount of insulin they take and the exercise they do. If the case is mild, certain drugs that cause the pancreas to increase its output of insulin may be given.

The Pituitary Gland

The **pituitary** (puh TEW uh ter ee) **gland** is an endocrine gland at the base of the brain that controls other glands. It is sometimes called the "master gland." This gland, about the size of a marble, hangs from a short stalk attached to the lower surface of the brain. The gland has two lobes. Only the front lobe produces hormones.

The pituitary gland makes several hormones. One of these controls the growth of bones. Too much of this hormone causes bones to grow too long. Too little of the hormone may result in dwarfism. Other hormones of the pituitary gland control the activities of the thyroid, adrenal, and reproductive glands. One hormone is released at the time of childbirth. Another controls the amount of water that is returned to the blood by the kidneys.

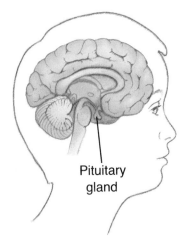

Pituitary gland

Figure 12–10. The pituitary gland is located at the base of the brain. It is called the "master gland."

Why is the pituitary gland sometimes called the "master gland"?

Figure 12–11. Two ten-month-old rats from the same litter differ in size, because the smaller one had its pituitary gland removed when both rats were 28 days old.

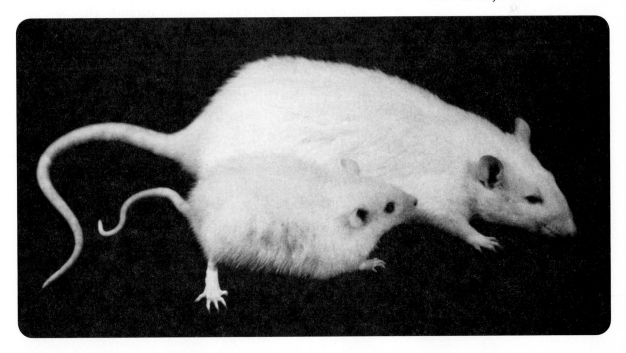

Table 12–1 Endocrine Glands

Gland	Location	Function
Pituitary	Base of brain	Controls other endocrine glands and bone growth
Thyroid	Throat	Controls rate at which cells use food
Parathyroids	Throat, on thyroid gland	Control amounts of calcium and phosphate ions in blood
Adrenals	Top of kidneys	Control emergency reactions by increasing heartbeat and releasing stored food, relieve sore bone joints, keep water balance, control amounts of sugar and salt in blood
Pancreas	Behind stomach	Controls glucose level in blood

Lesson Summary

- The endocrine system controls body processes by releasing chemicals called hormones.
- Hormones travel through the bloodstream from the endocrine glands to the target tissues.
- Glands of the endocrine system include the pituitary, the thyroid, the parathyroids, the adrenals, and part of the pancreas.
- Diabetes, brittle bones, and lack of growth are some of the problems that result from too little of some hormones.

Lesson Review

Review the lesson to answer these questions.

1. Explain the difference between an endocrine gland and a gland such as a sweat gland.
2. Name two endocrine glands located in the throat.
3. What substance is known as the "fight or flight" hormone? Why?
4. Which endocrine gland produces hormones that control several other glands?

Activity 12-1 Locating Endocrine Glands

QUESTION   Where are the endocrine glands located?

Materials

large sheet of paper
drawing paper
scissors
crayons

white glue or paste
masking tape
yarn
pencil and paper

What to do

1. Make a life-sized outline of the human body on a large sheet of paper.
2. In the spaces around your outline of the human body, write the name of each endocrine gland and what it does.
3. On other sheets of paper, draw, color, and cut out life-sized diagrams of endocrine glands. Use the following comparisons for reference:
pituitary—about the size of a marble
thyroid—about the size of a bar of soap
parathyroids—about the size of peas
adrenals—about the size of lemons
pancreas—about the size of a small banana
4. Paste the drawings in the correct locations on your outline of the human body.
5. Tape a length of yarn on the chart to connect each gland with its name and what it does.

What did you learn?

1. Where is each endocrine gland located?
2. What does the thyroid gland do?

Using what you learned

1. How does a hormone from the pituitary gland get to the thyroid gland?
2. Explain why this statement is false: the larger a gland is, the more it does in the body.

LESSON GOALS

In this lesson you will learn

- what activities are important for the health of all your body systems.
- the meaning of a balanced diet.

Figure 12–12. Fresh air, exercise, and sunshine are important for maintaining a healthy body.

It is important to develop habits that will keep all of your body systems healthy. All of your body systems are related. When a disease or an accident injures part of one system, other body systems are affected.

Each of the following activities is important for your overall health.

- Eat a balanced diet.
- Drink plenty of water.
- Exercise regularly.
- Get enough sleep.
- Spend time in the fresh air.

Name three activities that are important to health.

Diet

Food is the source of energy for your cells. Food is used to build and maintain all your body systems. The amount of food you need each day depends on your body size and your activities. A good diet is one that provides the right number of calories. Such a diet allows you to maintain a healthy weight. If you do not have enough calories, your body may not grow as it should. What may happen if a person's diet has too many calories? Too many calories add fat to a person's body. Extra fat may collect in blood vessels. Fat in the blood vessels may interfere with blood flow and may cause a heart attack.

A good diet must provide more than calories. It must also include the right types of food. The types of food you need come from five main groups. These are the milk group, the meat group, the fruit and vegetable group, the grain group, and a combination group. The combination group includes foods such as pizza and casserole dishes. The group contains foods that combine the other four groups. A balanced diet is one that includes correct amounts from each group. It is recommended that you have three servings from the milk group and two from the meat group each day. You should also have four servings each from the fruit and vegetable group and the grain group.

Grain, fruits, and vegetables contain fiber. Fiber supplied by food does not break down in the digestive system. Fiber provides bulk that aids the movement of food through the digestive tract. Thus, fiber is important for the health of your digestive system. The presence of fiber in your diet may prevent certain diseases of the digestive system.

Besides calories, what must a good diet provide?

Why is fiber important in the diet?

Figure 12-13. The five food groups contain all of the nutrients your body needs. It is important that your diet include food from the different food groups.

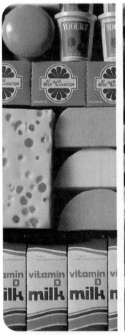

Figure 12–14. Water is lost from the body when you exhale.

Water

Give three ways your body depends on water.

Water makes up over half of your body weight. Your body uses water to break down foods. Water keeps the inside of your lungs moist. Water in the blood carries food to body cells. It also transports waste products to the kidneys. Water leaves the body in urine and sweat. A small amount is exhaled from the lungs. Your body needs to take in about two liters of water each day. All the body systems you have studied depend on water.

Exercise and Rest

What are some benefits of exercise?

When you exercise, you use the muscles of your body. Regular exercise is important to your health. Exercise improves blood circulation, and it can also make your heart muscle stronger. Swimming, skating, walking, and running are some good exercises to keep the circulatory system healthy. Exercise can also increase your lung volume. This allows your body to exchange more oxygen and carbon dioxide.

Exercise aids in weight control. As you exercise, your metabolism speeds up. Your cells must produce more energy. As a result, more food is used and less is stored as fat.

Your body also needs rest and sleep. Both help your body to build up again. During sleep your muscles relax and your body systems slow down. A growth hormone is released into your bloodstream. While you sleep, your body continues to grow. In adults the growth hormone aids in tissue repair.

Fresh Air

Breathing clean air is important for a healthy respiratory system. If air is polluted, it may contain particles and chemicals that can harm your lungs. Indoor air may become dirty because of cigarette smoke. The use of some household chemicals may also pollute the air. If you breathe polluted air, your body cells may not get enough oxygen. The cells cannot then supply enough energy for life activities. The air you breathe is partly cleaned by the mucus and cilia in your nasal passages. How else can you make the air you breathe cleaner?

Why is it not good to breathe polluted air?

Figure 12-15. Exercise in clean air promotes good health.

Lesson Summary

- A balanced diet, exercise, rest, plenty of water, and clean air are important for the health of all your body systems.
- A balanced diet is one that includes the proper number of calories and servings from the five main food groups.

Lesson Review

Review the lesson to answer these questions.

1. Name the five basic food groups, and state how many servings you should have daily from each group.
2. Give two reasons why exercise is important to health.

Science and Technology

Making More Milk

Like humans, all animals produce hormones to regulate their body systems. Recently, scientists have found a way to use one of these hormones to increase the amount of milk a cow produces.

Agricultural scientists performed careful experiments with a hormone called bovine growth hormone. The word *bovine* means that this growth hormone is found in cattle. The hormone regulates the growth of a cow's bones and controls the release of other hormones in the cow's body. It also controls the amount of milk that a cow can produce.

When cows were injected daily with a solution of bovine growth hormone, the scientists found that the cows could produce up to 25 percent more milk than cows that were not given the hormone treatments.

The scientists are continuing the experiments in order to be sure that the cows will not experience any health problems as a result of the hormone treatments.

The agriculture industry is eagerly awaiting the results of the final tests. If the treatment with bovine growth hormone is found to be entirely safe, then farmers who operate large dairy farms may be able to sell more milk. Many agricultural scientists feel that increasing the amount of milk produced in the United States may be helpful in providing food to poorer nations.

As the technology for producing more milk develops, scientists will work to educate farmers all around the world in the methods of raising healthy cattle. People everywhere may someday benefit from the use of bovine growth hormone in the dairy industry.

Chapter 12 Review

Summary

1. The endocrine system, along with the nervous system, helps to control other body systems. 12:1
2. The endocrine system is a system of ductless glands in the body that release hormones into the bloodstream. 12:1
3. Hormones pass into the blood from a gland in one part of the body, but have an effect elsewhere in the body. 12:1
4. Glands of the endocrine system include the thyroid, the parathyroids, the adrenals, part of the pancreas, and the pituitary. 12:1
5. The thyroid gland controls metabolism. 12:1
6. A parathyroid hormone regulates the amounts of calcium and phosphate ions in the blood. 12:1
7. The adrenal glands have an inner layer that produces adrenaline, a hormone that helps the body react to emergencies. 12:1
8. Outer layer adrenal gland hormones control water balance and the amounts of salt and sugar in the blood. 12:1
9. Special groups of cells in the pancreas produce hormones that control the amount of glucose in the blood. 12:1
10. The pituitary gland is sometimes called the "master gland" because it produces hormones that control other glands. 12:1
11. Diabetes, brittle bones, and lack of growth are some of the problems that result from too little of some hormones. 12:1
12. A balanced diet, exercise, rest, plenty of water, and clean air are important for the health of all your body systems. 12:2
13. A good diet includes the proper number of calories and the proper number of servings from the five main food groups. 12:2

Science Words

adrenal glands
adrenaline
diabetes
endocrine system

hormone
insulin
metabolism

parathyroid glands
pituitary gland
thyroid gland

Understanding Science Words

Complete each of the following sentences with a word or words from the Science Words that will make the sentence correct.

1. A chemical produced by an endocrine gland is a _____.

2. The total of all the chemical reactions that take place in the body is called _____.

3. The glands located on the back of the thyroid gland are the _____.

4. The hormone that allows glucose to move from the bloodsteam into body cells is _____.

5. The hormone that helps the body react to emergencies is _____.

6. The system of ductless glands that releases hormones into the bloodstream is the _____.

7. The butterfly-shaped endocrine gland in the throat is the _____.

8. The endocrine gland at the base of the brain that controls other glands is the _____.

9. The illness that occurs when the body does not produce enough insulin is called _____.

10. The endocrine glands on top of the kidneys are the _____.

Questions

A. Checking Facts

Determine whether each of the following is true or false. Rewrite the false statements to make them correct.

1. The endocrine system controls body processes by sending impulses along nerves.
2. The main function of the thyroid gland is to control glucose in the bloodstream.
3. Insulin is released in times of fear, anger, or pain.
4. Hormones of the pituitary gland control the activities of the thyroid, adrenal, and reproductive glands.
5. Fiber provides bulk that aids the movement of food through the digestive system.
6. The tissue controlled by a hormone is called endocrine tissue.
7. The adrenal glands hang from a short stalk attached to the lower surface of the brain.

8. To have a balanced diet, you should eat the proper number of servings from the five main food groups.

9. Iodine is needed to produce thyroid hormones.

B. Recalling Facts

Choose the word or phrase that correctly completes each of the following sentences.

1. Half of your body weight consists of
   (a) hormones.   (b) water.   (c) air.   (d) glands.

2. Adrenal gland hormones control all of the following EXCEPT
   (a) emergency reactions.   (c) blood glucose levels.
   (b) water balance.   (d) amount of salt in blood.

3. All of the following are endocrine glands EXCEPT the
   (a) pituitary.   (c) pancreas.
   (b) parathyroids.   (d) stomach.

4. A butterfly-shaped endocrine gland close to the trachea is the
   (a) pituitary.   (b) thyroid.   (c) pancreas.   (d) adrenal.

5. An illness that results when the body produces too little insulin is
   (a) diabetes.   (c) dwarfism.
   (b) goiter.   (d) kidney failure.

6. Which system controls body activities by producing hormones?
   (a) urinary system   (c) digestive system
   (b) respiratory system   (d) endocrine system

7. Which of the following is NOT a major food group?
   (a) grain group   (c) milk group
   (b) fiber group   (d) fruit and vegetable group

C. Understanding Concepts

Answer each of the following questions using complete sentences.

1. How do hormones get from the endocrine glands to other parts of the body?

2. Why is only part of the pancreas an endocrine gland?

3. Explain why exercise and proper amounts of sleep are just as important to good health as a balanced diet.

D. Applying Concepts

Think about what you learned in this chapter. Answer each of the following questions using complete sentences.

1. What is diabetes, and how might it be controlled?

2. Why might a very thin person have a thyroid problem?

UNIT 5 REVIEW

CHECKING YOURSELF

Answer these questions on a sheet of paper.

1. Five systems are described in this unit: circulatory, digestive, respiratory, urinary, and endocrine. Match the structures or descriptions below to the appropriate system.
   - (a) produces hormones
   - (b) exchanges oxygen and carbon dioxide in the lungs
   - (c) the heart, the blood, and blood vessels
   - (d) the esophagus, small intestine, and pancreas
   - (e) produces enzymes that aid in food breakdown
   - (f) transports oxygen to cells and carbon dioxide away from cells
   - (g) the pituitary, the thyroid, and the adrenal glands
   - (h) alveoli, bronchi, and trachea
   - (i) the kidneys, ureters, bladder, and urethra
   - (j) changes food to a form the body can use
   - (k) the aorta, capillaries, atria, and ventricles
   - (l) the diaphragm aids this system
   - (m) forms urea
   - (n) controls metabolism
   - (o) the "transportation system" of the body
2. How can you properly care for your body systems?
3. What is a balanced diet?
4. Beginning at the mouth, trace food through the structures of the digestive system.

RECALLING ACTIVITIES

Think about the activities you did in this unit. Answer the questions about these activities.

1. How does exercise affect your pulse rate?   10–1
2. How does diffusion take place?   10–2
3. What do we exhale?   11–1
4. How do kidneys work?   11–2
5. Where are the endocrine glands located?   12–1

IDEAS TO EXPLORE

1. Read about the digestive system of a cow. Make a poster comparing the cow's digestive system to the human digestive system. Point out the similarities and differences. Find out how chewing cud is related to digestion.

2. The factors in blood that give us the blood types, A, B, AB, and O, are just some of the substances present in blood. Another is the Rh factor. Blood is either Rh-negative or Rh-positive. Find out what this means and what the Rh factor is. Can Rh-positive blood be safely mixed with Rh-negative blood?

3. When a body organ stops functioning, it may be replaced by an organ from another person. It is necessary to match the tissues of the two persons as closely as possible, so that the donated organ is not rejected by the receiver's body. Today kidney transplants are not uncommon and are about 90 percent successful. Write a report on what is responsible for this high rate of success.

CHALLENGING PROJECT

During digestion, food undergoes both physical and chemical changes. The body breaks down large molecules into smaller molecules the body can use. The body has enzymes that aid in these reactions. Certain enzymes can break apart only protein molecules. Other enzymes work only on starches and sugars. Another group aids the breakdown of fat molecules. Using chemistry books or an encyclopedia, find out what it is about enzymes that makes them so specific. Write a report explaining how enzymes work.

BOOKS TO READ

Body Maintenance by Brian R. Ward, Franklin Watts, Inc.: Danbury, CT, © 1983.
    The function and importance of glands is the focus of this book.

Emergency Room by Bob Wolfe and Diane Wolfe, Carolrhoda Books: Minneapolis, © 1983.
    Read about the excitement of the emergency room.

The Human Body by Francene Sabin, Troll Associates: Mahwah, NJ, © 1985.
    Learn more about the human body.

UNIT 6
Earth Models

Coronado and his men explored much of the Southwest for Spain. They were in search of lengendary cities of gold. Although Coronado never found these cities, his travels provided factual information about the landscape of the Southwest. Modern explorers have used a variety of tools to accurately map the landscape of Earth. How did Coronado and other explorers contribute to our knowledge of Earth? What tools do modern scientists use to make maps?

Francisco Coronado—1540

Earth's solid surface

Chapter 13
Mapping Earth's Surface

Cameras and other special sensors on spacecraft, such as *Landsat,* produce vivid images of Earth features. The images provide information for making better maps. These images also provide data on crops, pollution, mineral resources, and many other aspects of Earth. What is the meaning of the red color in the photo? What is *Landsat?*

Landsat image of New York City

Using Maps

LESSON GOALS

In this lesson you will learn

- there are many kinds of maps.
- landscape features are shown with symbols on maps.
- scales are used to show distances on maps.

Kristi has invited you and some other friends to her house for a birthday party. Kristi lives in a nearby town and you are not sure where her house is located. Kristi offers to draw a map for you. What information would be the most helpful to you in finding Kristi's house?

There are many kinds of maps. Kristi's map in Figure 13–1 shows the streets and buildings near her house. When Kristi and her family go on vacation, they use a highway map. This map shows cities, towns, roads, and highways of many states. Maps can be used to show features of Earth such as mountains and plains. Other maps may show the kinds of plants growing in different areas. Still others show the features of the ocean floor. Any feature on Earth's surface can be shown on a map.

On maps, landscape features are shown with symbols. A **legend** (LEJ und) is the part of a map that explains the symbols for each feature. Look at the legends in Figure 13–2. Which legend explains the symbols on a city map? What kind of map might the other legend be used for?

Figure 13–1. Kristi's map to her house is a street map.

What does a map legend explain?

Figure 13–2. Map legends for two different areas

a

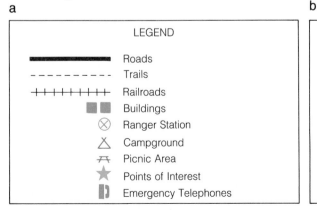

LEGEND	
▬▬▬▬▬	Roads
‑ ‑ ‑ ‑ ‑ ‑	Trails
+++++++++	Railroads
▪ ▪	Buildings
⊗	Ranger Station
△	Campground
⊼	Picnic Area
★	Points of Interest
▯	Emergency Telephones

b

	LEGEND
═⬡═	Interstate Highways
═⑭═	U.S. Highways
═⑮⑥═	State Highways
══════	City Streets
+++++++++	Railroads
‑ ‑ ‑ ‑ ‑ ‑	City Limits
△	Fire Stations
H	Hospitals
⌂	Court House
▪	Schools
⬦	Churches
★	Points of Interest

247

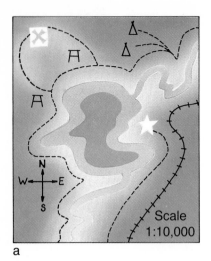

a

b

Figure 13-3. The scale on map (a) shows that the area represented is 10,000 times larger than the map. The scale on map (b) allows you to find the actual distance in kilometers between points on the map.

Maps are made smaller than the areas they represent. You can tell how much smaller a map is by looking at the map scale. A **map scale** is a ratio used to compare distances represented on a map to the actual distances on Earth.

Some map scales are written as fractions. The scale shows how many times smaller the map is than the area it represents. Look at the map shown at top left. The scale is 1 to 10,000. The scale may also be written as 1:10,000 or 1/10,000. A map scale of 1 to 10,000 shows that the map is ten thousand times smaller than the area it represents. No matter what units you use, one unit on this map represents ten thousand of the same units on Earth. One centimeter on the map represents how many centimeters on Earth?

Some map scales use line lengths. See Figure 13-3b. How do you find the distance to Boulder from Denver? Place a sheet of paper on the map so that one edge of the paper passes through both Boulder and Denver. Make a pencil mark on the edge of the paper where it touches Boulder. Make another pencil mark on the edge of the paper where it touches Denver. Then place the edge of the paper against the map scale to find the actual distance on Earth between Boulder and Denver. Line up one of the pencil marks with zero on the scale. The number that lines up with the other pencil mark is the distance from Boulder to Denver. What is it?

Lesson Summary

- There are different kinds of maps to show different features of Earth.
- A legend explains the symbols used on a map to show landscape features.
- A map scale is a ratio used to compare distances on a map to actual distances on Earth.

Lesson Review

Review the lesson to answer these questions.
1. What do maps show?
2. How is a map legend helpful?
3. What does a map scale of 1:10 mean?

Activity 13-1   Mapping Your Classroom

QUESTION   How can you make a classroom map?

Materials

meter stick   4 sheets of graph paper
tape   (1 cm grid)
pencil and paper

What to do

1. Measure the length of each classroom wall in meters. Record your data.
2. Tape four sheets of graph paper together.
3. Decide on your map scale. Let A equal the number of squares on the graph paper that represent one meter. Let B equal 100 centimeters. A/B or A:B is your map scale. Record the scale on your map.
4. Draw an outline of your classroom on the graph paper. Make the length of the walls the correct number of squares according to your map scale.
5. Measure the locations of other items in the classroom. Use symbols to show the locations of the items on your map. Then make a legend to complete your map.

What did you learn?

1. What are the length and width of the classroom in meters? In centimeters?
2. What is the scale of your map?
3. What does the legend show?

Using what you learned

1. Use your map, map scale, and ruler to estimate the distance from the classroom door to: (a) the teacher's desk, (b) the pencil sharpener, (c) your desk.
2. Check your estimates. How accurate is your scale?
3. Suppose you drew a map of the school on the same amount of graph paper. How would you change the map scale? The legend? Try it.

LESSON GOALS

In this lesson you will learn

- features of topographic maps.
- features of globes.

a

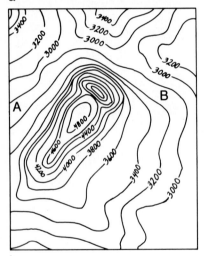

b

Figure 13–4. Map makers translate the features of a landscape (a) onto a flat map (b) using contour lines.

What is the meaning of the numbers on contour lines?

Look at Figure 13–4a. Suppose you wanted to walk from point A to point B. Use your finger to trace the easiest path from A to B. Now trace the most difficult path from A to B. Look at the map of this area in Figure 13–4b. It also shows points A and B. Use your finger to trace the easy path from A to B on the map. Now trace the more difficult path. Along which path did you cross the most lines? What do you notice about the lines on the map and the steep slopes in the photograph?

The word topography (tuh PAHG ruh fee) means "lay of the land." Mountains and grasslands have different topographies. The topography of Kansas, for example, is mostly flat. On the other hand, the topography of Colorado is very mountainous. A **topographic map** shows the surface features of the landscape in detail. These maps show height as well as distance. Features such as forests, lakes, bridges, and cities may also be shown.

Elevation is the height above sea level of a landscape feature. Elevation is shown on topographic maps by contour lines. A **contour line** is a line that joins all points on a map that have the same elevation. You can tell the general topography of an area by how the contour lines are drawn. When contour lines are drawn close together, the land varies greatly in elevation. Thus, the slope of the landscape is steep. The farther apart the contour lines are drawn, the flatter the land is. Look at the placement of the contour lines for the area shown in Figure 13–5a.

There are numbers on contour lines. The number is the elevation of the land where the contour line is drawn. The number shows how high the land is above sea level. Sea level has zero elevation.

a

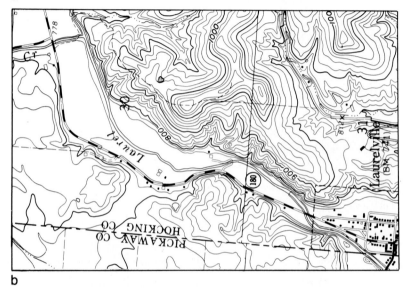

b

Figure 13–5. The contour lines on a topographic map of a flat, gradually sloping landscape are farther apart than the lines on a map of a steep landscape. The various elevations of the landscape in (a) are shown on the matching section of a topographic map in (b).

A **bench mark** is a place where the elevation has been measured exactly. A special metal cap is put at each place. On a map, a bench mark is shown with an X and its elevation. Find the bench mark on the map in Figure 13–5b. How many feet above sea level is the bench mark?

The difference in elevation between two contour lines on a topographic map is called the **contour interval.** The contour interval shows how much higher or lower the elevation of one contour line is than the one next to it. The size of the contour interval depends on the area being mapped. For example, if you were mapping Mount St. Helens, you would use a large contour interval because of the great changes in elevation. Otherwise, the contour lines would be so close together you could not read them. What kind of contour interval would you use to map a flat area such as Kansas?

What is a bench mark?

What is a contour interval?

251

Activity 13-2 Topographic Maps

What does a profile of a topographic map show?

Materials

ruler
pencil and paper

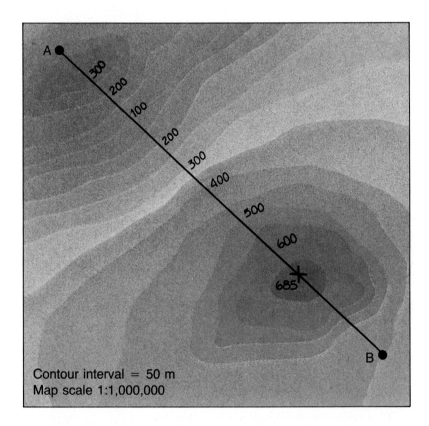

Contour interval = 50 m
Map scale 1:1,000,000

What to do

1. Line up the edge of a sheet of paper with the straight line on the topographic map.
2. Beginning at point A, make a pencil mark on the edge of the paper at each place a contour line crosses the straight line until you reach point B. Mark the bench mark also. Label each pencil mark with the elevation of the contour line or bench mark that it matches.
3. Make a graph like the one shown.

252

Distance (scale 1:1,000,000)

4. Line up the pencil-marked edge of the paper with the bottom of your graph.
5. Using a ruler, draw a straight line from each pencil mark up to its elevation on the graph.
6. Draw a smooth line to connect the top points of all the lines you drew on your graph. This is a map profile.

What did you learn?

1. What does your map profile show?
2. Describe the landscape shown by the topographic map.
3. What other information is shown on the map besides elevation?
4. Where would you need to be on the map in order to see the landscape as it appears on your profile?
5. Where is the lowest elevation on the contour map?
6. How would the landscape appear if you were at the bench mark?

Using what you learned

1. Suppose you were standing at point A and your friend was at point B. Could you see your friend? Explain why or why not.
2. How could you get from point A to point B and do the least amount of climbing?
3. From what point would you have the best view?

Figure 13-6. A sphere gives a more accurate view of Earth than a flat map.

Globes

Recall that models are used to represent real objects. Think about how you could make a model of Earth. What is the shape of Earth? Look at the map in Figure 13-6. How could the shape of this map be changed so it would be a more accurate model of Earth? Globes are spheres on which a map of Earth has been placed. Globes are usually divided into two halves by the equator, an imaginary line around the center of Earth. Each half of Earth is called a **hemisphere** (HEM uh sfihr). Hemisphere means half of a sphere. Which half of a globe represents the Southern Hemisphere of Earth? In which hemisphere are you?

People have constructed an imaginary grid system of lines to locate points on Earth. Most globes have this grid printed on them. The grid is made up of horizontal and vertical lines.

Lines of **latitude** (LAT uh tewd) are horizontal lines drawn parallel to the equator. The lines of latitude divide a globe into equal sections. Each section is a degree. The equator is 0° latitude. Each latitude line is a certain number of degrees north or south of the equator. Look at the lines of latitude in Figure 13-7a.

Figure 13-7. Lines of latitude (a) specify locations north or south of the equator. Lines of longitude (b) give locations east or west of the prime meridian.

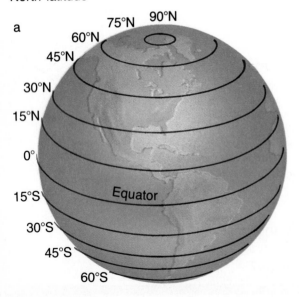

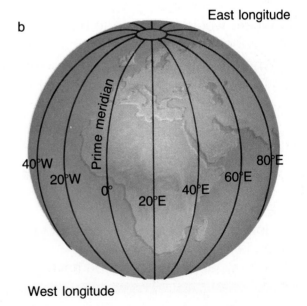

254

Lines of **longitude** (LAHN juh tewd) are vertical lines drawn through the north and south poles of a globe. Each line of longitude is a certain number of degrees from the prime meridian (muh RIHD ee un). The **prime meridian** is 0° longitude. It passes through Greenwich, England. Longitude is measured in degrees east or west of the prime meridian. Look at the lines of longitude in Figure 13–7b.

What do longitude lines measure?

Globes are the most exact models of Earth. World maps are models of Earth put on flat sheets of paper. When might you use a world map instead of a globe? Why is a world map not as accurate a model as a globe?

Which is more accurate, a globe or a world map?

Many world maps have latitude and longitude lines like globes. You can locate any place on Earth if you know which lines of latitude and longitude pass through it. Most globes and maps do not show every line of latitude and longitude. For instance, they may show a line for every five degrees only. To locate some places with these models, you may have to imagine the lines that are not drawn. Find the location of your community on a world map. Determine the line of latitude and line of longitude that cross at your location. Be sure to give the directions north or south for latitude and east or west for longitude. What confusion may occur if you do not state the direction with latitude and longitude?

Lesson Summary

- Elevation and other surface details are shown on topographic maps.
- A globe is a sphere-shaped model of Earth on which lines of latitude and longitude have been placed.

Lesson Review

Review the lesson to answer these questions.
1. What features are shown on a topographic map?
2. What is a bench mark?
3. What advantages does a globe have over a map?
4. How are latitude and longitude lines used?

People and Science

Mapping the Land

Marcos Rodríguez works for the United States Geological Survey. He has worked in many areas of the country. He and his co-workers are currently mapping an area of the southwestern United States. This area has deep canyons and steep, rocky mountains. It is located far away from any towns.

Mapmaking has changed over the years. The first maps were drawn by people who hiked all the way out to an area with mules. Nowadays, helicopters can take Marcos to almost any spot that needs to be surveyed.

Mapmaking tools have changed a lot, too. Mules used to be needed to carry heavy tripods, chains, and bulky transits. A transit is a surveying tool built around a telescope. Modern instruments are lighter and far more accurate. Geologists use electronic instruments to measure dis-

tances. For example, a Geodimeter uses light waves to measure from one point to another.

Marcos carries a compact calculator in his pack. It is one of his handiest tools. If he knows the exact locations of two points, he can use them to find the distance to a third point without going there. First, he measures the angles from the known points to the unknown point. Then he makes an imaginary triangle. With the help of his calculator, he uses trigonometry to find the missing lengths. Trigonometry is the mathematical study of the sides and angles of triangles.

Marcos enjoys getting out and learning about the land. After a day in the canyons, he knows the highest and lowest points. He knows how far apart peaks are. He also realizes how big his country really is.

Chapter 13 Review

Summary

1. There are different kinds of maps to show different features of Earth's surface.   13:1
2. A legend explains the symbols used on a map to show each feature.   13:1
3. A map scale is a ratio used to compare distances represented on a map to the actual distances on Earth.   13:1
4. A topographic map shows the surface features of a landscape in detail.   13:2
5. Contour lines and bench marks are used to show the height above sea level of landscape features.   13:2
6. A globe is a sphere-shaped model of Earth.   13:2
7. Lines of latitude and longitude drawn on maps and globes can be used to locate any place on Earth.   13:2

Science Words

bench mark	hemisphere	map scale
contour interval	latitude	prime meridian
contour line	legend	topographic map
elevation	longitude	

Understanding Science Words

Complete each of the following sentences with a word or words from the Science Words that will make the sentence correct.

1. The height of a landscape feature above sea level is its

   _____.

2. Vertical lines on a globe are lines of _____.

3. A place where an elevation has been measured exactly is a

   _____.

4. Zero degrees longitude is also called the _____.

5. The difference in elevation between two contour lines on a topographic map is the _____.

6. A ratio used to compare distances represented on a map to the actual distances on Earth is a _____.

7. A line that joins all points on a map that have the same elevation is a _____.

8. The part of the map that explains the symbols for each feature is the _____.

9. Each half of Earth, divided by the equator, is called a _____.

10. A map that shows the surface features of the landscape in detail is a _____.

11. Horizontal lines drawn parallel to the equator are lines of _____.

Questions

A. Checking Facts

Determine whether each of the following is true or false. Rewrite the false statements to make them correct.

1. Any feature on Earth's surface can be represented on a map.

2. A map legend is a ratio on a map that shows how many times smaller the map is than the actual areas on Earth it represents.

3. If you want to choose the easiest way to walk from point A to a point B on Earth, you should choose a path on a topographic map that crosses the most contour lines.

4. Bench marks on maps show points where the elevation of the landscape has been estimated.

5. You should use a larger contour interval for a topographic map of an area with flat topography than for a topographic map of an area with steep topography.

6. Lines of latitude and longitude represent an imaginary grid system of lines on a map or a globe.

7. The prime meridian is at 0° latitude.

8. Flat maps of the world are generally more exact models of Earth than are globes.

9. A map scale of 1:10 means that the actual area represented by the map is 10 times larger than the map.

10. Points of the same elevation are indicated on a topographic map by longitude lines.

B. Recalling Facts

Choose the word or phrase that correctly completes each of the following sentences.

1. Map symbols are found in the map
   (a) legend.   (b) scale.   (c) title.   (d) elevation.

2. If a map scale is 1:100, one centimeter on the map represents
   (a) one centimeter on Earth.   (c) 100 centimeters on Earth.
   (b) ten centimeters on Earth.   (d) 1,000 centimeters on Earth.

3. Contour lines spaced close together represent
   (a) a flat valley.   (c) a gentle slope.
   (b) the top of a hill.   (d) a steep slope.

4. The equator separates Earth into
   (a) north and south   (c) south and west
       hemispheres.   hemispheres.
   (b) north and east   (d) east and west
       hemispheres.   hemispheres.

5. The prime meridian separates Earth into
   (a) north and south   (c) south and west
       hemispheres.   hemispheres.
   (b) north and east   (d) east and west
       hemispheres.   hemispheres.

6. The most exact models used to represent the real shape of Earth are
   (a) hemispheres.   (c) lines of latitude and longitude.
   (b) globes.   (d) maps.

C. Understanding Concepts

Answer each of the following questions using complete sentences.

1. What is the difference between a contour line and contour interval?
2. What features are found on a topographic map?
3. How are latitude and longitude lines used?
4. What do all maps have in common?
5. Why is a map scale important?

D. Applying Concepts

Think about what you learned in this chapter. Answer each of the following questions using complete sentences.

1. List at least four kinds of maps. Describe how each is used.
2. Why is a globe a better model of Earth than a world map?

Chapter 14
Earth's Changing Crust

Glaciers are masses of ice in motion. In the past, large areas of Earth's surface were covered by glaciers. Many present-day landscapes were formed by the movements of glaciers. Both Long Island and the Great Lakes owe their existence to glaciers. Where do glaciers occur today? How do glaciers form?

Romanche Glacier, Chile

Continental Drift

14:1

LESSON GOALS

In this lesson you will learn
- about continental drift.
- the idea of continental drift was not supported by much evidence.
- new evidence has been found that has made continental drift a theory.

People have always wondered about the surface features and "arrangement" of landmasses on Earth. Throughout history, scientists have suggested many models to explain Earth's features. Many scientists once thought the cooling and shrinking of Earth's crust caused it to wrinkle. The scientists thought the crust of Earth was like the skin of a grape that wrinkles and dries into a raisin. According to this raisin model, many features such as mountains and ocean basins are "wrinkles" of Earth. They are caused by the cooling and shrinking of Earth's crust.

In 1912, Alfred Wegener suggested a new model to explain the arrangement of Earth's features. Wegener noticed that the Atlantic coastlines of South America and Africa looked like they would fit together. He thought the continents were like pieces of a giant puzzle that had moved apart. According to Wegener's model, many of Earth's features were the result of movement of the continents.

According to Alfred Wegener's model, what caused many of Earth's features?

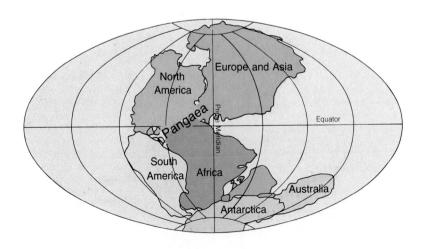

Figure 14-1. According to the idea of continental drift, all the continents were once part of one large continent called Pangaea.

261

Figure 14-2. *Mesosaurus*, an ancient swimming reptile

What evidence was provided by the fossil *Glossopteris*?

Wegener's model of the movement of continents became known as continental (kahnt un ENT ul) drift. The idea of **continental drift** states that the continents were once part of one large continent, called Pangaea, that broke into pieces and drifted apart. Wegener believed that about 200 million years ago Pangaea began to break up. It separated into smaller continents that drifted apart.

Wegener had some evidence for his idea of continental drift. Fossils of the same ancient plants were found on several continents. For example, the fossil fern *Glossopteris* has been found in Africa, Australia, South America, and Antarctica. Wegener believed this meant the climates in the four places must have been the same at one time. Think about the climates of Antarctica and Africa. How are they different today?

Fossils of a swimming reptile, *Mesosaurus,* were found on both sides of the South Atlantic. They have been found in eastern South America and western Africa and nowhere else in the world. Although the reptile could swim, scientists did not believe it could have swum through the thousands of kilometers of ocean that separate these two continents today. Scientists thought that a land bridge may have once joined South America and Africa. However, no evidence of this bridge exists. How does fossil evidence support the existence of Pangaea?

Surface features also provided clues to Wegener's puzzle. Many features that appear on one continent seem to be continued on another. Glaciers, as they

Figure 14-3. "Tracks" were left by melting glaciers (a). Parts of Pangaea were covered by glaciers (b).

a

b

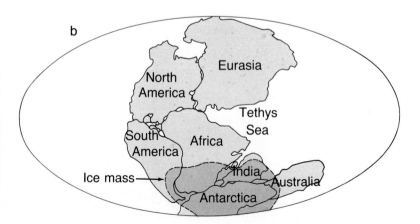

Figure 14-4. Features such as mountain chains and coal beds seem to continue from one continent to the other. Clues such as these support the idea of continental drift.

move across land, leave "tracks" such as grooves and loose rocks. The tracks of ancient glaciers have been found in South America, Africa, Antarctica, India, and Australia.

All mountains in a chain are of similar age and structure. The mountain chain in the eastern United States seems to continue through Canada and northern Europe. The mountains in all these areas are of similar age and structure. These kinds of evidence supported Wegener's idea.

The continents did seem to fit together like pieces of a puzzle. Yet, most scientists did not agree with Wegener's model of continental drift. He was not able to explain what caused the continents to move. Thus, scientists began to consider other models. But, enough new evidence was found to support Wegener's idea that it became a theory.

Why did most scientists not believe Wegener's model?

New Evidence

Compass needles are small magnets. Compass needles line up with Earth's magnetic field. The needles always point north to Earth's north magnetic pole. Some rocks contain magnetic minerals. These minerals line up with Earth's magnetic field the way compass needles do.

What causes compass needles to point north and south?

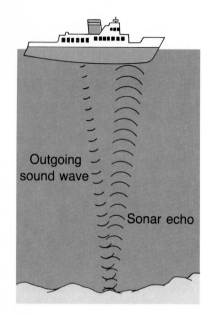

Figure 14–5. Sound waves are used to map the ocean floor.

Where along ocean floor ridges are the youngest rocks found?

Lava contains magnetic minerals. Magnetic minerals in recent lava flows line up with Earth's present magnetic poles. The magnetic minerals in ancient lava flows lined up with Earth's ancient magnetic poles. They do not line up with Earth's present magnetic poles. This is evidence that the continents moved after the rocks were formed.

Studies of the ocean floor have also provided new evidence. Scientists send sound waves from ships to the ocean floor. The sound waves bounce off the floor and return to the ship. These bouncing sound waves are called sonar echoes. Scientists record the amount of time it takes for the sound waves to return to the ship. The longer the echo time, the farther the floor is from the ship. Scientists use these data to map the ocean floor.

Large mountain ranges on the ocean floor were discovered using sonar. A mountain chain on the ocean floor is called a **mid-ocean ridge.** Large cracks were found in the centers of the ridges. The youngest ocean floor rocks are found at the edges of the cracks. Rocks become older as the distance from the ridge center becomes greater.

Figure 14–6. Map of ocean floor

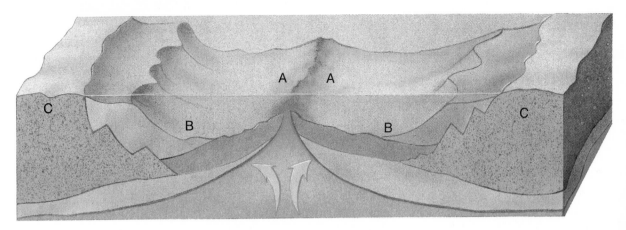

Figure 14-7. Seafloor spreading occurs at mid-ocean ridges as shown in this cross-section of ocean floor.

What process is occurring at mid-ocean ridge cracks?

The cracks in the ridges go through Earth's crust. Molten rock, or magma, from Earth's mantle moves through the cracks to the ocean floor. This process of adding new crust at mid-ocean ridges is called **seafloor spreading.**

Look at Figure 14-7. Where do you think the new ocean floor rocks are forming? What do you know about the age of rocks as you move from points A to B to C? What happens to the distance between the points labeled A as new rocks form between them?

Lesson Summary

- Wegener's idea of continental drift described the breakup of Pangaea and the movement of the continents.
- The continental drift idea was supported by evidence of fossils and surface features during Wegener's time.
- Magnetic data and seafloor spreading changed the idea of continental drift to a theory.

Lesson Review

Review the lesson to answer these questions.

1. How did fossils and glaciers support the idea of continental drift?
2. Why was Wegener's model of continental drift not believed by other scientists when it was suggested in the early 1900s?
3. What is seafloor spreading?

Activity 14-1 Solving a Continental Puzzle

QUESTION   How do surface features aid in solving the continental puzzle?

Materials

world map
5 sheets of white paper
1 large sheet of
   colored paper

scissors
colored pencils
pencil and paper

What to do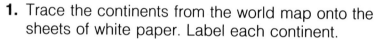

1. Trace the continents from the world map onto the sheets of white paper. Label each continent.
2. Cut out the continents you have traced.
3. Using their shapes, fit the continents together in as many ways as you can. They will not fit together perfectly the way the pieces of a puzzle do. Record the number of different ways you solved the puzzle.
4. Copy the features shown on the map below onto your continents. Color each feature. Use the same color for each feature that appears on more than one continent.

 Mountain ranges

 Coal beds

Glaciers

Humid climate

Dry climate

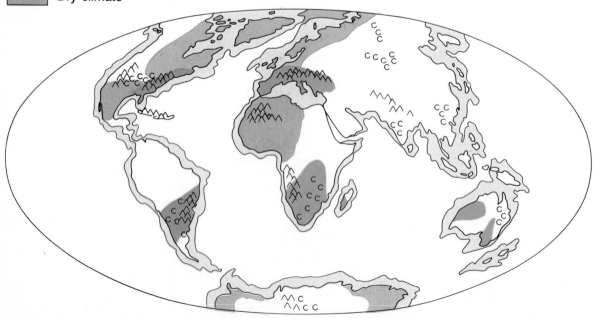

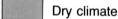

266

5. Place the continents on the colored paper. Fit them together again, using both the shape and surface features. Record the number of different ways you solved the puzzle.
6. When you have the best fit, trace around each continent with a colored pencil. Label each outline with the continent's name.
7. Move the continents to their present location. Using a different colored pencil, trace around each continent. Label each outline with the continent's name.
8. Make a legend to explain the features shown on your map. Copy the map scale shown on the world map that you used to trace the continents.

What did you learn?

1. How many different ways could you fit the continents together using only shape?
2. How many different ways could you fit the continents together using both shape and surface features?
3. How do you know which way is the best fit?
4. a. How does the map you produced in step 6 compare with the map in Figure 14–1?
   b. What did Wegener call this one large continent?
5. How did the placement of the continents change in the map you produced in step 7?

Using what you learned

1. a. Which continents have moved the farthest to their present positions?
   b. Which continents have moved the least to their present positions?
2. If the continents were once joined together, why do they not fit together perfectly?
3. a. Predict where the continents might be in the future.
   b. What evidence might aid scientists in solving a future continental puzzle?

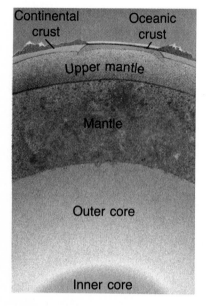

Figure 14-8. A cross-section of Earth showing its internal structure

LESSON GOALS

In this lesson you will learn
- the plate tectonics theory.
- that plates interact in three different ways.
- the locations of earthquakes and volcanoes support the plate tectonics theory.

Until the mid-1960s scientists continued to search for evidence that would prove or disprove continental drift. New technology allowed scientists to collect more data on magnetic minerals and seafloor spreading. These data, plus maps of the ocean floor and locations of earthquakes, aided scientists in developing a new theory concerning movements of Earth's crust. The **plate tectonics theory** states that Earth's crust and upper mantle are broken into plates. A **plate** is a large slab of Earth's crust and rigid upper mantle. Movements of these plates cause mountain building, earthquakes, and the activity of volcanoes. The plate tectonics model is not final. As scientists learn more, the theory may be altered.

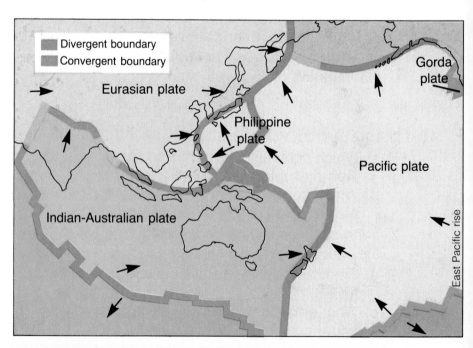

Figure 14-9. Earth's crust is broken into plates. Arrows show the directions of plate movements.

Scientists have determined that there are over 14 different plates. Figure 14–9 shows the major ones. The largest of these is the Pacific Plate. Plates vary in thickness. Under the continents, plates may be 100 to 400 kilometers thick. Under ocean crust, plates are only about 80 to 100 kilometers thick. Recall that plates are composed of the crust plus the rigid layer of the upper mantle. These plates rest on a layer of the mantle that is partially melted by heat and pressure within Earth. This partially melted layer of the mantle seems to be putty-like. Earth's plates "ride" on this layer.

On what do Earth's plates rest?

According to plate tectonics, each plate moves as a unit. A continent located on a plate moves as the plate moves. This is a major difference between continental drift and plate tectonics. The continents do not move *over* the ocean floor as required by continental drift. Instead they move *with* the ocean floor. Arrows on Figure 14–9 show the directions in which each plate moves. Movement is very slow. The rate varies among plates from about two to eighteen centimeters per year. If the plate carrying your school moved five centimeters per year to the west, where would it be in 100 years?

According to plate tectonics, how does a continent move?

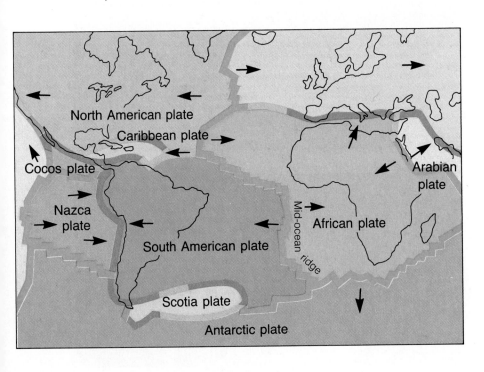

Name the three different types of plate boundaries.

Figure 14-10. The directions of plate movement differ in each type of zone: spreading zone (a), fracture zone (b), and converging zone (c). Each of the features shown formed as a result of movement in one of these zones.

The place where plates meet is called a **plate boundary.** There are three types of plate boundaries: spreading zones, fracture zones, and converging zones. Study Figure 14-10, which shows the directions of plate movement at each type of zone.

A **spreading zone** is a boundary where plates move apart or separate. Most spreading zones are located on ocean floors. Recall the previous lesson. What does seafloor spreading add to the ocean floor?

270

The mid-Atlantic ridge is a spreading zone. This mid-ocean ridge is an underwater mountain range in the Atlantic Ocean. Look at Figure 14–9. On which side of the North American plate is there a spreading zone?

A **fracture zone** is a boundary along which plates slide past one another. Earth material is neither made nor destroyed at a fracture zone. This kind of plate boundary connects a spreading zone with a converging zone. Fracture zones are also called fault zones. Fracture zones are associated with shallow earthquakes. The San Andreas fault in California is a fracture zone. Look at Figure 14–10b. How can you tell that movement has occurred?

What kind of plate boundary is found along the San Andreas fault?

A **converging zone** is a boundary where plates come together or converge. You know that new crust is formed and that the total surface area of Earth does not change very much. Therefore, crust must also be "destroyed." Two actions can occur at converging zones. Most often, when two plates collide, one plate is bent downward, allowing it to go beneath the other. Sometimes, however, the two plates collide and fold to produce mountain chains.

You can imitate these two actions using your hands. Place your hands, palms down, about four centimeters apart at the fingertips. Slowly bring your hands together, allowing one hand to ride over the other. In Earth, the bottom plate bends downward, moving deeper into the mantle, forming a trench. Heat and pressure at great depths cause the plate to partially melt. The resulting magma may rise and form volcanoes. Pressure from the "crash" may cause earthquakes.

What often happens to a plate that moves downward under another plate?

Repeat the plate collision model, but allow your fingertips to touch each other. Continue to push. Finally your fingers are forced to bend at the knuckles. You have just formed a folded mountain chain. Heat and pressure from the collision cause the plates to bend and fold. The Appalachians and the Alps are thought to have been built in this way. The Himalayas are still being built by the folding action caused by plate collision.

What mountains in the United States were formed by two colliding plates?

271

Activity 14–2 Mid-Ocean Ridge Model

QUESTION How is new crust added to ocean floors at mid-ocean ridges?

Materials
cardboard (21 × 28 cm)
scissors
metric ruler
2 sheets of yellow paper (21 × 28 cm)
1 sheet of brown paper (21 × 28 cm)
tape
brown crayon
pencil and paper

What to do

1. Cut 3 slits, each 11 cm long, in the cardboard as shown in diagram A.
2. Cut each sheet of paper in half lengthwise.
3. Tape the yellow strips end to end.
4. Tape one strip of brown paper to each end of the long yellow strip you formed in step 3.
5. Bend the strip of paper and poke the brown ends of the strips up through the center slit in the cardboard. Pull the ends through so all the brown is above the cardboard and all the yellow is below.

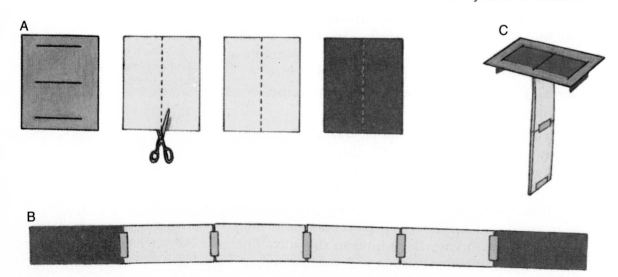

A

C

B

6. Bend the brown part of the strips so they lie flat against the top of the cardboard. Push the ends of the brown strips through the end slits. Let the yellow part of the strips hang below the cardboard.

7. Gently pull the ends of the brown strips through the center slit. Stop when part of the yellow paper shows above the cardboard.

8. Flatten the yellow part of each strip against the top of the cardboard. Color the yellow part that is showing on top with a brown crayon.

9. Repeat steps 6 and 7 at least two more times. Each time, label the section of each strip that you colored. Label the sections 1 for the first time, 2 for the second time, and so on. Be careful not to pull all of the yellow paper out of the slit the last time.

What did you learn?

1. What do the strips of brown paper in this model represent?
2. What does the yellow paper represent?
3. a. What does the center slit represent?
   b. What do the end slits represent?
4. What does coloring the yellow paper brown after it showed above the cardboard represent?
5. What happened to each labeled section of the paper as more yellow paper came up through the slit?

Using what you learned

1. How does your model show seafloor spreading?
2. According to your model, where would you find the youngest crust of Earth? The oldest?
3. What happens to the seafloor when it reaches the outer slits?
4. On which coast of the United States is there a spreading zone? Find out its spreading rate.
5. On which coast of the United States is there a converging zone? Find out the name of the plate with which the North American plate is colliding.

Plates, Earthquakes, and Volcanoes

What is an earthquake?

An earthquake is a vibration of Earth caused by sudden movements of rocks. The point where the movement starts, or the focus of the earthquake, may be in Earth's crust. The foci of other earthquakes may be found much deeper along a plate. Earthquake vibrations may be strong enough to topple large buildings. At other times, the vibrations are barely felt.

Using seismographs, scientists throughout the world keep records of where earthquakes occur. These earthquake data are recorded on the map in Figure 14–11. Compare these data with the map in Figure 14–9. Along what kinds of zones do earthquakes occur? Why?

What is a volcano?

A volcano is an opening in Earth through which magma or lava flows. Much volcanic activity occurs where there is seafloor spreading. Within the mid-Atlantic ridge, one place of volcanic activity formed a cone that rose above the ocean surface in 1963 off the coast of Iceland. The location of volcanoes worldwide has been recorded on the map in Figure 14–11. Compare these data with the map in Figure 14–9. Along what other kind of zone do volcanoes occur?

Figure 14-11. Locations of volcanoes and earthquakes throughout the world

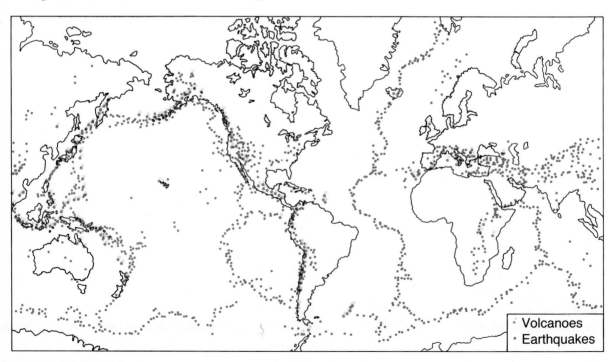

Volcanoes
Earthquakes

Figure 14–12. The volcanic island, Surtsey, rose above the surface of the North Atlantic Ocean near Iceland one November day in 1963.

Lesson Summary

- The plate tectonics theory states that Earth's crust and upper mantle are divided into plates.
- Plates move apart at spreading zones, slide past one another at fracture zones, and collide at converging zones.
- Most earthquakes and volcanoes occur along plate boundaries.

Lesson Review

Review the lesson to answer these questions.

1. Describe the structure of a plate.
2. Where are plates the thickest? The thinnest?
3. Where is new crust formed? Where is it destroyed?
4. At what type of plate boundary were these features formed?
   a. Appalachian Mountains
   b. San Andreas fault
   c. mid-Indian Ocean ridge
   d. ocean trench
5. What is the major difference between the models of continental drift and plate tectonics?

Science and Technology

Earthquake Detectors

Each year, earthquakes injure thousands of people. In order to prevent these injuries, scientists are trying to predict where and when earthquakes will occur. A seismograph is one tool that scientists use. It measures the strength and position of disturbances below Earth's surface. A new tool is fiber optics. Fiber optics is a technique for transferring light from one place to another through thin, flexible fibers of glass.

To use fiber optics, a hole is drilled about 80 meters deep in a fairly stable area of rock near a fault. A fault is an area of strain. A device with two fibers attached to it is placed in the hole. One fiber is inside the device, protected from movement. The other fiber is wrapped around the device.

The wrapped fiber acts as a sensing unit. It detects movement, or strain, in the rock. Laser light is sent along both fibers. When movement in the rock occurs, it bends or squeezes the wrapped fiber. The laser light takes longer to travel through this fiber. Scientists then study the light as it returns. Even slight movement can be detected by noting the differences in the speed and wavelength of the returning light.

With this method, scientists can monitor a fault zone and map a pattern of movement. They can detect small strains that may come before more powerful earthquake activity. If geologists can find patterns of movement that predict earthquakes, the loss of many lives and the destruction of property can be prevented.

Chapter 14 Review

Summary

1. Alfred Wegener proposed the model of continental drift to explain the arrangement of Earth's features.   14:1

2. The theory of continental drift states that the continents were once part of one large continent, called Pangaea, that broke into pieces and moved apart.   14:1

3. The idea of continental drift was supported by evidence of fossils and surface features during Wegener's time   14:1

4. New data on magnetic minerals and seafloor spreading supports the continental drift theory.   14:1

5. Seafloor spreading is the process of adding new crust at mid-ocean ridges.   14:1

6. Plate tectonics theory states that Earth's crust and upper mantle are broken into plates.   14:2

7. According to plate tectonics, each plate moves as a unit, and a continent located on a plate moves as the plate moves.   14:2

8. There are three types of plate boundaries: spreading zones, fracture zones, and converging zones.   14:2

9. Plates move apart at spreading zones, slide past one another at fracture zones, and collide at converging zones.   14:2

10. Most earthquakes and volcanoes occur along plate boundaries.   14:2

Science Words

continental drift	**mid-ocean ridge**	**plate tectonics theory**
converging zone	**plate**	**seafloor spreading**
fracture zone	**plate boundary**	**spreading zone**

Understanding Science Words

Complete each of the following sentences with a word or words from the Science Words that will make the sentence correct.

1. A large slab of Earth's crust and upper mantle is called a

   _____.

2. The process of adding new crust at mid-ocean ridges is known as

   _____.

3. The theory proposed by Wegener that the continents were once part of Pangaea, then broke into pieces and drifted apart, is known as _____.

4. A mountain chain on the ocean floor is a _____.

5. The place where plates meet is called a _____.

6. The model concerning movements of Earth's crust that states that Earth's crust and rigid upper mantle are broken into plates is _____.

7. The boundary where plates come together is a _____.

8. The boundary along which plates slide past one another is called a _____.

9. The boundary where plates move apart is called a _____.

Questions

A. Checking Facts

Determine whether each of the following is true or false. Rewrite the false statements to make them correct.

1. Scientists once thought that many features on Earth, such as ocean basins and mountains, were caused by the cooling and shrinking of Earth's crust.

2. The idea of continental drift states that the continents are all moving towards one another and will eventually form one large continent.

3. Magnetic minerals in ancient lava flows line up with Earth's present magnetic poles.

4. Related surface features and fossils found on a number of different continents that all appeared to "fit together" supported Wegener's idea of continental drift.

5. The plate tectonics theory states that the continents move over the ocean floor.

6. Seafloor spreading is the process that creates new crust at mid-ocean ridges.

7. Plate boundaries are always found at the edges of continents.

8. Most volcanic eruptions and earthquakes occur at the edges of continents.

B. Recalling Facts

Choose the word or phrase that correctly completes each of the following sentences.

1. Alfred Wegener was the first person to propose the idea of
   (a) Earth wrinkles.   (c) plate tectonics.
   (b) fracture zones.   (d) continental drift.

2. Seafloor spreading occurs at
   (a) spreading zones.   (c) converging zones.
   (b) fracture zones.   (d) continental drift zones.

3. Along the San Andreas fault, crustal plates are
   (a) moving apart.   (c) running into each other.
   (b) not moving.   (d) sliding past each other.

4. All of the following were used to support the idea of continental drift EXCEPT
   (a) glacier tracks.   (c) earthquakes.
   (b) mountain chains.   (d) fossils.

5. At mid-ocean ridges, plates
   (a) move together.   (c) move past each other.
   (b) move apart.   (d) slide underneath each other.

6. In which places are volcanoes NOT found?
   (a) mid-ocean ridges   (c) plate boundaries
   (b) convergent zones   (d) ocean shores

7. According to plate tectonics, movements of Earth's plates cause all of the following EXCEPT
   (a) mountain building.   (c) the activity of volcanoes.
   (b) magnetic fields.   (d) earthquakes.

C. Understanding Concepts

Answer each of the following questions using complete sentences.

1. Where would you find the youngest ocean floor rocks?

2. What causes earthquakes along plate boundaries?

3. What is the major difference between the models of continental drift and plate tectonics?

D. Applying Concepts

Think about what you learned in this chapter. Answer each of the following questions using complete sentences.

1. Why might plate tectonics theory change in the future?

2. What is happening to the distance between North America and Europe? Why?

Chapter 15

Earth History

Much of our knowledge of Earth history has come from the study of sedimentary rocks. Fossils, such as this trilobite, provide a means of determining the relative ages of rocks. Trilobites were invertebrate animals that lived mainly in the sea throughout the Paleozoic Era. What are fossils? What other methods might geologists use to date rocks?

Trilobite fossil

Rock Ages

LESSON GOALS
In this lesson you will learn
- how scientists determine relative ages of rocks.
- how fossils indicate rock ages.
- radioactive elements can be used to date rocks.

Earth is about 4.6 billion years old. Since its formation, Earth has changed. Mountains have been built and destroyed. Glaciers have advanced and retreated. Shallow oceans have covered much of Earth in the past. Recall from Lesson 14:2 that the continents have been plate "passengers." They have been carried to different parts of Earth through time. Earth is always changing. Scientists use different methods to unravel Earth history. Dating rocks and using fossils are two methods used to date events in Earth's past.

Earth's crust is made of rock layers. The layers can be distinguished from one another by color, rock type, and texture. In places where Earth's crust has not been disturbed, the rocks are found in nearly flat layers. These rock layers can be observed in road cuts and canyons. Each layer was deposited during a certain amount of time in a certain environment. In undisturbed areas, the oldest rock layer is on the bottom. The youngest rock layer is at the top of a rock sequence. The **law of superposition** states that the younger rock layer is on top of the older rock layer. Scientists use this law to determine relative ages of rocks. **Relative dating** is the process of determining that one event happened before or after another event. Relative dating does not give the age of the rock.

If rocks have been folded or faulted, the law of superposition may not apply. In some parts of the Appalachian Mountains, rock layers were folded and completely overturned. Look at Figure 15–1a. Why would it not be possible to tell the relative ages of these rocks using the law of superposition?

What is meant by the statement: the continents have been "plate passengers"?

When may the law of superposition not apply?

Figure 15–1. Rock is seen here in deformed (a) and undisturbed (b) layers.

a

b

Fossil Clues

Why have many species become extinct?

As Earth's environments changed through time, so did the kinds of living organisms. Organisms adapt to their environments. When the environment changes, the adaptations may no longer "fit" with the new conditions. Organisms that cannot change to fit the new conditions of the area in which they live will die. Environmental changes have caused many species to become extinct. An **extinct species** is one that has no living members.

A **fossil** is a track, a trace, or the remains of organisms preserved in rock. Many fossils are found in sedimentary rocks. Organisms that lived during a certain time period are found in the deposits formed at that time. A fossil found in one rock layer would be older than fossils found in rock layers above it. This is based on the law of superposition in undisturbed rock layers.

Suppose you find fossils in two rock layers. How can you tell which fossils are older?

Using the relative age of the fossils, it is then possible to tell the relative ages of sedimentary rocks. In the 1800s, William Smith, an English surveyor, noticed that the same kinds of fossils were found in different places. Smith showed how fossils could be used to find the relative ages of rocks over a wide area. Using fossil clues, he was able to match rock layers in France, the Netherlands, and England.

Figure 15–2. A geologist (a) examines sea shell fossils. The remains of an early fish (b) produced this fossil.

a

b

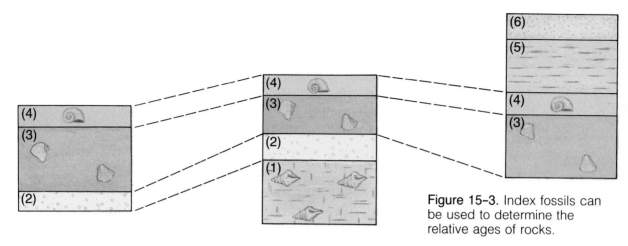

Figure 15-3. Index fossils can be used to determine the relative ages of rocks.

Certain fossils are better indicators of age than others. Organisms that lived in many places and became extinct after a short period of time formed **index fossils.** A trilobite is one example of an index fossil. Trilobites are hard-shelled invertebrates that lived about 570 million years ago. Ammonites are also shelled invertebrates. They are used as index fossils for a different time period. Study Figure 15–3. Which rock layer has the oldest relative age? The youngest?

Fossils of some organisms are not good clues to age because the species existed over a long period of time. These fossils are found in rocks that range from very old to quite young. Often these species lived only in certain kinds of environments. These kinds of fossils do not aid the process of relative dating. However, they do aid scientists in learning about how certain environments have changed over time.

Radiometric Dating

Radiometric dating is a technique that uses radioactivity to find the ages of certain rocks. Recall from Lesson 9:2 that a radioactive element is one whose atoms change naturally to form new atoms. The rate at which the radioactive element changes to the new atoms is constant. A **half-life** is the amount of time needed for one-half of the radioactive atoms to decay. The half-life of radioactive elements varies greatly. One form of uranium has a half-life of 4.5 billion years. On the other hand, one form of carbon has a half-life of only 5,730 years.

What is a radioactive element?

283

What mineral found in igneous rocks contains radioactive potassium?

Rocks are formed from minerals and other matter. Radioactive elements in the minerals can be used to date these rocks. Most igneous rocks contain the mineral feldspar. Feldspar contains radioactive potassium-40, which changes into argon-40. The half-life of potassium-40 is 1.3 billion years. Because of the long half-life of potassium-40, potassium-argon dating works best on very old rocks.

Scientists must assume that when an igneous rock first forms, it has no argon-40. The potassium-40 slowly changes to argon-40. Look at Figure 15–4. After one half-life, one-half of the potassium-40 atoms have changed to argon-40. Thus the mineral in the rock has only one-half of its potassium-40 left. An igneous rock with equal amounts of potassium-40 and argon-40 is about 1.3 billion years old. Suppose an igneous rock is found that has three times more argon-40 than potassium-40. What is the approximate age of the rock?

Figure 15–4. Potassium-40 has a half-life of 1.3 billion years. It decays to argon-40. The relative amounts of these two elements can be used to find the approximate ages of very old rocks.

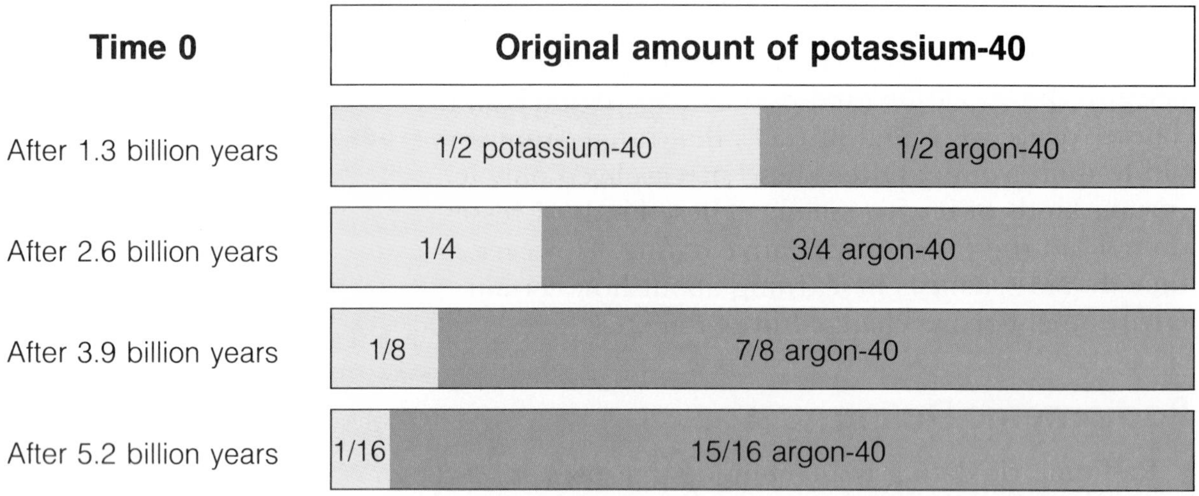

Time 0	Original amount of potassium-40	
After 1.3 billion years	1/2 potassium-40	1/2 argon-40
After 2.6 billion years	1/4	3/4 argon-40
After 3.9 billion years	1/8	7/8 argon-40
After 5.2 billion years	1/16	15/16 argon-40

How old are the oldest rocks so far found in Earth?

The oldest Earth rocks, so far, have been found in Australia. Radiometric dating has shown that these rocks formed about 4.2 billion years ago. Using data such as these, scientists estimate the age of Earth at 4.6 billion years.

Carbon-14 is also a radioactive element. It is used to date rocks and fossils younger than 35,000 years. Carbon-14 is found in all organic matter. Plants use

What rocks and fossils are dated with carbon-14?

small amounts of carbon-14 from carbon dioxide in the air. The carbon-14 becomes part of the bones and shells of animals when plants are eaten. After an organism dies, the amount of carbon-14 is no longer renewed. At that time, carbon-14 begins changing to nitrogen-14. The length of time since the organism died can be found by measuring the amount of carbon-14. Pieces of wood found in glacial deposits have been dated using carbon-14. The results have helped scientists learn more about the ice ages.

Radiometric methods of dating give approximate ages for Earth's rocks. Scientists must assume that no radioactive materials were gained or lost from the rocks they date. This could result in mistakes in ages.

Igneous rocks can be more accurately dated than other types of rocks. This is because of the way in which they are formed. Sedimentary and metamorphic rocks are formed from "recycled" materials. The ages of the minerals in these rocks can be found. However, dating methods may not determine the time at which the rocks themselves formed.

Figure 15-5. Petrified wood is the fossil remains of trees.

What type of rocks can be most accurately dated?

Lesson Summary

- The law of superposition states that, in undisturbed rock layers, younger rocks are on top of older rocks.
- Index fossils can be used to date some rocks.
- Rock or fossil ages may be found by radiometric dating methods.

Lesson Review

Review the lesson to answer these questions.
1. Describe two methods used to determine the relative ages of rocks.
2. How did scientists determine the estimated age of Earth?
3. Suppose a piece of granite is found to have seven times more argon-40 than potassium-40. How old is the rock?

Activity 15-1 Radiometric Dating Model

How are radioactive elements used to find the age of a rock?

Materials

32 paper squares
colored pencils, blue and yellow
pencil and paper

What to do

1. Make a table like the one shown.

Observations of Changes in Potassium-40		
Time Period	Number of Potassium-40 Atoms	Number of Argon-40 Atoms
0		
1		
2		
3		
4		

2. Color one side of the paper yellow and the other side blue.

3. Arrange the paper squares into one large square. Place all the yellow sides up. Each yellow side represents one potassium-40 atom. Each blue side represents one argon-40 atom. Record the numbers of potassium-40 and argon-40 atoms in the table.

4. As your partner counts to 10, turn every other square over. Record the numbers of potassium-40 and argon-40 atoms.

5. Repeat step 4 three more times.

6. Make a bar graph like the one shown. Using the blue and yellow pencils, color the bars to show the number of atoms of each element for each time period.

What did you learn?

1. What was represented by each time period?
2. What fraction of the model was potassium-40 when it was first formed?

Time	Type of Atoms	Number of Atoms
Time 4	Ar-40	
	K-40	
Time 3	Ar-40	
	K-40	
Time 2	Ar-40	
	K-40	
Time 1	Ar-40	
	K-40	
Time 0	Ar-40	
	K-40	

Type of Atoms   0 2 4 6 8 10 12 14 16 18 20 22 24 26 28 30 32
                          Number of Atoms

3. What happened to the number of potassium-40 atoms as time passed?
4. What happened to the number of argon-40 atoms as time passed?
5. What fraction of the potassium-40 changed to argon-40 during each time period?

Using what you learned

1. a. What is the half-life for this model of radiometric dating?
   b. What actual time period is represented by this model half-life?
2. Suppose you found a basalt that contained 7 times more argon-40 than potassium-40.
   a. How many half-lives have passed?
   b. How many billions of years old is the rock?
3. Uranium-238 changes to lead. This form of uranium has a half-life of 4.5 billion years. Suppose a granite was found that contained equal amounts of uranium-238 and lead-206. When was the rock formed?
4. Carbon-14 changes to nitrogen-14. This form of carbon has a half-life of 5,730 years. A fossil was found that contained 3 times more nitrogen-14 than carbon-14. When did the organism die?

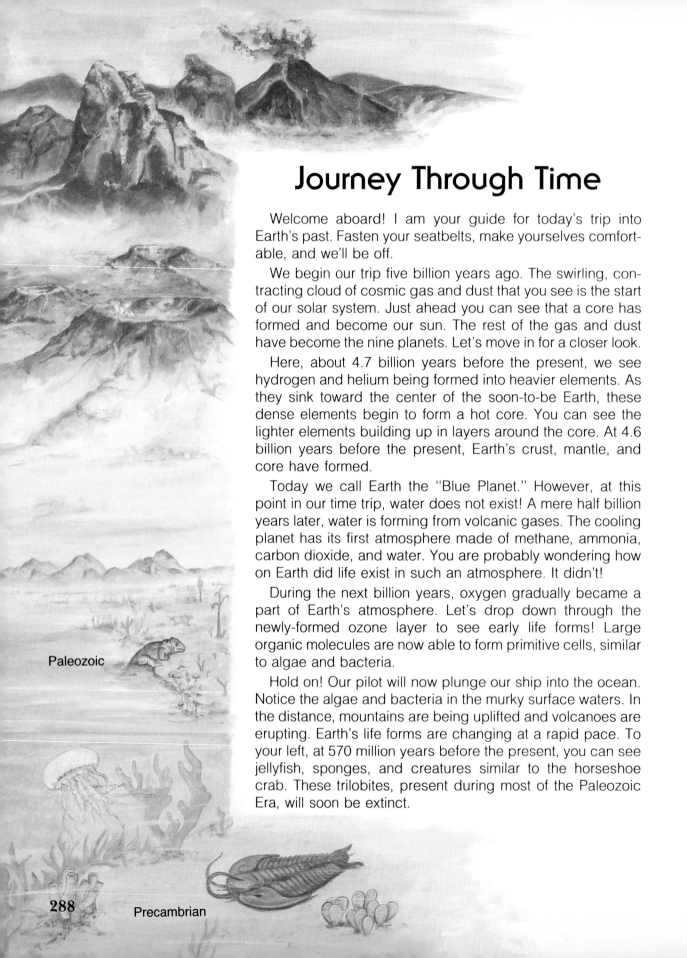

Journey Through Time

Welcome aboard! I am your guide for today's trip into Earth's past. Fasten your seatbelts, make yourselves comfortable, and we'll be off.

We begin our trip five billion years ago. The swirling, contracting cloud of cosmic gas and dust that you see is the start of our solar system. Just ahead you can see that a core has formed and become our sun. The rest of the gas and dust have become the nine planets. Let's move in for a closer look.

Here, about 4.7 billion years before the present, we see hydrogen and helium being formed into heavier elements. As they sink toward the center of the soon-to-be Earth, these dense elements begin to form a hot core. You can see the lighter elements building up in layers around the core. At 4.6 billion years before the present, Earth's crust, mantle, and core have formed.

Today we call Earth the "Blue Planet." However, at this point in our time trip, water does not exist! A mere half billion years later, water is forming from volcanic gases. The cooling planet has its first atmosphere made of methane, ammonia, carbon dioxide, and water. You are probably wondering how on Earth did life exist in such an atmosphere. It didn't!

During the next billion years, oxygen gradually became a part of Earth's atmosphere. Let's drop down through the newly-formed ozone layer to see early life forms! Large organic molecules are now able to form primitive cells, similar to algae and bacteria.

Hold on! Our pilot will now plunge our ship into the ocean. Notice the algae and bacteria in the murky surface waters. In the distance, mountains are being uplifted and volcanoes are erupting. Earth's life forms are changing at a rapid pace. To your left, at 570 million years before the present, you can see jellyfish, sponges, and creatures similar to the horseshoe crab. These trilobites, present during most of the Paleozoic Era, will soon be extinct.

Paleozoic

Precambrian

The turbulence we are experiencing is the moving together of the European and North American plates. The Appalachian Mountains are forming. Their building will go on for about 380 million years. When the water clears, observe the variety of ocean life. Coral reefs thrive in the warm, shallow seas. Notice that early fish are jawless. Their mouths are simply round holes.

We will now surface. It is 325 million years before the present. Many plants and animals are on the land. Flying insects, scorpions, and spiders are common. Amphibians roam the swampy areas. Reptiles arise from amphibian ancestors. Cotylosaurs are eating the conifers and ferns. We are at the close of the Paleozoic Era.

Just ahead, the Atlantic Ocean begins to form. Dinosaurs are stomping on gymnosperms such as cycads, conifers, and ginkgoes. Above the ship are flying reptiles called pterosaurs. *Brachiosaurus* and *Brontosaurus* are the large dinosaurs munching on the plants. *Tyrannosaurus* and *Triceratops* are battling to see who will be the other's dinner.

Be calm! The blackout is only temporary. This is a time when many marine and land animals became extinct. It is the end of the Mesozoic Era.

We now enter the Cenozoic Era. Looking to the west, you can see the beginnings of the Rocky Mountains. Below the ship, mammals are plentiful, and most plants are angiosperms. Let's leave the ship to look at that horse grazing in the grass. It is much smaller than modern horses and has three toes. It is getting chilly. Glaciers are forming. Let's return to the ship.

Look down at Earth. Large ice sheets cover much of the continents. Woolly mammoths and saber-toothed cats are looking for food. Now the climate is slowly warming. People have also appeared on Earth.

We have finished our trip through time. We hope you have enjoyed seeing the changes that have taken place over billions of years.

Mesozoic

Cenozoic

LESSON GOALS

In this lesson you will learn

- scientists have outlined Earth's history.
- life began as very simple forms and became more complex.
- geologic time is grouped into sections based on the life forms present and geologic events that occurred.

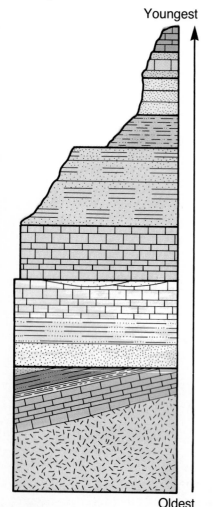

Figure 15–6. The pattern of fossils in the rock layers of the Grand Canyon has given scientists clues to Earth's history.

Youngest

Oldest

Scientists have built a time line of Earth's history. To do this, they compared rocks and fossils from all over the world. These data helped scientists to determine the relative ages of many types of rocks and fossils. This study resulted in the geologic time scale. The **geologic time scale** is an outline of Earth's history. It gives events in Earth's past in the order in which they happened. This time scale aids people in seeing how Earth and organisms on Earth have changed through time.

A record of the early part of the geologic time scale is found in the Grand Canyon. At the bottom of the canyon, the rocks are 1.3 billion years old. How do you think the ages of the rock layers near the top compare with the ages of the rocks near the bottom? A study of the fossils in these layers shows a pattern. Fossils in the oldest rocks are of very simple life forms such as monerans. Fossils from younger layers are more complex. Certain index fossils are found in each layer of the canyon. Recall that index fossils are of organisms that lived for short periods of time before becoming extinct. This pattern of fossils from the Grand Canyon aided scientists in piecing together a partial history of life on Earth.

The 4.6 billion years of Earth's history have been divided into four sections. The first 4 billion years have few fossils. Little detail about this time is known. The remaining years of Earth's history have been divided into eras. An **era** is the largest division of geologic time. Eras are periods of time during which certain rocks were deposited.

Precambrian Time

The oldest time period is called the Precambrian (pree KAM bree un). The **Precambrian** began about 4.6 billion years ago and lasted until about 570 million years ago. This represents about 75 percent of Earth's history. The oldest fossils found in Precambrian rocks are about 3.1 billion years old. These were fossils of cyanobacteria found in southern Africa. Fossils from younger Precambrian rocks include trails and burrows of wormlike animals. Scientists believe Precambrian life lived in warm, shallow seas. These simple life forms had no bones or shells. Their remains did not preserve easily, so fossils of Precambrian life are hard to find.

The oldest part of each continent is composed of Precambrian rocks and is called a **shield.** The shield of North America is called the Canadian Shield. Its formation has been dated at 2.5 billion years ago. Shields are composed of mostly metamorphic and igneous rocks. This is another reason fossils are hard to find in Precambrian rocks. In what kind of rocks are fossils usually found?

Why are Precambrian fossils hard to find?

What general type of animals lived during the Paleozoic Era?

Figure 15–7. Trilobites were extinct by the end of the Paleozoic Era.

Paleozoic Era

The **Paleozoic** (pay lee uh ZOH ihk) **Era** is the name given to the time period between 570 million and 225 million years ago. Paleozoic fossils indicate life was found in the oceans along the edges of continents. Early Paleozoic animals were invertebrates. Many of these animals had hard-shelled coverings that easily formed fossils. Paleozoic fossils include trilobites, brachiopods, and sponges. Why are trilobites good index fossils of the Paleozoic Era?

In the early Paleozoic, North America and Europe were separated by a shallow ocean. The Appalachian and Rocky Mountains did not exist. Much of North America was covered by warm, shallow seas. Fish developed in these shallow waters along the continents. Fish are considered to be the first vertebrates. Later, amphibians and land plants developed.

What environment led to the formation of coal deposits?

Late in the Paleozoic Era, vast swamps developed along the coastlines of the continents. Large trees and ferns grew in these swamps. Vegetation from these swamps became buried layer upon layer. Heat and pressure caused this buried organic matter to form coal. Many large coal deposits were formed from organisms that lived during this era. Why do you think coal is called a fossil fuel?

At the close of the Paleozoic Era, most of Earth's continental crust came together to form Pangaea. The Appalachians formed. The great tropical swamps dried up. Many species of amphibians became extinct. Why do you think this is so? During the late Paleozoic, the first reptiles appeared. Conifers became the main form of plant life during this time.

Mesozoic Era

The time period between 225 million and 65 million years ago is the **Mesozoic** (mez uh ZOH ihk) **Era.** In the early Mesozoic, Pangaea began to break up and separate. Reptiles became very abundant during the early part of this era. Reptiles are not as dependent on water as fish and amphibians. Therefore, scientists think the climate at this time was

Why do scientists believe that the Mesozoic Era was drier than the Paleozoic Era?

much drier than in the late Paleozoic. During the Mesozoic, many species of reptiles developed that were very large. The largest Mesozoic reptiles were the dinosaurs. The Mesozoic Era is often called the "Age of Dinosaurs" because dinosaurs were the major land animals. Fossils of dinosaurs have been found throughout the world. Among these are fossils of huge plant eaters like *Brontosaurus* and meat eaters like *Tyrannosaurus*. There were also small, fast-running dinosaurs. They were more like modern-day lizards. One group of dinosaurs had wings or winglike structures that enabled them to fly or glide.

What era is known as the "Age of Dinosaurs"?

Ammonites were ocean animals that lived during the Mesozoic. They had distinctive coiled shells that were covered with many lines. The pattern formed by the lines became more complex in species that developed later in the Mesozoic. Their shape and pattern of lines make ammonites easy to recognize. Ammonites are, therefore, good index fossils of the Mesozoic Era.

Why are ammonites easy to recognize?

By the end of the Mesozoic, many changes began to occur. Pangaea had broken apart. The Atlantic Ocean continued to open. There was mountain building along the west coast of North America. Climates began to change. Dinosaurs, ammonites, and many other kinds of organisms became extinct. Scientists have different explanations for the extinctions. Some believe the changes were sudden, perhaps caused by a meteorite striking Earth. Others believe the changes were gradual. Many ideas about the events that ended the Mesozoic Era are being tested.

What is one explanation for the extinction of dinosaurs?

Figure 15-9. The Mesozoic Era is often called the "Age of the Dinosaurs."

Activity 15-2 A Model of Geologic Time

QUESTION   How do the lengths of time periods within Earth history compare?

Materials
roll of adding machine paper (5 meters)
masking tape
meter stick
pencil and paper

What to do
1. Stretch the roll of paper out on the floor. Tape it down on each end.
2. Draw a line across the paper near one end. Write *TODAY* on the line. Begin at the *TODAY* line and measure 4.6 meters toward the other end. Draw a line across the tape at this point. Label the line *BEGINNING*. The distance from *TODAY* to *BEGINNING* represents the age of Earth, 4.6 billion years.

3. Look at the table. Notice the geologic event, number of years ago, and distance from *TODAY*. Measure and record each event on the paper.

	Geologic Event	Years Ago	Distance from *TODAY*
Cenzoic Era	ice ages, formation of Grand Canyon	2 million	0.2 cm
	first humans	3 million	0.3 cm
Mesozoic Era	last dinosaur	70 million	7 cm
	beginning of Rocky Mountains	136 million	13.6 cm
	first dinosaur	200 million	20 cm
	beginning of Mesozoic, Atlantic Ocean begins to form	225 million	22.5 cm
Paleozoic Era	first reptiles	350 million	35 cm
	first land plants and first amphibians	395 million	39.5 cm
	first fish	400 million	40 cm
	Appalachians begin to form	500 million	50 cm
	beginning of Paleozoic	570 million	57 cm
Precambrian Time	oldest life forms, several phases of mountain building	3.2 billion	320 cm

What did you learn?

1. When did the first organisms appear?
2. Compare the lengths of the different time units. Which unit is the longest? Which is shortest?
3. How long did dinosaurs live on Earth?
4. How long have people lived on Earth?

Using what you learned

1. What seems to be happening to the length of time between life events as Earth gets older?
2. What does this tell you about the rate of change in organisms today compared to early in Earth's history?
3. Compared to other life, like dinosaurs, how long have people been on Earth?

a

b

Figure 15-10. The Marshall gentian (a) is an extinct flower species. The Marshall pink (b) is a present-day relative.

When in the Cenozoic Era did the first evidence of human life appear?

Cenozoic Era

The time period between 65 million years ago and the present is called the **Cenozoic** (sen uh ZOH ihk) **Era.** During the Cenozoic, continents gradually took on the forms and positions they have today. North America continued to move westward on a large plate. A converging boundary between this plate and the Pacific Plate produced a series of volcanoes and mountains. The chain of volcanoes is in the Cascade Mountains of Washington and Oregon. The Rocky Mountains were uplifted during this time.

During the Cenozoic, mammals became the major land animals. Flowering plants and insects were important life forms. Fish, algae, and microscopic animals became the major ocean life. Late in the Cenozoic Era, a climate change occurred. The climate change resulted in the Ice Age. Glaciers covered much of North America and northern Europe. The glaciers advanced and retreated many times during the past two million years. Scientists have many ideas that might explain this period of glacier formation. The shape of Earth's orbit, the tilt of its axis, and the wobble of its axis are possible causes of temperature changes that formed vast glaciers. It was during the Ice Age that the first evidence of human life on Earth appeared.

Lesson Summary

- Earth's history is outlined by the geologic time scale.
- Fossils of monerans were found in early Precambrian time. Fossils show that organisms became more complex over time.
- Earth history is divided into Precambrian time, and the Paleozoic, Mesozoic, and Cenozoic Eras.

Lesson Review

Review the lesson to answer these questions.
1. How is the geologic time scale divided?
2. Describe the life forms and geologic events of Precambrian time and each of the three eras.

Chapter 15 Review

Summary

1. Earth is estimated to be about 4.6 billion years old. 15:1
2. Where rock layers are undisturbed, the law of superposition states that the younger rocks are on top of the older rocks. 15:1
3. Many species of organisms have become extinct as Earth's environments have changed over time. 15:1
4. Index fossils give clues to the relative ages of rock layers. 15:1
5. Radiometric dating gives the best estimate for the ages of fossils and some types of rocks. 15:1
6. The geologic time scale is an outline of Earth's history. 15:2
7. Early forms of life were simple organisms, and life forms have become more complex over time. 15:2
8. Earth history can be divided into four time periods, the Precambrian, the Paleozoic Era, the Mesozoic Era, and the Cenozoic Era. 15:2

Science Words

Cenozoic Era	**half-life**	**Paleozoic Era**
era	**index fossils**	**Precambrian**
extinct species	**law of superposition**	**relative dating**
fossil	**Mesozoic Era**	**shield**
geologic time scale		

Understanding Science Words

Complete each of the following sentences with a word or words from the Science Words that will make the sentence correct.

1. Fossils of animals that were widespread but lived only a short time are called _____.
2. A population that has no living members is called an _____.
3. The oldest part of each continent is the _____.
4. The amount of time needed for one half of a sample of radioactive atoms to decay is called a _____.
5. An outline of Earth's history that gives events in the order in which they happened is a _____.
6. Trilobites are good index fossils for the _____.
7. The "Age of Dinosaurs" occurred during the _____.

8. When rock layers are found with the oldest layers on the bottom and the youngest on the top, this demonstrates the _____.
9. A track, trace, or the remains of an organism preserved in rock is a _____.
10. The oldest time period of Earth's history is the _____.
11. The process of determining whether one event happened before or after another is called _____.
12. The first humans appeared on Earth during the _____.
13. The largest division of geologic time is an _____.

Questions

A. Checking Facts

Determine whether each of the following is true or false. Rewrite the false statements to make them correct.

1. The law of superposition states that the older rock layer is on top of the younger rock layer.
2. Certain species of organisms from Earth's past are extinct today because they could not adapt to the changes in their environments.
3. Using the techniques of radiometric dating, scientists can determine the exact ages of Earth's rocks.
4. The carbon-14 method of radiometric dating can be used to find the ages of fossils that are millions of years old.
5. The geologic time scale is an outline of Earth's history that was developed using relative dating techniques.
6. Most of Earth's history occurred in the Paleozoic, Mesozoic, and Cenozoic Eras.
7. The Rocky Mountains were uplifted during the Cenozoic Era.
8. Sedimentary rocks can be more accurately dated by radiometric methods than other types of rocks.

B. Recalling Facts

Choose the word or phrase that correctly completes each of the following sentences.

1. Rocks at the bottom of the Grand Canyon are
   (a) oldest.
   (c) above average age.
   (b) youngest.
   (d) just being formed today.

2. The oldest fossils are remains of
   (a) trilobites   (c) cyanobacteria.
   (b) dinosaurs.   (d) sponges.
3. The age of Earth is thought to be
   (a) 3.1 million years.   (c) 46 million years.
   (b) 3.5 billion years.   (d) 4.6 billion years.
4. The "Age of Dinosaurs" was the
   (a) Precambrian.   (c) Mesozoic Era.
   (b) Paleozoic Era.   (d) Cenozoic Era.
5. The Ice Age occurred during the
   (a) Precambrian.   (c) Mesozoic Era.
   (b) Paleozoic Era.   (d) Cenozoic Era.
6. The geologic time scale is divided into
   (a) the Precambrian and 3 eras.   (c) 5 eras.
   (b) the Cenozoic and 2 eras.   (d) 4 eras.
7. Which of the following does NOT apply to the Mesozoic Era?
   (a) Pangaea broke apart.
   (b) The Appalachian Mountains formed.
   (c) Ammonites are good index fossils for this era.
   (d) Dinosaurs were the major land animals of this era.

C. Understanding Concepts

Answer each of the following questions using complete sentences.
1. What are the characteristics of an index fossil?
2. Explain why the law of superposition is like building a large building.
3. Make a list of the four geologic time periods. Next to each, list the types of organisms and index fossils from that time period.
4. What are the major events in plate tectonics and continental movement and development, and when did they occur?
5. Describe the method of radiometric dating.

D. Applying Concepts

Think about what you learned in this chapter. Answer each of the following questions using complete sentences.
1. In which layer of the Grand Canyon would you expect to find the most complex animal fossils?
2. Suppose a radioactive element has a half-life of 1 million years. How old would a rock containing this element be when three-fourths of the element has decayed?

UNIT 6 REVIEW

Answer these questions on a sheet of paper.

1. What do maps show?
2. What is the difference between a map legend and a map scale?
3. How are lines of latitude and longitude useful?
4. Why was Wegener's idea of continental drift not believed by other scientists when it was first suggested?
5. What is the difference between plates of continental crust and plates of ocean crust?
6. At what type of plate boundaries is the crust of Earth made and destroyed?
7. What is the law of superposition?
8. What is radiometric dating?
9. What has happened to life forms since they first developed in the Precambrian?
10. Match each of the four major sections of geologic time, Precambrian, Paleozoic, Mesozoic, and Cenozoic, with the descriptions below.
    - (a) age of dinosaurs
    - (b) fish and amphibians developed
    - (c) began 225 million years ago
    - (d) oldest time period
    - (e) humans appeared
    - (f) Appalachians formed

RECALLING ACTIVITIES

Think about the activities you did in this unit. Answer the questions about these activities.

1. How can you make a classroom map?   13–1
2. What does a profile of a topographic map show?   13–2
3. How do surface features aid in solving the continental puzzle?   14–1
4. How is new crust added to ocean floors at mid-ocean ridges?   14–2
5. How are radioactive elements used to find the age of a rock?   15–1
6. How do the lengths of time periods within Earth history compare?   15–2

IDEAS TO EXPLORE

1. Locate topographic maps of your state. Use these maps to make profiles of various sections of the state. Identify valleys, ridges, hills, mountains, streams, and other features of Earth's crust.

2. Volcanism is an important process of plate tectonics. Use reference books to research how the Hawaiian Islands, the Columbia Plateau, and the Cascade Range in the western United States were formed. Choose one of these land features and write a report explaining its formation.

3. Choose one of the present continents. Use reference books to write a paper that describes the history of the continent through geologic time. Be sure to include the climate, fossils, and location(s) of the continent in the ancient past. Compare these data to the present climate, location, and life forms of the continent.

PROBLEM SOLVING

How can the motion of Earth's plates be explained using a model?
Most scientists believe that Earth's plates move due to convection currents in the upper mantle. Conduct an activity that demonstrates this idea. Fill a glass pot with water to 3 cm from the top. Put the pot on the center of a hot plate, and heat gently. **CAUTION:** *Do not touch the hot plate.* Add several drops of food coloring to the water directly above the center of the hot plate. Observe the currents that form in the water. Sketch what you see.

BOOKS TO READ

The Earth by Keith Brandt, Troll Associates: Mahwah, NJ, © 1985.
   Find out about the development of Earth's features.

Geology, 2nd Edition, by Robert E. Boyer and P. B. Snyder, Hubbard Scientific: Northbrook, IL, © 1986.
   This book is an interesting introduction to the study of Earth.

Our Earth by Huck Scarry, Wanderer Books: New York, © 1984.
   Learn about the planet we live on.

UNIT 7
Understanding Ecology

Rachel Carson, biologist and author, brought international attention to the environmental problems caused by pesticides. In her book, *Silent Spring*, she described how pesticides poison the food supply of many animals. One pesticide, DDT, was in the food supply of eagles. The DDT caused eagles to lay soft-shelled eggs that crushed when eagles sat on them. DDT is now banned and there are protected nest sites to encourage eagles to breed. What should be considered before using pesticides?

Rachel Carson—1962

302

Eagles

Chapter 16
Ecosystems

This sphere is a tiny ecosystem. In a 16.5-centimeter globe are an alga, coral, a red shrimp, seawater, and an atmosphere of gases. These living and nonliving things interact in a balanced manner. What is a possible food chain in this system? How is more of the alga produced?

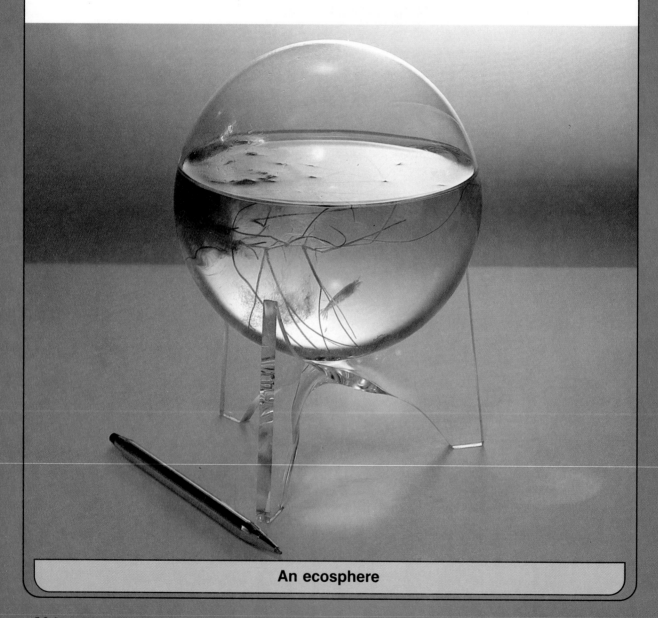

An ecosphere

LESSON GOALS

In this lesson you will learn

- organisms have certain roles in the environment.
- living things and nonliving factors interact.
- certain life substances are recycled in the environment.

You have learned that complex organisms are composed of organ systems. These organ systems work together so that the organism can carry on all life processes. Earth, too, is composed of interacting "systems."

There are five kingdoms of living things: monerans, protists, fungi, plants, and animals. Each of these groups of living things has an effect on the others. Some provide food. Others cause materials to be recycled. Some cause disease. All living things fulfill certain needs. Each organism has a special "role to play," or **niche,** in the environment.

What are some roles of living things in the environment?

Living things are affected by the nonliving parts of the environment. Air, water, rocks, light, and soil are some nonliving parts that affect organisms. How do you think organisms are affected by these nonliving parts of the environment?

Figure 16-1. Gannets on Bonaventure Island in Quebec, Canada. Each bird has its own niche in the community.

Figure 16–2. A rotting log in a forest is an ecosystem.

How large is an ecosystem?

What is a person who studies ecosystems called?

Figure 16–3. A garbage collector fills an important niche in the community.

Groups of living things interacting with each other and the environment compose an **ecosystem.** An ecosystem is one area in which all living and nonliving things interact. Earth may be considered one large ecosystem. A forest is an example of a smaller ecosystem. Often, though, much smaller areas are studied. The person who studies the ecosystem decides its size. A rotting log in a forest can be considered an ecosystem.

The study of how the living and nonliving parts of an ecosystem affect each other is called **ecology.** Therefore, the person who studies an ecosystem is called an ecologist. In the case of the rotting log ecosystem, an ecologist might study the following factors: the organisms in the log, the type of soil below the log, the chemicals in the area, the amount of rainfall in the area, and the amount of sunlight that strikes the fallen log. What kinds of living things do you think the ecologist might find in the rotting log ecosystem?

All of the different kinds of organisms in an ecosystem make up a **community.** Think about the community in which you live. Consider the different roles or niches of the people in your community. An ecologist studies the niche of each kind of organism in a community. Each niche must be filled for the ecosystem to continue "working."

Activity 16-1   Ecosystems

QUESTION   What is an ecosystem?

Materials
string
4 stakes
meter stick
hand lens
pencil and paper

What to do

1. Use the string and stakes to mark off a one-square-meter plot in the school yard or other area.
2. Locate a plant within the plot. Observe the plant carefully.
3. Write a description of how the nonliving parts of the environment affect the plant. Consider such things as water, air, rocks, and sunlight.
4. Use the hand lens to observe the plant carefully. Find other organisms that affect the plant. Write a description of how you think each organism affects the plant.
5. Draw a picture of your ecosystem.

What did you learn?
1. Describe the community in your ecosystem.
2. Describe the nonliving parts of your ecosystem.

Using what you learned
1. How do people affect ecosystems?
2. How does the ecosystem you observed affect you?
3. What happens in an ecosystem when organisms enter and leave it?
4. How is your ecosystem like those studied by other students?

Earth's Cycles

Organisms cannot live without certain nonliving substances. All organisms must have water, oxygen, and minerals or other chemicals to live. You have learned in Lesson 3:1 that according to the law of conservation of mass, matter cannot be created or destroyed in a chemical reaction. So, organisms must be using most of the same materials that have been used since life began.

a

b

Figure 16–4. Mushroom decomposers (a) and scavengers such as ants (b) and hooded vultures (c) are involved in the natural recycling of materials.

c

What is the process of recycling?

Life substances are available because of the process of recycling. After certain substances in the environment are used, they are returned to the environment to be used again. A cycle is completed each time a substance is used and returned to the environment. The complete cycle occurs again and again. Recycling of some substances occurs without involving organisms. It also occurs because of the life processes of certain organisms. Not all organisms recycle the same kinds of matter. Each kind of organism has a niche in the recycling of matter.

One important substance that is recycled in an ecosystem is water. The **water cycle** is the continuous movement of water in an ecosystem. Earth, as an ecosystem, has a water cycle. Water evaporates from Earth's surface and becomes water vapor in the atmosphere. Water vapor condenses into liquid water again. The water returns to Earth as dew, frost, rain, snow, sleet, or hail.

Organisms play a part in the water cycle. They take in water for life processes from the environment. Through the process of respiration, organisms give off water. This water may be returned to Earth in waste products. In photosynthesis, water is absorbed by plants and used to make food. Water not used in this way evaporates into the air through small pores in the leaves. About 7,000 liters of water may evaporate from one tree during a six-month growing season. The water that cycles through organisms is part of the water cycle. Water cycles that occur in small ecosystems are part of Earth's water cycle.

Describe what occurs in the water cycle.

Figure 16–5. The water cycle in this African ecosystem is part of Earth's water cycle.

The **nitrogen cycle** is the continuous movement of nitrogen in an ecosystem. Nitrogen cycles among organisms, the soil, and the atmosphere. Earth's atmosphere is composed of about 79 percent nitrogen. Most living things, however, cannot use the nitrogen in the air for life processes. This nitrogen must be changed to another form. Many bacteria and cyanobacteria can change the nitrogen in air to a form that can be used by plants. The animals, in turn, consume the plants to obtain nitrogen.

Some nitrogen returns to the ecosystem as waste products or from the decay of living things. Nitrogen present in organisms returns to the soil when they die. Nitrogen in the soil is changed by nitrogen-fixing bacteria found in nodules or lumps on the roots of certain plants called legumes. This "fixing" of the nitrogen allows it to be used by these plants, and when they decay, by other plants.

How is it possible for plants to use nitrogen from the air?

Figure 16–6. In this Canadian ecosystem, nitrogen cycles from air to plants to animals and back to the soil and air.

310

Carbon dioxide and oxygen are recycled in ecosystems. The **carbon dioxide-oxygen cycle** is the continuous exchange of carbon dioxide and oxygen among producers, consumers, and the atmosphere. Compare the simple formulas for photosynthesis and respiration shown in Figure 16–7. In which process is oxygen used? In which process is it produced? Look at the use and production of carbon dioxide.

Photosynthesis

What is produced in the process of photosynthesis?

$$6CO_2 \quad + \quad 6H_2O \quad \xrightarrow{\text{Light energy, chlorophyll}} \quad C_6H_{12}O_6 \quad + \quad 6O_2$$

Respiration

$$C_6H_{12}O_6 \quad + \quad 6O_2 \quad \xrightarrow{\text{Energy}} \quad 6CO_2 \quad + \quad 6H_2O$$

Figure 16–7. These chemical equations represent the overall reactions taking place in the processes of photosynthesis and respiration.

Many other substances in ecosystems also follow cycles. These substances are used by organisms. Some of the substances are returned to the environment in wastes. The substances may also be returned to the environment when organisms die and decompose. Then the substances may be used by other organisms. Many of the substances in your body have been used by other organisms before you.

Lesson Summary

- Each organism in an ecosystem has a niche.
- The living things and nonliving factors affect each other.
- Water, carbon dioxide, oxygen, nitrogen, and other substances are recycled in the environment.

Lesson Review

Review the lesson to answer these questions.
1. What is a niche?
2. What is an ecosystem?
3. Relate a community with an ecosystem.
4. How are living things involved in the water cycle? The nitrogen cycle? The carbon dioxide-oxygen cycle?

LESSON GOALS

In this lesson you will learn

- all organisms need energy.
- energy is transferred from one organism to another.
- models can be used to represent certain relationships in the environment.

Figure 16–8. Energy from the sun and nutrients from the soil pass through plants to consumers, the rabbit and then the hawk.

All organisms need energy to carry on life processes. This energy comes from the sun. Producers are the only organisms that can use the sun's energy in photosynthesis. Consumers get energy by eating producers or other consumers. Some consumers eat only producers. Others eat only consumers. Still others eat both producers and consumers. However, some consumers do not eat other organisms. A **decomposer** is a special consumer that gets energy by causing dead organisms to decay. The process of decay is important in recycling substances. Bacteria and fungi are two types of decomposers.

Energy passes from producers to consumers. The series of steps showing energy flow through a community is called a **food chain.** A food chain begins with a producer. The number of steps, or links, in a food chain can vary. Decomposers can be involved in each link. Look at the food chain in Figure 16–8. Trace the flow of energy through the food chain. How might the energy be used in each link? Describe a food chain of which you might be a part.

Most consumers eat more than one kind of food, so they are often part of many food chains. Producers and consumers that are eaten by a variety of other consumers are also part of many food chains. Food chains overlap when an organism is part of more than one food chain in an ecosystem. A **food web** is the combination of all overlapping food chains in a community. Ecosystems with many different producers and consumers have complex food webs. Describe two food chains from the food web in Figure 16–9 that involve a snowshoe hare.

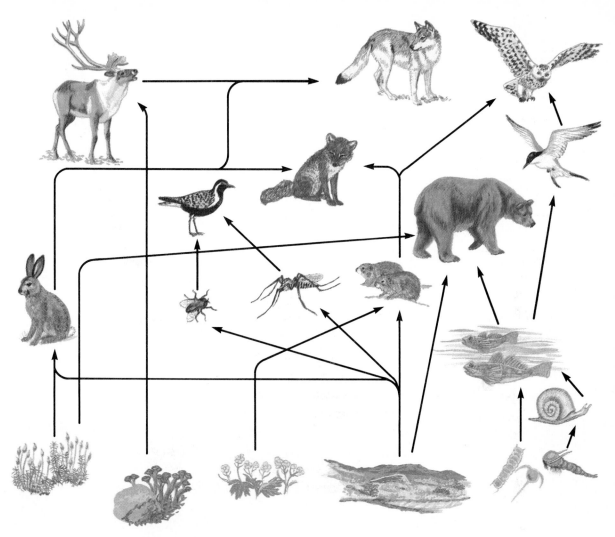

Figure 16-9. This arctic food web is a complex feeding system of many food chains.

Community Models

The amount of energy available to producers and consumers at each link in a food chain can be shown by using a pyramid. The pyramid is much broader at the base than at the top. The base always represents the energy available to the producers in a community. The next level is composed of consumers that eat producers. There is less energy available at this level than at the base. Each level of consumers has less energy available to it than the one before. Eventually, there is not enough energy to support life. Energy must be constantly added to an ecosystem for life to continue. *Organisms cannot recycle energy.*

In the pyramid model of a community, how is the amount of energy related to the level of consumers?

Look at the energy pyramid in Figure 16–10. The grass is at the base of the pyramid because it is one of the producers in this community. The grass, however, does not use all of the sun's energy that is available. The unused energy is "lost" in the form of heat. Some of the energy is used by the grass to make food. The grass uses some of the food it makes for its own life processes. Thus, the energy used by the grass cannot be passed along.

Cattle eat the grass. Many kilograms of grass are needed to feed each cow. Even so, most of the grass is not eaten. The amount of energy passed from the producers to the consumers is only a small part of what was available. The remaining energy in the grass plants is used by the grasses for growth, repair of tissues, and making seeds.

People are the final consumers in this energy pyramid. Still, not all the energy available is passed along. About half of each cow is eaten by humans.

How much energy is passed from producers to consumers?

Figure 16–10. Humans are at the top of this food pyramid. The meat being consumed was produced as the cattle consumed several times their weight in grasses.

The bones, hide, and many organs are not consumed by people. Therefore, some energy is lost to the human consumer. No energy transfer from one link in a food chain to another is complete. Some energy is always lost. This is why the pyramid has a peak. At this point there is not enough energy that can be passed along to support life.

A pyramid can also be used to show the total mass of organisms at each level in the energy flow. There is more mass at the producer level than there is at the consumer levels. The total mass of organisms at each level continues to decrease. In an ecosystem, there will be fewer large meat-eating animals than any other type of organism. Usually, predators are larger than prey. At what level do you think the most organisms will be present?

Besides energy, what else can be represented by the pyramid model of a community?

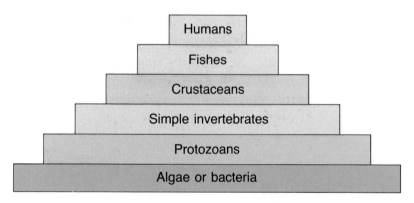

Figure 16-11. A food pyramid shows how mass decreases from producers to consumers and from one level of consumers to another.

Lesson Summary

- Energy from the sun is transferred throughout an ecosystem.
- Some of the energy that producers obtain from the sun is passed to consumers.
- The amount of energy available and the total mass of organisms present in a food chain can be represented by a pyramid.

Lesson Review

Review the lesson to answer these questions.
1. Compare a food chain and a food web.
2. At what level in a pyramid is the most energy available?

Figure 16-12. A population of a woodland flower species

What may limit the population in an ecosystem?

LESSON GOALS

In this lesson you will learn

- communities are composed of different populations.
- populations of living things interact with each other.
- certain factors limit the size of a population.

Communities are composed of different populations. A **population** is a group of organisms that are all the same species. A lawn community may have populations of different species such as grasses, dandelions, insects, worms, mushrooms, and other living things. The size of a population may be controlled by the environment. The amount of rainfall, for example, determines the kind and number of plants that can grow in the area. The population size of one species is also affected by populations of other species in the area.

Activity 16-2   Competition

QUESTION   How can you observe competition among plants?

Materials

3 small paper cups
potting soil
17 bean seeds
metric ruler
watering can
water
pencil and paper

What to do

1. Label the cups A, B, and C.
2. Fill each cup almost to the top with soil.

3. Plant 10 seeds in cup A, 5 seeds in cup B, and 2 seeds in cup C. The seeds should be planted about one centimeter below the surface of the soil. Record the number of seeds you plant in each cup.

4. Place the cups in a sunny location. Water the seeds as needed for 2 weeks. Keep the soil moist, but do not overwater.

5. Make a table like the one shown for recording what you observe after 5 days. Make similar tables for recording your observations after 10 and 15 days.

Competition Among Bean Plants				
		After 5 days		
Cup	Number of beans planted	Number of bean plants	Tallest bean plant (cm)	Average height (cm)
A	10			
B	5			
C	2			

6. Record the number of bean plants that appear in each cup after 5, 10, and 15 days.

7. Measure the height, in centimeters, of each bean plant in each cup after 5, 10, and 15 days. Record the heights of the tallest bean plants. Calculate and record the average height of the bean plants in each cup after 5, 10, and 15 days.

What did you learn?

1. After 15 days, how many bean plants were growing in each cup?
2. In which cups did all the seeds sprout?
3. In which cup did the tallest bean plant grow?

Using what you learned

1. In which cup was there the least competition? In which cup was there the most competition?
2. For what factors were the plants in each cup competing?
3. What effect did competition have on the growth of the bean plants in each cup?

a

b

Figure 16–13. Predator-prey relationships exist between a rock bass and a grasshopper (a) and a puffin and fish (b).

What organisms make up a lichen?

In an ecosystem, there are limited amounts of substances needed for life. There may also be limits on the amount of space available, places to live, the number of mates available, or other needs of living things. **Competition** is a relationship in which living things compete for life needs. Competition may occur among members of the same population or between populations.

Predator-Prey Relationships

Food chains limit the size of populations. A predator is an animal that feeds on another animal, which is called the prey. **Predation** (prih DAY shun) is the act of one animal killing and eating another animal. Predation is an important factor in controlling population size. Suppose, for example, that a community has plenty of food for insects. Because the insects do not need to compete for food, their population becomes large. Insects in the community are prey for spiders. A large spider population eats many insects. The number of insects will decrease as they are eaten by spiders. Then the spiders will have less food. Competition among spiders for food results in a smaller spider population. With fewer spiders, the insect population might increase again. What might then happen to the spider population? What might happen to the insect population if there were no insect predators?

Cooperation Among Organisms

Symbiosis (sihm bi OH sis) is a relationship between two different species of organisms that live in close contact. There are three basic forms of symbiosis. In one, both species benefit from the relationship. In another, one species benefits and the other is neither benefited nor harmed. In the third type, one species benefits at the expense of the other.

Mutualism (MYEW chuh lihz um) is a relationship that benefits both species. Lichens are an example of mutualism. Lichens are made up of a fungus and an alga. The alga may be a species of cyanobacteria or protist. The alga makes food and the fungus supplies water and nutrients that both organisms need.

318

Another example of mutualism occurs between certain ants and aphids (AY fihdz). Aphids eat plant juices. In fact, they eat more juice than they need. The extra juice flows out of their bodies. Ants eat the extra juice that flows from the aphids. The aphids thus provide food for the ants. During winter, cold temperatures would kill the aphids. The ants carry the aphids into small underground tunnels. In the tunnels, the aphids eat juices from the roots of plants. The ants eat the extra juice from the aphids. In spring, the ants carry the aphids back to the leaves and stems of plants. Because of this cooperation, the ants have food during the winter and the aphids are protected from the harsh weather.

How do ants and aphids benefit from mutualism?

The relationship in which one organism is helped and the other is not harmed is commensalism (kuh MEN suh lihz um). Birds build nests in trees. The trees shelter the nests. The building of the nests neither harms nor helps the trees.

Remoras (REM ur uhz) and sharks are two kinds of fish that live in the oceans. A remora attaches itself to the underside of a shark. The remora does not help or harm the shark. When the shark eats, pieces of leftover food are eaten by the remora. The remora benefits from its relationship with the shark because the remora does not need to find its own food. Also, the remora gets a "free ride" from the shark.

How does a remora benefit from its relationship with a shark?

Figure 16-14. Symbiotic relationships are found in lichens (a), ants and aphids (b), a shark and a remora (c), and in the protection that a sea anemone gives a clownfish (d).

a

b

c

d

Science and Technology

Tracking Starfish

Coral reefs, like the Great Barrier Reef, are very delicate ecosystems. The crown-of-thorns starfish seems to be taking a heavy toll on the coral of the Great Barrier Reef. The crown-of-thorns starfish population has increased rapidly in the past several decades. Studies are underway to determine if the starfish outbreak is part of a natural cycle or if there is another reason for the sudden increase in the number of starfish.

The crown-of-thorns starfish grazes on soft-bodied coral animals. As more and more coral animals are preyed upon by the starfish, whole portions of the reef ecosystem are destroyed.

Scientists are studying the movements of the starfish on the reef. Tiny radio transmitters are implanted in the bodies of the starfish. The transmitters produce a signal that is easily detected by radio receivers. Starfish movements can then be tracked.

As they track radio-tagged starfish, scientists collect data on the places where the starfish are found. Each of these places may have special environmental conditions that favor the growth of the starfish. For example, starfish were tracked to a part of the Great Barrier Reef where human activities had altered the structure of the reef. These changes removed some of the animals that preyed upon young starfish. Without the threat of predators, more starfish young survived and began feeding on the delicate coral.

There is still much to be learned about the crown-of-thorns starfish. The information obtained by radio tracking can be used to restore the balance between the starfish and its coral animal prey.

Parasite-Host Relationships

A parasite feeds on another living thing. The living thing on which the parasite feeds is called a host. **Parasitism** (PER uh suh tihz um) is a kind of symbiosis in which one organism is helped and the other is harmed. Many kinds of organisms may be parasites. Almost all organisms in a community are hosts for some parasites.

Parasites affect the size of host populations. Hosts are harmed in relationships with parasites. Sometimes a parasite kills its host. Even if a parasite does not kill its host, the host is weakened. Then the host may die of disease or be caught by predators. What might happen to a parasite population if its host population decreases? In a community, the parasite population is limited by the size of the host population.

One common parasite is a flea. You have probably seen a dog scratch because of fleas. Dogs are hosts for fleas. A flea burrows its mouth parts into the skin of a dog. The flea gets nourishment from the dog's blood. Ticks and mosquitoes are also parasites. They, too, live on blood from their hosts.

Not all parasites live on the outside of the bodies of their hosts. Some parasites live inside the bodies of their hosts. Some monerans may be parasites in your body. Perhaps you have had to stay home from school because you had strep throat. You were the host for a moneran parasite that had infected your body.

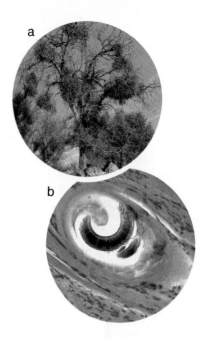

Figure 16–15. Mistletoe in an oak tree in winter (a) and trichina worms in pig muscle tissue (b) are examples of parasitism.

What limits the size of a parasite population?

What is the cause of strep throat?

Lesson Summary

- A population is a group of organisms within a certain area that are all the same species.
- The population size of one species is affected by populations of other species in the ecosystem.
- Competition, predation, and parasitism are factors that limit population size.

Lesson Review

Review the lesson to answer these questions.
1. How do nonliving factors affect population size?
2. Compare competition and symbiosis.

Language Arts Skills

Using Flow Charts

Flow charts present information in a way that is easy to see, to read, and to understand. Some of the flow charts you will use show the steps of a process. Others show relationships such as those between organisms.

Look at Figure 16–6, page 310. This flow chart illustrates the nitrogen cycle. The arrows show the movement of nitrogen through the cycle. Nitrogen in the air is fixed in the soil by clover. Moose eat the clover. When the moose die, their bodies decompose. In this way, nitrogen is returned to the air and soil.

Figure 16–9, page 313, is an example of a more complex flow chart. A food web in the summer Arctic tundra is described in this flow chart. A food web contains many food chains. The arrows show the relationships between various producers and consumers in a habitat. For example, phytoplankton in rivers and streams are eaten by snails. Fish eat the snails. The fish are food for brown bears and terns. The snowy owl preys on smaller animals, such as terns and lemmings.

A written description of all the information in this flow chart would be lengthy. Also, the variety of relationships would be difficult to visualize. The flow chart summarizes the information clearly and concisely.

The flow chart below shows how photosynthesis and cellular respiration aid in recycling materials through a community. Use this flow chart to answer the following questions.

1. What is used by plants in photosynthesis?
2. Where do plants get these materials?
3. What is produced during photosynthesis?
4. How are the products of photosynthesis used?

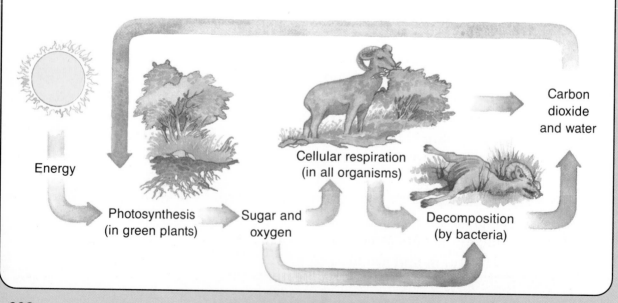

Energy

Photosynthesis (in green plants)

Sugar and oxygen

Cellular respiration (in all organisms)

Decomposition (by bacteria)

Carbon dioxide and water

Chapter 16 Review

Summary

1. Each organism in an environment has a certain role.   16:1
2. Living and nonliving parts of the environment affect each other.   16:1
3. Groups of living things interacting with each other and the environment compose an ecosystem.   16:1
4. Recycling causes life substances to be used and returned to the environment to be used again.   16:1
5. Water, carbon dioxide, oxygen, nitrogen, and other substances are recycled in the environment.   16:1
6. Energy from the sun supports life and is transferred throughout an ecosystem.   16:2
7. A food chain is a series of steps showing energy flow through a community.   16:2
8. Organisms cannot recycle energy.   16:2
9. A pyramid can be used to represent energy flow and the total mass of producers and consumers present in a food chain.   16:2
10. A population is a group of organisms within a community that is all of the same species.   16:3
11. The size of a population may be affected by competition, predation, or symbiosis.   16:3
12. Symbiosis is a relationship between two different species of organisms that live in close contact.   16:3

Science Words

carbon dioxide-oxygen cycle	**ecosystem**	**parasitism**
community	**food chain**	**population**
competition	**food web**	**predation**
decomposer	**niche**	**symbiosis**
ecology	**nitrogen cycle**	**water cycle**

Understanding Science Words

Complete each of the following sentences with a word or words from the Science Words that will make the sentence correct.

1. The study of how the living and nonliving parts of an ecosystem affect each other is _____.

2. A special consumer that obtains energy from dead organisms is a _____.

3. A relationship between two different species of organisms living in close contact is called _____.

4. A relationship in which an organism is harmed by living together with another organism is _____.

5. The total of all the organisms in an ecosystem make up a _____.

6. The continuous movement of water through an ecosystem is the _____.

7. The steps showing energy flow through a community form a _____.

8. Groups of organisms interacting with each other and the environment compose an _____.

9. Overlapping food chains in a community form a _____.

10. The continuous movement of nitrogen in an ecosystem is the _____.

11. A group of organisms of the same species is a _____.

12. An animal killing and eating another animal is _____.

13. The relationship in which living things all try to get the same life needs is _____.

14. The continuous exchange of oxygen and carbon dioxide among producers, consumers, and the atmosphere is the _____.

15. The role of an organism in the community is its _____.

Questions

A. Checking Facts

Determine whether each of the following is true or false. Rewrite the false statements to make them correct.

1. Consumers are the only organisms that use the sun's energy directly to carry on life processes.

2. A community is a group of organisms all of the same species.

3. Mutualism and commensalism are types of symbiosis in which neither organism is harmed.

4. The overlapping food chains in a community are an ecosystem.

5. Organisms cannot recycle energy.

6. Competition and predation can limit the size of a population.
7. A food chain always begins with a decomposer.
8. Almost all organisms in a community are hosts for parasites.
9. Ecology is a relationship between two different species of organisms that live in close contact.
10. Each organism has a niche in the environment.

B. Recalling Facts

Choose the word or phrase that correctly completes each of the following sentences.

1. Lichens are an example of
   - (a) parasitism.
   - (c) mutualism.
   - (b) predation.
   - (d) competition.
2. Bacteria that live in other organisms are
   - (a) hosts.
   - (b) parasites.
   - (c) producers.
   - (d) predators.
3. Nitrogen-fixing bacteria live in
   - (a) air.
   - (c) waste products from organisms.
   - (b) plant root nodules.
   - (d) soil.
4. The killing and eating of an insect by a spider is an example of
   - (a) symbiosis.
   - (c) predation.
   - (b) parasitism.
   - (d) competition.
5. All the brook trout in a certain stream are
   - (a) a population.
   - (c) a food web.
   - (b) a community.
   - (d) an ecosystem.
6. Squirrels and chipmunks trying to eat the same crop demonstrate
   - (a) predation.
   - (c) parasitism.
   - (b) mutualism.
   - (d) competition.

C. Understanding Concepts

Answer each of the following questions using complete sentences.

1. Describe how nitrogen in the air becomes available to plants and animals.
2. Explain the use of a pyramid model in representing a food chain.
3. Cite some of the factors that may limit the size of a population.

D. Applying Concepts

Think about what you learned in this chapter. Answer each of the following questions using complete sentences.

1. What factors might keep a population of mice in a cornfield from growing until it overruns a community?
2. Explain why the first link in a food chain is always a green plant.

Chapter 17
Biomes

The eerie, mournful "laughter" of the loon is again becoming a common sound on the lakes of the northern United States and Canada. During the first 75 years of this century, the loon population dropped drastically as people moved into loon habitats. Why do you think the loon population is now growing? How might acid rain affect the loons?

Common loon

LESSON GOALS

In this lesson you will learn

- organisms are adapted to certain habitats.
- changes in habitats may be natural or caused by people.
- changes in habitats have caused some populations to become very small.
- people have helped to save some species from extinction.

a

b

Figure 17-1. A fence row (a) and a small stream (b) provide different habitats for a variety of organisms.

Every kind of organism is adapted to a certain set of conditions. These conditions include temperature, amount of water and space, and other physical factors. These conditions make up the **habitat**, a place where an organism normally lives. The habitat provides all life needs. Within a community, the organisms may live in a number of different habitats. If the habitat is changed, some needs may not be met. The organisms may not survive.

The size of the habitat affects the population size within a community. Based on what you learned in Lessons 16:2 and 16:3, what other factors affect population size? The size of each population in a community is in balance with all of the others. If one population becomes larger or smaller than normal, other populations will be affected.

What conditions make up a habitat?

Name some natural processes that may change habitats.

Habitat changes may occur through natural processes. Fires, floods, volcanoes, and earthquakes are some ways in which habitats can be changed. Think of a forest suddenly burned up in a fire. Most of the shrubs and small plants are destroyed. Many of the trees are partly or totally burned. Animals that live on the ground or close to it either escape or are killed. After the fire is out, there is, at first, no habitat left for these ground-dwelling animals. Ground-nesting birds and small animals such as mice may die from lack of habitat. Their life needs can no longer be met. Larger animals such as deer and rabbits may be able to live in other places.

What are some organisms that may live in a burned area of a forest?

Food sources may no longer be present or may have changed. This does not mean, though, that no organisms can live in the burned area. Some conifers, for example, require the heat of a forest fire to open cones for seed dispersal. Clearing of trees may allow species of shrubs and grasses to grow that need much sunlight and space. As new plant populations grow, new types of animals move into the area. New habitats form. Populations that need these types of habitats will increase in size. After many years, a community like the one present before the fire may form again.

Figure 17-2. Forest fires destroy habitats. In time, new habitats form.

Activity 17-1   Observing Sidewalk Habitats

QUESTION   How are habitats specific to certain organisms?

Materials
hand lens   small jar
metric ruler   paper and pencil

What to do

1. Make a table like the one shown in which to record your observations.

Organisms Living in Sidewalk Crack	
Name/Description	Length/Height

2. Observe a crack in a sidewalk for organisms. Capture any animals in a small jar.
3. Identify or draw a picture of each type of organism.
4. Measure and record the length of each organism.
5. Count and record the number of each type of organism.
6. Release the animals in the spot from which they were taken.

What did you learn?

1. How many different types of organisms live in the sidewalk crack?
2. What organism did you observe most often?
3. What is the largest organism in the habitat?
4. What is the smallest organism you observed?

Using what you learned

1. What limits does the sidewalk habitat place on the size of the organisms you observed?
2. How do the nonliving factors of the sidewalk habitat affect the type of organisms present?
3. Suggest a possible food chain for some of the organisms living in the sidewalk habitat.

Human Influence

Habitat changes may be caused by humans. Whenever a road, home, or other building is built, the habitat is changed. Some industries can cause permanent habitat changes. Farming and logging are two examples. Changes caused by humans are often permanent because the land is not allowed to recover, as a burned forest can. The plants and animals of the original community do not return because their habitats have been destroyed. What do you think the original community might have been like where you live? How has it changed?

Figure 17–3. Some habitats are changed and others destroyed as houses are built.

Why do humans hunt or collect plants and animals?

Humans may directly affect the population size of an organism without destroying the habitat. One way they may do this is by hunting. Both plants and animals may be collected or hunted for various reasons. Plants or animals may be considered valuable for food or other products, recreation, or decoration. Whales, for example, supply meat, oil, and bonelike substances used in brushes and plastics. The whaling industry has greatly reduced the whale population. In 1900, there were about 4 million whales of different species. Today only about 1 million of these animals exist. The whale population may be so low that, in the great distances in the ocean, individual whales cannot find mates. As a result, reproduction cannot occur. Consider that the population size was decreased by 3 million in 100 years. If decreases continued at the same rate, how long would it take to reduce the current population to zero?

Hunting may be controlled by setting limits on the number of organisms to be collected at one time. Hunting seasons are another method of control. A hunting season is determined by the life cycle of the plant or animal. You cannot hunt some animals, for example, during the time that young are being raised. At what other times do you think hunting of animals should be limited? When would you limit the collecting of plants?

Disappearing Populations

The fossil record shows that there are many types of life that no longer exist. These organisms are said to be extinct. Recall from Lesson 15:1 that an extinct species is one with no members living anywhere in the world. The process of extinction happens naturally, usually over thousands of years.

During the last 400 years, the slow, natural process of extinction has been speeded up for many plants and animals. Records show many bird species, for example, are becoming extinct. Figure 17–5 shows the increasing extinction rate of bird species. Other vertebrate species are thought to be disappearing at the same rate as birds. The main reason for this increase in extinction rate is change in habitats. Most habitat changes are produced by the growing human population. What changes are people making to habitats?

Figure 17-4. Alligators are hunted for their hides.

What is the main reason for the increase in the extinction rate of some vertebrate species?

Figure 17-5. The rate at which some species of birds are becoming extinct has been increasing since the early 1700s. The dodo became extinct in the late 1600s.

The Rising Rate of Bird Extinctions

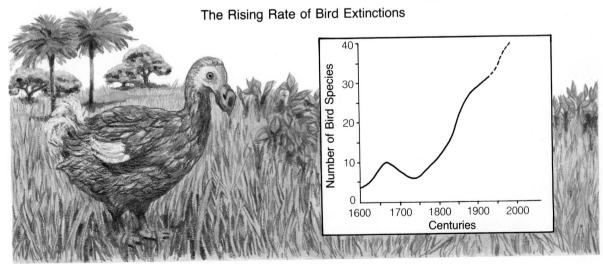

Studies of bird populations show that over 200 species found in the United States are nearing extinction. Each of these species is considered to be endangered. An **endangered species** is one that has very few members living anywhere in the world. Figure 17–6 shows examples of a variety of endangered species.

Figure 17–6. Endangered species include eastern cougar (a), leafy reed grass (b), red uakaris (c), short-branched beavertail (d), pine hill flannelbush (e), pine barrens tree frog (f), El Dorado morning glory (g), and komodo dragon (h).

Saving Wildlife

In the 1920s, a family living near a small lake in British Columbia in Canada began to feed the 35 trumpeter swans that wintered there. The family was not aware that this small population made up about one-third of all the trumpeter swans in the world at that time. Because the swans were helped through the harsh winter, more survived and reproduced. The family kept records of the number of swans returning each winter. The trumpeter swans wintering on this lake now number more than 400. This population brings the total number of trumpeter swans in North America to several thousand. One family helped to reverse the extinction of this bird species.

Many people are working to keep endangered species from becoming extinct. They also work to keep rare species from becoming endangered. Actions such as observing hunting laws, planting native plants, cleaning up trash from streams and parks, and building bird feeders are ways to aid plant and animal species. What are some other ways you can help keep species from disappearing?

What may be done to keep endangered species from becoming extinct?

Lesson Summary

- Habitat is a place where an organism usually lives.
- Natural events may destroy habitats, but people are the major cause of habitat destruction.
- Changes in habitat have caused populations to become extinct or endangered.
- People can help keep populations from becoming extinct.

Lesson Review

Review the lesson to answer these questions.

1. Why do changes in habitat cause problems for the organisms found there?
2. Compare the past rate of species extinctions with the present rate.
3. How can people help keep populations from becoming endangered?

Biomes

LESSON GOALS

In this lesson you will learn

- Earth is divided into large ecosystems with similar organisms and nonliving factors throughout.
- there are six land biomes.
- there are two water biomes.
- people have affected every biome in some way.

A biome (BI ohm) is a large ecosystem with characteristic organisms and nonliving factors throughout. Each biome has certain properties, such as the amount of sunlight, range of temperature, and

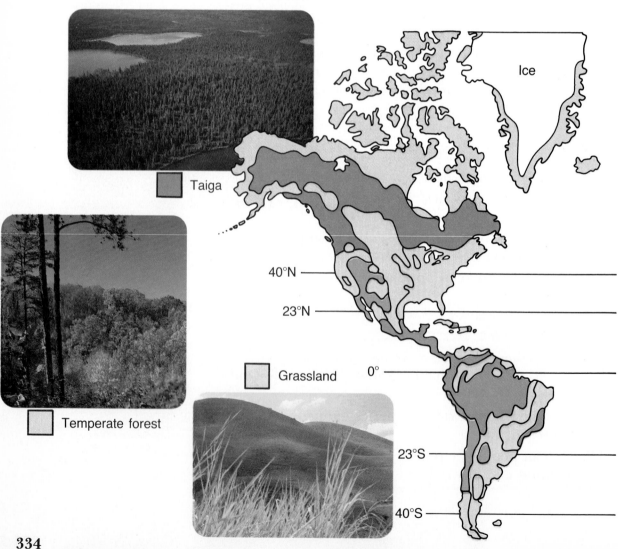

Figure 17-7. Six major land biomes of the world

the amount of precipitation. These factors determine the types of producers that can grow in the biome. The producers present, in turn, determine the type of consumers that can live there.

There are eight main types of biomes. The six major land biomes are shown in Figure 17–7. Notice that similar types of biomes are located at a given distance north and south of the equator. Each land biome can be described by its plant life. The characteristic plants vary from one biome to another.

There are two water biomes. They are salt water and fresh water. Different plants grow in freshwater biomes depending on the land biome that surrounds them. Saltwater plants and animals are specially adapted to live in this salty environment.

Name the two water biomes.

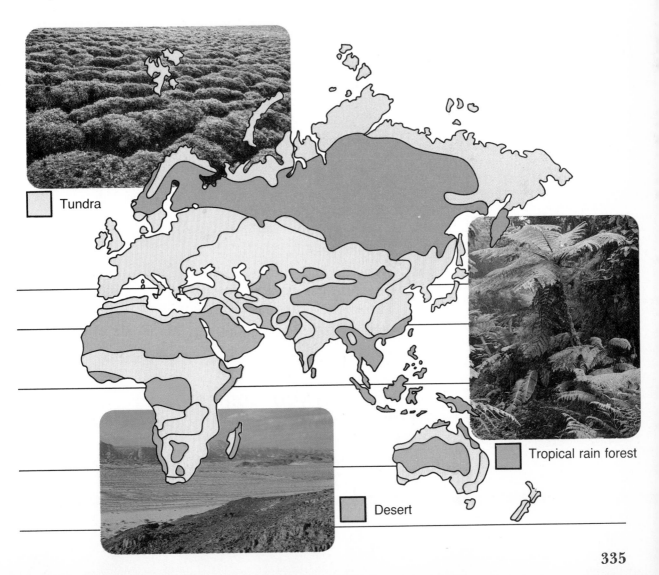

Tundra

Tropical rain forest

Desert

Activity 17–2 Comparing Biomes

QUESTION How do the climates of land biomes compare?

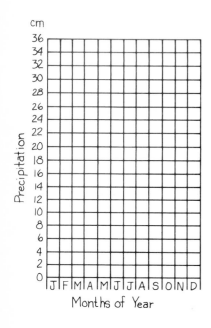

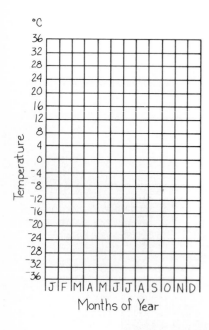

Materials

6 sheets of graph paper
2 pencils, different colors
pencil and paper

What to do

1. On six sheets of graph paper, copy the two diagrams shown at the left.
2. Label each sheet of paper with the name of one of the following biomes: tundra, taiga, temperate forest, tropical rain forest, grassland, desert.
3. The tables on the next page contain sample data about the precipitation and temperatures of the six biomes during one year. Plot the data given for each biome on the two graphs you made for that biome. Make bar graphs to show precipitation with one colored pencil and temperature with the other.

What did you learn?

1. What nonliving characteristics did you compare for each biome?
2. Consider that you are in the Northern Hemisphere. Describe the weather you would expect if you visited each of these biomes in June.
3. Write paragraphs describing the climate of each biome.

Using what you learned

1. What other characteristics could you compare for each biome?
2. If a type of organism could not live in temperatures below 4°C, in which biomes could it live?

Precipitation (cm)

Month	Biome					
	Tundra	Taiga	Temperate forest	Tropical rain forest	Grassland	Desert
January	0-1	2	13	28	3	3
February	1	2	12	28	3	3
March	0-1	2	13	33	6	2
April	0-1	1	9	29	9	1
May	1	2	10	18	12	1
June	2	2	8	10	12	1
July	3	3	10	5	9	0-1
August	3	6	8	4	12	0-1
September	3	7	7	6	8	0-1
October	2	5	7	12	6	2
November	1	2	9	15	5	2
December	0-1	2	11	20	4	2

Temperature (°C)

Month	Biome					
	Tundra	Taiga	Temperate forest	Tropical rain forest	Grassland	Desert
January	−25	−10	4	25	−1	−1
February	−27	−8	5	24	2	2
March	−26	−6	10	25	6	6
April	−18	2	14	25	10	9
May	−4	8	18	25	16	10
June	2	12	23	25	22	14
July	6	14	28	25	26	18
August	6	12	25	25	25	18
September	3	8	22	26	22	16
October	−4	2	18	26	14	10
November	−16	−6	10	26	10	4
December	−24	−10	5	25	2	0

Table 17–1	
Life in the Tundra	
Producers	Consumers
lichens	lemmings
liverworts	snowshoe hares
mosses	wolves
grasses	caribou
sedges	arctic foxes
small shrubs	musk oxen
small flowering	ptarmigans
plants	geese
	mosquitoes

In what parts of the world is tundra found?

Why can trees not grow in the tundra?

Figure 17–8. The habitats of the puffin, caribou, and tundra moss can be easily damaged.

Tundra

The **tundra** is a land biome with an annual precipitation of nearly 20 centimeters and with mosses and liverworts as the characteristic plants. The temperature in the tundra ranges from −60°C in the winter to 15°C in the summer. Tundra is found in the far northern parts of the world or on the tops of very high mountains. Look at the biome map in Figure 17–7. Why is there no tundra shown in the far southern regions?

Most precipitation in the tundra is in the form of snow. Most of the ground is also frozen. **Permafrost** is a layer of soil that is frozen all year. During the short summer, the soil thaws through just the top few centimeters. Because of the permafrost, no plants with deep-reaching root systems can grow. Trees cannot grow in the tundra. Table 17–1 in the margin lists some of the living things found in the tundra.

The tundra is a fragile biome. People who explore the tundra for natural resources such as oil can easily cause damage to the plant life. Once the plants are damaged, severe erosion occurs. Probably because of the short growing season, plant cover grows back slowly. A foot path used only one season may scar the landscape for years. Tire tracks can erode into gullies over three meters deep.

Figure 17-9. Logging in the taiga area of British Columbia may change the habitat of the white-tailed deer and the lodgepole pine.

Taiga

The **taiga** (TI guh) is a land biome with an annual precipitation of nearly 50 centimeters and with conifers as the characteristic plants. The temperature in the taiga ranges from −35°C in the winter to 20°C in the summer. Taiga is found in northern regions, south of the tundra. Look at Figure 17-7. In what countries is most of the taiga found?

Much of the precipitation is in the form of rain. There is also a lot of fog. Because the temperature is above 0°C for a longer period of time in the taiga than it is in the tundra, the soil thaws completely each year. The soil, though, is very wet and acidic. The acid condition is caused by peat mosses and conifers that grow in the taiga. Table 17-2 lists some of the living things in the taiga.

Conifers grow very well in the taiga. These large forests are used by people as a natural resource. Conifers are valued for their use as lumber and paper pulp. If careful logging methods are used, erosion and habitat destruction can be kept to a minimum.

Why is the soil in the taiga acidic?

Table 17-2 Life in the Taiga	
Producers	Consumers
lichens	deer
peat mosses	moose
grasses	grizzly bears
sedges	wolves
conifers	mice
willows	migrating birds
aspens	

Table 17–3 Life in the Temperate Forest	
Producers	Consumers
mosses	bears
ferns	owls
small flowering	deer
plants	mice
shrubs	foxes
maples	rabbits
oaks	raccoons
walnuts	opossums
hickories	squirrels

What are the characteristic plants of the temperate forest biome?

Temperate Forest

The **temperate forest** is a land biome with an annual precipitation of nearly 100 centimeters and with deciduous (dih SIHJ uh wus) trees as the characteristic plants. The temperature in the temperate forest ranges from −30°C in the winter to 40°C in the summer. The temperate forest biome has four distinct seasons each year: spring, summer, autumn, and winter. Look at Figure 17–7. Besides the United States, what other regions have four seasons?

Most temperate forests are composed of deciduous trees. What happens to the leaves of deciduous trees in the autumn? The temperature changes cause a slower recycling of substances needed for life than in forests near the equator. Therefore, the soil is very rich in these substances. Abundant plant life grows. The varied types of plants allow many types of consumers to live in these forests. Table 17–3 lists some of the living things found in temperate forests.

People have developed the temperate forest biome more than any other biome. Mild temperatures for most of the year make it easier for people to live in these areas. The rich soil is a natural resource for farmers. Much of the land has been cleared of trees so crops can be grown. Many types of deciduous trees are valuable for lumber. Careless logging methods have been used to clear much of this biome, causing severe erosion. If cleared areas are left alone, the forest community can regrow or regenerate. It may, however, take over 100 years for the forest community to return.

Figure 17–10. Temperate forest areas can regenerate and again become the home of animals like the weasel.

340

Tropical Rain Forest

The **tropical rain forest** is a land biome with an annual precipitation of nearly 250 centimeters and with vines and broadleaf trees as the characteristic plants. The temperature in the tropical rain forest is nearly the same all year, around 25°C. "Seasons" are marked in this biome by rainfall. Much more rain falls during the rainy season than during the dry season. Look at Figure 17–7. In which regions are tropical rain forests found?

The growing season lasts all year long in the tropical rain forest. Plants grow very well in the warm, wet climate. More kinds of plants grow in this biome than in any other biome. Table 17–4 lists some of the living things found in tropical rain forests.

The high temperature and humidity cause dead organisms to decay quickly. The life substances are then quickly recycled by the many living things. This causes very fast growth. Therefore, the soil is not very rich. If land is cleared for any reason, rain forest plants do not grow back. Without plant cover, the soil erodes easily. The hot sun causes the soil to bake into a claylike material. These scars of eroded and baked soil remain for many years.

Figure 17–11. Animals such as the spider monkey, the green python, and the eastern rosella are at home in a tropical forest.

How long is the growing season in the tropical rain forest biome?

Table 17–4 Life in the Tropical Rain Forest	
Producers	Consumers
palm trees	panthers
tree ferns	pythons
vines	insects
bromeliads	spiders
balsa trees	tree frogs
mahogany trees	monkeys
orchids	birds
	sloths

341

Table 17-6 Life in the Grassland	
Producers	Consumers
bluestem grass	lions
buffalo grass	moles
grama grass	prairie dogs
sagebrush	ground squirrels
rabbit brush	badgers
antelope brush	gophers
cottonwood	zebras
trees	bison
willow trees	deer
	coyotes
	wildebeests
	prairie chickens
	hawks

Grassland

The **grassland** is a land biome with an annual precipitation of nearly 75 centimeters and with grasses as the characteristic plants. The temperature in the grasslands ranges from −45°C in the winter to 50°C in the summer. Rain falls irregularly in the grasslands. Grasslands are called by many different names. Various names for grasslands are shown in Table 17–5. Locate each of these grassland areas on the biome map in Figure 17–7. How many seasons do you think the grasslands have each year?

Table 17–5 Grasslands Around the World		
Location	Name	Origin of Name
North America	prairies	French for meadows
Europe and Asia	steppes	Russian for plains
East Africa and Australia	savannahs	Spanish for plains
South Africa	velds	Dutch for fields
South America	pampas	Indian for flatlands

As you might expect from its name, the grassland biome contains many kinds of grasses. Small shrubs are also present. Because rain does not fall regularly, only a few kinds of trees can grow in the grasslands. These are often along the banks of streams. Table 17–6 lists some of the living things found in the grassland biome.

People have greatly changed the grasslands found in North America. By using irrigation and modern farming methods, many food grasses are grown. Wheat, oats, and corn have replaced many of the natural grasses. Large herds of cattle and sheep have also changed the plant life.

Figure 17–12. Grasslands provide homes for a variety of plant and animal species, such as bison and prairie dogs.

Figure 17–13. Species of cacti, burrowing owls, and the collared lizard live in the desert biome.

Desert

The **desert** is a land biome with less than 25 cm of rain per year and with euphorbia (yoo FOHR bee uh) and cactus as characteristic plants. Some deserts have warm to hot temperatures all year long. In other deserts, called cold deserts, temperatures range from −40°C in the winter to 45°C in the summer. In all deserts, the daytime temperature is much higher than the nighttime temperature. Look at the biome map in Figure 17–7. Locate the deserts of the world.

Desert plants and animals are adapted to the daily temperature extremes. Many animals are active only at night when the temperature is cooler. Table 17–7 lists some of the living things found in the desert.

Human influence is causing deserts all over the world to get larger. Because much water is used for irrigation of crops in desert areas, less water reaches the biomes bordering deserts. Therefore, the plants in the bordering biomes cannot grow. Without plants, desert conditions take over. When water is returned to these border areas, the original biome returns.

Deserts are also being destroyed by people. Because of the large open areas, many people drive vehicles anywhere they want. How does this damage the desert? Desert plants are collected by the thousands to sell for decoration. What could be done to stop people from destroying life in the desert?

Why are many animals in the desert active only at night?

Table 17–7 Life in the Desert	
Producers	Consumers
cacti	kangaroo rats
creosote	peccaries
bushes	jack rabbits
ocotillo	badgers
palo verde	elf owls
rabbit brush	cactus wrens
sagebrush	roadrunners
euphorbias	gila monsters
	rattlesnakes
	collard lizards
	scorpions

343

Table 17-8 Freshwater Life	
Producers	Consumers
cyanobacteria	bacteria
green algae	protozoans
elodea	fungi
duck weed	hydra
water lilies	insects
cattails	fish
diatoms	crayfish
	frogs
	herons
	muskrats

Of what does a freshwater biome consist?

What are the five factors that affect life in fresh water?

Fresh Water

Fresh water is a water biome in which the salt content is less than 0.005 percent. The freshwater biome is found within the other biomes. It consists of lakes, ponds, and streams. The climate of the freshwater biome is like that of the surounding biome. You probably have an idea of the kinds of living things found in fresh water. Look at Table 17-8 to see if you are correct.

There are five factors that affect the life in fresh water. Temperature, strength of current, and the amount of particles suspended in the water are three factors. The amount of dissolved gases and the kinds of minerals in the water also affect life. These five factors determine two freshwater habitats, standing water and moving water. How do you think each of these five factors compare in the two habitats: moving water and standing water?

Much fresh water is used for irrigation of cropland. As the water returns to the biome, it carries pesticides and fertilizers used on the crops. These chemicals can upset the balance among freshwater living things. They change the food chains and habitats, causing some populations to die and others to grow quickly. What are some other ways pollutants can enter fresh water?

Figure 17-14. A map turtle and water lilies live in freshwater biomes like this small lake.

Salt Water

Salt water is a water biome in which the salt content is around 3.5 percent. The saltwater biome consists of all the world's oceans. It covers about three-fourths of Earth's surface. Many kinds of life are found in the oceans. Look at the list of some saltwater living things found in Table 17–9. Think of as many other saltwater organisms as you can.

Certain factors affect life in the ocean. Light, temperature, salt content, and water pressure are the most important factors. Where is the most light present? Where would the water pressure be the greatest? How might these factors affect the type of life found in the ocean at different depths?

People affect the saltwater biome, too. Pollution from industry along coastlines, such as hot water and sewage, often enter the water. Ships, such as oil tankers, may also pollute the water if there is an accidental oil spill. Some large saltwater organisms, such as whales, have been threatened with extinction because of over-hunting. How can people help to protect the ocean?

Table 17–9 Saltwater Life	
Producers	Consumers
cyanobacteria	protozoans
green algae	crustaceans
diatoms	whales
red algae	tuna
dinoflagellates	jellyfish
kelp	clams
	starfish
	coral

What part of Earth's surface is the saltwater biome?

What are the most important factors that affect life in the oceans?

Lesson Summary

- A biome is a large ecosystem with similar organisms and nonliving factors throughout.
- The land biomes are tundra, taiga, temperate forest, tropical rain forest, grassland, and desert.
- The water biomes are fresh water and salt water.
- People have affected every biome in some way.

Lesson Review

Review the lesson to answer these questions.

1. How does the amount of annual precipitation affect the type of plants that grow in each biome?
2. Which land biome produces the most plant life? Why?
3. Why does light affect life in salt water more than life in fresh water?

People and Science

Bird-Watcher

The scientists waved to the pilot of the helicopter as he landed at their study site on the Alaskan tundra. The pilot brought supplies needed for a three-month study of the bird life of the tundra.

As leader of a team of five scientists, Ann Fields is responsible for organizing the research projects the team conducts. Most of the research focuses on the adaptations of birds living on the tundra. The team hopes to learn more about the ways in which certain birds, such as snow geese, raise their young. Snow geese spend the summer on the tundra to raise their young, but migrate south in the winter. In recent years, snow geese have declined in number but no one knows the reason.

Each day, Ann makes a survey of snow goose nests. She follows a special route plotted on a map of the area. The survey method she uses is called a grid census because the paths look like a checkerboard or grid pattern on the map. She walks from nest to nest, carefully urging each parent goose to leave. Then she counts the eggs in each nest. As she moves on, the parent geese return to continue incubating their eggs.

Ann looks for signs of predators. Snow geese are sometimes preyed upon by Arctic foxes. A broken egg far from a nest indicates that a fox may have preyed upon a nest.

Each night, Ann and the other scientists carefully review the data they have collected. They look for clues that may explain why the snow goose population is declining. It may take all summer, and perhaps longer, to solve the riddle of declining snow goose numbers.

Chapter 17 Review

Summary

1. A place where an organism normally lives is its habitat. 17:1
2. Populations may become extinct or endangered through changes in their habitats. 17:1
3. People can work to prevent endangered species from becoming extinct. 17:1
4. A biome is a large ecosystem having similar living and nonliving things. 17:2
5. The tundra is the northernmost land biome. 17:2
6. Taiga lies just south of the tundra and has large forests of conifers. 17:2
7. The temperate forest biome has four seasons, and deciduous trees are characteristic. 17:2
8. The tropical rain forest biome has nearly the same temperature all year round and an annual precipitation of around 250 centimeters. 17:2
9. Grasslands are characterized by various grasses and irregular rainfall. 17:2
10. Desert biomes are characterized by little precipitation and plants such as cactus and euphorbia. 17:2
11. Water biomes may be freshwater or saltwater systems. 17:2
12. Biomes are affected by humans in many ways. 17:2

Science Words

biome	grassland	taiga
desert	habitat	temperate forest
endangered species	permafrost	tropical rain forest
fresh water	salt water	tundra

Understanding Science Words

Complete each of the following sentences with a word or words from the Science Words that will make the sentence correct.

1. A land biome with a temperature range of $-30°$ to $40°C$ and an annual precipitation of nearly 100 centimeters is a _____.
2. A biome in which the dissolved salt content in the water is about 3.5 percent is _____.
3. A place where an organism normally lives is its _____.
4. A biome in which the salt content of the water is less than 0.005 percent is _____.

5. A land biome with less than 25 centimeters of rain per year and euphorbia and cactus as characteristic plants is a _____.
6. A fragile land biome found in the far northern parts of the world and on the tops of very high mountains is _____.
7. A land biome with a temperature range of $-35°$ to $20°C$ and an annual precipitation of nearly 50 centimeters is _____.
8. A layer of soil that is frozen all year is _____.
9. A land biome with temperatures around $25°C$ all year and an annual precipitation of nearly 250 centimeters is a _____.
10. A land biome called pampas in South America with an annual precipitation of nearly 75 centimeters is a _____.
11. A large ecosystem having similar organisms and nonliving factors is a _____.
12. A species of organism that has very few members living anywhere in the world is an _____.

Questions

A. Checking Facts

Determine whether each of the following is true or false. Rewrite the false statements to make them correct.
1. If a habitat is changed, an organism can always survive.
2. Pine trees grow in the tundra.
3. Similar kinds of biomes are found at the same distance north and south of the equator.
4. Humans can do nothing to keep endangered species from becoming extinct.
5. Besides a place for organisms to live, a habitat includes the temperature, amount of water and space, and other physical factors.
6. There is no record of any types of organisms that have become extinct.
7. Today the main reason for the increase in the extinction rate of a population is hunting.
8. The size of a population within a community is affected by the size of its habitat.
9. A hunting season is a way of controlling a population's size without killing too many of its members.

B. Recalling Facts

Choose the word or phrase that correctly completes each of the following sentences.

1. A habitat may be changed naturally by
   (a) hunting.   (b) logging.   (c) flooding.   (d) farming.
2. The daytime temperature during the month of January would probably be coldest in a
   (a) grassland.   (b) taiga.   (c) desert.   (d) tundra.
3. The amount of precipitation per year is highest in a
   (a) temperate forest.   (c) grassland.
   (b) tropical rain forest.   (d) taiga.
4. A way in which humans can directly affect a population's size without harming its habitat is by
   (a) hunting.   (c) road building.
   (b) logging.   (d) home building.
5. The biome that covers most of Earth's surface is
   (a) tundra.   (c) fresh water.
   (b) salt water.   (d) temperate forest.
6. The most fragile biome is the
   (a) tundra.   (b) taiga.   (c) grassland.   (d) temperate forest.
7. An organism found in a freshwater biome is
   (a) a cattail.   (b) a jellyfish.   (c) a whale.   (d) kelp.
8. Permafrost exists in the
   (a) desert.   (b) taiga.   (c) temperate forest.   (d) tundra.

C. Understanding Concepts

Answer each of the following questions using complete sentences.

1. State the major differences between a freshwater biome and a saltwater biome. List two organisms that could be found in each of these biomes.
2. Name three ways in which humans can help prevent extinction of a species.

D. Applying Concepts

Think about what you learned in this chapter. Answer each of the following questions using complete sentences.

1. If you were a biologist studying an endangered species of birds, what factors about the species' habitat might you consider?
2. Give some possible reasons why a cactus survives so well in a desert biome, but a deciduous tree does not.

UNIT 7 REVIEW

CHECKING YOURSELF

Answer these questions on a sheet of paper.
1. Distinguish an organism's niche from its habitat.
2. Explain the difference between a community and an ecosystem.
3. Describe three cycles that recycle important life substances.
4. What is the difference between a food chain and a food web?
5. What type of organism is at the beginning of a food chain and at the base of an energy pyramid? Why?
6. Define population and list three factors that may limit its size.
7. There are three basic forms of symbiosis: mutualism, commensalism, and parasitism. Match these three types of symbiosis with the following examples: (a) bacteria living in the large intestine of a healthy human; (b) mistletoe in an oak tree; (c) fleas on a dog; (d) ants living with aphids; (e) birds nesting in bushes.
8. For what might populations be in competition?
9. What is the main reason for the growing rate of extinctions of certain plant and animal species?
10. Name the biome that fits each of the following descriptions.
    (a) greatest variety of plant life
    (b) where permafrost keeps plants with deep root systems from taking hold
    (c) about three-fourths of Earth's surface
    (d) a northern biome with coniferous forests

RECALLING ACTIVITIES

Think about the activities you did in this unit. Answer the questions about these activities.
1. What is an ecosystem?   16–1
2. How can you observe competition among plants?   16–2
3. How are habitats specific to certain organisms?   17–1
4. How do the climates of land biomes compare?   17–2

IDEAS TO EXPLORE

1. Visit the local library to make a list of available natural history or nature magazines that are concerned with educating nonscientists about the world around us. Borrow one magazine that you find most interesting and share this with the class.
2. Write an essay that will answer one of the following questions.
   (a) How has the fur trade affected wildlife?
   (b) Why do people wear furs?
3. What are the Galapagos Islands, and how are they related to Charles Darwin's finches? Make a report that will show why scientists from all over the world are concerned for the future of the Galapagos.

CHALLENGING PROJECT

Ecological studies are a major part of conservation. To conserve any part of nature, people must understand how it works and how it affects other parts. Visit a water habitat in your region. It could be a creek, a pond, a lake, or a rock pool at the seashore. Make regular observations of plants and animals in this habitat. Use guide books to identify the species. Make an estimate of the numbers of individuals of each species present. Notice how the species interact. Estimate the space occupied by each species. Prepare a report and include bar graphs that demonstrate the changing nature of this water habitat.

BOOKS TO READ

One Day in the Desert by Jean George, Crowell Junior Books: New York, © 1983.
   Visit the desert on the hottest day on record. How do the plants and animals survive?

Scavengers and Decomposers: Nature's Clean-Up Crew by Pat Hughey, Macmillan Publishing Company: New York, © 1984.
   How are waste products cleaned up in the environment?

Tundra: The Arctic Land by Bruce Hiscock, Macmillan Publishing Co.: New York, © 1986.
   Look into life in the land without trees.

UNIT 8
Electricity and Electromagnetic Waves

In the mid-1700s, Benjamin Franklin reasoned that electricity and lightning were the same. Using this knowledge, he invented the lightning rod. During that time it became fashionable in Paris to wear anti-lightning hats or to carry portable lightning conductors. With advances in technology, people have learned to use electricity to do work. Modern factories use robots to do jobs that may be hazardous to employees. What are some ways to use electricity to do work?

Lightning rod "protectors"—1700s

Robots welding cars

Chapter 18
Electricity

The existence of electrical forces has been known for over 2,000 years. However, the first battery was made by Alessandro Volta only in the 1790s. Thomas A. Edison made the first light bulb in the late 1800s. What is electricity? How is electricity used today?

Electric light bulbs

Static Electricity

LESSON GOALS
In this lesson you will learn
- how positive and negative ions form.
- how static electricity occurs.
- the effects of like and unlike charges.
- what causes a static electric discharge.

Electricity is a popular and important source of energy. It is usually available at the flip of a switch. Scientists use the model of the atom to explain electricity. You know that the core of an atom is the nucleus. The nucleus contains particles called protons. Protons have a positive electric charge. Particles called electrons move around the nucleus. Electrons have a negative charge. An atom is neutral when the number of electrons equals the number of protons. A neutral atom has no electric charge, because the positive and negative charges balance.

What is the charge on a proton? On an electron?

When is an atom neutral?

Sometimes atoms gain electrons from other atoms. When this happens, the number of positive and negative charges is no longer equal. The atom takes on a negative electric charge. The atom that loses the electron also has an electric charge. It is positive, because it has more protons than electrons. Recall from Lesson 4:1 that an atom with a charge is called an ion. An atom becomes a positive ion when it loses one or more electrons. An atom becomes a negative ion when it gains one or more electrons.

What is an ion?

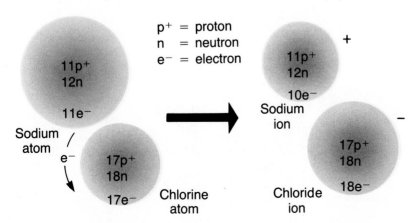

p^+ = proton
n = neutron
e^- = electron

Figure 18-1. A sodium atom is left with a positive charge when it loses an electron to chlorine. The chlorine atom takes on a negative charge.

Figure 18-2. Unless an anti-static agent has been used, clothes often cling together because of the buildup of charge on them in the dryer.

Why do clothes sometimes stick together in the dryer?

The positive or negative electric charges on objects are static electric charges. **Static electricity** is electric charge built up in one place. The charges on ions are static charges.

You may have observed the effects of static electricity while doing laundry. Clothes taken from the dryer often stick together. In the dryer the clothes rub against each other. Electrons move from one piece of clothing to another. A negative charge builds up on some clothes. Other clothes are left with a positive charge. Ions with different electric charges attract each other. This causes some of the clothes to cling together.

Objects with the same static charge repel one another. You may have noticed this while combing your hair. When you comb your hair, your hair loses electrons to the comb. As a result, your hair has more protons than electrons. Your hair has a positive charge. For this reason, the hairs repel each other. This repulsion causes your hair to stick up. Strands of hair may also move toward the comb. What is the charge on the comb?

If a balloon is rubbed with a piece of wool, electrons are rubbed off of the wool onto the balloon. This gives the balloon a negative charge. The balloons in Figure 18-3b have both been given a negative charge. What happens to them when they are brought near one another?

a   b

Figure 18-3. Two uncharged balloons hang side by side (a). After the balloons have been rubbed with wool, they are negatively charged and repel each other (b).

Static Discharge

Perhaps you have observed an effect of static electricity when you touched a metal doorknob after walking across a carpet. You may have felt a shock. If the room was dark, you may even have seen sparks. The shock was caused by electrons moving from your hand to the doorknob. These electrons came from atoms in the carpet. They were picked up by atoms in your body as you walked across the rug.

The movement of electrons from an object with negative charge to another object is called a **static discharge.** Only electrons move. Protons do not move. You may hear static discharges when you pull apart clothes after taking them out of the dryer.

What is a static discharge?

Sometimes there is a static discharge in the sky. Clouds have both negative and positive ions. Electrons may jump from one cloud to another cloud. They may also move from clouds to the ground. What do you observe when a static discharge from a cloud occurs?

Static electricity has many uses. For example, most copying machines use static electricity to produce copies. Static electricity is also used in special filters to remove smoke and dust particles from the air.

Lesson Summary

- Positive and negative ions form as electrons move from one atom to another.
- Static electricity is the buildup of charge in one place.
- Like charges repel and unlike charges attract one another.
- The movement of electrons from an object with negative charge to another object is static discharge.

Lesson Review

Review the lesson to answer these questions.

1. What happens when atoms lose or gain electrons?
2. Explain the difference between static electricity and static discharge.

Current Electricity

LESSON GOALS

In this lesson you will learn
- what current electricity is and how it flows.
- how a conductor differs from an insulator.
- how series and parallel circuits differ.
- how an electric motor operates.
- what is meant by power.
- how electricity use is measured.

Figure 18-4. Electric cords and plugs are covered with insulation, usually a rubber or plastic material. Only the metal wires and prongs in the plug conduct electricity.

Describe current electricity.

Name two sources of electrons for electric currents.

Sometimes electrons move from atom to atom through a material. This continuous movement of electrons is a current. Currents of electrons flow through some substances much like currents of water flow in a river. The flow of electrons through a material is **current electricity.**

A material through which electrons flow easily is a **conductor.** Copper wires are used as conductors of electric current in many homes. Most metals are good conductors. The electrons in metals flow easily from one atom to another. Both copper and aluminum are very good conductors. The nonmetal graphite is also a good conductor. Graphite is the form of carbon used in pencils.

Some substances are poor conductors of electricity. An **insulator** is a material that electrons do not flow through easily. Wood and plastic are good insulators. So are rubber and glass. Why do you think most wires that conduct electric current are covered with plastic?

A continuous source of electrons is needed to produce an electric current. A battery is one source of electrons. A chemical reaction inside the battery produces the supply of electrons. Electric current for most homes is produced at electric power plants. The source of electrons at these plants is a generator. Generators produce a flow of electrons by rotating coils of wire through a magnetic field. Generators at power plants can produce much more electric current than batteries can.

Circuits

Currents of electrons flow in circuits. An **electric circuit** is a continuous path over which electrons move. Race cars move in circuits called racetracks. When you go to and from school, you travel a circuit. In the morning you leave home and go to school. In the afternoon you complete the circuit when you leave school and go home. What other circuits can you name?

Conductors form circuits for current electricity. Electrons move from a place where there are more negative charges to a place where there are more positive charges. In Figure 18–5 the wires connect one terminal of the battery with the other. Electric current can flow only if there is a complete circuit. If the circuit is broken, the current will stop flowing.

Electricity flows through two types of circuits. A **series circuit** is one in which the electric current flows through only one pathway. A **parallel circuit** is one in which the electric current can flow through more than one pathway. The yellow and green bulbs in Figure 18–6 are part of a series circuit. Electric current must flow through the yellow bulb in order to flow through the green bulb.

In Figure 18–6 the red and blue bulbs are part of a parallel circuit. Electric current does not have to flow through the blue bulb in order to flow through the red one.

Figure 18–5. When the switch is closed, the circuit is complete and the bulb is lit.

Besides a conductor, what is necessary for the flow of current electricity?

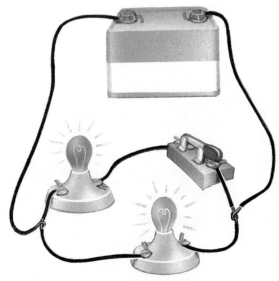

Figure 18–6. The yellow and green bulbs are part of a series circuit. The red and blue bulbs are connected in a parallel circuit.

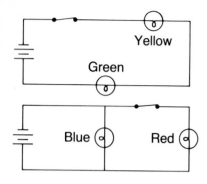

Figure 18-7. Symbols are used in electrical diagrams to represent parts of a circuit.

Table 18-1	Symbols for Electric Circuits	
Item	Purpose	Symbol
Wire	Conducts electric current	——
Battery	Stores and supplies electricity	⊦⊢⊦
Light bulb	Provides electric light	⊸◯⊸
Switch	Completes or breaks a circuit	•—•

People use symbols to draw electric circuits. The table shows some of the common symbols used. The circuits in Figure 18–6 are shown in Figure 18–7 using symbols. What electric devices are part of these circuits?

Electric Motors

An electric current flowing through a coil of wire produces a magnetic field. Look at Figure 18–8. A wire has been wrapped around an iron nail. When the wire is connected to a battery, a magnetic field is produced. This device is called an electromagnet.

If current flows through a wire around an iron nail, what does the nail become?

An electric motor is made of coils of wires wound on iron rods. The coils are surrounded by magnets. When the motor is switched on, electric current flows through the wire coils. A magnetic field is produced at the coils. This field interacts with the magnets around the coils. These magnetic forces cause the coils to rotate.

Figure 18-8. Electric current flowing through a wire coil around an iron nail forms an electromagnet.

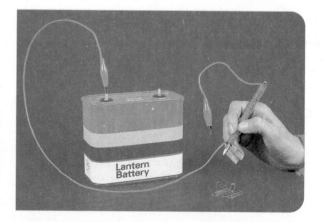

Activity 18–1   Comparing Circuits

Materials

2 flashlight batteries
  (size D)
insulated electric
  wire

2 light bulbs in sockets
masking tape
switch
pencil and paper

What to do

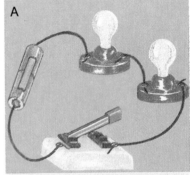

A

Part A

1. Tape two flashlight batteries together with the positive end of one touching the negative end of the other as shown. Tape wires to the ends of this "battery pack."
2. Connect the batteries, the sockets, and the switch to make the circuit shown in drawing A.
3. Turn the switch on and off. Observe.
4. Loosen one of the bulbs. Turn the switch on and off again. Observe.

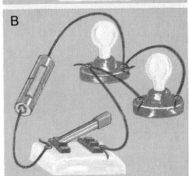

B

Part B

1. Make the circuit shown in drawing B.
2. Turn the switch on and off. Observe.
3. Loosen one of the bulbs.
4. Turn the switch on and off again. Observe.

What did you learn?

1. What happened when you loosened one bulb in the circuit in Part A?
2. What happened when you loosened one bulb in Part B?
3. Draw each circuit using the symbols in Table 18–1.

Using what you learned

1. Explain what you observed when you loosened the bulbs.
2. Circuit A is a series circuit. Circuit B is a parallel circuit. Are the lights in your home part of a series circuit or a parallel circuit?

Electric motors are very useful. The spinning motion of the motor can be used to move objects. A long rod attached to the coils can turn other objects, such as wheels. The blades of a fan are turned by an electric motor. The fans in furnaces and air conditioners are operated by electric motors. Perhaps you have a clock in your room that uses an electric motor. Where are other electric motors used?

Electricity in Our Homes

Electric current enters a home through wires. The wires are connected to a service panel or fuse box. The panel or box provides a place to connect different circuits to the outside wires. Each circuit provides electric current to an area of the home. Any electric device that is in use is part of a circuit. What are some electric devices that you use at home? Which devices have switches?

A simple **switch** is a device that makes it easy to complete or break an electric circuit. A switch is like a drawbridge. Suppose there is a drawbridge between your home and your school. In the morning, the drawbridge is down. You cross the drawbridge and go to school. On your way home after school, the drawbridge is up. You cannot get home until the drawbridge is lowered. As long as the drawbridge is

Figure 18-9. The opening and closing of a drawbridge is like the opening and closing of an electric circuit. Traffic cannot move while the drawbridge is up. Electric current cannot flow in an open circuit.

down, your circuit to and from school is complete. When the drawbridge is up, your circuit to and from school is broken.

When a switch is on, the electric circuit is complete, or closed. Current then flows through the circuit. When a switch is off, the electric circuit is broken and current does not flow. The circuit is said to be open.

Sometimes a circuit is broken in other ways. Perhaps you have been at home when all of the electricity was off. A circuit somewhere was broken. During storms, a circuit between your home and the electric power plant may break. Electricity cannot flow into your home until the circuit is repaired.

Sometimes a circuit is broken inside homes. You may hear someone say, "We blew a fuse." A **fuse** is a safety device with a metal strip that can break a circuit. Heat is produced when electric current flows through the wires of a circuit. Too much electric current flowing through a circuit can cause the wires to get too hot. The hot wires could cause a fire. Fuses help prevent fires. Before the wires of a circuit carry too much current, the metal strip in a fuse melts and breaks the circuit. The electric current stops flowing before the wires get too hot.

Some homes have circuit breakers instead of fuses. A **circuit breaker** is an automatic switch that breaks a circuit when electric wires carry too much current. A piece of metal holds the switch in the on position. If the circuit carries too much current, the metal becomes hot. As it gets hot, it expands and releases the switch. Fuses must be replaced after they have broken a circuit. Circuit breakers can be turned back on.

If a fuse or a circuit breaker breaks a circuit, you know there is a problem with that circuit. There may be too many appliances on the circuit. The problem should be corrected before the circuit breaker is turned on again or the fuse is replaced. Why do you think this is so?

We use electricity in many ways each day, and sometimes take it for granted. Because electricity is so common, we may forget that it can be dangerous. It is important to know how to use electricity safely.

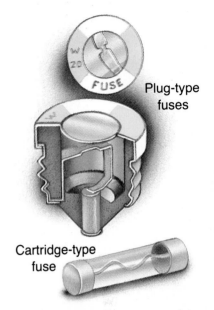

Plug-type fuses

Cartridge-type fuse

Figure 18-10. Fuses are safety devices in circuits. When a circuit becomes overloaded, the thin metal strip in the fuse melts and the circuit is broken.

How does a fuse break a circuit?

How is a circuit breaker like a fuse?

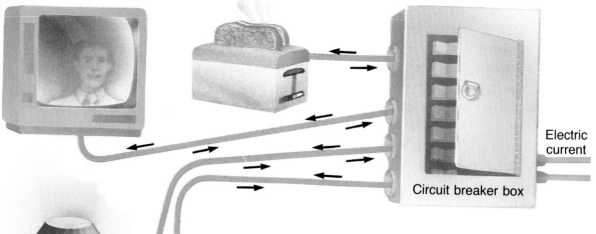

Electric current

Circuit breaker box

Figure 18-11. The electricity used by all the electrical devices in a home enters the house through a panel containing circuit breakers or fuses.

For what do electric companies charge their customers?

Measuring Electric Current

All electric devices use energy. A light bulb uses a small amount of energy. Much more energy is used by a toaster. If the toaster and the lamp were on all day, the toaster would use far more energy. The rate at which a device uses energy is called **power.** The **watt** is the unit used to measure power.

Most electric devices are labeled with the number of watts they use. Devices labeled with a low number of watts use electricity at a slower rate than those with a high wattage. Household light bulbs usually have power ratings of 25 to 100 watts. Small night-lights are usually 4 or 7 watts. An electric toaster may use energy at the rate of 1,000 watts.

The electric energy used in our homes is measured in kilowatt-hours. A kilowatt is equal to 1,000 watts. A **kilowatt-hour** is the energy produced by 1,000 watts of power in one hour. How many hours would a 100-watt light bulb have to burn to use one kilowatt-hour of electric energy?

Electric companies charge people for the number of kilowatt-hours they use. Suppose the cost of electricity is 12 cents for each kilowatt-hour. How much would it cost to use a 2,000-watt heater for four hours?

2,000 watts × 4 hours = 8,000 watt-hours or
8 kilowatt-hours

Eight kilowatt-hours at 12 cents each is 96 cents.

8 kilowatt-hours × $0.12 = $0.96

It would cost 96 cents to use the heater four hours.

MODEL 691-4
120 V. - 50-60 Hz. - WATTS 330
HAMILTON BEACH DIVISION
Scovill
Division of Scovill Mfg. Co.
MADE IN U.S.A.
LISTED
FOOD PREPARING MACHINE
917B

b

Figure 18-12. The amount of electricity used in a home is read from an electric meter (a). Electrical appliances have power ratings (b).

Homes have kilowatt-hour meters that measure the amount of electricity used in the home. The meter is read regularly, and the cost of electricity for the past month is calculated. How can you find out how many kilowatt-hours of electricity were used in your home last month?

Lesson Summary

- Current electricity is the flow of electrons in a conductor.
- Conductors are materials through which electrons flow easily, while insulators are the opposite.
- A series circuit provides one pathway for electric current, while a parallel circuit provides more than one.
- An electric motor is made of coils of wires wound on iron rods and surrounded by magnets.
- Power is the rate at which energy is used.
- Electricity use is measured in kilowatt-hours.

Lesson Review

Review the lesson to answer these questions.

1. Name two materials that are good conductors of electricity. Name two that are insulators.
2. What is meant by the wattage of an electric appliance?
3. What is the difference between a circuit breaker and a fuse? How are they alike?

Activity 18-2 Constructing an Electric Motor

QUESTION How can you make an electric motor?

Materials

1 enameled wire (150–160 cm)
2 flashlight batteries (size D)
sandpaper
2 giant paper clips
masking tape
foam board
3 plastic-insulated electric wires (1–25 cm, 2–15 cm)
2 brass fasteners
small paper clip
bar magnet
pencil and paper

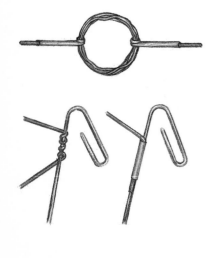

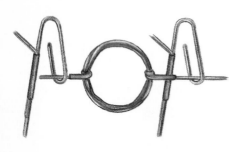

What to do

1. Using the enameled wire, make a coil by wrapping it 15 times around a flashlight battery.

2. Remove the coil from the battery. Loop each free end twice around the center of each side. Leave the ends sticking out as shown in the diagram. Sand the enamel off the free ends as shown. Save the coil for step 9.

3. Tightly wrap an end of one of the 15 cm wires around one end of a giant paper clip. Tape the end of the wire and paper clip together so they will not separate, as shown in the diagram. Do the same with the other 15 cm wire and giant paper clip.

4. Stick the paper clips into the foam board as shown in the diagram on page 367.

5. Make a loop on the free end of one 15 cm wire. Insert one prong of a brass fastener into the loop. Push the brass fastener *A* into the foam board.

6. Tape the batteries together with the positive end of one touching the negative end of the other. Tightly tape the free end of the other 15 cm wire to one end of the batteries.

7. Tape one end of the 25-cm piece of wire to the opposite end of the batteries.

8. Wrap around and then tape the free end of this wire to the small paper clip. Attach the wire to the foam board with the brass fastener *B* as shown in the diagram.

9. Place the coil in the paper clips as shown in the diagram. The coil should turn easily.

10. Complete the circuit by attaching the small paper clip switch to the top of brass fastener *A.*

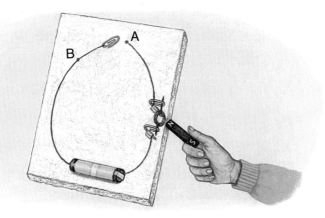

11. Hold one end of the bar magnet near the coil. Use your finger to gently spin the coil to start the motor. Move the magnet around until you find the position where the coil spins the fastest. Hold the magnet in this position.

What did you learn?

1. Why did you sand the enamel off the ends of the coil wires?
2. How did you make the circuit complete?
3. Describe the circuit you completed.

Using what you learned

1. Why did you not use a plastic or wooden strip for the switch?
2. Design and carry out an experiment that would change the speed of the spinning coil. Record your results.

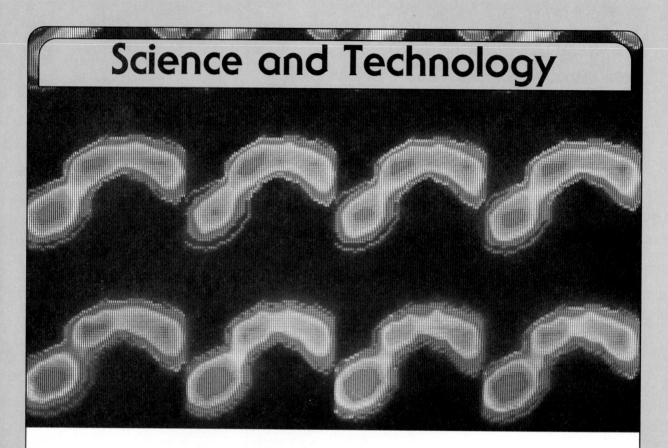

Pacemakers

Sixty to eighty times every minute your heart produces tiny electric pulses that cause your heart to beat. The electric pulses are produced by cells in a small region of the heart called the S-A node. The cells in the S-A node are sometimes called pacemaker cells, because the electric pulses they produce regulate the pace of the heartbeat.

People with heart disease may have pacemaker cells that fail to function properly. If the pacemaker cells do not send out the electric pulses properly, the heart will have an irregular beat or may stop beating. To correct this problem, medical scientists have invented a device to do the job of the pacemaker cells.

The electronic pacemaker produces regular pulses of electricity that start and control the rate of the heartbeat. Some electronic pacemakers produce pulses all the time. Other pacemakers operate only when the natural pacemaker cells do not work properly.

An electronic pacemaker has small electrodes that are implanted in or near the heart. The pacemaker itself is quite small (2 cm × 2 cm × 1 cm) and can be inserted just below the skin. A pacemaker may get its power from a battery. Another type of pacemaker uses the mechanical power of the beating heart to complete a circuit within the pacemaker mechanism. When the circuit is complete an electric pulse is produced.

Electronic pacemakers have helped thousands of people. Perhaps you know someone who has a pacemaker. This simple device can take over successfully when the heart's own electrical circuits fail.

Chapter 18 Review

Summary

1. Electricity is a popular and important source of energy.   18:1
2. Positive and negative ions form as electrons move from one atom to another.   18:1
3. Static electricity is the buildup of charge in one place.   18:1
4. The movement of electrons from an object with negative charge to another object is static discharge.   18:1
5. Current electricity is the flow of electrons in a conductor.   18:2
6. Conductors are materials through which electrons flow easily.   18:2
7. Insulators are materials like wood and plastic through which electrons do not flow easily.   18:2
8. A series circuit provides one pathway for electric current.   18:2
9. A parallel circuit provides more than one pathway for electric current.   18:2
10. An electric motor is made of coils of wires wound on iron rods and surrounded by magnets.   18:2
11. Power is the rate at which energy is used.   18:2
12. Electricity use is measured in kilowatt-hours.   18:2

Science Words

circuit breaker	insulator	static discharge
conductor	kilowatt-hour	static electricity
current electricity	parallel circuit	switch
electric circuit	power	watt
fuse	series circuit	

Understanding Science Words

Complete each of the following sentences with a word or words from the Science Words that will make the sentence correct.

1. One thousand watts of electric energy used for sixty minutes is called a _____.
2. How fast a device uses energy is called _____.
3. An automatic switch that stops the flow of electricity when a circuit is carrying too much current is a _____.

4. A continuous conducting path is an _____.
5. Electric charge built up in one place is _____.
6. A material such as glass through which electrons do not flow easily is called an _____.
7. Electric current can flow through only one path in a _____.
8. A device used to complete or break a circuit is a _____.
9. The flow of electrons through a conductor is called _____.
10. The movement of electrons from an object with negative charge to another object is _____.
11. Electric current can flow through two or more paths in a _____.
12. A material through which electrons flow easily is a _____.
13. The unit used to measure power is the _____.
14. A safety device with a metal strip that can melt to break an electric circuit is a _____.

══════════════════ Questions ══════════════════

A. Checking Facts

Determine whether each of the following is true or false. Rewrite the false statements to make them correct.

1. An atom forms a positive ion by gaining an electron.
2. Ions with the same static charge attract each other.
3. A continuous source of electrons is needed to produce an electric current.
4. Circuit breakers act as safety devices in electric circuits.
5. In a parallel circuit, if one bulb goes out so will all the others.
6. Electric devices labeled with a low number of watts use electricity at a faster rate than those with a higher wattage.
7. Most metals are good conductors of electricity.
8. Current flowing through a wire wrapped around an iron nail produces an electromagnet.
9. The kilowatt-hour is the unit used to measure power.
10. An atom is neutral when the number of protons in the nucleus equals the number of electrons.

B. Recalling Facts

Choose the word or phrase that correctly completes each of the following sentences.

1. An atom that has taken on an electric charge is called
   (a) a proton.   (b) an ion.   (c) neutral.   (d) an electron.
2. A material through which electrons flow easily is
   (a) a conductor.   (c) a fuse.
   (b) an insulator.   (d) a switch.
3. To produce an electric current, you need a continuous source of
   (a) electrons.   (b) protons.   (c) watts.   (d) static.
4. An electric circuit with more than one path for the current is
   (a) in series.   (b) balanced.   (c) in parallel.   (d) positive.
5. The buildup of charge in one place is called
   (a) static discharge.   (c) electromagnetism.
   (b) static electricity.   (d) a kilowatt.
6. Meters measure home electricity use in units of
   (a) kilograms.   (b) watts.   (c) kilowatt-hours.   (d) liters.

C. Understanding Concepts

Answer each of the following questions using complete sentences.

1. How does a conductor differ from an insulator? Give an example of each.
2. What are the advantages of a circuit breaker over a fuse?
3. Explain the difference between current electricity and static electricity.
4. How do switches control electricity?
5. Why are the circuits in your home parallel?

D. Applying Concepts

Think about what you have learned in this chapter. Answer each of the following questions using complete sentences.

1. Suppose the price of electricity is nine cents per kilowatt-hour. How much would it cost to operate
   (a) a 10,000-watt stove for one hour?
   (b) a 60-watt bulb for eight hours?
   (c) a 30-watt video cassette recorder for three hours?
   (d) a 1500-watt hair dryer for ten minutes?
2. A family's electric bill for one month is $60.50. Suppose one kilowatt-hour of electricity costs 10 cents. How many kilowatt-hours of electricity did the family use that month?

Chapter 19
Electromagnetic Waves

Electromagnetic waves surround you. You feel infrared waves as heat. Your eyes see the colors of visible light waves. Radio waves carry AM and FM broadcasts. Microwaves may cook your food. Like water waves, these electromagnetic waves transfer energy. How else are these two types of waves alike? How are they different?

Children making waves

LESSON GOALS

In this lesson you will learn
- how energy is transferred.
- how mechanical and electromagnetic waves are different.
- the characteristics common to waves.
- to define the electromagnetic spectrum.

Look at the photo on the left. The girl is throwing a rock into the water. Energy is needed to throw the rock. The girl is the source of this energy. The energy she transfers to the rock causes it to move. When the rock hits the water, it gives some of its energy to the water. How do you know that energy is transferred to the water?

Energy can be transferred from one object to another in a number of ways. All of these ways to transfer energy can be classified into two groups. Energy can be transferred by the movement of matter. Energy can also be transferred by waves. The transfer of energy as light is an example of transfer by waves.

What are two ways energy can be transferred?

Movement of Matter

Electric energy is transferred by the movement of matter. In static discharge, for example, electrons move from an object of negative charge to another object. In the process, energy is transferred. Electric energy may also be transferred through conducting wires. In the wires, electrons move from atom to atom as shown in Figure 19–1.

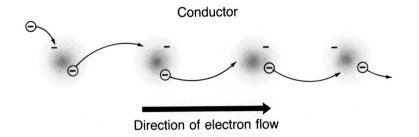

Conductor

Direction of electron flow

Figure 19–1. The movement of electrons from atom to atom transfers electric energy through a conductor.

373

When a soccer ball is kicked, energy is also transferred through matter. Energy is transferred from the person's foot to the soccer ball. When the ball hits the ground, energy is transferred from the ball to the ground. When all of the ball's energy of motion has been transferred to the ground, the ball comes to a stop.

Waves

A second way that energy can move from one place to another is by waves. When the rock was thrown into the water, some of the rock's energy was carried away by waves. Energy produced these waves. There are two types of waves. They are mechanical and electromagnetic.

A **mechanical wave** is a wave that transfers energy as it travels through matter. A water wave is an example of a mechanical wave. The wave travels through the water. The water moves up and down as the wave passes. Water is not carried out with the wave. A wave transfers only energy. It does not transfer matter.

In Figure 19–2 a wave is being transferred along a spring. The wave is formed by quickly moving one end of the spring up and down. The energy carried

What is transferred by a wave?

Figure 19–2. A wave is passed along a spring. Note that one wavelength is the distance from trough to trough.

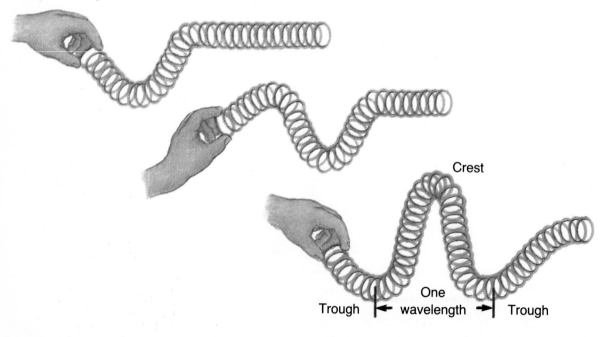

374

by the wave travels through the spring. The spring moves up and down as the wave passes. The spring does not move from left to right with the wave.

The highest point, or top, of a wave is its crest. The bottom of the wave, its lowest point, is the trough. See Figure 19-2. The distance from one wave trough to the next trough is known as **wavelength.** Different waves have different wavelengths.

How is wavelength determined?

The number of waves that pass a point in one second is the **frequency** of the wave. Imagine you are watching ocean waves come to the shore. If one wave hits the shore each second, the frequency of the waves would be one wave per second. If two waves hit the shore each second, the frequency would be two waves per second. What would the frequency be if three waves came to shore each second? What if ten waves hit the shore in five seconds?

What is the frequency of a wave?

Figure 19-3. These water waves strike the shore with a certain regularity, called their frequency.

Electromagnetic Waves

A wave that does not have to travel through matter in order to transfer energy is an **electromagnetic wave.** This type of wave can transfer energy through empty space. Energy from the sun is transferred through space to Earth by electromagnetic waves. Radio and TV make use of electromagnetic waves.

What is an electromagnetic wave?

Electromagnetic waves have different wavelengths. Their frequencies also differ. Each wave also transfers a different amount of energy. The speed at which these waves travel through space is the same. We refer to this speed as the speed of light. Figure 19–4 is a chart of the electromagnetic spectrum. The **electromagnetic spectrum** is an arrangement of electromagnetic waves according to their wavelengths. Notice that waves with high frequencies have short wavelengths. Waves with the lowest frequencies have the longest wavelengths. Visible light is only a small part of the spectrum. All the other wavelengths cannot be seen by people. What kind of waves have the longest wavelength? The highest frequency?

Which waves have the shortest wavelengths? The lowest frequencies?

Figure 19–4. The electromagnetic spectrum includes all electromagnetic waves.

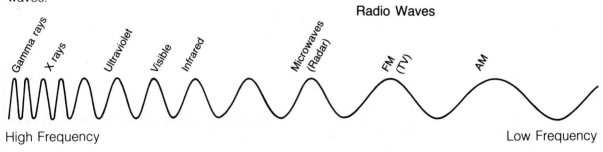

Radio Waves

Gamma rays X rays Ultraviolet Visible Infrared Microwaves (Radar) FM (TV) AM

High Frequency   Low Frequency

Lesson Summary

- Energy can be transferred by the movement of matter or by waves.
- Mechanical waves transfer energy as they travel through matter, while electromagnetic waves may transfer energy without matter.
- All waves have wavelength and frequency and can transfer energy.
- The electromagnetic spectrum is an arrangement of electromagnetic waves according to wavelengths.

Lesson Review

Review the lesson to answer these questions.
1. How is wavelength related to frequency?
2. What is the electromagnetic spectrum?
3. How does a water wave transfer energy?

Activity 19-1 Determining Wave Properties

QUESTION What are some properties of waves?

Materials
spring toy
meter stick
safety goggles
paper and pencil

What to do
1. Have a partner hold one end of the spring toy. Take hold of the other end and stretch the spring to a length of three meters along a smooth floor.
2. Give one quick side-to-side motion to your end of the spring. Observe the spring.
3. Make a steady side-to-side motion so that one wave is formed with the entire spring.
4. Now make the spring move twice as fast. Observe the wavelength.
5. Repeat, trying to move the spring twice as fast as in step 4. Note the wavelength.

What did you learn?
1. What happened in step 2 when the wave reached your partner?
2. How did the length of the wave in step 4 compare with the length of the wave in step 3?
3. How did the length of the wave in step 5 compare with the length of the wave in step 4?

Using what you learned
1. What evidence do you have that waves transmit energy?
2. If the frequency of a wave increases, what happens to its wavelength?
3. Based on what you observed, how does a wave behave when it reaches a barrier?

LESSON GOALS

In this lesson you will learn
- the names and characteristics of waves that make up the electromagnetic spectrum.
- some uses of electromagnetic waves.

You make use of electromagnetic waves every day. These waves make it possible for you to see. They can also keep you warm and cook your food. In fact, you are surrounded by electromagnetic waves. Waves are used to transmit information. When you turn on the radio or TV, you are able to detect some of these waves.

Radio Waves

At a radio station, sounds create vibrations in microphones. Microphones change the vibrations into electric currents. Special equipment changes the electric currents into radio waves. Transmitters broadcast the radio waves from an antenna. Radio waves travel through the atmosphere. Radio waves can also pass through some solid objects, such as the walls of your home. A **radio wave** is one of a group of waves that have the longest wavelengths of the electromagnetic spectrum. Radio waves have a large range of wavelengths. A radio wave may be as long as 10,000 kilometers. The shortest radio waves measure about one millimeter in length.

What makes radio waves different from all other types of electromagnetic waves?

Figure 19–5. Sound waves are changed to electric current and then to radio waves. The radio waves are transmitted through the atmosphere. Radios change the radio waves to electric current and then back to sound waves.

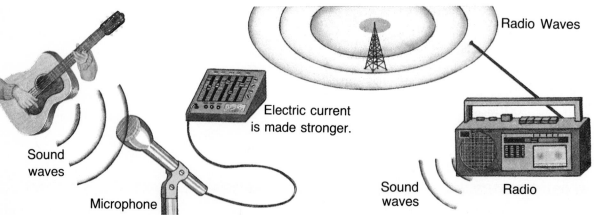

Sound waves

Microphone

Electric current is made stronger.

Radio Waves

Sound waves

Radio

An antenna in your radio receives the radio waves. The radio waves of many stations reach your antenna at the same time. You use the tuner on your radio to select one station or frequency at a time. In your radio, the radio waves from the station are changed into electric currents. Speakers change the electric currents into sound vibrations that you hear.

Radio waves are also used to broadcast television programs. Inside your TV, circuits separate the audio and video information. Speakers change the audio information into sounds. A picture tube changes the video information into patterns of light that appear as a picture on the screen.

Microwaves

A **microwave** is a radio wave with a wavelength between one millimeter and 30 centimeters. Microwaves have the highest frequencies of all radio waves. They have many uses. You are probably familiar with microwave ovens. Microwaves transfer their energy to food. This energy causes some molecules in the food to move more rapidly. As a result, the food becomes warmer. What is an advantage of microwave ovens over other ovens?

How do microwaves differ from other radio waves?

Microwaves pass easily through fog, smoke, and rain. This fact makes them well-suited for communication. Microwaves are used to transmit telephone calls. Certain types of radar units also use microwaves.

Figure 19–6. Mobile television units use microwaves to send information back to the station.

Language Arts Skills

Outlining

A good way to organize the material you read is to outline it. An outline is the general plan presented in the material. An outline gives the order of the various topics, their relative importance, and the ways the various parts are related.

There are different types of outlines. One type lists the main topics of each paragraph. Another more common type lists the main topics overall. This outline may be given in phrases, clauses, single words, or whole sentences. Each topic is called a heading, or head. There are main heads and subheads. These heads are given numbers or letters, based on importance.

What follows is one possible outline of pages 378–379 in Chapter 19.

Using Electromagnetic Waves (Title)
I. Radio Waves (Main head)
  A. Have the longest wavelengths in the electromagnetic spectrum (Subhead)

  B. Are used to broadcast radio and TV
  C. Travel through air and some solids
II. Microwaves (Main head)
  A. Have wavelengths between 1 millimeter and 30 centimeters (Subhead)
  B. Have many uses
    1. Microwave ovens (Sub-subhead)
    2. Communications
    3. Radar

In this outline, all main heads are marked by Roman numerals, all subheads with capital letters, and the sub-subheads with Arabic numbers. The phrasing within each type of head is parallel. The main heads, for example, are nouns. Each of the subheads is a phrase that modifies the noun heading. The first item of a group determines the form. All other items in the group must be phrased the same way.

Using the above outline as an example, outline the paragraph on radar in your text, page 381.

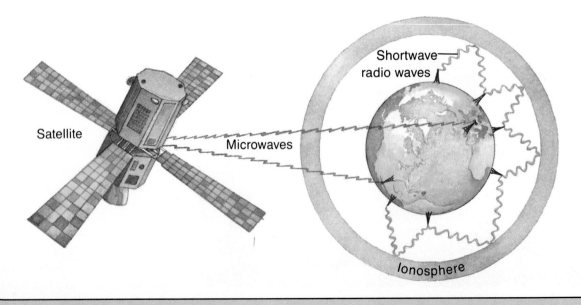
Shortwave radio waves

Satellite

Microwaves

Ionosphere

Figure 19-7. Radar is used to track airplanes.

Radar

The word radar is made from the first letters of the phrase "*ra*dio *d*etection *a*nd *r*anging." **Radar** is a device that uses radio waves to locate objects. Radar works like an echo. Radio waves are sent out from a transmitter. They travel through space until they meet an object. The waves bounce off the object and are received by an antenna when they return.

How is radar like an echo?

Flight controllers use radar to track airplanes. Waves are sent out from a transmitter in the observation tower. When the waves strike an airplane, they are reflected back to the tower. The airplanes appear as bright spots on radar screens. Why do you think many airplanes and ships have radar equipment?

Radar is also used to predict weather. It can be used to detect raindrops as far away as 400 kilometers. Strong radar echoes may mean hail. The use of radar allows meteorologists to forecast storms.

How do meteorologists use radar?

Radar is important in space missions. It is used for tracking spacecraft. Radar is also used to communicate with spacecraft in orbit. Scientists have used radar to find the distance from Earth to the moon and other objects in space.

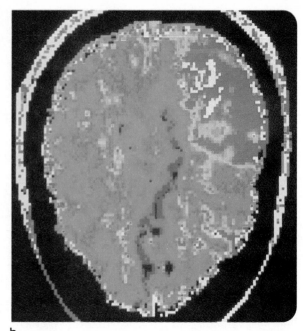

a   b

Figure 19-8. Thermograms are
records of infrared rays from
objects. They may be used to
show heat loss in buildings (a).
Red areas are warmest, purple
areas coolest. This brain
thermogram (b) has a red area
showing damage from a stroke.

How do infrared waves differ
from microwaves?

Infrared Waves

An **infrared wave** is an electromagnetic wave with a
wavelength slightly shorter than the wavelengths of
microwaves. Infrared waves have more energy than
microwaves. When objects absorb infrared waves, the
objects become warmer. Restaurants use infrared
lamps to keep cooked food warm.

All materials give off some infrared waves. The
hotter an object is, the more infrared waves it gives
off. The antennae of mosquitos can detect infrared
waves from your body. Places where heat leaks from
buildings can be detected by cameras sensitive to
infrared waves. See Figure 19-8a. Some tumors may
be located in the same way. Tumors are often warmer
than the tissue around them. How else could infrared
waves be used?

Visible Light

The part of the electromagnetic spectrum that
human eyes can see is called **visible light.** It is a very
small portion of the whole spectrum. What we see as
white light is a mixture of all colors. Each color of
visible light has different wavelengths. Red light has

What is white light?

Figure 19-9. A prism separates white light into all the colors of the visible spectrum.

the longest wavelengths. Violet light has the shortest. A prism can be used to separate white light into its colors. The prism causes light to bend. Light with shorter wavelengths is bent more than light of longer wavelengths. This causes the colors to separate. Rainbows are produced in a similar way. Drops of water in the sky act like tiny prisms.

How does a prism separate white light into colors?

Ultraviolet Waves

An **ultraviolet wave** is one that has a wavelength just shorter than the wavelengths of visible light. Ultraviolet waves are present in sunlight but cannot be seen by people. These waves do not pass through ordinary window glass. In fact, some ultraviolet waves do not pass through Earth's atmosphere.

Ultraviolet waves are both useful and damaging. These waves can cause your skin to darken as well as burn. Too much exposure may cause skin cancer. Ultraviolet waves produce vitamin D in your skin. Vitamin D is a nutrient that is important in forming teeth and bones. Ultraviolet waves are also used to kill germs. These waves are used in many hospitals to kill bacteria on equipment. Some hair stylists use ultraviolet waves to kill bacteria on their combs and scissors.

How are ultraviolet waves helpful?

X rays and Gamma Rays

An **X ray** is an electromagnetic wave with a wavelength just shorter than that of ultraviolet waves. X rays have a large amount of energy. They are able to penetrate many solid materials. X rays are used to examine luggage at airports. They are also used by dentists and other doctors to "see" inside the human body. X rays are partly absorbed by bones. When an X-ray picture is made, bones appear white on film. Other tissues appear dark. Doctors are able to locate breaks in bones using X rays. Some internal organs can also be examined. An X-ray picture can be made of the upper part of the digestive system by having a person drink a substance that will absorb X rays. In this way, the organs will show up on film.

How is it possible to take an X ray of the stomach?

X rays can be harmful to tissue. People should have only necessary X rays. Technicians who take X-ray pictures are careful not to expose themselves to X rays while they work. Have you ever had your teeth X-rayed? If so, the dentist probably covered your body with a lead apron. This apron protects the part of the body that it covers from X rays.

A **gamma ray** is a wave with the shortest of all wavelengths in the electromagnetic spectrum. Gamma rays have very high energy. They are the rays that are released in nuclear reactions. Both fission and fusion produce gamma rays. Gamma rays can damage body cells. Doctors use gamma rays to treat certain cancers.

From what kinds of reactions are gamma rays released?

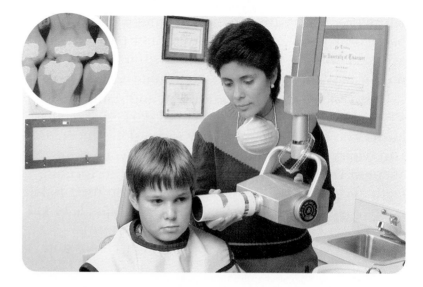

Figure 19-10. X rays aid dentists in locating problems with teeth. A lead apron protects other parts of the body from radiation.

Activity 19-2   The Spreading of Light

QUESTION   How much does light spread out from its source?

Materials
piece of paper
masking tape
flashlight
meter stick
paper and pencil

What to do
1. Tape a piece of paper on the wall. Mark an X in the center of the paper. Darken the room.
2. Hold the flashlight 1 cm from the X on the wall.
3. Have your partner mark the diameter of the circle of light on the wall.
4. Measure and record this distance.
5. Repeat steps 2, 3, and 4, placing the flashlight at 2, 4, 8, 16, and 32 cm from the wall. Keep the center of the beam on the X.
6. Graph your results. Put the distance of the flashlight from the wall across the bottom of the graph. Put the light circle diameter on the other axis.

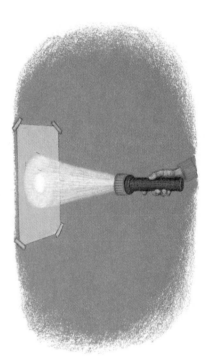

What did you learn?
1. What happened to the circle of light as you moved the flashlight farther from the wall?
2. What happened to the brightness of the circle of light as the flashlight was moved away from the wall?
3. Which increased more, the flashlight distance or the diameter of the circle?

Using what you learned
1. What caused the circle of light to change in size?
2. Why is it easier to read when a lamp is beside you on your desk than when the lamp is across the room?
3. What is the shape of your graph?

Lasers

What is a laser?

As you know, white light is a mixture of different colors. It is a mixture of waves of different wavelengths. If you turn on a light bulb, the light travels out in all directions. A **laser** is a device that produces an intense light beam of one wavelength that travels in only one direction. The laser produces a very narrow beam of light. Instead of spreading out, the laser light moves straight ahead for a longer distance than does ordinary light. These properties are the reason that the main use of lasers is to make exact measurements. Scientists have bounced lasers off the moon to measure the distance between the moon and Earth.

Laser light is used in communications, as well. Information from satellites can be sent to Earth with lasers. What property of lasers makes them useful for space communication? Some of the newest telephone cables are made of very small fibers. Messages may be sent through these fibers on laser beams.

How are lasers used in telephone communications?

Lasers have other important uses. One use is in medicine. Because a laser beam can be so sharply focused, it can be used to perform delicate surgery. Lasers are often used to repair parts of the eye. They are sometimes used in place of surgical knives. Lasers are also used to destroy some kinds of tumors.

Figure 19-11. Cable made of tiny optical fibers can act as a "pipeline" for laser light.

386

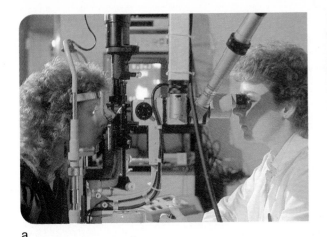

a

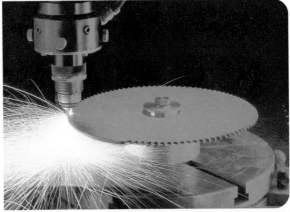

b

Figure 19–12. Lasers are used in eye surgery (a) because they are very precise. The concentrated energy in lasers may also be used to cut metal (b).

Lasers can produce extremely high temperatures. They can melt metals and bore holes through diamond. You may recall from Lesson 9:2 that nuclear fusion takes place at very high temperatures. Scientists are using lasers to reach the millions of degrees needed to start fusion reactions.

Modern supermarket checkouts use lasers to identify each item purchased. This information is sent to a computer that automatically records the price of each item sold. The price is then sent to the checkout register. This process produces a record of the total number of items sold. Managers use this record to reorder items as needed.

Lesson Summary

- Radio waves, infrared waves, visible light, ultraviolet waves, X rays, and gamma rays make up the electromagnetic spectrum.
- Electromagnetic waves have many uses, from space communication to medicine.

Lesson Review

Review the lesson to answer these questions.

1. How is visible light different from all other electromagnetic waves?
2. How does radar work?
3. What properties make laser light different from ordinary white light?

People and Science

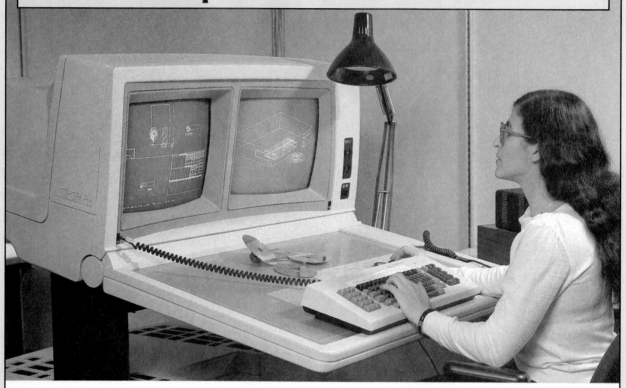

Laser Communications

Alicia Hernandez carefully placed the shiny compact disc on the turntable and turned on the disc player. Moments later, the sounds of her favorite musical group filled the room. As she sat at her work table, Alicia thought about the many recent developments in laser technology, such as the invention of the compact disc.

Alicia is an engineer who designs equipment for use in communications. Although most of the designs are very complicated, all of them rely on the intense beams of light produced by lasers. When telling about her work, Alicia often uses the compact disc player as an example of the use of lasers in communications technology.

In a compact disc player, a very narrow beam of light of one wavelength is pro-duced by a laser and is focused on the surface of the compact disc. The surface of the disc has microscopic wavy grooves. The laser beam, only as wide as one of the grooves, strikes the surface of the disc as the disc rotates on the turntable. Each time the beam strikes one of the ripples or waves within a groove, the beam changes in length. This change happens thousands of times per second. As the beam changes in length, an electronic signal is produced that is transferred through the circuitry of the disc player and, eventually, is re-produced as the sound we hear.

The laser communication devices Alicia designs may some day allow people to communicate with one another over great distances in space.

Chapter 19 Review

Summary

1. Energy is transferred by waves or moving matter. 19:1
2. A mechanical wave transfers energy as it moves through matter. 19:1
3. Electromagnetic waves can transfer energy through empty space. 19:1
4. Electromagnetic waves are arranged in the electromagnetic spectrum according to their wavelengths. 19:1
5. Radio waves have the longest wavelengths in the electromagnetic spectrum. 19:2
6. Microwaves are radio waves with wavelengths between one millimeter and 30 centimeters. 19:2
7. Infrared waves have wavelengths slightly shorter than those of microwaves. 19:2
8. Visible light is the small part of the electromagnetic spectrum that can be seen by human eyes. 19:2
9. Ultraviolet waves have wavelengths just shorter than those of visible light. 19:2
10. X rays and gamma rays are high energy waves with very short wavelengths. 19:2
11. Lasers are narrow beams of light having only one wavelength and traveling in one direction. 19:2

Science Words

electromagnetic spectrum
electromagnetic wave
frequency
gamma ray
infrared wave

laser
mechanical wave
microwave
radar
radio wave

ultraviolet wave
visible light
wavelength
X ray

Understanding Science Words

Complete each of the following sentences with a word or words from the Science Words that will make the sentence correct.

1. A wave that must travel through matter in order to transfer its energy is a _____.

2. An arrangement of electromagnetic waves according to their wavelengths is the _____.
3. Light of only one wavelength that travels in one direction can be produced by a _____.
4. The number of waves that pass a point in one second is the _____ of that wave.
5. A type of radio wave used to cook food and transmit telephone calls is a _____.
6. The part of the electromagnetic spectrum that includes the wavelengths from blue light to red light is _____.
7. A wave with very high energy that is released in nuclear reactions and can damage body cells is a _____.
8. The distance from one wave crest to the next wave crest is a _____.
9. A device that uses radio waves to locate objects is _____.
10. An electromagnetic wave having a wavelength just shorter than those of visible light is an _____.
11. A type of wave that can transfer energy through space is an _____.
12. An electromagnetic wave with a wavelength just shorter than those of microwaves is an _____.
13. An electromagnetic wave with a wavelength just longer than those of gamma rays is an _____.
14. A type of electromagnetic wave that can have wavelengths from one millimeter to 10,000 kilometers in length is a _____.

Questions

A. Checking Facts

Determine whether each of the following is true or false. Rewrite the false statements to make them correct.
1. In order to transfer energy, waves must travel through matter.
2. A prism can be used to separate infrared waves into colors.
3. Microwaves are a type of radio wave.

4. Waves with the highest frequencies have the longest wavelengths.
5. Gamma rays and ultraviolet waves travel through space at the same speed.
6. Ultraviolet waves produce vitamin D in the skin.
7. X rays are shorter than visible light waves, which are shorter than ultraviolet waves.
8. Gamma rays are released in nuclear fission and nuclear fusion.
9. Lasers can produce extremely high temperatures and can bore through diamond.

B. Recalling Facts

Choose the word or phrase that correctly completes each of the following sentences.

1. Waves that need matter in order to transfer energy are
   (a) electromagnetic. (c) mechanical.
   (b) infrared. (d) radio.
2. The waves produced by heat lamps are
   (a) mechanical. (c) microwaves.
   (b) X rays. (d) infrared.
3. A device that produces a narrow beam of light of one wavelength is
   (a) a laser. (b) radar. (c) a microwave oven. (d) a TV.
4. Waves that can be used to examine internal body parts are
   (a) ultraviolet. (b) X rays. (c) radio. (d) visible.
5. All of the following are used in communications EXCEPT
   (a) radar. (b) microwaves. (c) lasers. (d) gamma rays.
6. Microwaves are used in all of the following EXCEPT
   (a) ovens. (b) communications. (c) radar. (d) surgery.

C. Understanding Concepts

Answer each of the following questions using complete sentences.

1. How are mechanical and electromagnetic waves different?
2. List the waves of the electromagnetic spectrum in order from shortest to longest wavelengths.
3. How are microwaves used to cook food?

D. Applying Concepts

Think about what you have learned in this chapter. Answer each of the following questions using complete sentences.

1. List some uses of the various types of electromagnetic waves.
2. Why is it not possible to suntan while sitting in a sunny window?

UNIT 8 REVIEW

CHECKING YOURSELF

Answer these questions on a sheet of paper.
1. Explain how ions are formed.
2. Give an example of static discharge.
3. What is the difference between a series circuit and a parallel circuit? Using electrical symbols, draw and label a series circuit diagram and a parallel circuit diagram.
4. What is the purpose of a circuit breaker?
5. What does the power rating on an electrical appliance mean?
6. If you were charged 11 cents per kilowatt-hour, how much would it cost you to operate a 150-watt light bulb for 12 hours?
7. Why are the cords on electrical appliances wrapped in plastic or rubber materials?
8. What is the difference between static and current electricity?
9. What are the two ways that all energy can be transferred?
10. What is the difference between electromagnetic and mechanical waves?
11. How are waves on the electromagnetic spectrum arranged?
12. List three types of electromagnetic waves and one practical use of each type.
13. What is radar?
14. What is a laser, and how are laser beams used?
15. What is the frequency of a wave?

RECALLING ACTIVITIES

Think about the activities you did in this unit. Answer the questions about these activities.
1. How are circuits different? 18–1
2. How can you make an electric motor? 18–2
3. What are some properties of waves? 19–1
4. How much does light spread out from its source? 19–2

IDEAS TO EXPLORE

1. Laser light can be used to produce holograms. Do some library research to find out how pictures on flat surfaces can actually appear three-dimensional.
2. Make a bulletin board of the electromagnetic spectrum. Under each section, draw or paste a picture of a modern-day application using that region of the spectrum.
3. With the help of an adult, conduct a survey of the electrical appliances in your home. Make an estimate of how many hours each is used in a month. Obtain the cost to you of a kilowatt-hour of electricity. Then estimate the cost of operating these appliances for a month. Compare this estimate with your actual electric bill.

PROBLEM SOLVING

How can you build a circuit to control one light with two switches? Obtain or make two ordinary switches. Use a flashlight bulb, batteries, and wire to make a circuit in which the bulb may be turned on by either switch. If your circuit is correct, you will have to turn the light off using the same switch you used to turn it on. The other switch will have no effect when the light is on. Another type of switch is a double-throw switch. This switch allows you to switch current flow to one of two different wires. Ask your teacher to help you construct two double-throw switches. Use these switches to construct a circuit that allows you to turn the light on or off using either switch. If your circuit is correct, you should be able to turn the light on with one switch and off with the other switch. Draw diagrams of both circuits. Tell why the second circuit would be better for use in a home.

BOOKS TO READ

Electricity by Alan Cooper, Silver Burdett: Morristown, NJ, © 1983.
   Explore the world of electricity.
Computers: How They Work by Nigel Hawkes, Franklin Watts, Inc.: Danbury, CT, © 1983.
   RAM? ROM? This book will introduce you to computers.
TV and Video by Griffin Beale, EDC Publishing: Tulsa, OK, © 1983.
   Diagrams help you to understand how TV works.

UNIT 9
Patterns of Life

North American Indians developed many hybrid crops, such as corn. Today, scientists know that DNA molecules carry the genetic code that determines the characteristics of each organism. Scientists use computer-generated models of DNA to study ways to change this molecule in a process called genetic engineering. Early Indians and modern engineers used their knowledge to develop healthier, more productive crops. What pieces of DNA determine traits? What is genetics?

Indian village of Secotan

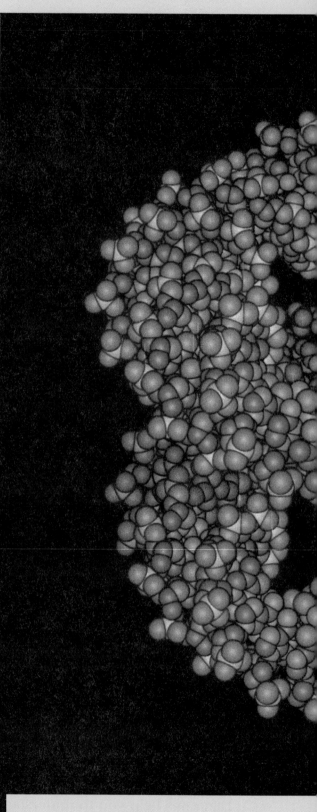

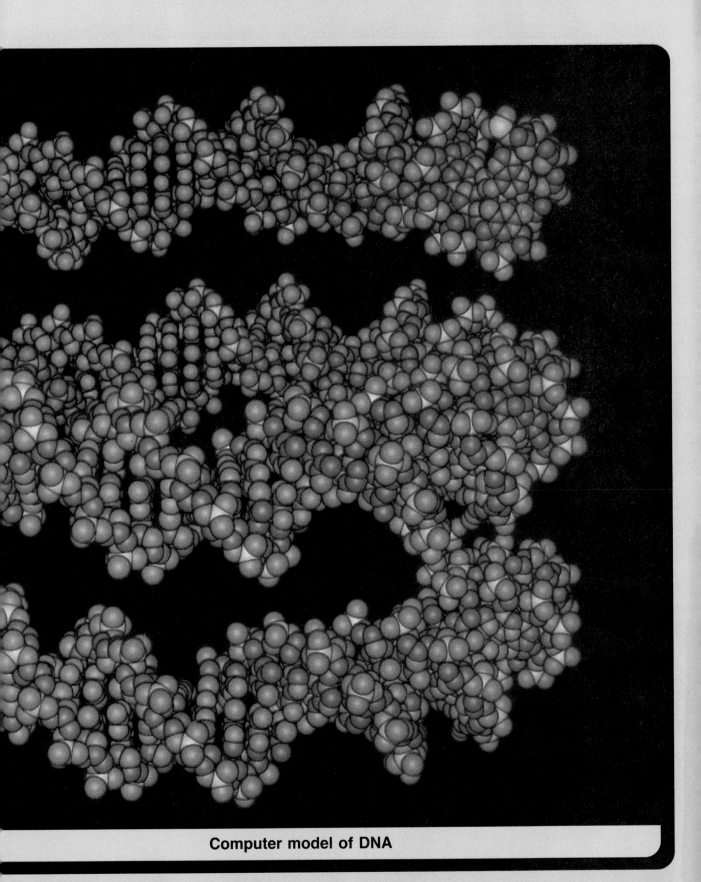

Computer model of DNA

Chapter 20
Producing New Organisms

Organisms reproduce more of their own kind. Reproduction may be by one parent or two. Every new organism begins life as a single cell, amoebas as well as these brown bear cubs. What structures in this single cell cause it to become a bear and not an amoeba? What is the name given to the process of cell division in single-parent reproduction?

Brown bear sow and cubs

Cells and Organisms

LESSON GOALS

In this lesson you will learn

- each cell of an organism has material that is different for each type of organism.
- how organisms grow.
- the stages of mitosis.
- about regeneration.

There are thousands of different kinds of organisms. Roses, frogs, mushrooms, amoebas, and bacteria are organisms. Each belongs to a different kingdom. Recall from Lesson 1:1 that all organisms have a similar basic structure. All organisms are composed of cells. An organism may be just a single cell such as an amoeba. An organism may be a group of similar cells such as a mushroom. An organism may be a complex system of different kinds of cells such as a frog.

Groups of similar cells make up the tissues of complex organisms. The muscles and skin of an animal are made of tissues. Tissues compose organs. The heart and brain are animal organs. The leaf of a plant is also an organ made up of several different tissues. The tissues of a leaf are made of groups of certain types of cells. Each cell, tissue, or organ aids in the survival of the organism.

What structures do all organisms have in common?

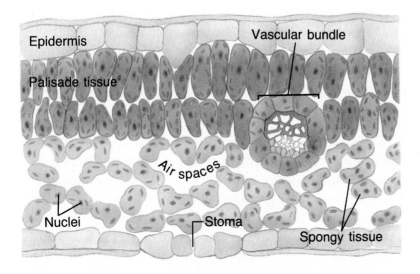

Figure 20-1. Organs such as leaves are composed of tissues.

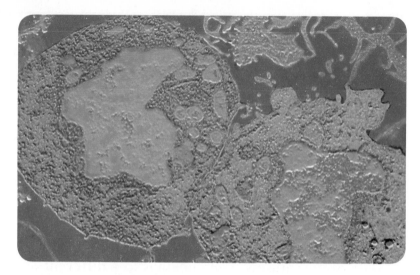

Parts of a Cell

Every organism begins life as a single cell. An amoeba is a one-celled organism throughout its life span. Complex organisms such as humans or orchids also begin life as one cell. All the complex tissues and organs of plants and animals develop from one cell.

All cells have similar parts. Look at the animal cell in Figure 20-2. Like most cells, it has a nucleus. The part of the cell that is outside the nucleus is called **cytoplasm.** Within the cytoplasm are many structures that control the features of life. The fluid part of the cytoplasm is called *cytosol.* Recall from Lesson 1:1 that the cell is surrounded by a covering called the cell membrane. The cell membrane regulates the movement of materials into and out of the cell. What are two other functions of the cell membrane?

The nucleus controls the activities of the cell. It is also surrounded by a membrane. The **nuclear membrane** separates the contents of the nucleus from those of the cytoplasm. This nuclear membrane has two layers and many tiny pores. Some products of the nucleus may pass through these holes into the cytoplasm. The nucleus contains chromatin. **Chromatin** (KROH mut un) is material in the cell that controls the appearance and type of the organism. The chromatin of a frog is different from that of a mushroom or a rose. Human chromatin is different from that of a dog or any other animal. Each type of frog, mushroom, or other organism has its own type

How do dogs and roses begin life?

Figure 20-3. Chromatin controls the appearance and type of an organism.

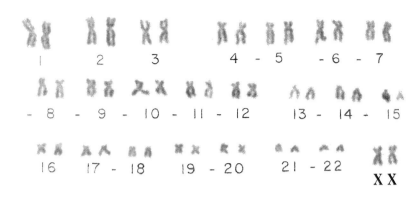

Figure 20-4. Human cells have 23 pairs of chromosomes.

of chromatin. Chromatin is spread throughout the nucleus. When a cell begins to divide, the chromatin becomes visible as fine threads that are called chromosomes (KROH muh sohmz).

A **chromosome** is a thread of chromatin that carries all the information about the organism. The chromosomes in a dividing cell can be seen with a light microscope. Each cell in the body of an organism has the same number of chromosomes. Each chromosome has a partner, and they form a pair. The number of chromosome pairs in species of plants and animals varies widely. For example, there are 4 chromosome pairs in a fruit fly, 500 pairs in one species of fern, 24 pairs in a potato, and 23 pairs in humans. Look at Figure 20-4. How many individual chromosomes are present in human cells? Each chromosome is able to make a copy of itself. A chromosome doubles by splitting down its length.

How many pairs of chromosomes does a human skin cell contain?

Figure 20-5. Cell division causes growth in many-celled organisms.

Cell Division

You know that kittens grow up to be cats. Oak trees grow from acorns. An increase in the number of cells of an organism causes growth. Many-celled organisms grow by cell division. When a cell divides, the chromosomes and the cytoplasm in the cell also divide. **Mitosis** (mi TOH sus) is the division of a cell into two new cells, each with the same number of chromosomes as the parent cell. In mitosis, the number of chromosomes is doubled, forming two pairs of each kind. The pairs are then divided equally between the two new cells.

Look at the process of mitosis in Figure 20–6. To make the process easy to follow, only three unpaired chromosomes are shown. The dividing cell passes through four stages of mitosis.

Stage 1. The chromosomes become visible. Each chromosome becomes doubled by splitting down its length. On each chromosome there is a structure called a **centromere.** Each doubled chromosome is held together at the centromere. At the end of this stage the nuclear membrane disappears.

Stage 2. The doubled chromosomes move to the center of the cell. The centromeres line up along the equator of the cell.

Stage 3. The centromeres split in half and each half moves to an opposite end of the cell. Each half of the doubled chromosomes is attached to one half of a centromere. The chromosomes move to the poles of the cell along with the centromeres.

Stage 4. The cytoplasm between the two sets of chromosomes becomes pinched apart. New cell membranes form between the two new cells. The cell divides into two. A nuclear membrane forms around each set of chromosomes. The chromosomes become invisible. Two new cells have formed. Each new cell has an exact copy of the original chromosomes.

What holds the doubled chromosomes together during the early stages of mitosis?

Figure 20–6. Mitosis has four stages.

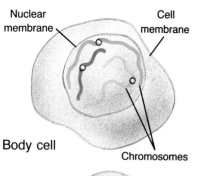

Nuclear membrane

Cell membrane

Body cell

Chromosomes

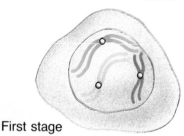

First stage

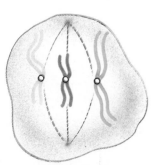

Second stage

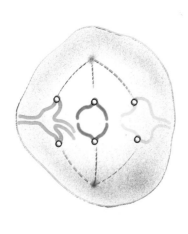

Third stage

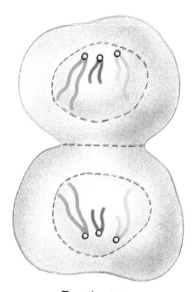

Fourth stage

Activity 20-1   A Model of Mitosis

QUESTION   How do cells divide?

Materials

1 50-cm string
construction paper
4 5-cm pieces blue yarn
4 5-cm pieces yellow yarn

scissors
tape
pencil and paper

What to do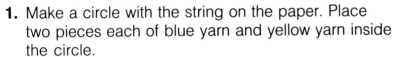

1. Make a circle with the string on the paper. Place two pieces each of blue yarn and yellow yarn inside the circle.

2. Place two more pieces each of blue and yellow yarn in the circle. Tape two pieces of blue yarn together at their center points. Tape the other two pieces of blue yarn together at their center points. Also tape the centers of the yellow yarn.

3. Remove the string circle from the paper. Place the pairs of blue and yellow yarn in the center of the paper so the tapes are together in a line.

4. Cut each tape lengthwise to separate the yarn pairs. Move one of each pair of blue and yellow yarn pieces to opposite sides of the paper.

5. Cut the string in half. Use each half to make a circle on the paper around each set of four yarn pieces.

6. Cut the paper in half between the two string circles.

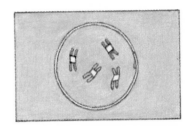

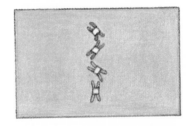

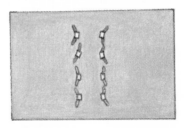

What did you learn?

1. What cell parts did the paper, the string, the tape, and the pieces of yarn represent?

2. Why were two yarn pieces of each color used in step 1?

3. How do steps 6 and 1 in your model compare?

Using what you learned

1. Use your model to explain how cells divide.

2. Explain how an organism, such as a human or a tree, grows larger.

What process allows an organism to grow and replace old cells?

Regeneration

Mitosis allows an organism to grow and to replace old or damaged cells. When the body of an organism is damaged, the cells around the area divide by mitosis until the tissue or organ is repaired. This process is known as regeneration. **Regeneration** is the regrowth of the damaged tissues of an organism. When a starfish loses an arm, when a salamander loses its tail, or when you scrape the skin on your knee, new cells are produced by regeneration. A starfish can regrow a missing arm, a salamander may regrow its tail, and the damaged skin on your knee will be replaced by new skin. Tissues and organs of plants, such as roots or stems, can also be regenerated.

Lesson Summary

- The nucleus of a cell contains chromatin that controls the appearance and type of each organism.
- Organisms grow by a method of cell division called mitosis.
- In mitosis, the chromosomes are copied and divided equally between the two new cells.
- Damaged tissues can be replaced by regeneration.

Lesson Review

Review the lesson to answer these questions.
1. What is chromatin?
2. Which types of chromosomes separate during mitosis: paired or doubled?
3. How many stages are there in mitosis?
4. How is the skin repaired over a scraped knee?

Artificial Skin

How does it feel when you burn your finger? Usually it becomes red and may be painful for a day. People with third-degree burns are not as fortunate. With a third-degree burn, the inner layer of skin, the dermis, and the outer layer, the epidermis, are both destroyed. A severely burned person needs an immediate supply of fluids, and pigskin is sometimes used as a temporary covering. The covering keeps fluids from being lost by exposed muscle tissue. Protection also reduces the possibility of infection.

Many people have died from third-degree burns. Once destroyed, the dermis and epidermis cannot grow back. If skin is replaced, it is by a process called skin grafting, which is slow, uncomfortable, and leaves scars.

Researchers are working to develop artificial skin. In one project, a piece of epidermis the size of a postage stamp is taken from a part of the patient's body that is not burned. It is put in a special growth solution in the laboratory. The cells divide by mitosis and the size of the patch grows. A newly-grown sheet of epidermis is placed on the burned area and covered. The wound develops a covering of epidermal cells. There is no dermis, however.

Other researchers are trying to make skin that will have both dermis and epidermis. Tiny samples of undamaged epidermis are taken from the patient and embedded or seeded in sheets of artificial dermis. These sheets are quickly bandaged to the patient. Results show that in less than two weeks, a new two-layered skin has begun to grow. This new skin has no hair follicles, sweat glands, or pigment cells. However, it may speed the healing of wounds and save lives.

LESSON GOALS

In this lesson you will learn

- organisms reproduce.
- reproduction may be from one parent or from two parents.
- methods of reproduction by one parent.
- the process of reproduction by two parents.
- a zygote develops into an embryo that is often protected during development.

What is reproduction?

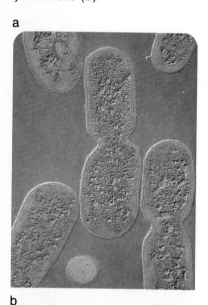
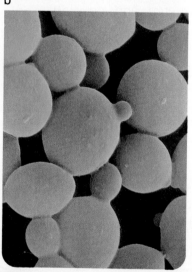

Figure 20–8. Reproduction by one parent occurs by fission in bacteria (a) and budding in yeast cells (b).

a

b

All organisms begin life as one cell. This single cell is formed from organisms that are mature. A mature organism may make new organisms that are copies of itself.

Reproduction is the process of organisms producing new organisms of their own kind. Recall from Lesson 1:1 that reproduction is one of the six features of life. Organisms reproduce. Reproduction allows the characteristics of an organism to be passed on from parent to offspring. Reproduction may require one parent or two parents.

Reproduction by One Parent

When one-celled organisms reproduce, they usually split in half. Each half grows and eventually reproduces again. **Fission** is the equal splitting by mitosis of a one-celled organism into two new one-celled organisms. Reproduction of organisms such as an amoeba or paramecium occurs by this simple method of mitosis. Reproduction by one parent is also common in bacteria and some algae. The offspring are exact copies of the parent. They have exactly the same kind of chromatin as the parent.

Some organisms can reproduce with one parent by budding. **Budding** is the production of offspring by outgrowths of the parent. In yeasts and some protozoans, the two cells formed by mitosis do not separate immediately. One cell is usually smaller than the other because the cytoplasm divides unequally.

Before the two cells pinch apart, a third cell may bud off from the larger cell. Budding also occurs in animals such as sea anemones. They reproduce by outgrowths of the body wall. The buds develop into young sea anemones. The outgrowths eventually fall off. The offspring are identical to the parent.

In plants, reproduction by one parent is common. New plants can develop from small pieces of a single plant. **Vegetative reproduction** is the formation of new plants from a body part of a single parent plant. There are many kinds of vegetative reproduction. Many plants in the tropical rain forest grow on tree branches. Some have runners that hang down from the parent. These runners are long thin stems that grow from the main stem of a plant. At the end of the runner, a new plant grows. As the runner gets longer, the young plant may touch another branch. The roots become attached to the new branch. Eventually the runner to the parent plant rots away.

Many grasses and weeds undergo vegetative reproduction by rhizomes. Rhizomes are stems that grow under the ground. New roots and leaves grow from this underground stem. Bulbs that you may plant in your garden, such as those for tulips and daffodils, are also organs of vegetative reproduction. At the end of flowering time, new bulbs form around the old bulb. The next spring there will be more flowers than there were the year before. A new plant grows from each new bulb. Look at Figure 20-9. What do you think happens when you put a potato into the ground?

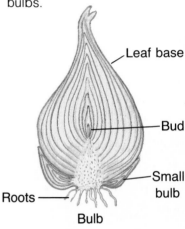

Figure 20-9. Vegetative reproduction may involve rhizomes, runners, tubers, or bulbs.

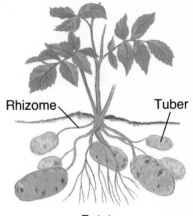

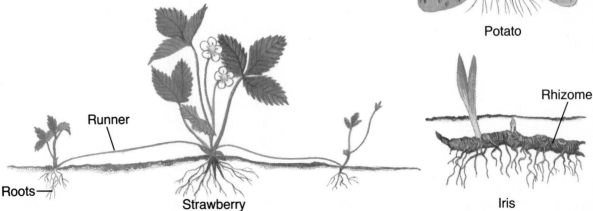

405

Activity 20-2 Vegetative Reproduction

QUESTION   How do plants reproduce from one parent?

Materials

sweet potato   small glass jar
large glass jar   water
toothpicks   pencil and paper
plant cutting

What to do

1. Place a sweet potato in a jar of water so at least half of it is underwater. Use toothpicks to hold the potato in position, if needed.
2. Keep the jar and potato in a dark place for a few days. After some roots have formed, place the jar in a warm, lighted area.
3. Place the plant stem cutting into another glass jar. Half fill the jar with water. Put the jar in a warm, lighted area.
4. Observe the sweet potato and plant cutting several times a week for three weeks. Add water to the sweet potato, if necessary. Replace the water around the plant cutting every other day.
5. Record your observations each week

What did you learn?

1. What changes did you observe in the sweet potato and the plant cutting?
2. What was the new growth in the sweet potato?
3. What was the new growth in the plant cutting?

Using what you learned

1. Compare the new growth of your plant cutting with those of your classmates.
2. If you planted the sweet potato and plant cutting into soil, what do you think would happen?
3. From what part of the sweet potato will new tubers grow?

Reproduction by Two Parents

Most species of plants, animals, and fungi reproduce by two parents. The offspring of this kind of reproduction are not exact copies of either parent. They have some characteristics of both parents. Different offspring of the same two parents usually have different characteristics. Think about sets of brothers or sisters you know. How are they different? Remember that all organisms develop from one cell. In organisms with two parents, this first cell is formed by the combination of one cell from each parent. The cells from the parents are formed by a special kind of cell division called meiosis (mi OH sus).

Meiosis is the process of cell division that results in cells with half the number of chromosomes of body cells. Body cells contain pairs of chromosomes. Each pair is made up of one chromosome from each parent. Both chromosomes in the pair control the same characteristics. One pair of chromosomes in an animal may control length of fur, color of eyes and hair, and size of ears. Another pair may control length of toes, type of teeth, and number of whiskers. The features of one species are controlled by pairs of chromosomes that are found in all individuals of that species. Meiosis ensures that the offspring receive the same number of chromosome pairs as their parents.

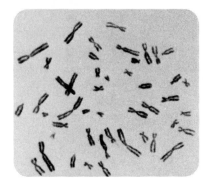

Figure 20-10. Body cells of organisms contain pairs of chromosomes.

What is the importance of meiosis in reproduction by two parents?

Figure 20-11. The traits of offspring are controlled by chromosomes from the parents.

In meiosis there are two cell division processes, not one as in mitosis. The first division is called meiosis I. This is followed by meiosis II. Look at Figure 20–12.

Meiosis I

How is the number of
chromosomes changed in
meiosis I?

In meiosis I, the chromosome number is halved. There are four stages.

Stage 1. The chromosomes become visible and pairs of similar chromosomes come together.

Stage 2. The chromosomes of each pair double. Each doubled chromosome is held together by the centromere. The pairs of chromosomes are not joined together but are positioned side-by-side. At the end of this stage the nuclear membrane disappears.

Stage 3. The pairs of doubled chromosomes move to the center of the cell. The centromeres line up on the equator.

Stage 4. The pairs of doubled chromosomes then move apart. They move to opposite poles of the cell. The centromeres do not split apart in this stage. Therefore, half the number of chromosomes are present in each half of the cell. The cytoplasm between the two groups of chromosomes is pinched apart. A new membrane forms between the two new cells. There are now two separate cells. This is the end of meiosis I.

Figure 20–12. There are two cell division processes in meiosis: meiosis I and meiosis II.

First Division

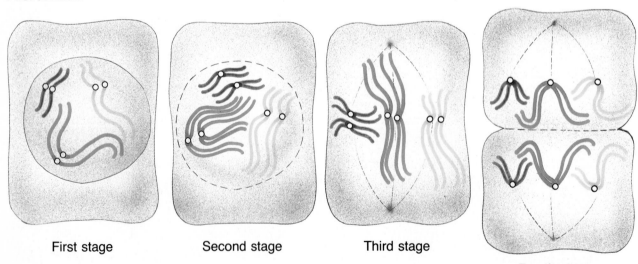

First stage   Second stage   Third stage

Fourth stage

Meiosis II

Meiosis II immediately follows meiosis I. The nuclear membrane does not form around the two new sets of chromosomes. In meiosis II, each of the two cells divides again. There are three stages, and they are similar to those in mitosis.

Stage 1. The centromeres of the doubled chromosomes line up along the equator of the cell.

Stage 2. The centromeres split in half and move to opposite poles. Each has one half of a doubled chromosome attached to it.

Stage 3. The cytoplasm between the two sets of chromosomes is pinched apart. Cell membranes form between the two cells. Nuclear membranes form around each of the four sets of chromosomes. Four cells are produced in this stage.

In what stage of meiosis does the nuclear membrane form?

Each cell has one half the original chromosome number for the species. Each cell has one unpaired chromosome of each type. Cells produced by meiosis in humans have 23 chromosomes in each. How do the four cells in the third stage of meiosis II compare with the first stage of meiosis I? In the males of a species, meiosis produces **sperm** cells. Meiosis in females of a species produces **egg** cells. How many chromosomes do egg cells have compared with sperm cells?

Second Division

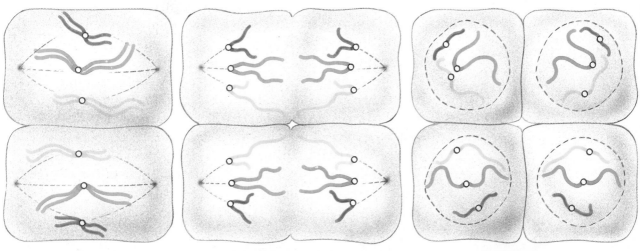

First stage   Second stage   Third stage

In two parent reproduction, what part of the offspring's chromosomes come from each parent?

Figure 20-13. Fertilization of an egg by a sperm (a) results in a zygote that divides (b) to form an embryo.

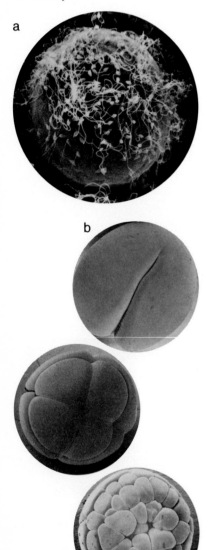

a

b

Some species, such as earthworms and many plants, can produce both sperm cells and egg cells in the same individual. Most animals and some plants produce sperm and eggs in separate male and female individuals. How many chromosomes do egg and sperm cells have compared with body cells? Each egg and each sperm contains one chromosome of each pair. During meiosis, small parts of chromosomes may be exchanged between the pairs. The characteristics of both parents are mixed in the offspring. This causes the offspring to be different from each other and from their parents. Differences in organisms cause changes in a species over time. Differences may aid the survival of all species if the environment changes. What may happen to a species that is no longer suited to its environment?

In reproduction, one egg unites with one sperm, bringing the pairs of chromosomes back together. **Fertilization** is the uniting of an egg with a sperm to form one cell. The **zygote** (ZI goht) is the cell that results from the combination of one egg and one sperm cell. A new organism grows from the zygote. The number of chromosomes in all the body cells of the new organism is the same as that in the body cells of each parent. In each offspring, exactly half of the chromosomes come from one parent and exactly half come from the other parent.

In the early stages of growth an organism is called an **embryo.** A mass of cells develops from the zygote as it divides by mitosis. Look at Figure 20-13. Observe the early divisions of a zygote. The mass of cells eventually develops into tissues and organs. Developing embryos are usually protected. The embryo may be protected by a layer of jelly, such as in fish and frogs. The fertilized eggs must be laid in water to prevent them from drying out. In reptiles and birds the embryos are protected by a shell. The shell protects the embryo from drying out on land. In most mammals, the body of the female parent is the protection for embryos.

The number of eggs produced by fish and amphibians is much greater than that produced by reptiles, birds, or mammals. There is generally very little care of the young by parent amphibians and fish. Mammals produce fewer offspring than reptiles and birds. Mammals provide more parental care for their young than other animals. Extra parental care increases the chance of offspring survival. As animals grow, they learn to take care of themselves.

The embryos of plants are also protected. Seed-bearing plants develop a thickened layer of cells called a seed coat around the embryo. Some seeds can remain in the soil for hundreds of years before germinating. Other seeds can live for only a few days. In many seed plants the number of seeds produced is very large. This increases chances of reproduction. An oak tree may produce hundreds of acorns but only a few will survive to grow into adult trees. Many will not drop onto suitable soil, while others are eaten by animals. Plants with a large number of seeds have a better chance of reproducing than do those with few seeds.

Figure 20-14. Lotus seeds are protected by a pod until they are scattered.

Why do hundreds of acorns result in only a few oak trees?

Lesson Summary

- Organisms reproduce new organisms of their own kind.
- Reproduction from one parent is by mitosis, and from two parents is by meiosis.
- Fission, budding, and vegetative reproduction are methods of reproduction by one parent.
- Fertilization of eggs by sperm and growth of the zygote occurs in reproduction by two parents.
- Animal embryos may be protected by jelly, shells, or the body of the female parent. Plant embryos are protected by a seed coat.

Lesson Review

Review the lesson to answer these questions.
1. How do sea anemones and yeast reproduce by one parent?
2. How is the third stage of the first division in meiosis similar to the first stage of the second division?
3. What is the protective layer of a plant embryo?

Language Arts Skills

Summarizing a Paragraph

The textbooks you use contain a large amount of useful information. You are not expected to remember every word of each book. You are, however, expected to learn the main points. One way to find the main points is to make a summary.

When summarizing a paragraph, you need to determine its main idea or theme. This idea may be stated in one or more sentences and may be located anywhere within the paragraph. Several details will usually be included in the paragraph to describe or support the main idea. When summarizing, you should select details that provide an example of the main idea.

Read the following paragraph. The main idea is underlined.

- In the early stages of growth, an organism is called an **embryo.** A mass of cells develops from the zygote as it divides by mitosis. Developing embryos are usually protected.[1] The embryo may be protected by a layer of jelly, such as in fish and frogs. The fertilized eggs must be laid in water to prevent them from drying out.[2] In reptiles and birds, the embryos are protected by a shell. The shell protects the embryo from drying out on land.[3] In mammals, the body of the female parent is the protection for embryos.

Notice that the boldfaced term and its definition are underlined. Boldfaced terms should always be included in a summary. Any one of the examples in the sentences marked 1, 2, or 3 could also be included. The other details are left out. A summary should be stated as simply as possible in your own words.

Write a one-sentence summary of
- paragraph 1, page 398, and
- paragraph 3, page 404.

Chapter 20 Review

Summary

1. The cell is the basic unit of organisms. 20:1
2. Most types of cells have cell membranes, cytoplasm, nuclei, nuclear membranes and chromatin. 20:1
3. Chromatin is a material in the nucleus of a cell that controls the appearance and type of each organism. 20:1
4. Organisms grow by a method of cell division called mitosis. 20:1
5. Mitosis is the division of body cells into two cells with the same number of chromosomes as the parent cell. 20:1
6. Organisms can replace damaged tissues by regeneration. 20:1
7. Organisms reproduce new organisms of their own kind. 20:2
8. Fission, budding, and vegetative reproduction are methods of reproduction by one parent. 20:2
9. Reproduction from one parent is by mitosis, and from two parents by meiosis. 20:2
10. Meiosis produces egg cells in the female and sperm cells in the male of the species. 20:2
11. In the early stages of development, an organism is called an embryo. 20:2
12. An embryo grows from the zygote formed when a sperm fertilizes an egg. 20:2
13. Animal embryos can be protected by jelly, shells, or the body of the female parent, while plant embryos are protected by a seed coat. 20:2

Science Words

budding	embryo	regeneration
centromere	fertilization	reproduction
chromatin	fission	sperm
chromosome	meiosis	vegetative reproduction
cytoplasm	mitosis	zygote
egg	nuclear membrane	

Understanding Science Words

Complete each of the following sentences with a word or words from the Science Words that will make the sentence correct.

1. An organism produces more of its own kind by _____.

2. The material that controls the kind and appearance of an organism is _____.
3. The production of a new organism from an outgrowth of the parent is known as _____.
4. In the female of the species, meiosis produces an _____ cell.
5. The part of the cell outside the nucleus is _____.
6. In the male of the species, meiosis produces _____ cells.
7. The regrowth of damaged tissues of an organism is _____.
8. The cell that results when an egg and sperm unite is a _____.
9. The formation of new plants from a body part of a single parent plant is _____.
10. The contents of the nucleus are separated from the cytoplasm by the _____.
11. A many-celled organism in the early stages of development is an _____.
12. One egg and one sperm join to form one cell in _____.
13. A thread of chromatin that carries all the information about an organism is a _____.
14. The equal splitting by mitosis of a one-celled organism into a two-celled organism is _____.
15. Cell division that produces cells with half the number of chromosomes in the parent cell is _____.
16. Doubled chromosomes are held together at the _____.
17. A cell divides into two cells, each having the same number of chromosomes as the parent cell, in the process of _____.

Questions

A. Checking Facts
Determine whether each of the following is true or false. Rewrite the false statements to make them correct.
1. Every organism begins life as a single cell.
2. Fertilization, fission, and budding are all forms of reproduction by one parent.
3. Cytoplasm is the fluid part of a cell.

4. In meiosis, the cells produced have half the number of chromosomes of the cell that divided.
5. Many-celled organisms grow by mitosis.
6. Damaged tissues can be replaced by budding.
7. Fission may involve rhizomes, runners, tubers, or bulbs.
8. Meiosis ensures that the offspring receive the same number of chromosome pairs as their parents.
9. As a group, mammals provide more parental care for their young than other animals.

B. Recalling Facts

Choose the word or phrase that correctly completes each of the following sentences.

1. How many pairs of chromosomes do human body cells have?
   (a) 150   (b) 46   (c) 23   (d)4
2. Organisms can repair damaged tissues or regrow body parts by
   (a) meiosis.   (b) budding.   (c) fission.   (d) regeneration.
3. The control center of the cell is the
   (a) nucleus.   (b) chromatin.   (c) cytosol.   (d) cytoplasm.
4. The process of combining an egg cell with a sperm cell is
   (a) meiosis.   (b) mitosis.   (c) fertilization.   (d) fission.
5. A potato reproduces by
   (a) fission.   (c) vegetative reproduction.
   (b) budding.   (d) bulbs.
6. Doubled chromosomes are held together at the
   (a) nuclear membrane.   (c) centromere.
   (b) chromatin.   (d) cytoplasm.

C. Understanding Concepts

Answer each of the following questions using complete sentences.
1. Briefly describe the process of mitosis.
2. What is fertilization, and why is meiosis important in this process?
3. List the methods of reproduction by one parent.

D. Applying Concepts

Think about what you have learned in this chapter. Answer each of the following questions using complete sentences.
1. How are mitosis and meiosis alike? How are they different?
2. How is the amount of protection an embryo has related to the number of embryos an organism produces?

Chapter 21
Inheriting Traits

In any population produced by two-parent reproduction, there is some variation in traits in the offspring. The one exception is identical twins. Even in this field of poppies, there are differences in plant height, leaf shape, and other features. What is the basic unit of heredity? Why may the offspring of two brown-eyed parents not always have brown eyes?

California poppies, New Mexico

LESSON GOALS

In this lesson you will learn

- offspring inherit traits from parents.
- traits are controlled by genes.
- genes may be dominant, recessive, or expressed equally.
- traits can be predicted using a Punnett square.

Organisms reproduce their own kind. The offspring have characteristics like those of their parents. A **trait** is a characteristic of an organism that is passed from parents to offspring. If you look closely at a population, such as oak trees, alligators, or students, you will notice individual traits. An offspring of two humans may inherit red hair, freckles, and a broad nose. An offspring of two other humans may inherit black hair, dark skin, and a narrow nose.

Heredity is the passing of traits from parents to offspring. Traits of an organism are controlled by the chromatin in the nucleus of each cell. Recall from Lesson 20:2 that half of the chromatin comes from one parent and half comes from the other parent.

The first well-known study of heredity was done by Gregor Mendel in the 1800s. He grew garden pea plants and made observations of the traits inherited by their offspring. To produce offspring of the pea plants, Mendel crossed one type of pea plant with another. Crossing is the process of transferring sperm from one parent to fertilize an egg of another parent. Mendel compared the traits of parent plants with those of their offspring. Mendel carried out careful scientific experiments using different parents to produce different offspring. From these data he hypothesized how traits are inherited. Mendel thought that traits were passed on by "factors." These factors later became known as genes. The science of heredity is now known as genetics. **Genetics** is the study of how genes are inherited.

What material in the cell controls the traits of an organism?

What is crossing?

Figure 21–1. All dogs have certain traits in common. They have other traits that make them different from one another.

Inheriting Traits

What is a gene?

What is the smallest number of genes that controls a trait?

Recall from Lesson 20:2 that during meiosis, the pairs of chromosomes are separated. An offspring receives one of each pair of chromosomes from each parent. The different traits of individual organisms are controlled by small portions of the chromosomes. A **gene** is a part of a chromosome that controls the traits of an organism. Genes on one chromosome control the same traits as those on the other chromosome of the pair. For example, the color of a flower may be controlled by one pair of genes. One gene is on one chromosome of the pair. It comes from one parent. The other gene is located on the second chromosome of the pair. The second gene is inherited from the other parent. In some flowers, the flower color may be only red or white. One pair of genes controls the color of these flowers. Most traits are controlled by two or more pairs of genes. Height in humans, coat color in guinea pigs, and leaf shape in many plants are all examples of traits controlled by more than one gene pair.

The traits of parents are passed on to their offspring by their genes. Offspring do not show all the traits of both parents. They have some traits like one parent and some like the other parent. Sometimes they have traits that are not like either parent. How might this occur?

Figure 21–2. Mendel studied crosses of violet-flowered and white-flowered pea plants.

Expressing Traits

When Mendel crossed a pea plant that had violet flowers with one that had white flowers, all the offspring had violet flowers. Similarly, when an orange Bengal tiger is crossed with a white Bengal tiger, the offspring may all be orange. All of the violet-flowered plant offspring and orange tiger offspring have hidden traits. The hidden trait in the violet-flowered plant offspring is the trait for white flowers. What is the hidden trait in the orange tiger offspring?

Mendel called a hidden trait a recessive trait. The gene that controls a hidden trait is said to be a **recessive gene.** The other genes of these pairs are

418

said to be dominant. A **dominant gene** is one whose trait is always expressed. The dominant gene hides the trait controlled by the recessive gene.

The recessive trait is expressed only when both genes in the pair are recessive. The recessive trait cannot be expressed in the presence of a dominant gene. White-flowered pea plants have a pair of recessive genes. If at least one gene of the pair is dominant, the pea flowers will be violet. The white tiger also has a pair of recessive genes that controls its fur color. What combinations of genes may be present in the gene pairs of the orange tiger?

Look at Figure 21–4. The genes for fur color in Bengal tigers occur on a pair of chromosomes. When the dominant gene is present, the tiger is orange. The white tiger has a pair of recessive genes for white fur. In each tiger, one gene for fur color came from its mother and one gene came from its father. A **pure trait** is a trait that results when both genes in the pair are alike. The pair of genes may both be recessive, as in the white tiger. A pure trait also results when both genes are dominant. A **hybrid trait** is a trait that results when the genes in a pair are different. Look at the tiger with the hybrid trait. The orange color in the tiger with one recessive and one dominant gene is a hybrid trait. An organism with a hybrid trait will look just like one that is pure for the dominant gene.

Consider another example. Striped and nonstriped silk moths are mated. Their offspring all have stripes. Thus, stripes are a dominant trait. The offspring have either the pure or hybrid trait for stripes.

Figure 21-3. White Bengal tigers are rare animals.

When does a hybrid trait result?

Figure 21-4. The genes present in chromosomes determine the fur color of Bengal tigers.

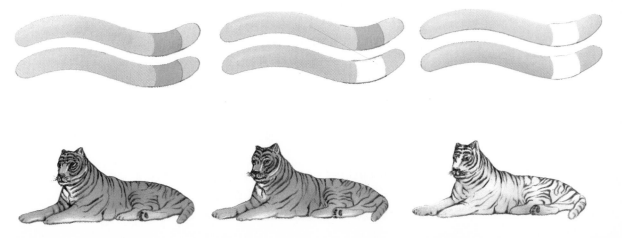

419

Activity 21-1   Inheritance

Materials

pencil and paper   mirror

What to do

1. Look at the dominant and recessive traits below.

Comparing Traits	
Dominant Trait	**Recessive Trait**
Dimples Free earlobes Can roll tongue into U-shape Hair on middle section of finger Space between front teeth Non-red hair	No dimples Attached earlobes Cannot roll tongue into U-shape No hair on middle section of finger No space between front teeth Red hair

2. Observe and record the number of people in your class that show the dominant or recessive traits listed in the table.

3. By using a mirror include your own traits in your observations.

What did you learn?

1. Which dominant traits are common in your class? Which recessive traits?
2. Are dominant or recessive traits more common?

Using what you learned

1. Why do you think some dominant traits are not common?
2. If two parents have red hair, predict the hair color of all their offspring. Explain.

Figure 21-5. Some genes are expressed together, as in the roan coat color of some cows.

Some genes are neither dominant nor recessive. The inheritance of red or white coat color in cows and horses is not like that of white or orange fur in tigers. When a red cow and a white cow are crossed, the offspring does not have a red or a white coat. The offspring will have red and white hairs, a coloring called roan. In this example, the red or white coat is a pure trait. The roan coat is a hybrid trait. The genes in the pair that control coat color are neither dominant nor recessive. When there is no dominance, the genes are expressed together. The offspring of two roan cows or horses are red, white, or roan. These offspring show that the roan coat color is not controlled by a separate gene.

What happens if there is no dominant gene?

Predicting Traits

Mendel hypothesized that factors, or genes, are inherited separately. Because genes in a pair are inherited separately, it is possible to predict the traits of offspring. In the cross between violet- and white-flowered pea plants, all the offspring had violet flowers. To show how a pair of genes are inherited, symbols are used. Each gene of a pair, such as for flower color, is given the same letter. When one gene is dominant, such as for violet pea flowers, it is written as a capital letter. The recessive gene, such as for white pea flowers, is written as a lowercase letter. In a pea plant that is pure for violet flowers, the two dominant genes may be written as *VV*. The pair of recessive genes in the pea plants pure for white flowers is then written as *vv*. The gene pair for hybrid violet flowers is written as *Vv*.

Figure 21-6. Symbols are used to represent the genes found in chromosomes.

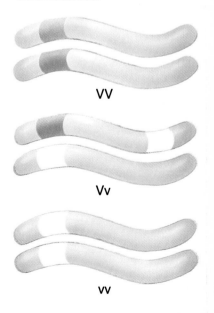

VV

Vv

vv

421

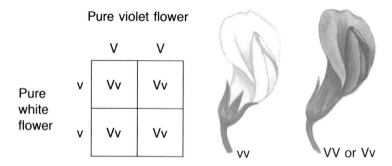

Figure 21-7. Punnett squares are used to predict traits of offspring.

Pure violet flower

	V	V
v	Vv	Vv
v	Vv	Vv

Pure white flower

vv   VV or Vv

The offspring of a cross between a pure, violet-flowered pea plant, and a pure, white-flowered pea plant can be predicted in a checkerboard diagram called a Punnett square. Look at Figure 21–7. The genes of the parents are shown outside the Punnett square. These genes are inherited in the sperm or egg of the parents.

The four boxes within the square show every possible combination of gene pairs that an offspring could inherit. All the offspring, or 100 percent, of a cross between pure, violet-flowered pea plants and pure, white-flowered pea plants will have the hybrid trait. What color will all of the flowers be? From a Punnett square such as this, you can predict the genes in the pair and the traits of the offspring. Recall from the table in Activity 21–1 that the gene for dimples is dominant. What percentage of offspring will inherit dimples in a cross between a person with the pure trait for dimples and a person with the hybrid trait for dimples?

A Punnett square can also be used to predict the percentage of offspring with a certain trait when both parents are hybrid for that trait. The symbol L can be used to represent the dominant gene for free earlobes in a person. The symbol l represents the recessive gene for attached earlobes. Consider a cross between two people, both with the hybrid trait. The gene pairs and appearance of the offspring can be predicted in a Punnett square. Look at Figure 21–8.

Notice that only one of the boxes has a recessive gene pair. The offspring that receive this pair will have the pure recessive trait of attached earlobes. We can predict that one in every four offspring will have

What do the four boxes of a Punnett square show?

If both parent gene pairs are hybirds, what part of the offspring will have the pure recessive trait?

422

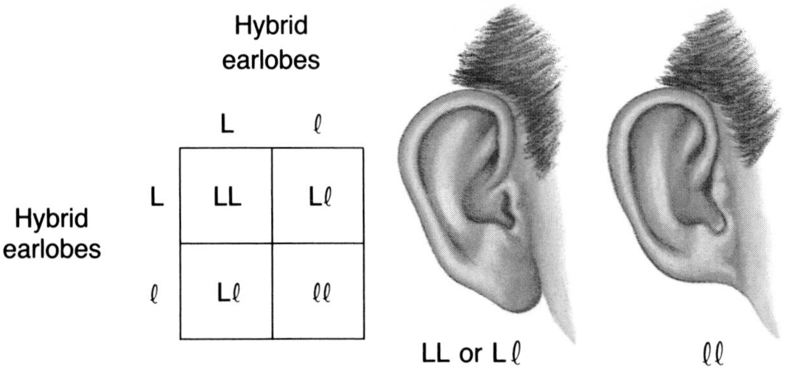

Hybrid earlobes

	L	ℓ
L	LL	Lℓ
ℓ	Lℓ	ℓℓ

Hybrid earlobes

LL or Lℓ   ℓℓ

Figure 21-8. The percentage of all offspring with a certain trait, such as free earlobes, can be predicted using a Punnett square.

attached earlobes. This is the same as saying that 25 percent of the offspring will have the pure recessive trait of attached earlobes. What percentage of the offspring will have free earlobes? What percentage will have the hybrid trait for earlobe types?

The results in Figure 21-8 do not mean that out of four offspring, one *will always* have attached earlobes. The prediction means that each offspring has one *chance* in four of having attached lobes. Consider tossing a coin. Though the chance of heads is 50%, many tosses may be needed to show this.

Lesson Summary

- Individuals of a population inherit different traits.
- Pairs of chromosomes contain pairs of genes that control traits.
- Dominant genes may be expressed over recessive genes, or expressed together with the recessive gene.
- A Punnett square can be used to predict the gene pairs and appearance of offspring.

Lesson Review

Review the lesson to answer these questions.
1. What is heredity?
2. Why is the white Bengal tiger rare?
3. Predict the percentage of offspring that will have attached earlobes when there is a cross between a pure recessive and a hybrid for attached earlobes.

LESSON GOALS

In this lesson you will learn

- genes in a population may be changed over time.
- some inherited traits may be altered.
- how humans have carried out selective breeding of plants and animals.
- genes of one species can be transferred to a different species.

Figure 21-9. Desert plants are specially adapted to dry conditions and may not reproduce if grown under different conditions.

How are the genes of a population passed on?

The gene pairs that control the different forms of traits are present throughout populations of organisms. For example, in a field of clover some plants may be short and some tall, some flowers may be red and some white, some stems may be hairy and some smooth. Most of the differences in traits can be seen in a population. Individual differences are evidence of the inheritance of dominant and recessive genes. The genes in a population are passed on in the chromosomes of egg and sperm cells from one generation to the next.

When an organism is adapted or suited to its environment it has a better chance of survival. Recall from Lesson 17:1 that organisms are adapted to certain habitats. Adaptations allow organisms to survive and reproduce. If a desert cactus were planted in a tropical rain forest, it would not survive. The conditions are too dark and wet. A cactus is adapted to a dry, hot habitat. Changes in habitats are common. Many changes are caused by humans. If species of organisms cannot adapt to changes in the environment, what will happen to them?

Mutations

What is a mutation?

Changes in genes occur often in populations. A **mutation** is a change in the genes that can cause a new trait to appear. Most mutations produce very small changes in each organism. The effect of these small mutations may not be seen for several generations.

424

Many genes control minor traits that neither harm nor benefit an organism. For example, the number of hairs on a stem of a clover plant may not harm or benefit the plant. Other genes are more important to the survival of an organism. For example, certain insects may be attracted by a particular flower color such as red. If an individual plant did not have red flowers, it would not be visited by as many insects. The flowers might not be pollinated, and seeds might not form. When this plant died, there would be no offspring carrying its genes. Suppose the plant that died had yellow flowers. Because the gene for yellow flowers would still be present in hybrid plants, it would remain in the population. If the insect population in the field of flowers changed, the yellow flower color might become an advantage in attracting a different kind of insect.

Some gene mutations are more harmful than the flower color-insect example. In some plants, such as corn, offspring may form that have no green pigment or chlorophyll. Without chlorophyll the plant cannot make food. As soon as the stored food in the seed is used up, the plant dies. The corn and flower color are two examples of natural selection. **Natural selection** is the process by which organisms less adapted to their environment tend to die, and better-adapted organisms tend to survive. Natural selection ensures the passing on of genes that are most adapted to a particular environment.

Why is chlorophyll important to a plant?

What is the importance of natural selection?

Figure 21-10. Mutations can make organisms less adapted to their environments and less likely to survive or reproduce.

Parent

	A	A
A	AA	AA
a	Aa	Aa

Parent

Figure 21-11. This cross shows how a recessive trait can remain hidden in a population.

Figure 21-12. Each species of woodpecker is adapted to a certain habitat and food source.

Natural Selection

All organisms in a population are not equally adapted to a habitat. Some do not survive, while others are more likely to reproduce. For example, in a population of plants with the gene pair *AA*, a mutation in the sperm or eggs may form the new gene pair *Aa*. Look at Figure 21-11 for the predicted offspring of a cross between the *Aa* plants and the more common *AA* plants. What percentage of the offspring would you expect to be *Aa*? The new gene *a* can remain in the population as a hidden trait even though it may be harmful to the individual in the pure form. Which parents could be crossed to produce pure recessive offspring? The survival of individuals with the recessive *a* gene is important if the environment changes. The pure *aa* trait may make the organism better adapted than the *AA* trait.

The importance of mutations to the survival of a species has been shown in studies of many plants and animals. Changes in the genes of a population cause changes in the traits of individuals. When their environments change, populations gradually become extinct or adapt to the new environment. Hidden and uncommon traits in a population aid the adaptation of a species. Recall from Lesson 15:2 that types of organisms have changed throughout Earth's history. Changes in the types of organisms on Earth are the result of adaptations and natural selection.

What processes have brought about changes in the types of organisms on Earth?

Figure 21-13. A mutation in gray peppered moths to a dark-colored form aided their survival in a changing environment.

Changes in a population caused by changes in the environment have been shown in peppered moths in England. Peppered moths occur throughout Europe. In rural areas of England they are gray and spotted. The moths are hard to see when they rest on trees. In the 1800s many factories were built in the northern cities of England. Pollution from the factories caused the bark of trees to turn black. By the 1950s, the populations of peppered moths in cities with factories were found to have large numbers of dark-colored mutant moths. Birds that fed on the moths could see the gray spotted moths but not the black ones. More black moths than gray moths survived and reproduced. The change in the city environment made the black moths better adapted than the gray moths. In the 1960s, pollution control laws were passed in England. The cities became less polluted. Data from studies done since the laws were passed show that there are now more gray moths than black moths. Once the easy prey of birds in the polluted cities, more gray peppered moths can now survive in the cleaner cities.

Mutations in populations of organisms can be observed in many species. In some species, such as the peppered moths, the studies take many years. In simple organisms, such as bacteria, several generations may be produced in a few hours. Therefore, the chances of observing mutations in bacteria are higher than in more complex organisms. Mutations in bacteria have decreased the effects of the drug penicillin. Bacterial infections are sometimes treated with penicillin. Some bacteria that cause infections have mutated and become resistant to penicillin. Other drugs must be used to treat these infections.

Why is it easier to observe mutations in bacteria than in other organisms?

Figure 21-14. Some bacteria have mutated, becoming resistant to the penicillin on the central disc in the agar plate.

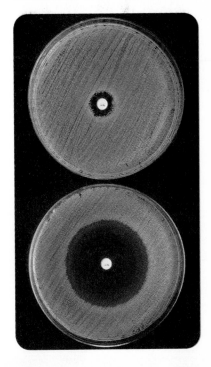

Activity 21-2 Gene Inheritance

Materials

masking tape
two coins
pencil and paper

What to do

Part A

1. Tallness is a dominant trait in pea plants. Let *T* represent tallness. Let *t* represent shortness.
2. Two plants that are hybrid, *Tt,* for the tallness trait are mated. Draw a Punnett square to show the possible gene pairs that may occur in the offspring.

Part B

1. Put a small piece of tape on each side of two coins. Let each coin represent one of the plants in part A.
2. Mark a *T* on one side of each coin. Mark a *t* on the other side of each coin. The letters represent the genes of the plants.
3. Put one coin in each hand. Shake the coins loosely and drop them on a table.
4. Record both letters observed face up on the coins. These two letters represent the genes of one offspring of the plants.
5. Repeat steps 3 and 4 nineteen more times.

What did you learn?

1. Look at your Punnett square. How many of the twenty offspring would you predict to be tall?
2. How many of the offspring in Part B were tall?

Using what you learned

1. Are the two parent plants, *Tt,* tall or short? Explain.
2. What are the chances that the first offspring would be tall?
3. What are the chances that the last offspring would be tall?

Changes Caused by the Environment

The final appearance of an organism's traits may not be a result of genes. Changes can be caused by the environment. Traits such as skin color can be changed. Human skin contains a brown pigment called melanin. Sunlight causes the skin to produce more melanin, which makes the skin darker. The food a person eats is part of the environment. Studies show that the average height of people in the United States today is greater than the average height of earlier generations. The increase in average height of the population is thought to be due to a more nutritious diet. Describe the traits of your hair. How could these traits be changed? How do you think your genes for hair color and texture would be affected by these changes?

The shape of leaves in a water crowfoot plant is affected by the environment. This plant lives in ponds. The leaves that are produced in deep water are finely divided. Leaves that develop near the surface of the water are rounded or lobed. Because of their shape, the leaves under the water have a large surface exposed to the weak light rays. The floating leaves have less surface from which to lose water and, therefore, do not dry out. Some animals of the tundra, such as the snowshoe hare, have dark coats that change to white in the winter.

Using Genetics

Natural selection produces changes in species. Changes in species of organisms have also been caused by humans. Since people began to grow plants for food, over 11,000 years ago, they have selected the plants with the most desirable traits. Over thousands of years this selection process has caused great changes in food plants. Similarly, animal species have been changed by human selection. With the present knowledge of genetics, scientists have been able to breed better crop plants and livestock. **Selective breeding** is the crossing of organisms with desirable traits to produce offspring with a combination of these desirable traits. Some of the traits that breeders select include resistance to disease, greater food production, and faster growth rate.

Figure 21-15. Changes in the leaf shape of the water crowfoot are in response to the environment.

Besides genes, what else may be responsible for the appearance of an organism's traits?

What are some traits that are selectively bred?

429

a

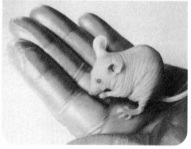

b

Figure 21–16. Selective breeding has produced seedless fruit (a) and hairless mice used for research (b).

In selective breeding, a record is kept of the offspring of each individual. The offspring with the most desired traits are chosen. Organisms with desirable traits are crossed. The traits become pure after several generations. The development of organisms with many pure traits means that few hidden traits will occur in the population. Many "improved" species have been developed with selective breeding. A variety of wheat that can be grown in colder climates has been produced. Cows with high milk production or better quality beef have been developed. Many types of animals, such as cats and dogs, have been selected for their outward appearance. Unlike natural selection, selective breeding does not necessarily make the organism better adapted to its natural environment. Some traits that are selected by people might be harmful to the plant or animal if the species were not cultivated. Plants that have seedless fruits or colorless leaves, or animals with little fur, could not survive in the wild.

Transferring Genes

Selective breeding of crops and livestock takes many years. Many generations of a breed are necessary before a pure strain of a desirable trait is produced. Until recently, it was not possible to select a desirable trait from one species and transfer it into another. With new technology these problems have been overcome. Scientists can move a single gene from one organism of one species to an organism of a different species. This process is being done in one-celled organisms such as bacteria and yeasts.

A gene is part of what substance?

Each gene is part of a *deoxyribonucleic acid* molecule, or DNA. A piece of the DNA of one organism with a desirable trait is inserted into the DNA of another organism. The pieces of DNA combine to form a new DNA molecule. This new DNA is called recombinant DNA. **Recombinant DNA** is DNA that is made by the movement of genes from one organism into another to form new combinations. The gene that causes insulin to be produced in humans can be placed into bacteria. Bacteria reproduce quickly. They are able to make large

What is recombinant DNA?

quantities of insulin in a very short time. For what does the body use insulin? What disease keeps the body from producing enough insulin?

Bacteria have also been used to produce human growth hormone and interferon. A lack of human growth hormone may result in dwarfism. Interferon has been found useful in the treatment of viral diseases and white blood cell cancer. In 1986, the first vaccine produced with recombinant DNA was made for hepatitis B. The vaccine was made in yeast cells. Before this time there was no reliable method of preventing the hepatitis B virus infection that causes a liver disease.

Scientists hope that recombinant DNA can be used to produce many desirable traits. For example, some crop plants such as peas and beans have bacteria in their roots that allow the plants to grow without nitrogen fertilizer. Instead they use nitrogen from the air. Genes that allow plants to form this relationship with bacteria may one day be developed. They could then be moved into other species of crop plants, such as corn. The use of expensive fertilizers would not then be needed.

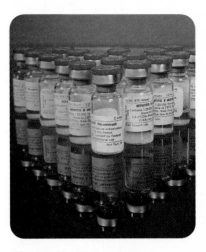

Figure 21-17. Hepatitis B vaccine is produced by recombinant DNA techniques.

In what type of organism was recombinant DNA used to produce the hepatitis B vaccine?

Lesson Summary

- Gradual changes in the genes present in populations over time are caused by natural selection.
- The environment can change the appearance of some inherited traits.
- Selective breeding has produced changes in traits of plants and animals that are useful to humans.
- Medicines have been produced by recombinant DNA techniques.

Lesson Review

Review the lesson to answer these questions.
1. Why are black peppered moths rare in rural England?
2. What chance is there for a pure recessive trait in a cross of a pure dominant and a hybrid?
3. What organisms are used to produce recombinant DNA?

Genes and Color

Some people cannot tell the difference between red and green traffic lights. These people are color-blind. Color blindness is inherited.

Hanako Lam is a medical student doing research on DNA. Hanako has located the genes that are responsible for making molecules needed for seeing different colors.

In the laboratory, Hanako had already discovered the gene that makes light-absorbing molecules in the eyes of cows. How could she find the gene that does the same thing in humans?

A DNA molecule resembles a spiral ladder. Hanako knew that if DNA is split at the rungs of the ladder, each strand would be able to combine with other DNA strands. Using a research method called the recombinant DNA technique, she split cow DNA into two strands. Then she put a strand of human DNA in with it. Hanako watched as the color-vision gene from the cow DNA lined up with genes on the human DNA. With the cow DNA as a road map, Hanako was able to see where genes that produce color-vision molecules in humans are located.

Hanako's research will not eliminate color-blindness. Hanako wants to use the recombinant DNA technique to locate other genes that cause harmful inherited traits. The more scientists know about the work of each gene, the more they can detect harmful genes.

Hanako's research is in the field of genetics. This work demands many hours of careful examination of chromosomes and genes. She will be a doctor/scientist who sees many of her patients through a microscope.

Chapter 21 Review

Summary

1. A trait is a characteristic of an organism passed from parents to offspring. 21:1
2. Individuals in a population inherit different traits. 21:1
3. Pairs of chromosomes contain pairs of genes that control traits. 21:1
4. Genes that control hidden traits are called recessive genes. 21:1
5. A dominant gene may be expressed over a recessive gene, or expressed together with the recessive gene. 21:1
6. If the genes in a pair are both dominant or both recessive, the inherited trait is pure. 21:1
7. If a dominant gene is paired with a recessive gene, the inherited trait is a hybrid. 21:1
8. A Punnett square can be used to predict the gene pairs and appearance of offspring. 21:1
9. Mutations are changes in genes that can cause the appearance of a new trait. 21:2
10. Changes in the types of organisms on Earth are the result of adaptations and natural selection. 21:2
11. The final appearance of an organism's traits may not be the result of genes but, rather, the environment. 21:2
12. With their knowledge of genetics, scientists have been able to select and breed desirable traits in plants and animals. 21:2
13. Medicines have been produced using recombinant DNA. 21:2

Science Words

dominant gene	**hybrid trait**	**recessive gene**
gene	**mutation**	**recombinant DNA**
genetics	**natural selection**	**selective breeding**
heredity	**pure trait**	**trait**

Understanding Science Words

Complete each of the following sentences with a word or words from the Science Words that will make the sentence correct.

1. An inherited characteristic of an organism is a _____.

2. A pair of recessive genes or a pair of dominant genes will produce a _____.
3. The passing of traits from parents to offspring is _____.
4. The part of a chromosome that controls the traits of an organism is a _____.
5. A gene that controls a hidden trait is a _____.
6. A molecule made by the movement of genes from one organism to another to form new combinations is _____.
7. A trait that results when a dominant gene is paired with a recessive gene is a _____.
8. The study of how traits are inherited is _____.
9. A gene whose trait is always expressed is a _____.
10. The process by which organisms less adapted to their environment die, and better adapted organisms survive is _____.
11. A change in genes that can cause a new trait to appear in a population is a _____.
12. The crossing of organisms with desirable traits to produce offspring with a combination of these desirable traits is called _____.

Questions

A. Checking Facts

Determine whether each of the following is true or false. Rewrite the false statements to make them correct.

1. The combination of a dominant and a recessive gene results in a mutation.
2. Most traits are controlled by two or more pairs of genes.
3. A Punnett square can be used to predict the percentage of offspring that will have a certain trait.
4. A pure gene is one whose trait is always expressed.
5. Natural selection is a change in genes that can cause a new trait to appear in a population.
6. The final appearance of an organism's traits may not always be the result of genes.
7. Scientists can move a single gene from one organism of one species to an organism of a different species.

8. A hybrid trait cannot be expressed in the presence of a dominant gene.

B. Recalling Facts

Choose the word or phrase that correctly completes each of the following sentences.

1. A characteristic passed from parent to offspring is a
   (a) gene.   (b) chromosome.   (c) zygote.   (d) trait.
2. If the gene for white is dominant and the gene for red recessive, the offspring of a pure white flower and a pure red flower will be
   (a) all white.   (b) all red.   (c) all pink.   (d) 25% red.
3. A trait that results when both genes in a pair are dominant is
   (a) a hybrid.   (b) pure.   (c) a mutation.   (d) recombinant.
4. The small portions of chromosomes that control the traits of an organism are called
   (a) centromeres.   (b) sperm.   (c) genes.   (d) cells.
5. Some genes are neither dominant nor recessive, and the trait they express together is
   (a) a hybrid.   (b) a mutation.   (c) dominant.   (d) pure.
6. The crossing of organisms to produce certain desirable traits is
   (a) natural selection.   (c) mutation.
   (b) selective breeding.   (d) heredity.

C. Understanding Concepts

Answer each of the following questions using complete sentences.

1. What factors in the environment change the final appearance of an organism without changing the genes of that organism?
2. When will the trait of recessive genes be expressed?
3. An offspring has long eyelashes. One parent has long eyelashes and the other parent has short eyelashes. Neither parent is a hybrid. Which gene is dominant?

D. Applying Concepts

Think about what you have learned in this chapter. Answer each of the following questions using complete sentences.

1. One parent has a hybrid trait *(Tt)*, the other the pure trait *(TT)*. List the possible gene pairs of the offspring.
2. What is the chance that the offspring in question 1 will have the pure trait?

UNIT 9 REVIEW

Answer these questions on a sheet of paper.

1. What are different ways organisms protect their embryos?
2. Where is chromatin found in a cell, and why is it important?
3. What is mitosis?
4. What is the difference between one-parent and two-parent reproduction?
5. What is the difference between a sperm cell and an egg cell?
6. What is heredity?
7. How are genes passed from parents to offspring?
8. How are traits passed from parents to offspring?
9. How does a recessive gene differ from a dominant gene?
10. How does a hybrid trait compare with a pure trait?
11. Why is a blue lobster rare?
12. Predict the percentage of offspring that will have attached earlobes when there is a cross between two parents with hybrid earlobe traits.
13. How does natural selection differ from selective breeding?
14. What is a mutation?
15. What organisms are used to produce recombinant DNA?
16. How is fission related to regeneration?
17. If two-parent organisms each have 500 pairs of chromosomes, how many chromosomes will be present in a cell produced by meiosis?
18. What is the difference between a zygote and an embryo?

RECALLING ACTIVITIES

Think about the activities you did in this unit. Answer the questions about these activities.

1. How do cells divide? 20–1
2. How do plants reproduce from one parent? 20–2
3. How common are dominant and recessive traits? 21–1
4. What are the chances for tallness? 21–2

IDEAS TO EXPLORE

1. Use books to find out what a pedigree is and why it is useful. Choose a domesticated animal such as a dog, cat, cow, or horse to illustrate your answer.
2. Select one of the following genetic diseases and research its causes and symptoms.
   (a) Down's syndrome
   (b) sickle-cell anemia
   (c) cystic fibrosis
3. What is the structure of deoxyribonucleic acid? Give a report on the history of its discovery and its importance in heredity.

CHALLENGING PROJECT

Simple Mendelian inheritance can be observed in many organisms, such as pea plants or humans. It can, however, be studied more easily in an organism that has a shorter lifespan. Bacteria are often used for inheritance studies, but *Drosophila,* commonly called fruit flies, are easier to count. Thus, it is easier to record their inheritance of traits. From your teacher, obtain a population of *Drosophila* that have winged or wingless individuals. Observe and record the types of offspring over a few weeks. Make a report on their inheritance of the winged or wingless trait.

BOOKS TO READ

Birth and Growth by Brian R. Ward, Franklin Watts, Inc.: Danbury, CT, © 1983.
   Read this fascinating book about birth and human growth.
Genetics: From Mendel to Gene Splicing by Caroline Arnold, Franklin Watts, Inc.: Danbury, CT, © 1986.
   Learn about the present and future of genetics.
The Story of Life by Cuillin Bantock, Peter Bedrick Books: New York, © 1984.
   Learn how different organisms reproduce.

UNIT 10
Conserving Our Environment

In the 1800s, George Washington Carver found that the cotton and tobacco crops grown in the southern United States robbed the soil of important nutrients. He grew peanut and sweet potato crops to enrich the soil. He then developed hundreds of uses for these crops so nothing would be wasted. Today we recognize the importance of preserving the land and other valuable resources. How can industries and individuals work to protect and preserve resources?

George Washington Carver—1900

Water reclamation project, Akron, Ohio

Chapter 22
Soil and Land

Next to air and water, soil may be our most important natural resource. It is needed for supplying food. Topsoil may take thousands of years to form, but it can be destroyed in minutes. It is necessary to plan our use of land and soil. How can soil erosion be controlled? What is land use management?

Rice terrace-farming, Philippines

Soil and Its Conservation

LESSON GOALS

In this lesson you will learn
- that soil is an important natural resource.
- that a soil profile describes soil layers.
- the importance of humus.
- methods of soil management and conservation.

Think of the materials you need for life. Air provides you with oxygen. Food provides you with energy to maintain your body and to grow. You need water to drink. You need clothes and shelter to protect you from the weather. What else do you need to stay alive?

All of these materials must come from natural resources. A natural resource is a material in the natural environment that is useful to people. Trees and animals are natural resources. Soil is a natural resource. Soil is, in fact, one of our most important natural resources. How is soil important to you?

What is a natural resource?

Figure 22-1. Many materials we use everyday depend on the soil.

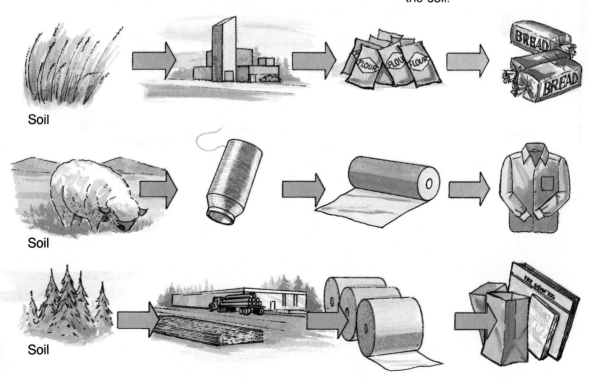

Soil

Soil

Soil

Soil: A Natural Resource

Many things we eat come from plants that grow in the soil. Trees and other plants help maintain our oxygen supply. Lumber, paper, and some clothing fibers come from plants. Other products come from animals that eat plants that grow in soil. Without soil, life outside the oceans would probably not be possible.

Soil is a resource that forms slowly. It takes about 300 years for one centimeter of soil to form in some areas. Soil is made up of both inorganic and organic materials. The inorganic materials are mostly rock and mineral particles. These particles are formed by weathering by wind, water, and ice. Water and air are other inorganic materials present in soil. The organic part of soil includes plants and other organisms that are alive or were once alive. Certain organisms aid in soil formation. Plant roots can grow into cracks in rocks. As they grow, they wedge the rocks apart. This exposes more rock to weathering processes. Burrowing animals, such as earthworms, make tunnels as they move through the soil. Water and air can get into the soil through the tunnels and cause further weathering. Decayed organisms produce acids that contribute to chemical weathering.

Soil Profile

Soils vary in different biomes. Most soils are made of three basic layers. If you were to dig a deep ditch, you could see the layers. The depth and color of the layers and their composition may differ from place to place. The layers form a soil profile as shown in Figure 22-2. A soil profile includes the topsoil, the subsoil, and a layer of parent material.

The top layer in the soil profile is topsoil. Topsoil contains most of the humus that is in soil. **Humus** is the dark organic material in soil. It is formed from the decay of various organisms. Topsoil rich in humus is important. It is in this soil that most plants grow best. Humus is rich in minerals that plants need. Humus also holds water in the topsoil and keeps soil from becoming too alkaline.

What does the organic part of soil include?

Figure 22-2. Layers of soil form a soil profile. Parent material is on the bottom. Above this are the subsoil and topsoil.

The thick layer of soil below topsoil is the subsoil. Subsoil is usually lighter in color than topsoil. Subsoil often contains much clay. Water carries minerals and other materials down into this layer from the topsoil. The roots of most trees grow down into the subsoil.

The bottom layer in a soil profile contains large rocks. This is the material from which the soil above was partly formed. This bottom layer is the parent material. These rocks break down into gravel, sand, and clay that become part of the subsoil.

Figure 22-3. Unprotected soil can be easily eroded.

Soil Management

Good topsoil is needed for growing plants. Earth is covered with only a thin layer of topsoil. Soil can be destroyed easily. For these reasons, care must be taken to use soil wisely. Care of the soil is known as soil conservation. The methods people use to conserve soil are called **soil management.**

Soil management is needed to prevent erosion. Erosion is the removal of soil by wind, water, ice, or gravity. Knowing how to plant crops is important in preventing erosion. Bare topsoil is easily eroded by wind and rain. Plants may prevent erosion by shading the soil and keeping it moist. The roots of plants also hold the soil in place.

What is erosion?

One way to prevent soil erosion is to plant cover crops. A **cover crop** is a fast-growing plant with many shallow roots. Cover crops keep topsoil from becoming dry and being eroded. Alfalfa and clover are often planted as cover crops. Many farmers plant cover crops after the autumn harvest. These crops protect the topsoil during winter and also add nutrients to the soil.

Another method of soil management is strip cropping. **Strip cropping** is the planting of several rows of a cover crop between rows of a main crop. A farmer may plant a strip of corn, then a strip of clover, then another strip of corn, another strip of clover, and so on. The cover crop holds water in the soil. The water retained in the soil helps the main crop grow better.

Figure 22-4. In strip cropping, rows of a cover crop are planted between rows of the main crop.

How does contour planting
prevent erosion?

What is a shelter belt?

Some farmers combine strip cropping with contour planting. **Contour planting** is the planting of crops in rows that follow the shape, or contour, of the land. If crops were planted in rows up and down a hillside, rain would carry topsoil from the top of the hill down the rows to the bottom of the hill. Planting the crops in rows around the hill keeps the topsoil in place.

Shelter belts reduce erosion by wind. A **shelter belt** is a row of trees or shrubs planted to prevent wind from blowing soil away. Shelter belts are sometimes called windbreaks. The trees or shrubs are usually planted along the side of a field. In winter, shelter belts also prevent snow from blowing off a field. When the snow melts, it adds moisture to the soil.

Soil may still need improvement after erosion has been stopped. Plants remove nutrients from the soil. The materials used by plants must be replaced to keep the soil fertile. Soil management includes methods of replacing nutrients, such as nitrogen and phosphorus compounds, used by plants.

Figure 22-5. The use of contour planting (a) and shelter belts (b) aid in preventing soil erosion.

a

b

One way to replace nutrients is to rotate crops. **Crop rotation** is the planting of one crop one year and a different crop the next year in the same soil. For example, a farmer may plant alfalfa in a field the first year. Alfalfa plants add more nitrogen compounds to the soil than they take from it. The second year the farmer may plow the alfalfa under and plant wheat in the same field. Wheat uses a lot of nitrogen compounds. The third year the farmer would plant alfalfa in the field again.

Nutrients can be added to soil in other ways. A **fertilizer** is a material added to soil to replace nutrients. Fertilizers can be natural or synthetic. Natural fertilizers contain organic matter, such as dead plants and animal wastes. They add humus to the soil. Synthetic fertilizers are mixtures of minerals made in laboratories. Synthetic fertilizers add mineral nutrients to soil, but they do not add humus.

Adding water to soil that is too dry is called **irrigation.** Irrigation has made it possible to grow crops in places that do not receive much rain. Watering a lawn is an example of irrigation. What other examples of irrigation have you seen?

Figure 22-6. Irrigation is used in agricultural areas where annual precipitation is low.

How do synthetic fertilizers differ from natural fertilizers?

What is irrigation?

Lesson Summary

- Soil is an important natural resource because it is used to provide food, lumber for housing, materials for clothes, and other items.
- Most soil profiles have three layers: the topsoil, the subsoil, and the parent material.
- Humus in topsoil is important because it holds water, conserves minerals, and keeps the soil from becoming too basic.
- Irrigation, use of fertilizers, and good farming practices improve and conserve soil.

Lesson Review

Review the lesson to answer these questions.
1. Name some inorganic materials in soil.
2. How is humus formed?
3. Explain several methods of soil management.

LESSON GOALS

In this lesson you will learn
- how land is used for the disposal of refuse.
- some methods to dispose of refuse.
- the value of biodegradable materials.
- the value of recycling.

What is refuse?

Figure 22-7. These barges are hauling trash to a landfill near New York City.

How is refuse handled in a sanitary landfill?

Any material that is a waste product is **refuse** (REF yooz). Each day millions of tons of solid waste are produced. These wastes must be disposed of. Getting rid of refuse is a big problem.

Today large amounts of land are being used for disposal of refuse. These areas are called landfills. In the past many landfills have been open dumps. They have polluted air and water. More and more landfills are now sanitary landfills. A **sanitary landfill** is a disposal site where trash is processed so that it will harm the environment as little as possible.

At a sanitary landfill, the refuse is covered with layers of soil. In time, some of the refuse decomposes and becomes part of the soil. If a landfill is well cared for, the land can later be put to another use.

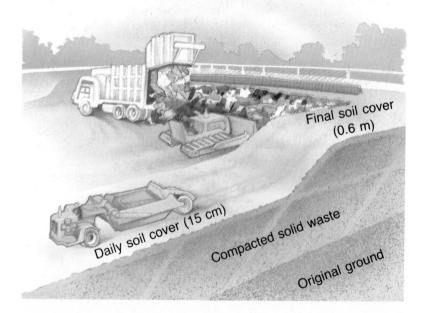

Figure 22-8. In a sanitary landfill, refuse is spread in a thin layer, compacted, and then covered with soil. Portable fences catch and hold trash blown by the wind.

Final soil cover (0.6 m)

Daily soil cover (15 cm)

Compacted solid waste

Original ground

Figure 22-9. A trash burning power plant provides electricity for a nearby city.

Sometimes, however, the refuse from landfills may leak into the ground and pollute groundwater. Refuse that can be harmful is known as **hazardous waste** or toxic waste. Hazardous wastes must be kept from entering the environment.

Refuse that can be broken down into harmless compounds by organisms is **biodegradable.** Many paper and wood products are biodegradable. Some detergents, soaps, and industrial cleaning materials are also biodegradable. The natural resources used to make biodegradable items are broken down and returned to the environment.

What is a biodegradable material?

Some cities use refuse as fuel. Refuse that will burn is separated from refuse that will not burn. What kinds of refuse will burn? Burnable refuse is mixed with some other fuel such as coal and burned to produce energy. Using refuse as a fuel helps reduce the demand for fossil fuel energy resources. What problems might result from using refuse as a fuel?

Many communities have laws that govern the ways refuse can be disposed of. Some communities do not allow refuse to be burned. Most communities do not allow refuse to be dumped in water or placed in an open dump on land. How do your community's methods of refuse disposal affect the environment?

447

Science and Technology

Hazardous Wastes—At Home

Many people have collected aluminum cans or newspapers for recycling, but few have thought about recycling some of the potentially hazardous products they use around their homes. Cleaning products, paint, and used automobile oil are among the items that people may throw away without thinking of the harm these materials cause to the environment.

In some parts of the country, communities have organized recycling drives to encourage people to be more responsible when disposing of dangerous household products. During these recycling drives, people bring the products they need to throw away to a central location, such as a community center or meeting hall. At the center, the products are sorted into different categories, such as automotive oil, paint, old batteries, garden pest killers, and floor waxes.

As the products are sorted, experts on hazardous waste disposal determine the ways in which each type of waste should be handled. Some products, such as certain plastics, cannot be recycled at the present time and must be transported to special waste disposal sites. Other products, such as automotive oil, can be recycled quite easily and are sent off to an industrial recycling center. There, they are recycled into new, useful products.

Community recycling programs are becoming more and more popular. As we learn more about the potential dangers of careless waste disposal, community recycling programs will help assure that our environment will become safer for all of us.

Recycling

Reducing the amount of refuse is another solution to the problem of waste disposal. One way to reduce refuse is to use fewer disposable packages and products. When we shop, we can choose products and packages that can be used more than once. We can buy items with less packaging.

Reusing items or resources is called recycling. Aluminum or steel cans can be recycled. They are collected and melted. The metal is then used to make new products of aluminum and steel. Paper and glass products can also be recycled. Several states have passed laws that require most beverage containers to be recycled. When you buy a beverage, you pay a small deposit. When you take back the empty can or bottle to be recycled, the deposit is returned.

Making a compost pile is an example of recycling biodegradable items. **Compost** is a mixture of decaying organic matter. Some people have compost piles in their yards. Autumn leaves, grass clippings, and food wastes may be added to the compost pile. The compost contains humus that may be used as a natural fertilizer for a farm or garden.

Figure 22–10. In recycling plants, aluminum cans are melted for reuse.

What is recycling?

What is compost?

Lesson Summary

- Landfills are land areas set aside for the disposal of refuse.
- Refuse is disposed of by burning, as well as in landfills.
- Biodegradable materials return resources to the environment when they are broken down by organisms.
- Recycling of material decreases the amount of refuse.

Lesson Review

Review the lesson to answer these questions.
1. What is refuse?
2. How is a sanitary landfill different from an open dump?
3. Explain the term *biodegradable*.

449

Activity 22–1 Biodegradable Materials

QUESTION   Which items are biodegradable?

Materials
rubber gloves
safety goggles
refuse: soft drink can, glass jar, plastic bag, paper
 napkin, orange peel, milk carton, discarded ink pen
4 stakes
string
meter stick
shovel
pencil and paper

What to do

1. Wear rubber gloves and goggles whenever you handle the refuse and when digging.
2. Examine each refuse item. Predict which ones are biodegradable and which ones are not. Record your predictions.
3. Use stakes and string to mark off a one square meter area in the schoolyard. Remove the soil to a depth of 30 cm in the area.
4. Place the refuse in the bottom of the pit you have made. Separate the refuse items so they do not touch each other.

5. Make a top-view map of the pit. Label the location of each refuse item.

6. Carefully replace the soil in the pit. Do not disturb the refuse as you cover it with soil. Wait 30 days.

7. Carefully reopen the pit. Observe and write a description of each refuse item.

8. Remove any items that are not biodegradable and dispose of them in a refuse container. Replace the soil in the pit. Try to make the area look as good or better than it did before you dug the pit.

What did you learn?

1. How did the items in the pit change?
2. How did your predictions compare with your actual results?

Using what you learned

1. Suppose you put all of the items back in the pit and closed it. What would you expect to observe if you reopened it after 30 more days?
2. What items could you use in place of the items that are not biodegradable?
3. What happens to nonbiodegradable items that are disposed of in a sanitary landfill?

Language Arts Skills

Understanding Cause and Effect

When one event happens, another event has caused it to happen. For example, if water is polluted, chemicals or other wastes have entered the water. To stop the pollution, its cause must be known.

Scientists and others often seek to learn why an event occurs. The relationship between an event and why it occurred is known as cause and effect. What happened is the *effect*. Why it happened is the *cause*.

Read the following description of how building a new neighborhood changed the environment. Then answer the questions about causes and effects.

A few years ago, this area was a forest. Builders came in to build houses. They built streets with bulldozers. They cut down trees to make space for houses. With the trees gone, the soil began to lose moisture and dry out. Small plants began to die, because there was little moisture. The plants also had little food, because there were no leaves to enrich the soil. The sun further dried out the ground. Then a windstorm blew much of the topsoil away. The ground was dug up for house foundations, and more soil blew away each day. Rains washed even more soil away. When I moved into my new house, the yard was clay. I thought I could work with it, and sowed grass seed. I've lived here for three months and worked in the yard every day. No grass will grow.

1. What first caused the ground to lose moisture?
2. What two events caused small plants to die?
3. What events caused the loss of topsoil?
4. What effect did the loss of topsoil have on the remaining soil?
5. What effect did the loss of topsoil have on the grass?

Summary

1. Soil is a natural resource that is important for life. 22:1
2. Soil is made of organic and inorganic materials. 22:1
3. Layers of soil form a soil profile, and most soil profiles have three layers: topsoil, subsoil, and parent material. 22:1
4. Humus is a part of topsoil that holds moisture and adds nutrients to the soil. 22:1
5. Soil management includes preventing erosion and improving the quality of soil. 22:1
6. Cover crops, strip cropping, contour planting, and shelter belts are used to prevent erosion. 22:1
7. Crop rotation, fertilization, and irrigation are used to improve the quality of soil. 22:1
8. Refuse is any material that is a waste product. 22:2
9. Refuse is disposed of mainly in sanitary landfills or by burning. 22:2
10. Biodegradable refuse can be broken down by organisms into harmless compounds. 22:2
11. By recycling and using biodegradable materials, the amount of refuse can be decreased. 22:2

Science Words

biodegradable

compost

contour planting

cover crop

crop rotation

fertilizer

hazardous waste

humus

irrigation

refuse

sanitary landfill

shelter belt

soil management

strip cropping

Understanding Science Words

Complete each of the following sentences with a word or words from the Science Words that will make the sentence correct.

1. Refuse is dumped and covered with layers of soil at a

   _____.

2. Refuse that can be broken down by organisms into harmless compounds is called _____.

3. Refuse that can be harmful to people is _____.

4. The methods people use to conserve soil are called _____.
5. Any matter that is a waste product is _____.
6. The planting of different crops year after year in the same soil is called _____.
7. The planting of a cover crop between rows of a main crop is called _____.
8. A row of trees or shrubs planted to prevent wind erosion is a _____.
9. A material added to soil to replace nutrients is _____.
10. Planting crops in rows that follow the shape of the land is known as _____.
11. A fast-growing plant with many shallow roots that is planted to prevent erosion is called a _____.
12. The dark, organic part of topsoil that holds water and is rich in minerals is _____.
13. Adding water to soil that is dry is _____.
14. A mixture of decaying organic matter such as food wastes, leaves, and grass clippings is _____.

Questions

A. Checking Facts

Determine whether each of the following is true or false. Rewrite the false statements to make them correct.

1. Subsoil is the bottom layer in a soil profile.
2. If hazardous wastes are not disposed of properly, they can pollute groundwater.
3. Strip cropping is the planting of one crop one year and a different crop the next year in the same soil.
4. Soil is a nonrenewable resource.
5. Erosion is the removal of soil by wind, water, ice, or gravity.
6. Synthetic fertilizers add mineral nutrients and humus to the soil.
7. A disposal site where trash is processed so that it will harm the environment as little as possible is a landfill.
8. Biodegradable products can be put into a compost pile, and later the decayed material can be used for fertilizer.

9. A natural resource is a material in the natural environment that is useful to people.

B. Recalling Facts

Choose the word or phrase that correctly completes each of the following sentences.

1. Which of the following is NOT an example of soil management?
   (a) irrigation
   (b) contour planting
   (c) strip cropping
   (d) erosion

2. A soil mixture of decayed organisms is
   (a) inorganic.
   (b) a soil profile.
   (c) humus.
   (d) subsoil.

3. A shelter belt is used to prevent erosion of soil by
   (a) gravity.
   (b) wind.
   (c) water.
   (d) ice.

4. The soil layer that contains the most humus is the
   (a) topsoil.
   (b) subsoil.
   (c) rock layer.
   (d) parent material.

5. The planting of crops in rows that follow the shape of the land is
   (a) strip cropping.
   (b) crop rotation.
   (c) contour planting.
   (d) cover cropping.

6. The layer of soil that is most important to crops is
   (a) parent material.
   (b) rock layer.
   (c) subsoil.
   (d) topsoil.

7. Fertilizers may add all of the following to the soil EXCEPT
   (a) minerals.
   (b) water.
   (c) humus.
   (d) nutrients.

C. Understanding Concepts

Answer each of the following questions using complete sentences.

1. How is soil affected by the organisms that live in it?
2. Describe the layers in a soil profile.
3. What happens at a sanitary landfill?
4. List six methods of soil conservation.

D. Applying Concepts

Think about what you have learned in this chapter. Answer each of the following questions using complete sentences.

1. Name some products you use daily that are related to soil.
2. How can you conserve soil around your home?
3. What are some possible solutions to the problem of too much refuse?

Chapter 23
Water and Air

Fresh, clean water is a prized natural resource. Most of our drinking water contains pollutants. An experimental water treatment plant uses water hyacinths to produce 20,000 gallons of sparkling clean water from wastewater each day. What is an advantage of this method over chemical methods of water treatment? What are some common water pollutants?

San Diego, California, water treatment plant

LESSON GOALS

In this lesson you will learn
- the importance of conserving air and water.
- some sources of water pollution.
- some sources of air pollution.

Water and air are important natural resources. All organisms need water. Except for a few species, all organisms also need air. You could not survive without a supply of clean water and air.

There are plentiful supplies of water and air on Earth. Although air is available to everyone, water is not. Some areas of the world have very little water. Many places on Earth have neither clean air nor clean water. The water must be cleaned before it is used for drinking and other purposes. Air is partly cleaned by rain and snow. Recall from Lesson 8:3 that acid-forming compounds in the air fall to Earth as acid precipitation. People often pollute air and water faster than it can be cleaned by nature.

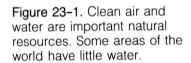

Why are water and air important natural resources?

Figure 23–1. Clean air and water are important natural resources. Some areas of the world have little water.

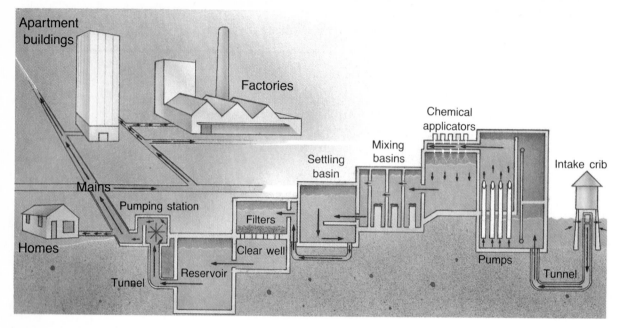

Figure 23-2. Water is treated before it is used.

Where do people get drinking water?

How are reservoirs used?

What chemical is usually used to kill bacteria in water treatment plants?

Water Treatment

Half the people in the United States obtain their drinking water from groundwater supplies. Most of the rest comes from rivers and lakes. A small amount comes from the oceans. Over half of the rain and melted snow soaks into the ground, adding to the groundwater supply. About 40 percent of the water from rain and snow flows over the surface and runs off into rivers and oceans.

Most water must be treated before use. Often the water for a community is collected in a reservoir. A **reservoir** is a large artificial or natural lake used to collect and store water. During storage some materials in the water settle to the bottom of the reservoir. Water from the top of the reservoir flows through a filter and is pumped to a water treatment plant. The filter keeps sticks, fish, and other large objects out.

In the water treatment plant, chlorine is usually added to water to kill bacteria. Other chemicals are added to remove color and small particles. The water is filtered again and more chlorine is added. Some water treatment plants also add compounds of fluorine to the water. The fluorine compounds are important for healthy teeth. The water is then pumped to the community through pipes.

Water Pollution

Water pollution occurs when impurities are added to water. Groundwater in many areas has become polluted by chemicals and radioactive wastes. Thousands of wells that supply drinking water across the United States have been closed because of pollution. Surface water is polluted by sewage, excess nutrients, sediments, chemicals, and excess heat. Polluted water must be cleaned before it can be used.

One type of water pollution is sewage. **Sewage** is liquid and solid waste that is carried in sewers or drains. A large amount of sewage is human wastes. Human wastes contain bacteria that can cause disease if the wastes are left untreated. Sewage also contains food and cooking wastes. Some chemical wastes are also part of sewage. What chemicals may be in the sewage that comes from your home?

Agricultural wastes come from farms. Wastes from farm fields sometimes seep into rivers and lakes. The wastes can cause diseases and decrease the amount of oxygen in the water. How might organisms in the water be affected by this pollution?

Fertilizers and pesticides are agricultural wastes that may pollute groundwater. Fertilizers and pesticides dissolve in surface water that runs off farmlands into rivers and lakes. A **pesticide** is a chemical farmers use to kill organisms that harm crops. Many fertilizers and pesticides are hazardous chemicals. Lawn chemicals, such as weed killers and insect poisons, may also be toxic. They can pollute the water supply in the same way agricultural chemicals do.

Figure 23–3. Much surface water has become badly polluted.

What are some pollutants in surface water?

How do pesticides get into rivers and lakes?

Figure 23–4. Agricultural pesticides can be a source of both air and water pollution.

Another source of water pollution is industrial wastes. Many industries use cleaning agents and other chemicals. Often water is used during the production process to wash away excess chemicals. The polluted water from an industry may be dumped into a nearby river, lake, or ocean. These industrial wastes may poison organisms that use the water.

Water used by some industries to cool machines gets very hot. Some industries dump the hot water into nearby rivers or lakes. Dumping hot water into a body of water is **thermal pollution.** Thermal pollution can raise the temperature in parts of the body of water. The heat may kill organisms and increase the evaporation rate of the water. Thermal pollution reduces the amount of oxygen dissolved in water. Some organisms may die from lack of oxygen. Dissolved oxygen is very important for decomposing organic wastes in water. A lack of oxygen prevents the wastes from decomposing quickly. As a result, the water stays polluted for a long time.

Water Conservation

Earth has a total water supply that is about 200,000 times greater than present demands. However, less than one percent provides the water needed by people, cities, and industry. Thus, we must use water wisely. Preventing water pollution is an important part of water conservation. What might happen if all the water on Earth became polluted?

What is thermal pollution?

How may organisms be affected by thermal pollution?

Figure 23-5. Cooling towers are used to cool hot water before it is released into bodies of water. This decreases the risk of thermal pollution.

460

Thermal pollution can be prevented by cooling the water before it is dumped into bodies of water. The use of cooling towers and ponds is one way to cool the water. In some places, the hot water is used to heat buildings instead of being dumped into lakes and rivers.

Harmful chemicals can be removed by industries before water flows into waterways. Sewage can be treated in sewage treatment plants before it is dumped into a body of water. Sewage treatment plants remove some impurities and bacteria from wastewater before it is returned to the environment.

Some farmers practice organic farming. Organic farming is a method that uses only natural fertilizers and no pesticides. Farm animal wastes can be used as fertilizers instead of dumping them in waterways. Many organisms that harm crops can be reduced with biocontrols. A **biocontrol** is an organism that prevents other organisms from harming crops. For example, ladybugs eat certain insects such as aphids that destroy crops. How does organic farming help prevent water pollution?

Figure 23–6. Ladybugs act as biocontrols when they eat aphids that may damage crops.

What is organic farming?

Air Pollution

Air pollution occurs when harmful particles and gases are added to air. It comes from many sources. Seed particles, pollen, forest fires, and volcanoes are natural sources of air pollution. What other natural sources of air pollution can you name?

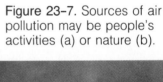

Figure 23–7. Sources of air pollution may be people's activities (a) or nature (b).

a

b

461

Most air pollution is caused by people. Cigarette smoking is a cause of harmful indoor air pollution. Most industries that burn fossil fuels for energy produce smoke that pollutes air. You may have seen smoke pouring out of smokestacks. The smoke may contain harmful gases such as sulfur and nitrogen oxides that can form acid precipitation. Small particles of solid matter called particulates (par TIHK yuh layts) are also found in the smoke.

In one recent example, a factory polluted the air with particulates. Many cattle on nearby farms became sick and died. Scientists found that the cattle became sick from grazing in a pasture where the grass was coated with the particulates.

Motor vehicles are a major source of air pollution. Many city streets and highways are crowded with automobiles and trucks. The exhaust from these vehicles pollutes air with harmful hydrocarbons, lead, nitrogen oxides, and carbon monoxide. Some of these substances combine with elements in air to form other dangerous compounds. Vehicles that burn diesel fuel add large amounts of particulates to the air.

In some parts of the southwestern United States, increasing air pollution from motor vehicles has caused fruit trees to produce only half as much fruit as they once produced. Air pollution from cities has been rising into the mountains, producing acid precipitation and killing millions of pine trees.

What types of air pollution are caused by motor vehicles?

Figure 23-8. Motor vehicles are a major source of air pollution.

Conserving Clean Air

Air pollution is very harmful and costly. Many materials, such as concrete, steel, and nylon, wear out faster because of air pollution. It damages crops and harms livestock. Air pollution causes respiratory illnesses, such as asthma and bronchitis, to get worse. Scientists have found that people who breathe some kinds of polluted air are more likely to get cancer. Conserving clean air is important. We cannot live healthful lives without clean air. We may not be able to end all air pollution, but we can control it.

Laws have been passed to combat the sources of air pollution. Some states forbid the open burning of trash within city limits. Some cities require that people form car pools. This reduces pollution from cars in urban areas. The federal government has set limits on air pollutants from car exhaust.

One way industries prevent particulates and smokestack gases from polluting air is to use scrubbers. A **scrubber** is a device that fits in a smokestack or chimney and uses water to remove particulates and some polluting gases. Some of the materials removed by a scrubber can be used to make other products.

Air pollution from motor vehicles can be reduced by changing the way engines burn fuels. Particulates could be cleaned from engine exhaust before the exhaust is released into air. Fuels that do not contain lead can be used. Special equipment called catalytic converters are used on vehicles to reduce the amounts of harmful gases in the exhaust.

Figure 23–9. Riding bicycles and using electric vehicles help to prevent air pollution.

How can some particulates be removed from industrial smoke?

463

One way you can help prevent air pollution is to share a ride whenever possible. You can also walk or ride a bicycle to nearby places. In what other ways can people reduce air pollution?

Lesson Summary

- Water and air are important natural resources needed for life.
- Sewage, chemicals from industry and agriculture, radioactive wastes, and waste heat are some sources of water pollution.
- Cigarette smoke, smoke from industries, and vehicle exhaust are some sources of air pollution.

Lesson Review

Review the lesson to answer these questions.

1. How is water treated so it is fit to drink?
2. List three ways to prevent water pollution.
3. List three ways to prevent air pollution.

Activity 23–1   An Air Pollution Detector

QUESTION   Where can you locate air pollution?

Materials

scissors
thin cardboard
metric ruler
hole punch
string

nickel
transparent tape
hand lens
pencil and paper

What to do

1. Cut five strips of cardboard, 10 cm × 25 cm. Punch a hole in one end of each strip.
2. Cut five pieces of string, each 15 cm long. Put a piece of string through the hole in each strip. Tie the string to make a loop for hanging the strip.

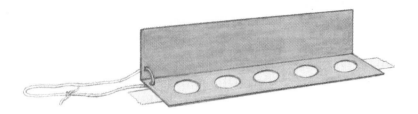

3. Fold each strip in half lengthwise. Trace five nickel-sized circles in a row on one half of each strip. Then cut out the circles.

4. Put tape on the outside of each strip so that the sticky side of the tape shows through the holes in the strip. Then fold the strip in half to cover the holes. Seal with tape.

5. Find a different place to hang each strip. Choose some places that are inside and some places that are outside. Label each strip with the location where you are going to hang it.

6. Open the strips so the sticky part of the tape is exposed. Hang the strips in the locations you chose. Note the time when you hang each strip.

7. The next day, return to the places and collect the strips. As you collect each strip, fold it up again and seal it.

8. Return to your classroom. Use a hand lens to observe any particles that collected on the tape. Record your observations.

What did you learn?

1. What did you observe on the strips?
2. Where did you find the least air pollution?
3. What type of air pollution occurred most often?

Using what you learned

1. What can you do to help reduce air pollution in these locations?
2. Would you expect to detect more or less pollution on a windy day?
3. What types of pollution might not be detected with your strip?

LESSON GOALS

In this lesson you will learn
- how population growth affects resource use.
- what is meant by environmental impact.

Look around your classroom. Everyone has a chair, books, and school supplies. Suppose that one day each of the students in your class brought one friend to school. Where would the friends sit? Who would share books and school supplies with them?

Imagine what would happen if everyone brought two friends to your classroom on the next day. The classroom would probably be very crowded and it might be noisy. There would not be enough chairs, books, or school supplies for everyone.

Population Growth

The human population on Earth is a little like the population of this classroom. Long ago, few people lived on Earth. In 1650, the world population was about 550 million. The population had doubled by 1850. How many years did it take for the population to double? By 1930, the world population was about two billion. By 1980, it was about four billion. The population doubled in the 50 years between 1930 and 1980. Some people predict that the population of Earth may double again by 2015. How many people would be living on Earth then?

We use Earth's resources to meet our needs for air, water, food, clothing, and shelter. More and more people on Earth need more and more space and resources. Recall from Lesson 16:3 that there is competition within an ecosystem. Competition is a relationship in which living things compete for life needs. The larger the population, the more competition there is for resources. Earth can be viewed as one very large ecosystem. You might think of it as a spaceship on which we are all passengers. The natural resources on this spaceship are limited, so they must be used wisely.

Figure 23–10. In large populations, people must compete for resources. The population on Earth increased from 4 billion in 1980 to 5 billion in 1986.

What is competition?

Figure 23–11. Earth is an ecosystem with limited resources. Wise use of these resources will allow all people a good quality of life.

The quality of our future environment depends on the choices people make today. The way we live affects our environment. The effect of people's activities on the total environment is called **environmental impact**. It is possible to make our impact a good one. Careful planning and wise use of resources is important. It may be possible to produce more goods for a growing population and still maintain a clean environment. Science gives us much of the knowledge we need to do this. How can you make a positive impact on your environment?

What is environmental impact?

Lesson Summary

- As our population increases, more of Earth's limited resources are being used up.
- The effect of people's activities on the total environment is called environmental impact.

Lesson Review

Review the lesson to answer these questions.

1. How does population growth affect the environment?
2. What is meant by environmental impact?

Protecting the Taiga

Far from the busy city, biologist James Kabotie often paddles his canoe across a serene wilderness lake. From the far end of the lake the laughing cry of a common loon may ring out. Not long ago, Jim was concerned that the loon's voice would no longer be heard echoing across the wilderness lakes of the taiga.

Jim has studied the ecology of the taiga for nearly 20 years. In that time, he has observed alarming changes in the freshwater and conifer forest ecosystems. Many trees died and the lakes produced fewer and fewer fish. Common loons and other fish-eating birds became rarer as their food supplies dwindled.

After years of intense investigation, Jim learned that the pH of the lakes was very acidic. The source of the problem was acid rain. Acid rain forms when nitrogen oxides and sulfur dioxide are released into the atmosphere. A major source of nitrogen oxides is the exhaust from automobiles. Sulfur dioxide is produced from coal or oil fired power plants. When these oxides combine with water vapor in the air, acids form. Eventually, acid rain or snow falls to earth many miles from the place it first formed.

Taiga lakes cannot neutralize the acid rain. A procedure called liming has been undertaken to protect the lakes. Lime is a chemical that reacts with acid and neutralizes its effect on lakes. Lime is sprayed onto lakes while they are still frozen so it can act before the acidic snow and ice melt into the lake in the spring.

Jim agrees with other conservationists that air pollution from factories and automobiles must be reduced in order to prevent acid precipitation. Until then, liming must continue. As if in agreement, a loon calls out, its loud voice echoing across a lake encircled by towering pines.

Chapter 23 Review

Summary

1. Water and air are important natural resources. 23:1
2. Organisms need clean water and air to survive. 23:1
3. Most water undergoes special treatment before it can be used. 23:1
4. Groundwater and surface waters are polluted by chemicals, sewage, radioactive wastes, sediments, excess nutrients, and heat. 23:1
5. Industrial wastes, agricultural wastes, and sewage are major sources of water pollution. 23:1
6. Preventing water pollution is an important part of water conservation. 23:1
7. Transportation, industry, and heating are major sources of air pollution. 23:1
8. Major air pollutants include sulfur and nitrogen oxides, lead, hydrocarbons, carbon monoxide, and particulates. 23:1
9. Acid rain is one of the damaging effects of air pollution. 23:1
10. Air pollution can be reduced by using scrubbers, catalytic converters, and unleaded gasoline, by not burning trash in the open, and by using automobiles less. 23:1
11. As Earth's population grows, there is greater competition for Earth's limited resources. 23:2
12. The quality of our future environment depends on the choices we make today. 23:2
13. People's activities have an impact on the environment. 23:2

Science Words

biocontrol
environmental impact
pesticide
reservoir

scrubber
sewage
thermal pollution

Understanding Science Words

Complete the following sentences with a word or words from the Science Words that will make the sentence correct.

1. The effect of people's activities on the environment is _____.
2. An organism that prevents other organisms from harming crops is a

_____.

3. Dumping hot water into a body of water is _____.
4. Liquid and solid waste that is carried in sewers or drains is

   _____.

5. A chemical used to kill organisms that may harm crops is a

   _____.

6. A device in a chimney or smokestack that uses water to remove
   particulates and some polluting gases from the smoke is a

   _____.

7. A large lake used to store water is a _____.

Questions

A. Checking Facts

*Determine whether each of the following is true or false. Rewrite the false
statements to make them correct.*

1. Chlorine is added to water in water treatment plants to remove color
   from the water.
2. There are no natural sources of air pollution.
3. Earth's natural resources are unlimited.
4. Some farmers use biocontrols in place of fertilizers.
5. Thermal pollution reduces the amount of oxygen that is dissolved in
   water.
6. The total population on Earth is increasing at a faster rate than ever
   before.
7. Organic farming is a method that uses no pesticides and no
   fertilizers.
8. Motor vehicles are only a minor source of air pollution.
9. There is competition among people for the resources in Earth's
   ecosystem.

B. Recalling Facts

*Choose the word or phrase that correctly completes each of the following
sentences.*

1. Between 1980 and 2015, scientists expect world population to
   (a) double.   (b) triple.   (c) stay the same.   (d) decrease.
2. Which of the following is NOT a water pollutant?
   (a) sewage   (b) chemicals   (c) reservoirs   (d) heat

3. What percent of the total amount of water on Earth provides the water needed by people, cities, and industry?
   (a) one   (b) ten   (c) twenty   (d) fifty
4. Organisms used in place of pesticides to prevent other organisms from harming crops are
   (a) particulates.   (c) yeasts.
   (b) fertilizers.   (d) biocontrols.
5. A chemical added to water in a water treatment plant to kill bacteria is
   (a) sulfur.   (c) chlorine.
   (b) nitrogen oxide.   (d) sediment.
6. Earth's resources are
   (a) nonrenewable.   (c) unlimited.
   (b) limited.   (d) none of these.
7. Which of the following air pollutants is a cause of acid precipitation?
   (a) lead   (c) particulates
   (b) hydrocarbons   (d) sulfur oxides
8. Which of the following pollutants does NOT come from a natural source?
   (a) pollen   (b) seed particles   (c) nitrogen oxides   (d) dust

C. Understanding Concepts

Answer each of the following questions using complete sentences.
1. Why is water an important natural resource?
2. Explain how thermal pollution affects water organisms.
3. How can pollution of water by sewage be controlled?
4. List several sources of air pollution.
5. What are some harmful effects of air pollution?
6. What is the environmental impact of population growth?
7. How has the human population changed since 1650?

D. Applying Concepts

Think about what you have learned in this chapter. Answer each of the following questions using complete sentences.
1. Why is water pollution dangerous?
2. How can organic farming reduce water pollution?
3. Tell what might be done about each of these instances of pollution.
   (a) a power plant dumping hot water into a river
   (b) air pollution caused by heavy traffic near a school
   (c) a city dumping untreated sewage into a lake

UNIT 10 REVIEW

CHECKING YOURSELF

Answer these questions on a sheet of paper.

1. What are some of the inorganic materials in soil?
2. What is the difference between an open dump and a sanitary landfill?
3. List the ways that topsoil can be eroded.
4. What is refuse?
5. Why are some wastes considered hazardous?
6. What is a biodegradable material?
7. Why are natural resources important to people?
8. What is pollution, and what causes air and water pollution?
9. What is meant by environmental impact?
10. What are biocontrols, and how are they better than pesticides?
11. Describe the layers in a soil profile.
12. What is the importance of humus?
13. Match each of these types of soil management with one of the descriptions that follow: irrigation, use of fertilizer, crop rotation, contour planting, cover crop, shelter belt.
    (a) prevents wind from blowing soil away
    (b) rows of crops around a hill that prevent rain from washing topsoil away
    (c) crop planted to protect soil during winter
    (d) makes it possible to grow crops in areas that do not receive much rain
    (e) adding nutrients to soil
    (f) planting of one crop one year and a different crop the next year in the same field

RECALLING ACTIVITIES

Think about the activities you did in this unit. Answer the questions about these activities.

1. Which items are biodegradable? 22–1
2. Where can you locate air pollution? 23–1

IDEAS TO EXPLORE

1. Some items normally referred to as "wastes" and "pollution" are really valuable resources. They are thrown away because there has been a lack of planning for their use. Gasoline was once considered a waste product of petroleum refining. Choose three "wastes" or "pollutants" and research how these could be used, or how they could be prevented from becoming "wastes" or "pollutants."

2. In the past few years, scientists have become aware of an increasing indoor air pollution problem. Cigarette smoke is just one of many possible sources of pollutants in indoor air. Research the problem of indoor air pollution. Write a report on the types of indoor air pollutants, including possible solutions to the problem.

3. Visit the water treatment plant in your community. Find out the source of drinking water for the community and how the water is purified. Make a poster showing all the steps in the treatment of water for your community.

PROBLEM SOLVING

How can salt be removed from water so that the water can be drunk? In some areas of the world, fresh water is scarce, and salt water must be used for drinking water. Before one can drink salt water, the salt must be removed. One means of doing this is to evaporate the salt water and then condense the water vapor. Devise a means of purifying some salt water or muddy water by solar evaporation.

BOOKS TO READ

More With Less: The Future World of Buckminster Fuller by Nathan Asseng, Lerner Publications Co.: Minneapolis, © 1986.
Read about this inventor who discovered new ways of thinking.

Toxic Threat: How Hazardous Substances Poison Our Lives by Stephen J. Zipko, Julian Messner Co.: New York, © 1986.
Learn more about environmental issues such as radioactive waste, water and air pollution, pesticides, and acid rain.

Wastes by Christina G. Miller and Louise A. Berry, Franklin Watts, Inc.: Danbury, CT, © 1986.
Learn more about the disposal of waste materials in our society.

Glossary

This book has words that you may not have read before. Many of these words are science words. Some science words may be hard for you to read. You will find the science words in **bold print.** These words may appear two ways. The first way shows how the word is spelled. The second way shows how the word sounds. The list below shows the sounds each letter or group of letters makes.

Look at the word **alveolus** (al VEE uh lus). The second spelling shows the letters "ee." Find these letters in the list. The "ee" has the sound of "ea" in the word "leaf." Anytime you see "ee," you know what sound to say. The capitalized syllable is the accented syllable.

a . . . back (BAK)
er . . . care, fair (KER, FER)
ay . . . day (DAY)
ah . . . father (FAHTH ur)
ar . . . car (KAR)
ow . . . flower, loud (FLOW ur, LOWD)
e . . . less (LES)
ee . . . leaf (LEEF)
ih . . . trip (TRIHP)
i (i + consonant + e) . . .
   idea, life (i DEE uh, LIFE)
oh . . . go (GOH)
aw . . . soft (SAWFT)
or . . . orbit (OR but)
oy . . . coin (KOYN)

oo . . . foot (FOOT)
yoo . . . pure (PYOOR)
ew . . . food (FEWD)
yew . . . few (FYEW)
uh (u + consonant) . . .
   comma, mother (KAHM uh, MUTH ur)
sh . . . shelf (SHELF)
ch . . . nature (NAY chur)
g . . . gift (GIHFT)
j . . . gem, edge (JEM, EJ)
ing . . . sing (SING)
zh . . . vision (VIHZH un)
k . . . cake (KAYK)
s . . . seed, cent (SEED, SENT)
z . . . zone, raise (ZOHN, RAYZ)

A

acid: a substance that forms hydrogen ions as it dissolves in water

acid precipitation (prih sihp uh TAY shun): rain or snow in which sulfur or nitrogen oxides have combined with water in the air

adrenal (uh DREE nul) **gland:** one of a pair of endocrine glands on top of the kidneys

adrenaline (uh DREN ul un): a hormone secreted by the adrenal glands that helps the body react to emergencies

474

alveolus (al VEE uh lus): an air sac in the lungs where gases are exchanged; plural is alveoli

antibody (ANT ih bahd ee): a chemical produced in the blood when foreign matter is present

antiseptic (an tih SEP tihk): a disinfectant used on living things

artery: a blood vessel that carries blood away from the heart

atoms: the tiny particles that make up all matter

B

base: a substance that forms hydroxide ions as it dissolves in water

bench mark: a place on Earth where the elevation has been measured exactly

big bang theory: a model stating that all matter in the universe was together in one place more than 10 billion years ago and then exploded, scattering pieces of matter everywhere in a constantly expanding pattern

biocontrol: an organism that prevents other organisms from harming crops

biodegradable (bi oh dih GRAYD uh bul): can be broken down into harmless compounds by organisms

biome (BI ohm): a large ecosystem with characteristic organisms and nonliving factors throughout

black dwarf: a small, cold, dense star; the last stage in the life cycle of some stars

black hole: a star with a gravity field so strong that light cannot escape

bladder: a sac that stores urine for a few hours

blood transfusion (tranz FYEW zhun): the process of receiving blood from a donor

bronchi (BRAHN ki): short tubes in the chest that connect the trachea with the right and left lungs

budding: the reproduction of a new organism from an outgrowth of the parent

C

capillary (KAP uh ler ee): a small blood vessel that connects an artery and a vein

carbon dioxide-oxygen cycle: the continuous exchange of carbon dioxide and oxygen among producers, consumers, and the atmosphere

cell: the basic unit of life

cell membrane: a flexible structure that encloses a cell and holds the contents of the cell together

cell wall: a stiff structure that provides protection and support for the cell

Cenozoic (sen uh ZOH ihk) **Era:** the geologic time period between 65 million years ago and the present; mammals became dominant land animals and flowering plants and insects were important

centromere (SEN truh mihr): the structure on a doubled chromosome where the chromosomes are held together

chemical (KEM ih kul) **change:** the formation of a new substance with different chemical properties

chemical property: a property that relates to how a substance changes to a new substance

chemical reaction: the process by which a chemical change occurs

chromatin (KROH mut un): material in a cell that controls the appearance and type of the organism

chromosome (KROH muh sohm): a thread of chromatin that carries all the information about the organism

cilium (SIHL ee um): a tiny hairlike structure that enables movement

circuit (SUR kut) **breaker:** an automatic safety switch that breaks an electric circuit when wires are carrying too much current

circulatory (SIHR kyuh luh tor ee) **system:** a system that transports materials in the blood to and from the cells of the body

classification (klas uh fuh KAY shun): the process of grouping organisms by their characteristics

colony (KAHL uh nee): several cells stuck to each other in a group or chain

communicable (kuh MYEW nih kuh bul) **disease:** a disease that can be passed from one person to another

community (kuh MYEW nut ee): all of the different kinds of organisms in an ecosystem

competition (kahm puh TIHSH un): a relationship in which living things compete for life needs

compost: a mixture of decaying organic matter that can be used as a natural fertilizer

compound: a substance formed from the chemical combination of atoms of different elements

conductor (kun DUCT ur): a material through which electrons flow easily

consumer (kun SEW mur): an organism that eats other organisms

continental (kahnt un ENT ul) **drift:** an idea that states that the continents were once part of one large continent, called Pangaea, that broke into pieces and drifted apart

contour interval: the difference in elevation between two contour lines on a topographic map

contour line: a line that joins all points on a map that have the same elevation

contour planting: planting crops in rows that follow the shape of the land

converging zone: a boundary where Earth's moving plates come together

cover crop: a fast-growing plant with many shallow roots that help keep topsoil from becoming dry and being eroded

crop rotation (roh TAY shun): method of replacing soil nutrients by planting one crop one year and a different crop the next year in the same soil

current electricity (ih lek TRIHS ut ee): the flow of electrons through a material

cytoplasm (SI toh plaz um): the part of the cell outside the nucleus

D

decomposer (dee kum POH zur): a special consumer that gets energy by causing dead organisms to decay

dehydration (dee hi DRAY shun): the removal of water from a material

desert (DEZ urt): a dry land biome with cactus and euphorbia as the characteristic plants

diabetes (di uh BEET us): an illness that occurs when the body does not produce enough insulin

diaphragm: (DI uh fram): a sheet of muscle between the chest and lower part of the body that aids in breathing

diffusion: (dihf YEW zhun): the movement of molecules from where they are present in large amounts to where they are present in small amounts

digestive system: the body system that changes food to forms that cells can use for life activities

disinfectant (dihs ihn FEK tunt): a chemical that kills many simple organisms

dominant (DAHM uh nunt) **gene:** a gene whose trait is always expressed

E

ecology (ih KAHL uh jee): the study of how living and nonliving parts of an ecosystem affect each other

ecosystem (EE koh sihs tum): the interaction of groups of living things with each other and with the environment

egg: cell produced by meiosis in female organisms

electric circuit: a continuous path over which electrons move

electromagnetic (ih lek troh mag NET ihk) **spectrum:** an arrangement of electromagnetic waves according to their wavelengths

electromagnetic wave: a wave that does not have to travel through matter in order to transfer energy

electron (ih LEK trahn): particle with a negative electric charge that moves around the nucleus of an atom

element (EL uh munt): matter made of one kind of atom

elevation (el uh VAY shun): the height above sea level of a landscape feature

embryo (EM bree oh): an organism in the early stages of growth

endangered species: a species that has very few members living anywhere in the world

endocrine (EN duh krun) **system:** a system of ductless glands in the body that produce and release hormones

energy alternative (awl TUR nut ihv): an energy resource that is not a fossil fuel

environmental (ihn vi run MENT ul) **impact:** the effect of people's activities on the total environment

enzyme (EN zime): a molecule that speeds up a chemical reaction in an organism

era: the largest division of geologic time

esophagus (ih SAHF uh gus): a tube that connects the mouth with the stomach

excretion (ihk SKREE shun): the process by which wastes are removed from the body

extinct (ihk STINGT) **species:** a population that has no living members

477

F

fertilization (furt ul uh ZAY shun): the uniting of an egg with a sperm to form one cell

fertilizer (furt ul I zur): natural or synthetic material added to the soil to replace nutrients

fibrin (FI brun): a threadlike protein that forms a blood clot

fission (FIHZH un): the process in which the nucleus of an atom is split, releasing energy; the equal splitting by mitosis of a one-celled organism into two new one-celled organisms

flagellum (fluh JEL um): a long whip-like structure used for movement

food chain: the series of steps showing energy flow through a community

food web: the combination of all over-lapping food chains in a community

formula: a group of symbols used to show the elements in a compound

fossil (FAHS ul): a record of past life in the form of a track, a trace, or the remains of organisms preserved in rock

fossil fuel: an energy resource formed from the remains of plants and ani-mals that lived millions of years ago

fracture (FRAK chur) **zone:** a bound-ary along which Earth's plates slide past one another

frequency (FREE kwun see): the number of waves that pass a point in one second

fresh water: a water biome, with very little salt content, consisting of lakes, ponds, and streams

fungus (FUN gus): a consumer with a cell wall

fuse: a safety device with a metal strip that can break an electric circuit when too much current flows through it

fusion (FYEW zhun): the combination of the nuclei of two atoms to form the nucleus of a different atom

G

gamma ray: a wave with the shortest wavelength in the electromagnetic spectrum; released in nuclear reactions

gene: a part of a chromosome that controls a trait of an organism

genetics (juh NET ihks): the study of how genes are inherited

geologic (jee uh LAHJ ihk) **time scale:** an outline of Earth's history, arranging events in the order in which they occurred

geothermal (jee oh THUR mul) **en-ergy:** heat from rocks and water deep inside Earth

grassland: land biome where most of the plants are grasses; known also as prairies, steppes, savannahs, velds, and pampas

H

habitat (HAB uh tat): the place where an organism normally lives

half-life: the amount of time needed for one half of the atoms in a radio-active element to decay

hazardous waste: refuse that can be harmful; toxic waste

heat value: a measure of the heat released when a certain amount of fuel is burned

hemisphere (HEM uh sfihr): one half of Earth; half of a sphere

heredity (huh RED ut ee): the passing of traits from parents to offspring

hormone (HOR mohn): one of the chemical messengers produced by the endocrine glands; controls the activity of a specific target tissue

humus (HYEW mus): the dark organic material in soil

hybrid (HI brud) **trait:** a trait that results when the genes in a pair are different

hydrocarbon (HI droh kar bun): an organic compound that contains only carbon and hydrogen

hydroelectric (hi droh ih LEK trihk) **energy:** electricity produced when water falls from a high place to a lower place

I

index fossil: fossil of an organism that lived in many places, but over a short time period; used to date the rock layer in which it is found

indicator (IHN duh kayt ur): a compound that changes color when added to acids and bases

infrared (IHN fra red) **wave:** an electromagnetic wave with a wavelength slightly shorter than those of microwaves; used in heat lamps and to detect certain tumors and heat loss from buildings

inorganic (ihn or GAN ihk) **compounds:** all compounds made from any elements, except those carbon compounds classified as organic

insulator (IHN suh layt ur): a material through which electrons do not flow easily

insulin (IHN suh lun): a hormone that allows glucose to move from the bloodstream into body cells

ion (I ahn): an atom that has gained or lost an electron

irrigation (ihr uh GAY shun): the addition of water to soil that is too dry

K

kerogen (KER uh jun): a rubbery hydrocarbon mixture that releases oil when heated

kidney: one of two bean-shaped organs in humans that filter waste from the blood

kilowatt-hour: the energy produced by 1,000 watts of power in one hour

kingdom: the largest division of living things used in classification

L

larynx (LER ingks): a structure at the top of the trachea that contains the vocal cords

laser (LAY zur): a device that produces an intense light beam of one wavelength that travels in only one direction

latitude (LAT uh tewd) **lines:** horizontal lines drawn parallel to the equator around a globe; used to describe locations north or south of the equator

law of conservation (kahn sur VAY shun) **of mass:** a law that states that mass is neither created nor destroyed in a chemcial reaction

law of superposition (sew pur poh ZIHSH un): a law that states that the younger rock layer is on top of the older rock layer

legend (LEJ und): part of a map that explains the symbols for each feature represented on the map

longitude (LAHN juh tewd) **lines:** vertical lines drawn through the north and south poles of a globe; used to describe locations east or west of the prime meridian

M

map scale: a ratio used to compare distances represented on a map to actual distances on Earth

mechanical (muh KAN ih kul) **wave:** a wave that transfers energy as it travels through matter

meiosis (mi OH sus): the process of cell division that results in cells with half the number of chromosomes of body cells

Mesozoic (mez uh ZOH ihk) **Era:** geologic time period between 225 million and 65 million years ago when reptiles became abundant; "Age of Dinosaurs"

metabolism (muh TAB uh lihz um): the total of all the chemical reactions that take place in the body

microwave: a radio wave with a wavelength between one millimeter and 30 centimeters; useful in heating food, communication, and radar

mid-ocean ridge: mountain chain on the ocean floor

mitosis (mi TOH sus): the division of a cell into two new cells, each with the same number of chromosomes as the parent cell

mixture: a combination of substances that forms without a chemical reaction

molecule (MAHL ih kyewl): particle formed when two or more atoms combine by sharing electrons

moneran (muh NIHR un): a one-celled organism with no nucleus

mucus (MYEW kus): a moist, sticky fluid that is found, for example, in the nasal cavity

mutation (myew TAY shun): a change in the genes that can cause a new trait to appear

N

natural selection: the process by which organisms less adapted to their environment tend to die and better-adapted organisms tend to survive

nebula (NEB yuh luh): a large cloud of dust and gas in space

nephron (NEF rahn): the filtering unit of the kidneys

neutral (NEW trul): a substance with a pH of 7; neither an acid nor a base

neutron (NEW trahn): a particle in the nucleus of an atom that has no electric charge

neutron star: a very small, dense star formed by a supernova

niche (NIHCH): the place or role of an organism in the environment

nitrogen (NI truh jun) **cycle:** the continuous movement of nitrogen in an ecosystem

nonrenewable resource: a resource, such as a fossil fuel, that cannot be replaced within the foreseeable future

nova: a star that bursts into brightness, then fades

nuclear (NEW klee ur) **membrane:** a cell structure that separates the contents of the nucleus from that of the cytoplasm

nucleus (NEW klee us): the control center of a cell; the core of an atom

O

oil reservoir (REZ urv wor): an area where oil is trapped in the ground

optical (AHP tih kul) **telescope:** a tube with magnifying lenses or mirrors that collect, transmit, and focus light

organic (or GAN ihk) **compound:** a compound that contains carbon

organism (OR guh nihz um): anything that has all the features of life

oxide (AHK side): a compound of oxygen and one other element

P

Paleozoic (pay lee uh ZOH ihk) **Era:** geologic time period between 570 million and 225 million years ago; the first fish, amphibians, and land plants appeared

parallel circuit (PER uh lel • SUR kut): an electric circuit in which the current can flow through more than one pathway

parasitism (PER uh suh tihz um): a kind of symbiosis in which one organism is helped and the other is harmed

parathyroid (per uh THI royd) **glands:** a set of four glands at the back of the thyroid that produce a hormone that controls the amounts of calcium and phosphate ions in the blood

pasteurization (pas chuh ruh ZAY shun): the process of heating and quickly cooling milk to kill the disease-causing bacteria

periodic (pihr ee AHD ihk) **table:** a chart used by scientists to classify elements

permafrost (PUR muh frawst): a layer of soil that is frozen all year; found in the tundra

pesticide (PES tuh side): a chemical used to kill organisms that harm crops

pharynx (FER ingks): a passage that connects the nasal cavity with the trachea

pH scale: a scale used to indicate the strength of acids and bases

physical (FIHZ ih kul) **change:** a change in the size, shape, or state of matter; does not cause a new substance to be formed

physical property: a property that can be observed without referring to another substance

pituitary (puh TEW uh ter ee) **gland:** an endocrine gland at the base of the brain that controls other glands

plasma (PLAZ muh): the liquid part of the blood

plate: a large slab of Earth's crust and rigid upper mantle

plate boundary: a place where plates of Earth's crust meet

platelet: small cell in the plasma that causes blood clots to form

plate tectonics (tek TAHN ihks) **theory:** a theory that states that Earth's crust and upper mantle are broken into plates

population (pahp yuh LAY shun): a group of organisms in a community that are all the same species

power: the rate at which a device uses energy

Precambrian (pree KAM bree un): the earliest period of geologic time; 4.6 billion to 570 million years ago

predation (prih DAY shun): the act of one animal killing and eating another animal

prime meridian (muh RIHD ee un): 0° longitude; passes through Greenwich, England

producer (proh DEW sur): an organism that makes its own food

protist (PROH tihst): a one-celled organism with a nucleus

proton (PROH tahn): a particle in the nucleus of an atom that has a positive electric charge

pseudopodium (sewd uh POHD ee um): a fingerlike extension of a cell that enables movement and feeding

pulsar: a neutron star that spins quickly and gives off radio waves

pulsating theory: a model stating that the universe will expand and shrink, over and over

pure trait: a trait that results when both genes in the pair are alike

R

radar: a device in which radio signals sent out from a transmitter bounce off objects and are received by an antenna; used to locate objects

radioactive element: an element whose atoms have nuclei that change naturally to form nuclei of different atoms

radio telescope: an antenna used to collect radio waves from space

radio wave: one of a group of waves that have the longest wavelengths of the electromagnetic spectrum

recessive (rih SES ihv) **gene:** a gene that controls a hidden trait

reclamation (rek luh MAY shun): the reconstruction of strip-mined land

recombinant (ree KAHM buh nunt) **DNA:** DNA that is made by the movement of genes from one organism into another to form new combinations

red blood cell: a cell in the plasma that transports oxygen to the body cells and carbon dioxide away from the body cells

red giant: a very large red star that develops in the life cycle of a star

refinery (rih FINE uh ree): a place where crude oil is separated into different products

refuse (REF yooz): any waste product

regeneration (rih jen uh RAY shun): the regrowth of the damaged tissues of an organism

relative dating: the process of determining that one event occurred before or after another

renewable resource: a resource, such as trees, which can be replaced within the foreseeable future

reproduction (ree pruh DUK shun): the process by which organisms produce new organisms of their own kind

reservoir (REZ urv wor): a large artificial or natural lake used to collect and store water

respiration (res puh RAY shun): the process of using oxygen to combine with food molecules and release energy

rocket: a device used to launch objects into space

S

salt water: a water biome with a salt content of around 3.5%; consists of all the world's oceans

sanitary (SAN uh ter ee) **landfill:** a waste disposal site where trash is processed so that it will harm the environment as little as possible

saturated solution (SACH uh rayt ud • suh LEW shun): a solution in which no more of a substance can be dissolved at that temperature

scrubber (SKRUB ur): a device in a smokestack or chimney that uses water to remove particulates and some polluting gases

seafloor spreading: the process of adding new crust to Earth at mid-ocean ridges

selective breeding: the crossing of organisms with desirable traits to produce offspring with a combination of these desirable traits

series circuit (SUR kut): an electric circuit in which the electric current flows through only one pathway

sewage: liquid and solid wastes carried in sewers or drains

shelter belt: a row of trees or shrubs planted to prevent wind from blowing soil away

shield (SHEELD): the oldest part of each continent, composed of Precambrian rocks

soil management: the methods people use to conserve soil

solar cell: a device used to concentrate solar energy and produce electricity

solar collector: a device that gathers the energy from the sun

solar energy: energy from the sun

solar reflector (rih FLEK tur): a curved shiny surface that reflects and focuses sunlight on one spot

solution (suh LEW shun): a mixture in which a substance is spread evenly throughout another substance

space: all the area beyond Earth's atmosphere

spacecraft: a vehicle, made by people, that travels through space

space probe: a spacecraft sent beyond Earth to gather data about space objects

space shuttle: a system composed of a giant fuel tank, two large rockets, and an orbiter which can glide and land like a plane; the orbiter can be launched and returned to Earth many times

space station: a spacecraft used for living and working in space

sperm: cell produced by meiosis in male organisms

spreading zone: a boundary where Earth's plates move apart or separate

static discharge: the movement of electrons from an object with negative charge to another object

static electricity: the positive or negative electric charges on objects

stomach: a small, saclike organ that holds and digests food

strip cropping: the planting of several rows of a cover plant between rows of a main crop

strip mining: removal of the rock and soil above a coal seam

substance: pure matter, always the same in composition

supernova: a very large exploding star

suspension (suh SPEN chun): a mixture in which the substances are not dissolved

switch: a device that makes it easy to complete or break an electric circuit

symbiosis (sihm bi OH sus): a relationship between two different species that live in close contact; mutualism, commensalism, and parasitism are all forms of symbiosis

T

taiga (TI guh): a land biome south of the tundra, with annual precipitation of about 50 cm and conifers as characteristic plants

technology (tek NAHL uh jee): using science knowledge to develop new products

temperate forest: a land biome with four distinct seasons and an annual precipitation of about 100 cm; characteristic plants are deciduous trees

thermal pollution (THUR mul • puh LEW shun): the dumping of hot water into a body of water

thrust: the force exerted by gases that pushes rockets forward

thyroid (THI royd) **gland:** a butterfly-shaped gland in the throat whose main function is to control cell metabolism

tidal energy: energy of moving water caused by tides

topographic (tahp uh GRAF ihk) **map:** a map that shows the surface features of the landscape in detail

trachea (TRAY kee uh): the windpipe, a stiff tube that leads from the nasal cavity to the bronchi

trait: a characteristic of an organism that is passed from parents to offspring

tropical (TRAHP uh kul) **rain forest:** a warm, rainy, land biome; vines and broadleaf trees are characteristic plants

tundra: a cold biome located in the far northern part of the world and on the tops of very high mountains

turbine (TUR bun): a machine with blades like a fan that turns generators to produce electricity

U

ultraviolet (ul truh VI uh lut) **wave:** an electromagnetic wave with a wavelength just shorter than that of visible light

universe (YEW nuh vurs): space and all matter and energy in it

urea (yoo REE uh): cell waste containing nitrogen

ureter (YOOR ut ur): tube leading from the kidney to the bladder through which urine passes

urethra (yoo REE thruh): a duct through which urine leaves the body

urinary (YOOR uh ner ee) **system:** a group of organs that remove liquid wastes from the body

urine (YOOR un): a liquid produced by the kidneys and made up of water, urea, salts, and other wastes

V

vaccine (vak SEEN): a dead or weak virus that is used to help your body produce antibodies to fight against a certain disease

vegetative reproduction (vej uh TAY tihv • ree pruh DUK shun): the formation of new plants from a body part of a single parent plant

vein (VAYN): a blood vessel that carries blood to the heart

virus (VI rus): a particle that has characteristics of both living and nonliving matter

visible light: the part of the electromagnetic spectrum that can be seen by human eyes

W

water cycle: the continuous movement of water in an ecosystem

watt: the unit used to measure power

wavelength: the distance from one wave trough to the next wave trough

weightlessness: the absence of feeling the pull of gravity; the condition of objects that are falling freely in space

white blood cell: a cell in the plasma that destroys foreign matter in the blood

white dwarf: a very old, hot, white star about the size of Earth

X

X ray: an electromagnetic wave, having a wavelength just shorter than ultraviolet waves, and able to penetrate many solid materials

Z

zygote (ZI goht): the cell that results from the combination of one egg with one sperm cell

Index

Physical property, 51; *illus.,* 51

Pituitary gland, 231; *illus.,* 231; *table,* 232

Planet, 130-131; *illus.,* 120, 131

Plant: classification of, 9; fuel-producing, 157; nonvascular, 12; reproduction of, 405, 406, 411; vascular, 12; *act.,* 316-317, 406; *illus.,* 9, 12, 405, 411

Plant cell, *illus.,* 6

Plasma, 195

Plate, 268-269; *illus.,* 268

Plate boundary, 270-271; *illus.,* 270

Platelets, 195; *illus.,* 195

Plate tectonics, 268-274; *illus.,* 268, 270

Pollution: air, 461-465; thermal, 460, 461; water, 459-460; *act.,* 464-465

Polymers, 78

Population, 316; disappearing, 331-332; and environment, 466-467; and habitats, 327, 328; and humans, 330-331

Potassium-40, 284; *table,* 284

Power, 364

Precambrian time, 291; *table,* 295

Precipitation, acid, 87, 159-160, 462, 468

Predation, 318; *illus.,* 318

Prime meridian, 255; *illus.,* 254

Prism, 383; *illus.,* 383

Producer, 8

Propane, 85

Property, chemical, 48; physical, 51; *act.,* 53; *illus.,* 51

Protist, 9, 30-33; *illus.,* 8, 30, 31; *table,* 32

Proton, 55, 355; *illus.,* 55

Protozoans, 31-32; *illus.,* 31; *table,* 32

Proxima Centauri, 103

Pseudopodia, 31; *illus.,* 31

Pulsar, 109

Pulsating theory of universe, 115

Pulse, 193, *act.,* 194

Punnett square, 422; *illus.,* 422, 423

Pure trait, 419

R

Radar, 381; *illus.,* 381

Radioactive element, 176-177, 283-287; *act.,* 286-287; *table,* 284

Radiolarians, 2; *illus.,* 3

Radiometric dating, 283-287; *act.,* 286-287; *table,* 284

Radio telescope, 123-124; *illus.,* 123, 124

Radio wave, 378-379; *illus.,* 378

Recessive gene, 418-423; *act.,* 420

Reclamation, 163

Recombinant DNA, 430-431

Recycling, 308-311, 449

Red blood cell, 195; *illus.,* 189, 195

Red giant, 107; *illus.,* 108

"Red tide," 31; *illus.,* 31

Refinery, 151

Refuse disposal, 446-449; *act.,* 450-451; *illus.,* 446, 447

Regeneration, 402; *illus.,* 402

Relative dating, 281

Renewable resource, 154

Reproduction, 396-411; budding, 404-405; fission, 404; meiosis, 407-411; mitosis, 399-402; vegetative, 405, 406; *act.,* 401, 406; *illus.,* 399, 400, 404, 405, 407, 408, 410

Reservoir, 458

Respiration, 212, 311; *act.,* 212

Respiratory system, 208-214; breathing, 209-210; parts of, 210-211; *illus.,* 210, 211, 213

Rock: ages of, 281-287, 290; on ocean floor, 264, 265; *act.,* 286-287; *illus.,* 281, 290

Rocket, 126; *act.,* 124-125; *illus.,* 126

S

Saliva, 198

Salmonella, 25

Salt, 69, 91-92; *illus.,* 69, 92

Salt water, 345; *tables,* 337, 345

Sanitary landfill, 446-447

Satellite, 127-129; *illus.,* 127, 128

Saturated solution, 73; *illus.,* 73

Saturn, 130

Scrubber, 162, 463

Sea anemone, *illus.,* 4, 319

Seafloor spreading, 265; *illus.,* 265

Seed, 411; *illus.,* 411

Selective breeding, 429-430; *illus.,* 430

Sequence, 215

Series circuit, 359; *act.,* 361; *illus.,* 359

Sewage, 459

Shelter belt, 444; *illus.,* 444

Shepard, Alan, 134; *illus.,* 134

Shield, 291

Silicon dioxide, 86; *illus.,* 86

Silver nitrate, *illus.,* 49

Simple organisms, 10, 22-37; fungi, 34-37; monerans, 23-29, 33; protists, 30-33; *act.,* 28-29, 36-37; *illus.,* 8, 22, 23, 24, 25, 30, 31, 34, 35; *tables,* 10, 25, 32

Skin, 220; artificial, 403; *illus.,* 220

V

Vaccine, 17
Vascular plant, 12; *illus.,* 12
Vegetative reproduction, 405; *act.,* 406; *illus.,* 405
Vein, 193, 196; *illus.,* 193
Ventricle, 192
Venus, 120; *illus.,* 120
Viking 1 and 2, 130
Villi, 200
Virus, 16-18; *illus.,* 16, 17; *table,* 17
Volcano, 271, 274; *illus.,* 274, 275
Volta, Alessandro, 354
Voyager 1 and 2, 130-131

W

Waste, 201, 216-220; hazardous, 447, 448; industrial, 460

Water, 48; in body, 236; conservation of, 460-461; formula for, 71; fresh, 344; salt, 345; states of, 51
Water conservation, 460-461
Water cycle, 309; *illus.,* 309
Water energy, 172-173; *illus.,* 172
Water pollution, 459-460; *illus.,* 459
Water reclamation, *illus.,* 439
Water treatment, 456, 458; *illus.,* 456, 458
Watt, 364
Wave, 374-375; electromagnetic, 372, 375-388; frequency of, 375; gamma ray, 384; infrared, 382; mechanical, 374; microwave, 379; radio, 378-379, 381; ultraviolet, 383; X ray, 384; *act.,* 377; *illus.,* 372, 374, 375, 378
Wavelength, 375
Weather satellite, 128

Wegener, Alfred, 261-263
Weightlessness, 135-136; *illus.,* 135
Whale, 208
White blood cell, 195; *illus.,* 195
White dwarf, 107
Wind energy, 146, 169-171; *act.,* 171; *illus.,* 146-147, 169, 170
Windmill, 146, 170; *illus.,* 146-147, 170

X

X ray, 384; *illus.,* 384

Z

Zygote, 410; *illus.,* 410

PHOTO CREDITS

15 16 17 18—98